**Ready-to-Use
Activities & Materials for**

IMPROVING CONTENT READING SKILLS

Wilma H. Miller

Illustrations by Eileen Ciavarella

JOSSEY-BASS
A Wiley Imprint
www.josseybass.com

4/04

Published by Jossey-Bass
A Wiley Imprint
989 Market Street, San Francisco, CA 94103-1741   www.josseybass.com

Jossey-Bass books and products are available through most bookstores. To contact Jossey-Bass directly call our Customer Care Department within the U.S. at 800-956-7739, outside the U.S. at 317-572-3986 or fax 317-572-4002.

Jossey-Bass also publishes its books in a variety of electronic formats. Some content that appears in print may not be available in electronic books.

Library of Congress Cataloging-in-Publication Data
Miller, Wilma H.
     Ready-to-use activities & materials for improving
content skills / Wilma H. Miller
          p.   cm.
     Rev. ed. of : Reading & writing remediation kit. c1997.
     Includes bibliographical references.
     ISBN 0-13-007815-8
     1. Language arts—Correlation with content subjects—United
States.   2. Content area reading—United States.   3. English
language—Composition and exercises—Study and teaching—United
States.   4. Language arts—Remedial teaching—United States.
5. Teaching—United States—Aids and devices.   I. Miller, Wilma H.
Reading & writing remediation kit.   II. Title.   III. Title: Ready-to-use activities
and materials for improving content reading skills.
LB1576.M52   1999
372.6—dc21   99-19057

FIRST EDITION
HB Printing 10 9 8 7 6 5 4 3 2

To the memory of my beloved parents, William and Ruth Miller,
and
Win Huppuch, Vice-President of C.A.R.E. and
my dear friend and professional advisor for twenty-seven years

Acknowledgments

I would like to gratefully acknowledge a number of people who have made it possible for me to write this resource. I first would like to acknowledge the memory of my beloved late mother Ruth K. Miller who worked with me on all my writing projects until the age of eighty. She remains an inspiration to me in all of my writing projects. I also would like to thank all of my present and former undergraduate and graduate students at Illinois State University for being a constant source of information and motivation for me. I too would like to express my deepest gratitude to the following people at the Center for Applied Research in Education for their help and inspiration: Win Huppuch, Susan Kolwicz, Diane Turso and Ellen Ciavarella, who drew the illustrations. Without their help, this manuscript would not have been possible. In addition, I would like to thank Fred Dahl and his associates at Inkwell Publishing Services for their help.

About the Author

A former classroom teacher, Wilma H. Miller, Ed.D., has been teaching at the college level for more than 30 years. She completed her doctorate in reading at the University of Arizona under the direction of the late Dr. Ruth Strang, a nationally known reading authority.

Dr. Miller has contributed numerous articles to professional journals and is the author of more than sixteen other works in the field of reading education. Among the latter are *Identifying and Correcting Reading Difficulties in Children* (1972), *Diagnosis and Correction of Reading Difficulties in Secondary School Students* (1973), *Reading Diagnosis Kit* (1975, 1978, 1986), "Corrective Reading Skills Activity File" (1977), *Reading Teacher's Complete Diagnosis & Correction Manual* (1988), *Reading Comprehension Activities Kit* (1990), *Complete Reading Disabilities Handbook* (1993), and *Alternative Assessment Techniques for Reading & Writing* (1995), all published by The Center for Applied Research in Education.

She is also the author of an inservice aid for teachers entitled *Reading Activities Handbook* (1980), several textbooks for developmental reading, *The First R: Elementary Reading Today* (1977), and *Teaching Elementary Reading Today* (1983), published by Holt, Rinehart & Winston, Inc., and of a guide to secondary reading instruction, *Teaching Reading in the Secondary School* (1974), published by Charles C. Thomas.

The Practical Help This Book Offers

Do you believe most students in the upper primary grades, intermediate grades, middle school, and secondary school read effectively? If one equates reading with lower-level comprehension of narrative material, the answer may well be *yes* for the majority of students. However, if one considers reading as higher-level comprehension and retention of content material in literature, social studies, science, and mathematics, the answer may well be *no* for far too many students. A number of students just are not competent in understanding and retaining content material.

For example, data from the National Assessment of Educational Progress (NEAP) indicates that while younger elementary school students are fairly competent in the basics of reading, older students have declining higher-level comprehension skills. Other data indicate that students in the middle and secondary schools can write to communicate only at a minimal level and have difficulty using critical thinking and organizational skills. Therefore, although the United States may not necessarily have a basic illiteracy problem, we do have a *literacy problem*. Many other surveys indicate that students need to learn how to learn. All of the data indicate that students experience difficulty with higher-level reading and writing skills such as critical thinking, drawing inferences, summarizing, and applying what is read. In addition, many students do not have mastery of a large body of content material which is considered essential for informed readers.

Reading, writing, studying, and test-taking in the content areas also are difficult for many students for a number of reasons. As an example, each of the content areas of literature (language arts), social studies, science, and mathematics contains its own unique specialized vocabulary which may be difficult for even able readers. In addition, expository material generally is much more difficult to comprehend than is narrative material because of the unique patterns of organization used in various content materials. To compound the problem even further, many of the content textbooks are written above the grade level of the students who are to read them. They also are not always written in a "reader friendly" fashion since they usually are written by experts in the content area without input from reading specialists. They also may contain many difficult concepts and may be uninteresting to the students who are to read them, unless the content teacher makes a concerted effort to teach the material in a truly interesting, motivating manner with active student involvement, such as in thematic units of instruction.

In addition, even an excellent reader may be a disabled reader in some aspects of content reading. For example, I always have been a very good reader who really enjoys reading. However, even today I consider myself to be a disabled reader in the reading skills of reading and carrying out directions and in comprehending and solving mathematical verbal problems. Even now I simply "freeze" when I am confronted with either of these two reading tasks. Perhaps there also are some elements of content literacy in which you consider yourself to be disabled. That should not be the case with any of the students whom we teach. The techniques and activities in this resource can prevent many students from falling short of realizing their full potential when reading, writing, and studying the content areas of literature (language arts), social studies, science, and mathematics at all grade levels from the primary-grade level on through the secondary school level.

This book should greatly help teachers assess, present, and reinforce all of the important skills required for effective *comprehension, retention, writing,* and *test-taking* in the content areas. If such assessment, instruction, and practice were to occur with all students beginning in the primary grades, but with increasing emphasis in the intermediate grades, middle schools, and secondary schools, students would be much better able to profit from their content area instruction.

This book has been written for classroom literacy teachers, content teachers, Title I literacy teachers, teachers of all types of "at-risk" students, reading specialists and supervisors, and administrators. Everyone involved in the teaching of content literacy (reading, writing, and studying) should find it a valuable source of information since it stresses reading, writing, and studying in the content areas of literature (language arts), social studies, science, and mathematics.

This book has been written in a *practical and easy-to-understand manner.* It contains a multitude of classroom-tested *strategies and activity sheets* of all kinds that are designed to assess and to improve the ability of all students to read, comprehend, write, and study in the content areas of literature (language arts), social studies, science, and mathematics. The descriptions and reproducible examples of a wide variety of devices should save any literacy or content teacher countless time and energy in teaching content reading and writing skills to his or her students.

Chapter 1 stresses the importance of teaching the vocabulary and skills required for effective reading and writing in the content areas. The chapter makes the point that different content areas have different requirements in reading and writing and that, without mastery of the specialized vocabulary and skills needed in that content area, a student cannot read and write successfully in the area. Chapter 1 also describes in detail the classification scheme used to categorize the literacy-study skills used in this handbook. In this teacher's resource, the literacy-study skills are classified in the following way: *Information-Location Skills, Ability to Read and Carry Out Directions, Ability to Interpret Graphic Aids,* and *Reading Rate and Flexibility.* In addition, this chapter describes in detail the specialized vocabulary and skills required for effective reading, writing, and study in the content areas of literature (language arts), social studies, science, and mathematics. You will learn that there is considerable variation in the requirements of these four content areas.

Chapter 2 is devoted to ready-to-use strategies and activity sheets for assessing competencies and weaknesses in content reading, writing, and study skills in both whole language and traditional literacy programs. The chapter briefly explains the importance of using mainly *informal,* but also some standardized assessment devices, in an assessment program. The importance of "kid-watching" and holistic assessment is emphasized in this chapter. The chapter then briefly describes the advantages and limitations of both informal and standardized assessment devices for literacy programs. The chapter contains many reproducible checklists of various types including literacy-study observational checklists at various levels from the primary-grade level through the middle-upper grade level, student self-assessment checklists at the same grade levels, several parent surveys at various grade levels, and a checklist for literature response groups at the intermediate-grade and middle-upper grade levels. In addition, this chapter lists and describes standardized tests of various types that are designed to assess competencies in the reading-study skills; contains reproducible examples of group and individual reading-study inventories of various types; explains miscue analysis and the running record for the assessment of reading competencies and weaknesses; and explains the value of using portfolios in assessment of the literacy-study skills along with a number of other reproducible devices of various kinds. This chapter should help both literacy and content teachers to make a very effective assessment of a student's competencies and weaknesses in the various literacy-study skills.

Chapter 3 is devoted to improving vocabulary in the content areas and opens by describing meaning vocabularies. It also provides many classroom-tested strategies for vocabulary improvement in the content areas such as the use of word structure, questioning strategies, and the five-step guide to vocabulary independence; and contains many reproducible devices designed to improve vocabulary in the content areas, such as a semantic map or web, a semantic features analysis grid, a Predict-o-Gram, Magic Squares, and word puzzles of various types.

Chapter 4 contains countless ready-to-use strategies and activity sheets for improving all elements of comprehension, critical (evaluative) reading, and creative (applied) reading in the various content areas. The chapter opens by describing all of these very important elements and provides many strategies for improving ability in them. Some of the strategies included in this chapter are: teaching the content areas in thematic units such as in whole language programs, effectively using cooperative learning in thematic units of instruction, various pre-reading strategies, various types of reading guides, a five-phase instructional sequence for comprehension and retention in the content areas, visual imagery, self-questioning about the main idea, the herringbone technique, expository paragraph frames, self-monitoring of comprehension, and a comprehension rating model. Chapter 4 also contains a multitude of reproducible devices such as an anticipation guide, K-W-L and K-W-H-L activity sheets, a jot chart, a three-level guide, the guided reading procedure, a self-questioning about the main idea activity sheet, a cause–effect story map, a cause–effect story guide, and an activity sheet for the explicit teaching of determining between fact and opinion. Literacy and content teachers should find this chapter to be *extremely* helpful in improving all elements of comprehension in the different content areas.

Chapter 5 is devoted to the improvement of writing skills in the content areas. It stresses the importance of teaching writing as a process during thematic units in social studies and science. The chapter also suggests many useful strategies and reproducibles that can be used to improve writing ability in the content areas, including: reading response journals, the GLOBAL method, the language-experience approach (LEA), REAP technique, biopoems and cinquains, writing a content-focused melodrama, writing the "Eyewitness Action Nightly News," writing a one-paragraph essay, the GIST Procedure, and K-W-L Plus.

Chapter 6 is devoted to ready-to-use strategies and activity sheets for adapting literacy-study skills to the unique demands of literature, social studies, science, and mathematics. The chapter opens by explaining the more *general* literacy-study skills. It also describes how to use the school library/media center to improve competency in content literacy-study skills. Then the chapter presents the general goals for teaching literature and contains many ready-to-use strategies and reproducible devices for improving competency in various aspects of literature; some of the activity sheets contained in this part of the chapter are related to dealing with feelings about words, the use of heteronyms, and using figurative language. Next the chapter describes the general goals for teaching social studies and discusses the importance of using *multicultural literature* in thematic units. *The chapter also contains a list of multicultural tradebooks that can be used in social studies thematic units.* The chapter provides many strategies that can be used to improve reading, writing, and study skills in social studies. The chapter also describes the general goals for teaching science, discusses why science should be taught as part of thematic units as much as possible, and presents strategies and reproducibles for improving competency in reading, writing, and studying in science. The final part of Chapter 6 is devoted to improving competency in mathematics, and explains strategies and offers reproducibles that will improve a student's competency in mathematical literacy.

Chapter 7 is devoted to the improvement of test-construction and test-taking strategies in the content areas. It opens by explaining some of the reasons that students need to take tests and the importance of giving valid tests in the content fields. It then describes the importance of using good techniques in test construction in the content areas and provides some test construction tips; contains a reproducible teacher checklist for designing a content area test; discusses test-taking skills and "testwiseness" in detail and provides suggestions for improving both of them; describes the PORPE checklist to help students evaluate essay test responses; and closes by including reproducibles.

Chapter 8 provides ready-to-use strategies for teaching content reading and writing to various kinds of *"at-risk"* students. The chapter opens by briefly describing the characteristics of many different types of "at-risk" students such as the following: learning disabled (LD), attention deficit hyperactivity disordered (ADHD), ESL, LEP, bilingual, culturally or linguistically diverse, mildly mentally handicapped, visually impaired, hearing impaired, and speech or language disordered. The chapter discusses the inherent danger of labeling these students in any way; discusses the issue of *inclusion* and "at-risk" students; includes a number of classroom-tested strategies for improving the content reading, writing, and study abilities of different kinds of "at-risk" students; contains a list of professional resource books for teachers of "at-risk" students; and closes by including a number of reproducibles.

Literacy and content teachers will find the following to be unique about *Ready-to-Use Activities and Materials for Improving Content Reading Skills:*

- It is published in a spiral-bound format that makes reproducing the material very simple.

- It contains numerous classroom-tested strategies and activity sheets for improving *reading, writing, studying,* and *test-taking* in the content areas of literature (language arts), social studies, science, and mathematics. A number of these strategies and activity sheets are innovative.

- It emphasizes the whole language (thematic unit teaching) philosophy as much as possible. The content areas are best taught and reinforced in thematic units.

- It is the only resource of which I am aware that contains *reproducible examples* of many of the strategies that are only discussed in other more theory-based teachers' resource books.

- It contains a comprehensive classification scheme for categorizing the reading, writing, and study skills that should be emphasized at the appropriate grade levels from the primary-grade level through the secondary-school level.

- It contains an inclusive list of all the unique literacy skills that should be presented and reinforced in the content areas of literature (language arts), social studies, science, and mathematics.

- It contains many reproducible assessment devices for ascertaining competencies and weaknesses in literacy-study skills in the content areas. It emphasizes informal assessment as much as possible, which is in keeping with the whole language philosophy.

- It presents strategies and reproducible activity sheets for improving ability in the specialized vocabulary that is crucial to comprehension in the different content areas of literature (language arts), social studies, science, and mathematics.

- It presents a multitude of classroom-tested strategies and reproducible activity sheets for improving higher-level comprehension skills. It is at this level that a number of elementary and secondary students lack competence.

- It provides a number of classroom-tested strategies and reproducible activity sheets for improving ability in writing in the content areas of literature (language arts), social studies, science, and mathematics. It is very important that the teaching and reinforcement of reading, writing, and spelling be integrated.

- It contains strategies and reproducible activity sheets for presenting and reinforcing the unique skills required for effective reading, writing, and studying in the content fields of literature (language arts), social studies, science, and mathematics. These strategies should prove very helpful to both classroom literacy teachers and content teachers.

- It contains a list of multicultural tradebooks that should be beneficial to all students.

- It provides strategies and checklists for improving test-construction and test-taking skills in the content areas.

- It contains an entire chapter devoted to ready-to-use strategies and activity sheets for teaching content reading and writing skills to various kinds of "at-risk" students.

- All of the reproducible materials in this book should save literacy and content teachers countless time and effort in providing optimum instruction and reinforcement in content reading—certainly a very important task.

   All types of literacy and content teachers must provide more effective instruction and reinforcement in content reading, writing, studying, spelling, and test-taking skills. The data of the recent past show that this instruction and practice is absolutely essential, especially in a technological society that demands a much higher level of literacy than in the past. Far too many students just are not able to read, write, and study content materials effectively. If this handbook can help literacy and content teachers to present and reinforce content literacy skills more effectively, it will have served its purpose very well. It is my hope that this resource can be very helpful to many students at all grade levels.

Wilma H. Miller

Contents

**Chapter 3   READY-TO-USE STRATEGIES AND
ACTIVITY SHEETS FOR IMPROVING
VOCABULARY IN THE CONTENT AREAS**   *128*

Teaching the Required Vocabulary and Skills for Effective Reading and Writing in the Content Areas

At the present time I teach a nontraditional student named John in one of my undergraduate classes. He has retired from the United States Navy and has returned to college to prepare to become a teacher of learning disabled students. He is a good, conscientious, highly motivated student. However, he now is having great difficulty in a mathematics class for prospective teachers because of his inability to read math verbal problems effectively. As I wrote in the preface of this resource, I share John's inability to read such problems very effectively. John told me that he just "freezes" when he is required to read this kind of material. I am sure you know many students who have similar difficulties in reading all types of expository (content) material whether it be in literature, social studies, science, or mathematics. We have tutored countless students especially in the intermediate grades and junior high school who evidenced such problems to an extreme degree. Yet most of these students were at least adequate readers of narrative material. Most of them could have been taught to read all types of content material effectively *if* they had been given the proper instruction and practice early in their school careers. This teachers' resource is designed to provide literacy teachers with this kind of help.

After reading this chapter, literacy teachers will better understand the reasons why effective reading, writing, and studying in the various content fields present such a challenge to otherwise able readers. Literacy teachers also will more clearly understand that if otherwise adequate readers have great difficulty with content literacy skills, why they present almost insurmountable difficulties for below-average readers and many other "at-risk" students.

THE IMPORTANCE OF TEACHING THE REQUIRED VOCABULARY AND SKILLS FOR EFFECTIVE READING, WRITING, AND STUDY IN THE CONTENT AREAS

It is a commonly-heard statement in the field of literacy education that students "first learn to read and then read to learn." The first part of this statement means that beginning readers must first learn the basic word identification and comprehension skills. The second part of the statement—that students "read to learn"—means that their major purpose for learning to read is to understand and remember content (the facts and concepts) that are found in subject matter assignments. The idea this statement misses is that students must learn *how* to read to learn.

As you will learn from the extensive list of specialized skills included later in this chapter, the content fields of literature, social studies, science, and mathematics each require unique skills for effective comprehension, retention, and writing in that field. Although it is true that there is some commonality among the skill requirements of all of these areas, it is equally true that there are great differences in their requirements. If a reader is very competent in comprehending narrative material at his or her instructional reading level, it is not a certainty that he or she will be equally competent in reading another type of content material. Both John and I are good examples that this is not always the case. For example, I am an excellent reader of both literature and social studies, have considerable difficulty in comprehending scientific materials, and have extreme difficulty in understanding mathematical verbal problems. In fact, it is virtually impossible for me to do so, which caused me great difficulty in both undergraduate and graduate school. Yet I had the capability of becoming a competent reader of both science and mathematics materials *if* a teacher in elementary school or secondary school had presented the appropriate strategies for reading these content fields. Unfortunately, this never happened, and I have never attained true competency in reading either scientific or mathematical materials. That is why it is so important for any literacy teacher to present the strategies and materials that will enable each student to be as competent a literacy learner as possible. This resource should help you teach content literacy skills as effectively as possible.

Then, too, a number of content textbooks are written well above the reading level of the students who are to read them. For example, a sixth-grade science textbook may well be written at the seventh-grade readability level or above. Such a textbook often contains many difficult specialized vocabulary terms and concepts and may not be very "reader-friendly." Thus, even the above-average readers may find such a textbook fairly difficult to comprehend, while it is even more difficult for average readers to comprehend and virtually impossible for below-average readers and many kinds of "at-risk" students (such as learning disabled students) to understand. Many content textbooks are written by experts in that field such as the scientific field, and literacy specialists do not provide any input into the process which might have made them somewhat easier to comprehend. However, contemporary content textbooks generally are providing more aids that may make it somewhat easier to comprehend them. In any case, students still should be presented with the strategies and other activities that will enable them to understand the textbooks more effectively.

As you are well aware, typical content textbooks are written in an expository style that is vastly different from the narrative style typical of easy-type reading material. Expository reading often contains many very difficult specialized vocabulary terms; a heavy, concentrated concept load; unique patterns of paragraph organization (all of which are explained later in Chapter 6); and symbolism and formulae. In addition, some of the paragraphs may lack a directly stated main idea and may also lack unity and purpose. All of these elements make most types of expository reading much more difficult for a good reader to comprehend, while causing extreme difficulty for below-average readers.

In addition, the graphic aids—such as maps, various types of graphs, charts, timelines, pictures, and diagrams—in content textbooks may cause all readers some difficulty, but cause the greatest amount of difficulty for below-average readers of various kinds. All students need meaningful instruction and practice in the use of these graphic aids beginning at the primary-grade level within the limits of their capability and prior knowledge. This resource provides many meaningful strategies and activity sheets for presenting and reinforcing graphic aids in later chapters.

It is a certainty that without competency in the specialized vocabulary and skills needed in a specific content area, a student cannot read, write, and study successfully in that area. As stated earlier in this section, each student *has to be taught to read and write to learn*. Without such appropriate instruction and practice, even otherwise good readers will not be competent literacy learners in all of the content areas as John and I clearly illustrate in the area of mathematical verbal problems. However, it is especially important for below-average readers and "at-risk" students to have meaningful instruction and reinforcement in all of the specialized vocabulary and literacy skills that comprise the content reading and writing skills. This teachers' resource will help literacy teachers to provide this instruction and practice.

SEVERAL CLASSIFICATION SCHEMES USED TO CATEGORIZE THE LITERACY-STUDY SKILLS NEEDED IN CONTENT READING AND WRITING

There are several different classification schemes that can be used to categorize the literacy-study skills needed for effective content reading and writing. Although all of them undoubtedly are equally useful, this teachers' resource describes only one in detail.

In any case, one such classification scheme is found in the following teachers' resource:

Wilma H. Miller, *Reading Teacher's Complete Diagnosis & Correction Manual.* West Nyack, New York: The Center for Applied Research in Education, 1988, pp. 266-275.

It very briefly includes the following major elements:

- Selection of Information
- Organization of Information
- Following Directions
- Location of Information
- Use of Graphic Aids
- Reading Rate and Flexibility

The literacy-study skills also can be categorized in the following way:

- Locating Information
- Using Library Resources
- Selecting Information
- Organizing Information

- Following Directions
- Reading Charts, Maps, and Graphs

However, after extensive research in the area, I have chosen to use another scheme for classifying or categorizing the literacy-study skills. This classification scheme is now listed and briefly discussed.

I. ***Information—Location Skills:*** The elements that comprise this type of literacy-study skills enable students to locate and use the various resources that help them to effectively comprehend and study content textbooks and other materials.

   A. *Selection of Information*

   1. *Locate Directly Stated Main Idea in a Paragraph.* Some paragraphs in expository (content) textbooks and other materials contain a directly stated main idea that usually is found in the first sentence. It can be called the topic sentence.

   2. *Locate Significant Details in a Paragraph.* If a paragraph in a content textbook or other materials has a directly stated main idea, it usually also contains significant details that support the main idea.

   3. *Locate Irrelevant Details in a Paragraph.* Some paragraphs in content textbooks and other materials contain irrelevant or unimportant details that do not amplify the main idea.

   4. *Locate the Implied Main Idea in a Paragraph.* In some paragraphs in content textbooks and other materials, the main idea is merely implied, not directly stated, and therefore must be inferred by the reader. This often makes the paragraph fairly difficult to understand.

   5. *Locate the Main Idea of a Longer Selection.* Students must be able to infer the major idea or main point of a longer selection in a content textbook or other content materials such as a section, an entire chapter, or an entire book.

   6. *Locate Information by the Use of Book Parts.* Students must be able to use the parts found in a content textbook or other materials in order to comprehend and study it effectively. The following are the important textbook parts that should be presented to students:

Title	Name of series
Author or Editor	Edition
Publisher	Copyright date
City of publication	

   7. *Locate and Understand the Function of the Following Book Aids.* Students should be able to understand the function of and effectively use the following aids contained in content textbooks and other materials:

Preface	Footnotes
Introduction	Bibliography
Table of contents	Glossary
List of figures	Index
Chapter headings	Appendices
Subtitles	

8. *Locate Information in Various Kinds of Reference Works.* Students should be able to use all of the following reference works effectively in order to ensure that they can locate important content information related to thematic units of instruction or for other important school and personal purposes.

Dictionary

Encyclopedia

Encyclopedia on CD-ROM computer software

Other types of reference works

Newspapers of various kinds

Magazines of various kinds

Telephone directories

Atlases

Television listings as found in the *TV Guide* and the television section of the local newspaper

Various periodical indices such as *The Reader's Guide to Periodical Literature*

9. *Locate Information in the School and Public Libraries.* Students should be able to use all of the resources found in school and public libraries to locate information needed for thematic units of instruction in content areas and for personal information and pleasure related to the learning of content material.

Library card catalog

On-line computer listing of works found in some larger libraries

10. *Ability to Study Information and Remember It.* Students should be able to comprehend, retain, and retrieve important information found in content textbooks or other types of content materials.

Highlight or underline important information

Use oral repetition to increase retention

Ask and answer questions as an aid to remembering

Employ a systematic study technique such as Survey Q3R, Survey Q4R, PQRST, POINT, C2R, or OK4R.

11. *Demonstrate Effective Study Habits.* Students should learn and apply effective study habits while comprehending and remembering content material found in textbooks and other materials.

Set a regular study time

Have adequate time for test or project preparation

Recognize the importance of self-motivation in learning

12. *Ability to Organize Information.* Students must learn how to effectively organize information learned from content textbooks and other content materials so that they can use the learned information for school or personal purposes.

Take useful notes

Note sources of information

Write a summary of a paragraph

Write a summary of a short selection

Write a summary for integrating information from more than one source

Write a summary of a longer selection

Make graphic aids to summarize information

Write an outline of a paragraph

Write an outline of a short selection

Write an outline of a longer selection

Write an outline integrating information from more than one source

Use an outline to write a report or make an oral report

Make an acceptable semantic map (web) as an alternative to a traditional outline

II. *Ability to Read and Carry Out Directions:* The elements in this category deal with the students' ability to effectively read and carry out various kinds of directions.

Read and carry out simple directions (one-, two-, three-, four-, and five-step directions)

Read and carry out a more complex series of directions (directions that contain more than five steps or are complicated in some other way)

III. *Ability to Interpret Graphic Aids:* The elements in this category deal with students' ability to effectively interpret various types of graphic aids that are found in content textbooks and other content materials.

A. *Ability to Interpret the Following Graphic Aids:*

Map

Graph (circle or pie graph, picture graph, bar graph, line graph)

Chart

Flow chart

Timeline

Picture

Cartoon

Venn diagram

IV. *Reading Rate and Flexibility:* The items in this group deal with students' ability to vary their reading rate depending upon the difficulty of the material and their purpose(s) for reading it.

Skim for a general impression

Scan for a particular fact

Rapid reading of easy, motivating material

Study-type reading

Careful, analytical reading

A LISTING OF THE REQUIRED SPECIALIZED VOCABULARY AND SKILLS FOR EFFECTIVE READING, WRITING, AND STUDY IN THE CONTENT AREAS

As stated earlier, various content areas require competence in different literacy-study skills. Although there is some overlap in the ways these skills are needed in the different content fields, there also are some differences that should be carefully considered by the literacy teacher. Content materials do not normally contain the narrative reading material that is most commonly found in basal readers but instead contain mainly expository material.

Literature (English or Language Arts)

Although the content area of literature does contain some narrative material comparable to the reading material found in basal readers, it also contains a number of unique literacy-study skills that should be presented to students when applicable.

Literature (Language Arts or English) includes the following unique literacy-study skills:

- Ability to understand the unique vocabulary in various genres such as the novel, short story, essay, biography, autobiography, drama, and poetry
- Ability to interpret figurative language
- Ability to notice and analyze the theme

- Ability to analyze characters
- Ability to read dialect
- Ability to recognize mood and tone
- Ability to recognize a climax and anticlimax
- Ability to read a play
- Ability to recognize an author's style and how a selection fits into the writing of the period in which it was written
- Ability to follow a plot
- Ability to vary the reading rate for various genres of literature (novel, short story, essay, biography, autobiography, drama, or poetry)
- Ability to understand word origins, slang, connotations of words, and words with multiple meanings
- Ability to identify a story line
- Critical (evaluative) reading ability
- Creative (applied) reading ability (creative responses to literature such as creative writing of prose and poetry and reading response logs)
- Making inferences about characters, events, and settings
- Using the library card catalog, library on-line computer system, other reference books such as *The Reader's Guide to Periodical Literature,* encyclopedias, and encyclopedias on CD-ROM computer software
- Ability to use computer databases and the INTERNET

Social Studies

The content area of social studies requires a number of unique literacy-study skills if students are to be able to read effectively in the field. Effective reading of social studies materials is essential if students are to develop an understanding of how people interact in culture, societies, and the world. The content materials in this area are especially difficult because social studies textbooks often are written on a higher reading level than the reading level of most of the students who are required to read them. This is an especially difficult problem for disabled readers and other "at-risk" readers who may be reading significantly below grade level anyway.

The content area of *social studies* includes the following literacy-study skills:

- Ability to understand specialized vocabulary (sometimes general vocabulary terms also have unique meanings in social studies)
- Ability to understand these textbook patterns of organization:

  Sequential

  Enumeration

  Cause-effect

  Comparison-contrast
- Ability to interpret maps, graphs, tables, diagrams, and pictures effectively
- Ability to read critically

- Ability to critically evaluate propaganda techniques
- Ability to read creatively
- Ability to understand the meanings of word roots, prefixes, and suffixes for vocabulary development
- Ability to locate main ideas and significant details in the material
- Ability to identify sequence of events especially in history
- Ability to use the following aids found in social studies textbooks:
  Chapter introductions
  Vocabulary lists
  Italicized words
  Marginal notes
  Highlighting
  Study aids of various kinds
  Footnotes
  Glossaries
- Ability to understand time and space relationships
- Ability to effectively use a study strategy such as Survey Q3R, Survey Q4R, PQRST, POINT, C2R, or OK4R
- Ability to use computer databases and the INTERNET

Science

The content area of science is difficult even for otherwise able readers; thus, it is extremely difficult for disabled readers and learning disabled students. The science textbooks that are selected for a grade level often are above the reading level of many of the students in that grade. They then are *much above* the reading level of the below-average readers in that grade. In addition, they are difficult for several other reasons, not the least of which is the large number of specialized, polysyllabic terms that they contain.

The content area of *science* includes the following unique literacy-study skills:

- Ability to understand these patterns of organization:
  Sequential
  Explanation of a technical process
  Directions for performing an experiment
  Detailed statement of facts
  Problem-solving
  Pattern of abbreviations and equations
- Ability to understand the difficult technical vocabulary
- Ability to use word roots, prefixes, and suffixes to determine the meaning of the polysyllabic specialized vocabulary
- Ability to understand and retain many important details
- Ability to differentiate between fact and opinion

- Ability to read and carry out directions
- Ability to perform a scientific experiment (demonstrate a scientific phenomenon) after reading how it should be conducted
- Ability to organize ideas from reading and understand the relationships between ideas in order to draw appropriate conclusions
- Ability to understand such cue words as *some, a few,* and *many*
- Ability to use library and computer skills to research a scientific topic
- Ability to interpret graphs and visual materials
- Ability to identify symbols, abbreviations, and formulae
- Ability to use the Survey Q3R study technique or an equivalent study strategy such as Survey Q4R, PQRST, POINT, C2R, or OK4R
- Ability to use computer databases and the INTERNET

Mathematics (Arithmetic)

The content area of mathematics (arithmetic) contains a number of unique elements that makes it very difficult for many students to comprehend effectively. As stated at the beginning of this chapter, the reading of mathematical verbal problems often presents a very difficult challenge for even able readers, including this author. Therefore, just imagine how extremely difficult this reading skill is for disabled readers and learning disabled students. In reading in mathematics (arithmetic), the student must know how to read mathematical materials of all types *and* must understand the concepts and their applications.

The following are some of the unique literacy-study skills required for effective reading and problem-solving in the content field of *mathematics (arithmetic)*:

- Ability to understand the specialized vocabulary (both unique terms and ordinary terms used in unique ways such as the terms *plus, minus, divide,* and *multiply*)
- Ability to understand the meanings of relevant word roots, prefixes, and suffixes
- Ability to comprehend mathematical symbols
- Ability to read for details
- Ability to read analytically and carefully
- Ability to generalize from what is read
- Ability to note relevant and irrelevant data in a mathematical problem
- Ability to comprehend different kinds of graphic and tabular materials
- Ability to read and follow directions precisely
- Ability to critically analyze statistical material
- Ability to locate and comprehend reference materials such as those about famous mathematicians
- Ability to interpret formulae, equations, principles, and axioms
- Ability to comprehend visual materials such as diagrams and geometric forms
- Ability to use a study technique in mathematics such as SQRQCO
- Ability to pronounce mathematical terms

- Ability to solve mathematics verbal problems (a very difficult skill for most students)
- Ability to estimate an answer to a mathematical problem
- Ability to use computer databases and the INTERNET

Each content area of literature (English or language arts), social studies, science, and mathematics (arithmetic) contains its own unique specialized terminology and skills that a student must master in order to be competent in reading, writing, and studying in that field. In addition, there are a number of more general literacy-study skills students also must master in order to be successful in reading, writing, and studying in the content areas. As stated earlier, a number of these skills are difficult for many students. In addition, the difficulty level of the content textbooks in these fields makes them very challenging for many students to read and study.

The ready-to-use, classroom-tested assessment devices, teaching strategies, reproducible materials, and games described and presented in this book will make the learning of these important literacy-study skills much more effective and easy for all students. In addition, literacy and content teachers will save much time and effort by using them to present and reinforce all of these important literacy-study skills.

Ready-to-Use Strategies and Activity Sheets for Assessing Competencies and Weaknesses in Content Reading, Writing, and Study Skills in Both Whole Language and Traditional Literacy Programs

Do you believe standardized reading/achievement tests are effective in assessing students' abilities in reading, writing, and study skills? Although it is certainly true that school districts must administer some standardized achievement tests in order to gather data about students' performance which then can be given to school boards, state boards of education, and parents, such standardized devices are not very effective in evaluating the everyday performance of most students. Although this also is the case in traditional literacy programs such as the basal reader or phonic approach, it is even more certainly the case in the *whole language programs* that today are so common in elementary schools. Indeed, whole language proponents consistently emphasize the crucial need for access to many useful types of *informal assessment devices* that can be used to effectively evaluate the actual outcomes of whole language programs.

This chapter contains numerous classroom-tested assessment strategies and devices of all types for evaluating students' performance in all aspects of the content reading, writing, and study skills in both whole language and traditional literacy programs. Although I have also written the following teachers' resource which entirely contains informal assessment devices for ascertaining students' abilities in reading, writing, and spelling, this chapter deals mainly with informal assessment devices for evaluating abilities in *content reading, writing, and study.*

Wilma H. Miller, *Informal Assessment Techniques for Reading & Writing.* West Nyack, New York: The Center for Applied Research in Education, 1995.

Literacy and content teachers should find this chapter to be extremely helpful in trying to assess a student's competencies and weaknesses in reading, writing, and study skills at all grade levels from the beginning stages of literacy through the middle-upper levels. The use of the reproducible assessment strategies and devices included in this chapter will save both literacy and content teachers immeasurable time and help them to make an accurate assessment of students' abilities in all of the literacy-study skills.

USING MAINLY INFORMAL BUT ALSO SOME STANDARDIZED ASSESSMENT DEVICES IN ASSESSING COMPETENCIES AND WEAKNESSES IN CONTENT READING, WRITING, AND STUDY SKILLS

Although standardized assessment devices of various kinds can serve a purpose in the assessment of the literacy-study skills, informal assessment devices generally are much more effective in assessing competencies and weaknesses in the various content reading, writing, and study subskills. In addition, they are much more relevant for use in contemporary whole language programs than are any type of standardized assessment devices. Indeed, the use of informal assessment devices should always be considered an essential part of instruction and therefore should occur continuously. Informal assessment often is more useful in determining a student's content literacy strengths and weaknesses than are standardized tests such as norm-referenced and criterion-referenced tests of various types, especially if the informal assessment is made by experienced literacy or content teachers.

Process-oriented assessment of reading, writing, and spelling weaknesses is much more likely to be accurate and useful than are the results of standardized testing. Far too many people place unjustified faith in standardized tests scores that correspondingly discourages the use of informal teacher assessment. However, such tests can be influenced by far too many extraneous factors to ever be used as a *sole criterion* for grouping students, promoting students, grading students, or evaluating teachers, schools, or school districts. Standardized test scores can be greatly influenced by factors such as examiner-examinee rapport, the student's health on the day of the test, the format of the test, physical conditions in the classroom, or even the time of the year when the test is given.

However, standardized tests do have a place in evaluating a student's competencies in the various elements of content reading, writing, and spelling. They may be useful in determining if a school district has met its goals or objectives or possibly the goals or objectives of some outside agency such as a state board of education. In addition, standardized tests may be useful in helping a teacher indicate a student's achievement to parents in a more scientific-appearing, but not necessarily more accurate, manner.

It certainly is always essential to integrate or link *literacy-study skills assessment with literacy-study skills instruction.* All informal and standardized assessment always should direct subsequent instruction. Without such direction, assessment of any type has no place in the school curriculum. Appropriate assessment followed by appropriate instruction can save a teacher and student much time and effort. Why, for example, should a student spend time and effort on learning literacy-study skills he or she already knows or that are relatively unimportant?

In summary, although both informal and standardized assessment devices are important in evaluating a student's competencies and weaknesses in the various literacy subskills required for effective comprehension, retention, and study in literature (language arts or English), social studies, science, and mathematics, *informal assessment devices are generally much more useful.*

"KID-WATCHING" AND HOLISTIC ASSESSMENT IN CONTENT READING, WRITING, AND SPELLING PROGRAMS

The term "kid-watching" was coined by Yetta Goodman of The University of Arizona, a proponent of the whole language philosophy. ("Kid-Watching: An Alternative to Testing," *National Elementary Principal,* 57, June 1978, pp. 41-45.) She has stated that "kid-watching" is direct or informal observation of a student in various classroom settings. "Kid-watching" enables teachers to explore these two questions:

1. What evidence exists that literacy development is occurring?
2. What does the student's unexpected production of literacy behaviors say about his or her knowledge of literacy?

"Kid-watching" or informal teacher assessment consists of these three aspects:

Observation—Carefully watching activities of a single student's, a group of students', or the entire class's literacy use and social behaviors.

Interaction—This occurs when the teacher raises questions, responds to journal writing, and conferences with students in order to stimulate further literacy and cognitive growth.

Analysis—The teacher obtains information by listening to a student read or discuss what was read and by examining the student's written work. The teacher then applies knowledge of learning principles to analyze his or her various literacy-study abilities.

Expert "kid-watchers" demonstrate the following behavior:

- They understand the reading, writing, and spelling processes in great detail.
- They also have an excellent knowledge of children's and adolescents' literature.
- They recognize the important patterns of behavior differences in competencies and weaknesses exhibited by different students.
- They listen attentively and perceptively to students.
- They *continuously evaluate* while teaching.
- They accept responsibility for curriculum development; they do not place undue emphasis on standardized test scores.
- They keep detailed records of a student's strengths and limitations in reading comprehension, writing, and spelling. Such records can take the place of completed checklists, paper-and-pencil tests of various types, videotapes, audiotapes, graphs or other records of progress, self-assessment devices, "working and show" portfolios, and teacher anecdotes.

I acknowledge that "kid-watching" or the informal assessment of reading, writing, and spelling abilities in the content fields is a difficult, demanding task with demands for great teacher expertise. However, it can be made easier and more effective by the reproducible assessment devices included in this *Handbook* and other useful resources.

THE ADVANTAGES AND LIMITATIONS OF INFORMAL AND STANDARDIZED ASSESSMENT OF CONTENT READING, WRITING, AND SPELLING SKILLS

There are a number of advantages for using *informal assessment devices* which often make them more useful than standardized tests. However, as stated earlier, they usually should be used along with some standardized tests since the latter are often mandated by administrators, school boards, state boards of education, and parents.

Here are the *major advantages* of using **informal assessment devices** in any literacy or content program:

- They are often more *authentic* in evaluating most of the subskills of reading comprehension, writing, and spelling in the content fields.
- They emphasize the *process aspects* of the literacy-study skills rather than the product aspects as traditionally is done by standardized tests of various types.
- They often are more relevant to the information that is being taught in a literacy classroom or content classroom.
- They are able to assess the affective (emotional or attitudinal) aspects of reading, writing, and spelling more effectively than can standardized devices.
- They usually more accurately reflect the accomplishments and attitudes of "at-risk" students of various types than do standardized tests. "At-risk" students such as minority group students, learning handicapped students, students who speak a nonstandard dialect, and slow-learning students often are penalized by standardized tests.
- They do not have the prescribed directions and time limits typically found on standardized tests. Such tests, for example, often penalize the slow, but accurate, reader.

Here are some of the *major limitations* of using **informal assessment devices** of various types:

- They usually are neither statistically reliable nor valid. However, this does not indicate that they are not useful. They usually simply do not meet the statistical requirements for reliability and validity.
- Their results often do not meet the requirements of administrators, school boards, state boards of education, or parents.
- They can be time-consuming to construct and/or evaluate and can be fairly difficult to learn how to administrate and especially to evaluate accurately.
- They may make it difficult to evaluate students' abilities in reading, writing, and spelling in the content fields by using predetermined criteria such as traditional report cards and grades.

- They are not always easy to locate. However, the informal assessment devices in reading comprehension, writing, and spelling in the content fields contained in this *Handbook* and other useful resources should greatly help literacy and content teachers to locate and reproduce many appropriate, useful informal assessment techniques.

Here are the *main advantages* of using **standardized tests** in any literacy content program:

- They serve as a useful screening device to locate the students who need additional testing of various informal and standardized types.
- They usually are statistically reliable and valid.
- They usually are easy to administer and to score. Often this kind of test takes from about 45 minutes to 60 or 90 minutes to give, and the scoring can be done entirely by computer.
- They reflect the content materials in the areas of literature (language arts or English), social studies, science, and mathematics of most elementary, middle, and secondary schools.
- They are formulated by test experts and experts in the field of literacy and the content field in which they are attempting to evaluate.
- They can be given by a virtually untrained examiner.

However, all **standardized devices** have the following *significant limitations*:

- They are not free of cultural bias and often discriminate against various types of "at-risk" students such as students from minority groups, learning-handicapped students, students who speak nonstandard English, or slow-learning students.
- They sometimes are not *passage dependent*. The student may well be able to answer the comprehension questions without even reading the material since they are based upon prior knowledge.
- They use only short reading passages to evaluate reading comprehension. This is unlike the reading materials required in actual school content reading in the fields of literature (language arts or English), social studies, science, or mathematics.
- They often do not evaluate a student's actual meaning vocabulary knowledge in the content fields very well since the student may not know the meaning of the vocabulary term in isolation when he or she would be able to determine the meaning in the context of content materials.
- They have considerable difficulty in evaluating a student's ability in *implicit (higher-level) comprehension* since only one answer is possible for any question.
- They may well *overestimate* the student's actual instructional reading level due to the guessing factor and to the difficulty of obtaining a true estimate of a student's abilities at the upper and lower ends of the scale.

These limitations indicate why a student's score on any standardized device should always be considered as only a *tentative indicator* of his or her performance in the skill(s) that device is attempting to evaluate.

USING TEACHER-PUPIL CONFERENCES IN THE ASSESSMENT OF CONTENT READING, WRITING, AND SPELLING SKILLS

Teacher-pupil conferences can be very helpful in the assessment of competencies and weaknesses in content reading, writing, and spelling skills in the fields of literature (English or language arts), social studies, science, and mathematics. They can be used effectively for this purpose in both regular classrooms and content classrooms from the upper primary grades through the secondary school level. They normally should only be used occasionally for this purpose instead of on a daily basis due to the time constraints in such classrooms, although their regular use could certainly be very helpful. Teacher-pupil conferences can mainly be used to assess, present, or reinforce many different literacy-study concepts and skills. However, the teaching of literacy-study concepts and skills usually takes place in a total-class or small-group setting due to the time that such group instruction saves.

Although teacher-pupil literacy-study conferences can take place at the upper primary grade level, they more typically occur in middle and secondary schools. There should be occasionally scheduled one-on-one conferences, and the literacy or content teacher should have a sign-up sheet that a student can sign in order to request a conference when it is needed or wanted. However, in addition each student should be scheduled to have individual literacy-study conferences with his or her teacher on specified occasions.

When a teacher uses teacher-pupil literacy-study conferences as part of content instruction, he or she may be able to meet with several students each day. The conferences usually last from several minutes to about fifteen minutes with most conferences lasting about five to ten minutes.

Recordkeeping is a very important part of any program of teacher-pupil literacy-study conferences. The literacy or content teacher can have a notebook with a section for each student. The student's records should include the dates of the conferences, the titles and authors of the content-related trade books or other content materials the student has read, the specific literacy-study skills in which the student is competent and weak, and observations about how the student feels about literacy in general and specifically about reading, writing, and spelling in the content fields of literature (English or language arts), social studies, science, and mathematics. The student also should be encouraged to keep his or her own records. Often the student's records can be kept in a notebook or on index cards. Have the student simply list the title and author of each trade book, content textbook chapter, other content materials, or computer software and his or her reaction to the material on a separate page of the notebook or index card. There also are many creative ways in which a student can keep literacy-study conference records.

Very briefly, teacher-pupil literacy/study conferences can be used for the following general purposes:

- to assess a student's competency in the various literacy-study skills in the content fields of literature (English or language arts), social studies, science, and mathematics

- to specifically evaluate a student's competency in the comprehension skills required in the content fields

- to help the student in locating more information on a content topic from sources such as trade books, other content textbooks, other content reading materials, and computer software

- to help the student obtain feedback about his or her literacy-study skills
- to share an enjoyable trade book or other content materials related to a content topic he or she is studying
- less commonly, to teach and/or reinforce a specific literacy-study skill in which the student lacks competence

The typical teacher-pupil literacy-study conference has the following parts:

- listening to the student speak
- talking with the student
- listening to the student read
- assessing a student's competencies and weaknesses in the targeted literacy-study skills
- presenting and/or reinforcing a needed literacy-study skill or skills

This is the format most teachers in a content literacy program use when having literacy-study content conferences:

- discussing the trade book, content textbook chapter, other content materials, or related computer software the student has read, thus ensuring his or her comprehension and mastery of the requisite literacy-study skills
- having the student *on occasion* read aloud from the selected content material and providing instruction/reinforcement as needed
- discussing additional activities or readings from related trade books, content-related textbooks, other content materials, or computer software

   Note: It is often important to allow the student to take the lead in teacher-pupil literacy-study conferences if possible.

Here are some questions you can ask during a teacher-pupil literacy-study conference to evaluate a student's literacy-study skills in an effective way:

- How do you feel about the trade book or other content material you're reading (you have just read)?
- What are some of the *most interesting* things you learned from reading this trade book or other content material?
- What are some of the *most important* things you learned from reading this trade book or other content material?
- What did you like *the best (the least)* about reading this trade book or other content material?
- Will you please read *your favorite (the most important)* part of this tradebook or other content material aloud? **Note:** Do not use this request on a regular basis. Oral reading in content material should only be done occasionally.

   Note: If the student is reading his or her favorite portion of the trade book or other content material out loud, note the kind of miscues he or she makes. You can also note the type of word attack strategy the student uses when meeting an unknown word. In most instances, *semantic cues along with graphophonic cues and syntactic (grammar) cues* provide the best method of word identification in content reading. The student always should be encouraged to use *multiple cuing systems and to read for meaning.*

Reproducible Literacy-Study Skills Observational Checklists

These reproducible literacy-study skills observational checklists are at the upper primary, the interemediate, and the middle-upper grade levels. You can duplicate and use any of these useful checklists in their present form or modify them to meet the needs and interests of your own students.

LITERACY-STUDY SKILLS OBSERVATIONAL CHECKLIST
(Upper Primary Grade Level)

I. Information—Location Skills

A. Is able to substitute words for unknown words that make sense in sentence context and that are grammatically correct while reading content material at the second- or third-grade reading level ❏

B. Is able to orally state the main idea of a paragraph, a short passage, or a longer selection ❏

C. Is able to orally state the most important details in a paragraph, a short passage, or a longer selection ❏

D. Is able to locate information by using the following book parts: title, author, illustrator, and date of publication ❏

E. Is able to use a table of contents from a second- or third-grade content textbook ❏

F. Is able to use the page numbers in a content textbook to locate the required page ❏

G. Is able to use the guide words and entry words in a simplified dictionary to locate the targeted words ❏

H. Is able to use a simplified dictionary to locate the meaning or pronunciation of an unknown word ❏

I. Is able to use alphabetical sequence by the first letter in a series of words such as the following: ❏

afternoon

between

cane

door

eight

J. Is able to use appropriate resources to locate information required in such content areas as social studies and science. Some of these resources may be as follows: trade books, a children's encyclopedia, content textbooks at the appropriate reading level, computer software, or children's magazines ❏

K. Is able to answer literal (explicit) and interpretive (implicit) comprehension questions to help remember the content material read ❏

L. Is able to orally give a brief summary of a trade book or content textbook chapter ❏

M. Is able to write a one- or two-sentence summary of a trade book or content textbook chapter using invented spelling if necessary ❏

LITERACY-STUDY SKILLS OBSERVATIONAL CHECKLIST
(Upper Primary Grade Level)

(cont.)

N. Understands the purpose of a semantic map or web and can complete one with some teacher or peer assistance if necessary ❏

II. Ability to Read and Carry Out Directions

A. Is able to listen carefully and then carry out directions of two to four steps ❏

B. Is able to read and carry out directions of two to four steps ❏

III. Ability to Interpret Graphic Aids

A. Is able to interpret the pictures found in social studies and science textbooks ❏

B. Is able to understand and interpret simple maps such as a map of his or her neighborhood or those found in a content textbook ❏

C. Is able to interpret a simple picture graph ❏

D. Is able to interpret simple cartoons and comic strips within the limits of his or her prior knowledge ❏

IV. Reading Rate and Flexibility

A. Is able to vary his or her reading rate depending upon his or her purpose for reading the material and the difficulty of the reading material within the limits of his or her reading level and prior knowledge; i.e., reads a predictable book more rapidly than a chapter from a social studies or science textbook ❏

B. Generally avoids reading in a word-by-word manner, which can slow his or her reading rate ❏

V. Uses the Necessary Specialized Vocabulary and Skills Required for Effective Reading, Writing, Spelling, and Study in the Content Areas

A. Literature (Language Arts or English)

1. Understands such elements of story grammar as *theme, plot, characters,* and *resolution* ❏

2. Is able to predict story content before reading and then effectively confirm or disconfirm his or her predictions ❏

3. Is able to retell a story or trade book at the second- or third-grade reading level in approximately correct sequence ❏

4. Is able to interpret such figurative language as the following: ❏

   hungry as a bear

   eat like a pig

   Katie *caught a cold* on Monday.

LITERACY-STUDY SKILLS OBSERVATIONAL CHECKLIST
(Upper Primary Grade Level)

(cont.)

5. Is able to differentiate between fact and fantasy (real and make-believe) in *most,* but not necessarily all material ❑

6. Is able to recognize the feelings, actions, and motives of story characters with some degree of competence ❑

7. Is able to follow up narrative or content reading in a problem-solving manner such as by creative dramatics, dramatic play, art activities, construction activities, creative writing of prose or poetry, cooking or baking activities, or a simple reading response journal ❑

B. Social Studies

1. Is able to understand simple cause-effect relationships ❑

2. Is able to place 3 to 5 items from social studies material in correct order or sequence ❑

3. Is able to interpret the pictures, simple maps, and diagrams correctly from a second- or third-grade social studies textbook ❑

4. Is able to distinguish between fact and opinion from social studies topics at a rudimentary level ❑

5. Is able to understand the meanings of simple prefixes such as *-un* and *-re* ❑

C. Science

1. Is able to read the directions for performing a *very simple* scientific experiment and then carry it out successfully independently, or more likely, with one or more partners ❑

2. Is able to understand such cue words as *some, a few,* and *many* ❑

3. Is able to use simple resources such as appropriate trade books, content textbooks, a children's encyclopedia, or computer software to research a unit in science independently, or more likely, with one or more partners ❑

4. Is able to place 3 to 5 items from science reading materials in correct sequence ❑

5. Is able to interpret a simple graph from science materials ❑

D. Arithmetic

1. Is able to understand the basic vocabulary and symbolism of simple arithmetic at the second- or third-grade level such as *add* and *subtract* (+ and −) ❑

2. Is able to differentiate between the main ideas and the details in a simple arithmetic verbal problem ❑

LITERACY-STUDY SKILLS OBSERVATIONAL CHECKLIST
(Upper Primary Grade Level)

(cont.)

3. Is able to comprehend and solve a simple arithmetic verbal problem independently or with one or more partners ❑

4. Is able to determine whether or not the answer to an arithmetic verbal problem is correct (makes sense) ❑

LITERACY-STUDY SKILLS OBSERVATIONAL CHECKLIST
(Intermediate Grade Level)

I. Information—Location Skills

A. Is able to substitute words for unknown words that make sense in sentence context and that are grammatically correct while reading content material at the fourth-, fifth-, or sixth-grade level ❏

B. Is able to locate directly stated main ideas from paragraphs in content material at the fourth-, fifth-, or sixth-grade level ❏

C. Is able to locate significant (important) details in paragraphs from content material at the fourth-, fifth-, or sixth-grade level ❏

D. Is able to locate irrelevant (unimportant or inaccurate) details in paragraphs from content material at the fourth-, fifth-, or sixth-grade level ❏

E. Is able to state implied main ideas from paragraphs with some degree of competence from content material at the fourth-, fifth-, or sixth-grade level ❏

F. Is able to state the main idea of a longer selection from content material at the fourth-, fifth-, or sixth-grade level ❏

G. Is able to locate information by using the following book parts: title, author or editor, illustrator, publisher, city of publication, and date of publication ❏

H. Is able to locate, understand the function of, and use the following content textbook parts: table of contents, chapter subheadings, typographical aids, glossary, appendices, and index ❏

I. Is able to use all of the elements of an intermediate-grade dictionary to locate the pronunciation, spelling, and meaning of unknown words encountered in content reading—including alphabetical sequence, guide words, entry words, diacritical markings, and selecting the correct definition for use in the context of content material ❏

J. Is able to use a thesaurus effectively to locate synonyms for targeted terms ❏

K. Is able to effectively use such elements of an encyclopedia as key words, volume numbers, guide words, entry words, section headings, and cross-references ❏

L. Is able to use alphabetical sequence by the first several letters in a series of words such as the following: ❏

abstain

admit

aisle

amber

anchor

LITERACY-STUDY SKILLS OBSERVATIONAL CHECKLIST
(Intermediate Grade Level)

(cont.)

appetite

astute

attitude

M. Is able to use appropriate resources to research information required in the content areas of literature (language arts or English), social studies, science, and mathematics (arithmetic). Some of these resources may be as follows: trade books, content textbooks at the appropriate reading level, computer software including software on a CD-ROM, newspapers, magazines, a telephone directory, an atlas, *The Guinness Book of Records,* and *The Reader's Guide to Periodical Literature* ❏

N. Is able to use the school library, a local public library, a library card catalog, and an on-line computer system (if available) to locate information for use in content learning ❏

O. Is able to answer literal (explicit) and interpretive (implicit) comprehension questions to help remember content material read at the fourth-, fifth-, or sixth-grade level ❏

P. Is able to highlight or underline the important information in the content material that is being read and studied ❏

Q. Is able to employ a systematic study strategy such as Survey Q3R (or any variation of it) to help comprehend and retain content material at the fourth-, fifth-, or sixth-grade level ❏

R. Is able to employ such effective study habits as setting a regular study time and having enough time for test and project preparation ❏

S. Is able to take usable notes from content reading material at the fourth-, fifth-, or sixth-grade level ❏

T. Is able to write an acceptable one-sentence summary of a paragraph ❏

U. Is able to write an acceptable one-paragraph summary of a short or a longer selection ❏

V. Is able to write an outline of a short or a longer selection ❏

W. Is able to use an outline to prepare an oral report or to write an acceptable report ❏

X. Is able to construct an acceptable semantic map or web as an alternative to a traditional outline while reading and studying content material at the fourth-, fifth-, or sixth-grade level ❏

LITERACY-STUDY SKILLS OBSERVATIONAL CHECKLIST
(Intermediate Grade Level)

(cont.)

II. Ability to Read and Carry Out Directions

    A. Is able to listen carefully and then carry out directions of four to six steps   ❏

    B. Is able to read and carry out directions of four to six steps   ❏

III. Ability to Interpret Graphic Aids

    A. Is able to interpret the types of maps found in content material at the fourth-, fifth-, or sixth-grade level   ❏

    B. Is able to interpret the following types of graphs from content material at the fourth-, fifth-, or sixth-grade level: ❏

        circle or pie graphs

        picture graphs (pictographs)

        bar graphs

        line graphs

    C. Is able to interpret charts of various types, including flow charts, from content material at the fourth-, fifth-, or sixth-grade level   ❏

    D. Is able to interpret a timeline from content material at the fourth-, fifth-, or sixth-grade level   ❏

    E. Is able to interpret diagrams of various kinds, including Venn diagrams, from content material at the fourth-, fifth-, or sixth-grade level   ❏

    F. Is able to interpret cartoons and comic strips from content material at the fourth-, fifth-, or sixth-grade level   ❏

IV. Reading Rate and Flexibility

    A. Is able to vary his or her reading rate depending upon his or her purpose for reading and the difficulty of the reading material; i.e., reads a chapter book more rapidly than a chapter from a social studies or science textbook   ❏

    B. Is able to skim material to gain a general impression   ❏

    C. Is able to scan material to locate a specific fact such as a time, date, or place   ❏

    D. Is able to read appropriate content material at a study-type rate of reading   ❏

    E. Is able to read appropriate content material at a careful, analytical, slow rate of reading   ❏

    F. Avoids reading in a word-by-word manner which can slow his or her reading rate   ❏

LITERACY-STUDY SKILLS OBSERVATIONAL CHECKLIST
(Intermediate Grade Level)

(cont.)

G. Avoids inhibiting factors such as lip movements, head movements, and finger-pointing while reading content material at the fourth-, fifth-, or sixth-grade level ❏

V. Uses the Necessary Vocabulary and Skills Required for Effective Reading, Writing, Spelling, and Study in the Content Areas

A. Literature (Language Arts or English)

1. Understands such elements of story grammar as *theme, plot, characters,* and *resolution* with some degree of sophistication ❏

2. Is able to make correct inferences about characters, events, and settings ❏

3. Is able to understand the unique vocabulary and style of the various genres of literature such as the young adolescent novel, the short story, the essay, the biography or autobiography, drama, and poetry at the fourth-, fifth-, or sixth-grade level ❏

4. Is able to interpret such figurative language as the following: ❏

   as cool as a cucumber

   stood out like a sore thumb

   Jimmy must *use kid gloves* while handling that situation.

   Molly hardly *cracked a book* during the entire spring vacation.

5. Is able to understand an author's style and how the selection fits into the writing of the period in which it was written ❏

6. Is able to understand word origins, slang, word connotations, and words with multiple meanings at the fourth-, fifth-, or sixth-grade level ❏

7. Is able to make inferences about characters, events, and settings ❏

8. Is able to vary the reading rate for the various genres of literature such as young adolescent novel, short story, essay, biography or autobiography, drama, and poetry at the fourth-, fifth-, or sixth-grade level ❏

9. Is able to critically analyze what was read from literature at the fourth-, fifth-, or sixth-grade level ❏

10. Is able to make creative responses to literature such as creative dramatics, Reader's Theater, reading response journals, cooking or baking activities, rhythm activities, or creative writing of prose or poetry ❏

LITERACY-STUDY SKILLS OBSERVATIONAL CHECKLIST
(Intermediate Grade Level)

(cont.)

B. Social Studies

1. Is able to identify and interpret the specialized vocabulary from social studies material at the fourth-, fifth-, or sixth-grade level ❏

2. Is able to read social studies material critically at the fourth-, fifth-, or sixth-grade level ❏

3. Is able to understand the following patterns of organization that are commonly found in social studies material at the fourth-, fifth-, or sixth-grade level: *sequential, enumeration, cause-effect,* and *comparison-contrast* ❏

4. Is able to distinguish fact from opinion in social studies material at the fourth-, fifth-, or sixth-grade level ❏

5. Is able to critically analyze such propaganda techniques as *testimonials, emotionally-toned words,* and the *bandwagon technique* ❏

6. Is able to use word roots, prefixes, and suffixes to determine the meaning of unknown words from social studies materials at the fourth-, fifth-, or sixth-grade level ❏

7. Is able to read creatively in social studies; i.e., apply what was read from social studies materials to his or her own life to change it in some positive way ❏

8. Is able to understand time and space relationships ❏

9. Is able to use such textbook aids as the following while reading social studies materials at the fourth-, fifth-, or sixth-grade level: *chapter introduction, targeted vocabulary terms, italicized words, marginal notes, highlighting, study aids,* and *footnotes* ❏

10. Is able to use a study strategy such as Survey Q3R, Survey Q4R, PQRST, POINT, C2R, or OK4R while reading social studies materials at the fourth-, fifth-, or sixth-grade level ❏

C. Science

1. Is able to identify and comprehend the difficult specialized vocabulary from science materials at the fourth-, fifth-, or sixth-grade level ❏

2. Is able to understand the following patterns of organization from science materials at the fourth-, fifth-, or sixth-grade level: *sequential, classification, explanation of a technical process, directions for performing an experiment, detailed statement of facts, problem-solving,* and *pattern of abbreviations and equations* ❏

LITERACY-STUDY SKILLS OBSERVATIONAL CHECKLIST
(Intermediate Grade Level)

(cont.)

3. Is able to use word roots, prefixes, and suffixes to determine the meaning of the polysyllabic specialized vocabulary from science materials at the fourth-, fifth-, or sixth-grade level ❏

4. Is able to read and carry out directions for performing a scientific experiment from science materials at the fourth-, fifth-, or sixth-grade level ❏

5. Is able to differentiate between fact and opinion while reading science materials at the fourth-, fifth-, or sixth-grade level ❏

6. Is able to understand and retain many important details while reading science materials at the fourth-, fifth-, or sixth-grade level ❏

7. Is able to successfully perform a scientific experiment independently or with one or more partners after reading how it should be carried out ❏

8. Is able to organize ideas from reading science materials at the fourth-, fifth-, or sixth-grade level and understand the relationships between ideas in order to draw appropriate conclusions ❏

9. Is able to understand such cue words in science materials as *some, a few,* and *many* ❏

10. Is able to interpret graphs and visual materials from science materials at the fourth-, fifth-, or sixth-grade level ❏

11. Is able to use library and computer skills to research a scientific topic ❏

12. Is able to identify and understand symbols, abbreviations, and formulae from science materials at the fourth-, fifth-, or sixth-grade level ❏

13. Is able to use a study strategy such as Survey Q3R, Survey Q4R, PQRST, POINT, C2R, or OK4R while reading science materials at the fourth-, fifth-, or sixth-grade level ❏

D. Mathematics (Arithmetic)

1. Is able to understand the specialized vocabulary and symbolism of mathematics such as *plus, minus, multiply, divide,* and *equal* $(+, -, \times, \div, =)$ ❏

2. Is able to understand the meanings of relevant word roots, prefixes, and suffixes in determining the meaning of mathematical terms at the fourth-, fifth, or sixth-grade level ❏

3. Is able to read mathematical material at the fourth-, fifth-, or sixth-grade level very carefully and analytically for details ❏

4. Is able to understand and to follow directions precisely while reading a mathematical problem at the fourth-, fifth-, or sixth-grade level ❏

LITERACY-STUDY SKILLS OBSERVATIONAL CHECKLIST
(Intermediate Grade Level)

(cont.)

5. Is able to note relevant and irrelevant data in a mathematical problem at the fourth-, fifth-, or sixth-grade level in order to attempt to solve it ❏

6. Is able to comprehend and solve mathematical verbal problems at the fourth-, fifth-, or sixth-grade level ❏

7. Is able to critically analyze graphs and tables while reading mathematical material at the fourth-, fifth-, or sixth-grade level ❏

8. Is able to successfully comprehend visual materials such as diagrams while reading mathematical material at the fourth-, fifth-, or sixth-grade level ❏

9. Is able to use a study technique in mathematics such as SQRQCO ❏

LITERACY-STUDY SKILLS OBSERVATIONAL CHECKLIST
(Middle–Upper Grade Level)

I. Information—Location Skills

A. Is able to substitute words for unknown words that make sense in sentence context and that are grammatically correct while reading content material at the seventh-, eighth-, ninth-, tenth-, eleventh-, or twelfth-grade level ❏

B. Is able to locate directly stated main ideas from paragraphs in content material at the seventh-, eighth-, ninth-, tenth-, eleventh-, or twelfth-grade level ❏

C. Is able to locate significant (important) details in paragraphs from content material at the seventh-, eighth-, ninth-, tenth-, eleventh-, or twelfth-grade level ❏

D. Is able to locate irrelevant (unimportant or inaccurate) details in paragraphs from content material at the seventh-, eighth-, ninth-, tenth-, eleventh-, or twelfth-grade level ❏

E. Is able to competently formulate implied main ideas from paragraphs from content material at the seventh-, eighth-, ninth-, tenth-, eleventh-, or twelfth-grade level ❏

F. Is able to state the main idea of a long selection from content material at the seventh-, eighth-, ninth-, tenth-, eleventh-, or twelfth-grade level ❏

G. Is able to locate information by using the following book parts: title, author or editor, illustrator, publisher, city of publication, name of series, edition, and copyright date ❏

H. Is able to locate, understand the function of, and use the following content textbook aids: preface, introduction, table of contents, list of figures, chapter headings, subtitles, typographical aids, headnotes, footnotes, bibliography, glossary, index, and appendices ❏

I. Is able to use all of the elements of a middle- or upper-level dictionary to locate the pronunciation, spelling, and meaning of unknown words encountered in content reading—including alphabetical sequence, guide words, entry words, diacritical markings, and selecting the correct definition for use in the context of content material ❏

J. Is able to use a thesaurus effectively to locate synonyms and antonyms for targeted terms ❏

K. Is able to use such elements of an encyclopedia effectively as key words, volume numbers, guide words, entry words, section headings, and cross-references ❏

L. Is able to use alphabetical sequence by any of the letters in a long series of words: ❏

LITERACY-STUDY SKILLS OBSERVATIONAL CHECKLIST
(Middle–Upper Grade Level)

(cont.)

aardvark

absolute

admire

aerial

aft

aggregate

ahead

airborne

ajar

akin

album

ambassador

anthem

aorta

apology

aquatic

arbitrary

assimilate

atmosphere

audible

avalanche

awkward

axis

aye

azure

LITERACY-STUDY SKILLS OBSERVATIONAL CHECKLIST
(Middle–Upper Grade Level)

(cont.)

M. Is able to use appropriate resources to research information in the content areas of literature (language arts or English), social studies, science, and mathematics. Some of these resources may be as follows: trade books, content textbooks at the appropriate reading level, a dictionary, an encyclopedia, computer software including software on a CD-ROM, newspapers, magazines, a telephone directory, an atlas, *The Guinness Book of Records,* and *The Reader's Guide to Periodical Literature.* ❑

N. Is able to use the school library, a local public library, a library card catalog, and an on-line computer system (if available) to locate information for use in content learning ❑

O. Is able to answer literal (explicit) and interpretive (implicit) comprehension questions to help in remembering content material at the seventh-, eighth-, ninth-, tenth-, eleventh-, and twelfth-grade level that was read ❑

P. Is able to highlight or underline the important information in the content material that is being read and studied ❑

Q. Is able to use oral repetition to increase retention of the content material that is being read and studied ❑

R. Is able to employ a systematic study strategy such as Survey Q3R (or any variation) to help in comprehending and retaining content material at the seventh-, eighth-, ninth-, tenth-, eleventh-, or twelfth-grade level ❑

S. Is able to employ such effective study habits as setting a regular study time and having enough time for test and project preparation ❑

T. Recognizes the importance of *self-motivation* in learning content material ❑

U. Is able to take usable notes from content material at the seventh-, eighth-, ninth-, tenth-, eleventh-, or twelfth-grade level ❑

V. Is able to write an acceptable one- or two-sentence summary of a content paragraph ❑

W. Is able to write an acceptable one-paragraph or several-paragraph summary of a short or long content selection ❑

X. Is able to write an acceptable summary integrating content material from more than one source ❑

Y. Is able to construct an outline to prepare an oral report or write an acceptable report ❑

Z. Is able to construct an outline to integrate information from more than one source ❑

LITERACY-STUDY SKILLS OBSERVATIONAL CHECKLIST
(Middle–Upper Grade Level)

(cont.)

AA. Is able to construct an acceptable semantic map or web as an alternative to a traditional outline while reading and studying content material at the seventh-, eighth-, ninth-, tenth-, eleventh-, or twelfth-grade level ❏

II. Ability to Read and Carry Out Directions

A. Is able to listen carefully and then carry out directions containing multiple steps ❏

B. Is able to read and then carry out directions containing multiple steps ❏

III. Ability to Interpret Graphic Aids

A. Is able to interpret all of the types of maps found in content material at the seventh-, eighth-, ninth-, tenth-, eleventh-, or twelfth-grade level ❏

B. Is able to interpret the following types of graphs from content material at the seventh-, eighth-, ninth-, tenth-, eleventh-, or twelfth-grade level: ❏

circle or pie graphs

pictures graphs (pictographs)

bar graphs

line graphs

C. Is able to interpret charts of various types including flow charts from content material at the seventh-, eighth-, ninth-, tenth-, eleventh-, or twelfth-grade level ❏

D. Is able to interpret a time line from content material at the seventh-, eighth-, ninth-, tenth-, eleventh-, or twelfth-grade level ❏

E. Is able to interpret diagrams of various kinds including Venn diagrams from content material at the seventh-, eighth-, ninth-, tenth-, eleventh-, or twelfth-grade level ❏

F. Is able to interpret cartoons from content material at the seventh-, eighth-, ninth-, tenth-, eleventh-, or twelfth-grade level ❏

IV. Reading Rate and Flexibility

A. Is able to vary his or her reading rate depending upon his or her purpose for reading and the difficulty of the reading material; i.e., reads a novel more rapidly than a chapter from a social studies or science textbook ❏

B. Is able to skim material to gain a general impression ❏

C. Is able to scan material to locate a specific fact such as a time, date, or place ❏

LITERACY-STUDY SKILLS OBSERVATIONAL CHECKLIST
(Middle–Upper Grade Level)

(cont.)

D. Is able to read appropriate content material at a study-type rate of reading ❏

E. Is able to read appropriate content material at a careful, analytical, slow rate of reading ❏

F. Avoids reading in a word-by-word manner which can slow his or her reading rate ❏

G. Avoids inhibiting factors such as lip movements, head movements, and finger-pointing while reading content material at the seventh-, eighth-, ninth-, tenth-, eleventh-, or twelfth-grade level ❏

V. Uses the Necessary Vocabulary and Skills Required for Effective Reading, Writing, Spelling, and Study in the Content Areas

A. Literature (Language Arts or English)

1. Understands such elements of *story grammar* as *theme, plot, characters, climax, anticlimax,* and *resolution* with a high degree of sophistication ❏

2. Is able to orally read and understand the various types of dialects found in different genres of literature ❏

3. Is able to make correct inferences about characters, events, and settings ❏

4. Is able to understand the unique vocabulary and style of the various genres of literature such as the novel, the short story, the essay, the biography or autobiography, drama, and poetry at the seventh-, eighth-, ninth-, tenth-, eleventh-, or twelfth-grade level ❏

5. Is able to interpret such figurative language as the following: ❏

as slow as molasses in January

acts like a bull in a china shop

When Ellen's mother died, she *shouldered the burden* of raising her younger brother and sister.

Ralph and his mother don't see *eye to eye* on anything.

6. Is able to understand an author's style and how the selection fits into the writing of the period in which it was written ❏

7. Is able to make inferences about characters, events, and settings ❏

8. Is able to vary the reading rate for the various genres of literature such as novels, short stories, essays, biographies or autobiographies, drama, and poetry at the seventh-, eighth-, ninth-, tenth-, eleventh-, or twelfth-grade level ❏

LITERACY-STUDY SKILLS OBSERVATIONAL CHECKLIST
(Middle–Upper Grade Level)

(cont.)

9. Is able to understand word origins, slang, connotations of words, and words with multiple meanings from literature at the seventh-, eighth-, ninth-, tenth-, eleventh-, or twelfth-grade level ❑

10. Is able to identify a story line from literature at the seventh-, eighth-, ninth-, tenth-, eleventh-, or twelfth-grade level ❑

11. Is able to make creative responses to literature such as creative dramatics, Reader's Theater, reading response journals, cooking or baking activities, rhythm activities, or creative writing of prose or poetry ❑

B. Social Studies

1. Is able to identify and interpret the specialized vocabulary from social studies material at the seventh-, eighth-, ninth-, tenth-, eleventh-, or twelfth-grade level ❑

2. Is able to read social studies material critically at the seventh-, eighth-, ninth-, tenth-, eleventh-, or twelfth-grade level ❑

3. Is able to understand the following patterns of organization commonly found in social studies material at the seventh-, eighth-, ninth-, tenth-, eleventh-, or twelfth-grade level: *sequential, enumeration, cause-effect,* and *comparison-contrast* ❑

4. Is able to distinguish fact from opinion from social studies material at the seventh-, eighth-, ninth-, tenth-, eleventh-, or twelfth-grade level ❑

5. Is able to critically analyze such propaganda techniques as *testimonials, emotionally-toned words, cardstacking, the halo effect,* and the *bandwagon technique* ❑

6. Is able to use word roots, prefixes, and suffixes to determine the meaning of unknown words from social studies materials at the seventh-, eighth-, ninth-, tenth-, eleventh-, or twelfth-grade level ❑

7. Is able to read creatively in social studies; i.e., apply what was read from social studies to his or her own life to change it in some positive way ❑

8. Is able to understand time and space relationships ❑

9. Is able to use such textbook aids as the following while reading social studies materials at the seventh-, eighth-, ninth-, tenth-, eleventh-, or twelfth-grade level: *chapter introduction, vocabulary list, italicized words, marginal notes, highlighting, study aids, headnotes, footnotes, glossary,* and *index* ❑

10. Is able to use a study strategy such as Survey Q3R, Survey Q4R, PQRST, POINT, C2R, or OK4R while reading social studies material at the seventh-, eighth-, ninth-, tenth-, eleventh-, or twelfth-grade level ❑

LITERACY-STUDY SKILLS OBSERVATIONAL CHECKLIST
(Middle–Upper Grade Level)

(cont.)

C. Science

1. Is able to identify and comprehend the difficult specialized vocabulary from science materials at the seventh-, eighth-, ninth-, tenth-, eleventh-, or twelfth-grade level ❏

2. Is able to understand the following patterns of organization from science materials at the seventh-, eighth-, ninth-, tenth-, eleventh-, or twelfth-grade level: *sequential, classification, explanation of a technical process, directions for performing an experiment, detailed statement of facts, problem-solving,* and *pattern of abbreviations and equations* ❏

3. Is able to use word roots, prefixes, and suffixes to determine the meaning of the polysyllabic specialized vocabulary from science materials at the seventh-, eighth-, ninth-, tenth-, eleventh-, or twelfth-grade level ❏

4. Is able to read and carry out directions for performing a scientific experiment at the seventh-, eighth-, ninth-, tenth-, eleventh-, or twelfth-grade level ❏

5. Is able to differentiate between fact and opinion while reading science materials at the seventh-, eighth-, ninth-, tenth-, eleventh-, or twelfth-grade level ❏

6. Is able to understand and retain many important details while reading science materials at the seventh-, eighth-, ninth-, tenth-, eleventh-, or twelfth-grade level ❏

7. Is able to successfully perform a scientific experiment independently or with one or more partners after reading how it should be carried out ❏

8. Is able to organize ideas from reading science materials at the seventh-, eighth-, ninth-, tenth-, eleventh-, or twelfth-grade level and understand the relationships between ideas in order to draw appropriate conclusions ❏

9. Is able to understand such cue words in science materials as *several, some, a few, a number of,* and *many* ❏

10. Is able to interpret graphs and visual materials from science materials at the seventh-, eighth-, ninth-, tenth-, eleventh-, or twelfth-grade level ❏

11. Is able to use library and computer skills to research a scientific topic ❏

12. Is able to identify and understand symbols, abbreviations, and formulae from science materials at the seventh-, eighth-, ninth-, tenth-, eleventh-, or twelfth-grade level ❏

13. Is able to use a study strategy such as Survey Q3R, Survey Q4R, PQRST, POINT, C2R, or OK4R while reading science materials at the seventh-, eighth-, ninth-, tenth-, eleventh-, or twelfth-grade level ❏

LITERACY-STUDY SKILLS OBSERVATIONAL CHECKLIST
(Middle–Upper Grade Level)

(cont.)

D. Mathematics

1. Is able to understand the specialized vocabulary and symbolism of mathematics such as *axis, hypotenuse, parallel, equation, correlation, median, mean,* and *standard deviation* ❏

2. Is able to understand the meanings of relevant word roots, prefixes, and suffixes in determining the meaning of mathematical terms at the seventh-, eighth-, ninth-, tenth-, eleventh-, or twelfth-grade level ❏

3. Is able to read mathematical material at the seventh-, eighth-, ninth-, tenth-, eleventh-, or twelfth-grade level ❏

4. Is able to locate and comprehend reference materials such as about famous mathematicians ❏

5. Is able to critically analyze statistical material ❏

6. Is able to understand and to follow directions precisely while reading a mathematical problem at the seventh-, eighth-, ninth-, tenth-, eleventh-, or twelfth-grade level ❏

7. Is able to note relevant and irrelevant data in a mathematical problem at the seventh-, eighth-, ninth-, tenth-, eleventh-, or twelfth-grade level in order to attempt to solve it ❏

8. Is able to comprehend and solve mathematical verbal problems at the seventh-, eighth-, ninth-, tenth-, eleventh-, or twelfth-grade level ❏

9. Is able to critically analyze graphs and tables while reading mathematical material at the seventh-, eighth-, ninth-, tenth-, eleventh-, or twelfth-grade level ❏

10. Is able to successfully comprehend visual materials such as diagrams while reading mathematical material at the seventh-, eighth-, ninth-, tenth-, eleventh-, or twelfth-grade level ❏

11. Is able to use a study technique in mathematics such as SQRQCO ❏

Name _____ Grade _____ Teacher _____ Date _____

STUDENT SELF-ASSESSMENT CHECKLIST OF LITERACY-STUDY SKILLS
(Upper Primary Grade Level)

Put an X in the box beside each sentence that is *true*.

1. I listen in school to my teacher and to the other children in my class. ❑

2. I read the directions before I begin to do my work. ❑

3. I ask questions when I don't know what to do. ❑

4. I can guess what might happen in a book or story before I begin to read it. ❑

5. I can tell my teacher or the other children in my class what I have read about. ❑

6. I can find what I need from the books I read. ❑

7. I can usually tell if a book or a story is real or make-believe. ❑

8. I can use a dictionary when I need to. ❑

9. I can write a story on my own when I want or I need to. ❑

10. I can understand a map I may see in one of my books. ❑

11. I can read how to do an experiment found in one of my science books and then do it alone or with a friend. ❑

12. I know what to do when I see these signs in an arithmetic book: + – ❑

13. I can solve most of the problems found in my arithmetic book. ❑

14. I usually do my homework if I have any. ❑

15. I remember to bring my homework back to school. ❑

16. I have a special place at home to do my homework. ❑

17. I think I am a good reader. ❑

18. I think I am a good student. ❑

STUDENT SELF-ASSESSMENT CHECKLIST OF LITERACY-STUDY SKILLS
(Intermediate Grade Level)

Put an X in the book beside each statement that is *correct*.

1. I am able to find the main idea in most of the paragraphs I read. ❑

2. I am able to find the important details in most of the paragraphs I read. ❑

3. I am able to use the various aids that are found in my textbooks such as the table of contents, chapter subheadings, highlighting, glossary, and index. ❑

4. I am able to use a dictionary whenever I need it to do my schoolwork. ❑

5. I am able to use such resources as encyclopedias, an encyclopedia on CD-ROM, trade books, newspapers, magazines, a telephone directory, *The Guinness Book of Records,* and *The Reader's Guide to Periodical Literature* to locate the information I need to do my schoolwork. ❑

6. I am able to use the school library and/or a public library to locate the information I need to do my schoolwork. ❑

7. I usually am able to remember the information I read in the books at school. ❑

8. I do my homework every night when I have homework to do. ❑

9. I have a special place to do my homework. ❑

10. I usually remember to bring my homework back to school. ❑

11. I can listen and follow most of the directions my teacher gives at school. ❑

12. I usually can understand the maps, tables, and graphs my textbooks contain. ❑

13. I change my speed of reading depending upon how hard the material is and why I am reading it. ❑

14. I am able to read different kinds of material such as chapter books, biographies, plays, poems, social studies textbooks, science textbooks, and arithmetic textbooks fairly well. ❑

15. I am able to react to what I read by such activities as creative dramatics, reading response journals, or creative writing of stories or poems. ❑

16. I usually am able to distinguish between fact and opinion ❑

17. I can read and follow the directions to perform an experiment from my science textbook. ❑

18. I am able to understand the following symbols in arithmetic: $+ - \times \div =$ ❑

19. I usually am able to understand and solve the word problems are found in my arithmetic textbook. ❑

20. I think I am a good reader. ❑

21. I think I am a good student. ❑

STUDENT SELF-ASSESSMENT CHECKLIST OF LITERACY-STUDY SKILLS
(Middle–Upper Grade Level)

Place an X in the box beside each statement that is *correct.*

1. I am able to locate the main ideas in the paragraphs I read from all of my books at school. ❏

2. I am able to locate the important details in the paragraphs I read from all of my books at school. ❏

3. I am able to locate the following parts of a book: title, author or editor, illustrator (if one), publisher, city of publication, edition, and copyright date. ❏

4. I am able to use the following aids contained in my content textbooks: preface, introduction, table of contents, list of figures, chapter headings, chapter subheadings, highlighting, italicized words, footnotes, bibliography, glossary, index, and appendices. ❏

5. I am able to use a dictionary for whatever purposes I need in order to do my schoolwork. ❏

6. I am able to use other resources such as trade books, other textbooks, encyclopedias, an encyclopedia on CD-ROM, other computer software, newspapers, magazines, telephone directories, atlases, *The Guinness Book of Records,* and *The Reader's Guide to Periodical Literature* to locate the information I need to do my schoolwork. ❏

7. I am able to use the school library, public libraries, and the library card catalog to locate the information I need to do my schoolwork. ❏

8. I usually am able to remember the information I read in the textbooks at school. ❏

9. I usually can understand the maps, graphs, diagrams, tables, and charts found in reading material of various kinds. ❏

10. I do my homework every night that I have homework to do. ❏

11. I have a special place to do my homework. ❏

12. I remember to bring my homework back to school. ❏

13. I listen to and follow the directions my teacher gives at school. ❏

14. I am able to study effectively for the tests I have in school. ❏

15. I can take notes or highlight the important information I read from my books at school. ❏

16. I can write a summary of the material I read about. ❏

17. I change my speed of reading depending upon how difficult the material is and my purposes for reading it. ❏

STUDENT SELF-ASSESSMENT CHECKLIST OF LITERACY-STUDY SKILLS
(Middle–Upper Grade Level)

(cont.)

18. I am able to read different types of books such as novels, biographies, drama, poetry, social studies textbooks, science textbooks, and mathematics textbooks effectively. ❏

19. I am able to react to what I read by such activities as creative dramatics, Reader's Theater, reading response journals, or creative writing of prose or poetry. ❏

20. I understand the different paragraph patterns found in content textbooks such as **sequence, cause-effect,** and **comparison-contrast.** ❏

21. I usually can distinguish fact from opinion. ❏

22. I can read and follow the directions to perform an experiment from my science textbook. ❏

23. I am able to understand such special vocabulary in mathematics as **axis, hypotenuse, parallel, equation, correlation, median, mean,** and **standard deviation.** ❏

24. I usually am able to understand and solve the word problems found in my mathematics textbook. ❏

25. I think I am a good reader. ❏

26. I think I am a good student. ❏

Name _____ Grade _____ Teacher _____ Date _____

PARENT SURVEY OF LITERACY-STUDY SKILLS
(Primary Grade Level)

Put an X in the box after each statement that is correct.

	Yes	No
1. I read to my child on a regular basis.	❏	❏
2. I listen to my child read on a regular basis.	❏	❏
3. My child has a definite time at home each day when he or she reads for pleasure.	❏	❏
4. I discuss with my child how he or she is doing in school. We also talk about what is going well and what is causing problems at school for him or her.	❏	❏
5. My child has a special place to read and study.	❏	❏
6. I always require my child to finish his or her homework if he or she has any homework.	❏	❏
7. I sometimes help my child with his or her homework.	❏	❏
8. My child is allowed to watch television while he or she is doing homework.	❏	❏
9. My child usually watches two or more hours of television in the evenings.	❏	❏
10. I usually check over my child's homework.	❏	❏
11. My child has a special place to put the materials that must be returned to school.	❏	❏
12. My child has a regular bedtime. What time is it? _____	❏	❏
13. My child eats a good breakfast every morning.	❏	❏

Name _____ Grade _____ Teacher _____ Date _____

PARENT SURVEY OF LITERACY-STUDY SKILLS
(Intermediate Grade Level)

Put an X in the box after each statement that is correct.

	Yes	No
1. I listen to my child read aloud on a regular basis.	❏	❏
2. I discuss with my child how he or she is doing in school. We also talk about what is going well and what is causing problems at school for him or her.	❏	❏
3. My child has a definite time at home each day when he or she reads just for pleasure.	❏	❏
4. My child has a special place at home for reading and studying.	❏	❏
5. I am always certain that my child completes his or her homework if he or she has any homework to do.	❏	❏
6. I often help my child with his or her homework if he or she needs any help.	❏	❏
7. My child is usually allowed to watch television while he or she is doing his or her homework.	❏	❏
8. My child usually watches two or more hours of television in the evenings.	❏	❏
9. My child usually likes to do homework in social studies (history or geography).	❏	❏
10. My child usually likes to do homework in science.	❏	❏
11. My child usually likes to do homework in arithmetic.	❏	❏
12. I usually check over my child's homework.	❏	❏
13. My child has a special place to put the materials that must be returned to school.	❏	❏
14. My child has a regular bedtime. What time is it? _____	❏	❏
15. My child eats a good breakfast every morning.	❏	❏

© 1997 by John Wiley & Sons, Inc.

PARENT SURVEY OF LITERACY-STUDY SKILLS
(Middle–Upper Grade Level)

Put an X in the box after each statement that is correct.

		Yes	No
1.	I listen to my child read aloud once in a while just to monitor his or her oral reading progress.	❏	❏
2.	I discuss with my child how he or she is doing in school. We talk about what is going well and what may be causing problems at school for him or her.	❏	❏
3.	My child has a definite time at home each day when he or she reads just for pleasure.	❏	❏
4.	My child has a special place at home for reading and studying.	❏	❏
5.	I am always certain that my child completes his or her homework if he or she has homework to do.	❏	❏
6.	I sometimes help my child with his or her homework if he or she needs any help.	❏	❏
7.	My child is usually allowed to watch television while he or she is doing his or her homework.	❏	❏
8.	My child usually watches two or more hours of television in the evenings.	❏	❏
9.	My child usually likes to do homework in English (literature or language arts).	❏	❏
10.	My child usually likes to do homework in social studies (history, government, or geography).	❏	❏
11.	My child usually likes to do homework in science.	❏	❏
12.	My child usually likes to do homework in mathematics.	❏	❏
13.	I usually check over my child's homework.	❏	❏
14.	My child has a special place to put the materials that must be returned to school.	❏	❏
15.	My child has a regular bedtime. What time is it? _____	❏	❏
16.	My child eats a good breakfast every morning.	❏	❏

Reproducible Checklist for Literature Response Groups

The following is a reproducible checklist for literature response groups and is applicable for use at the intermediate or middle–upper grade levels. As the literacy teacher joins a group of students reading the *same trade book,* he or she enters the discussion and also keeps a record of each student's status on a checklist. Such a checklist helps the teacher gain a great deal of information over a period of time about students' abilities to gain insights about characters and plot development, interests and needs, and skill in interacting within a group. These informal records can serve as a basis for parent-teacher conferences and entries on report cards.

Name _____ Grade _____ Teacher _____ Date _____

CHECKLIST FOR LITERATURE-RESPONSE GROUPS
(Intemediate and Middle–Upper Grade Levels)

Title of Book Date	Attended	Read to page	Shared number of items	Questions asked	Made connections to real-life situations	Responded to others in the group	Comments about reading from response journal
Child's Name							
Child's Name							
Child's Name							
Child's Name							
Child's Name							
Child's Name							
Child's Name							
Child's Name							
Child's Name							
Child's Name							

Description, Advantages, and Limitations of the Standardized Survey Reading/Achievement Tests That Have Subtests Devoted to the Literacy-Study Skills

A number of the standardized survey reading/achievement tests commonly given at the intermediate and middle–upper grade levels have subtests that attempt to assess competencies and weaknesses in some of the elements of the literacy-study skills. Although they may be useful for this purpose, the results from such a standardized test *always should be used along with* a number of informal assessment techniques such as teacher observation of daily classroom performance, teacher observation using structured checklists, informal assessment devices of various types, and the use of portfolios. All of these devices are discussed in other parts of this chapter.

In any case, any standardized device is only a *very tentative indicator* of those qualities it is attempting to assess. It must *never* be thought of as an *infallible measure* of those qualities since a student's performance on any standardized test can be influenced by a countless number of factors. In addition, a student should *never* be placed into a group, classroom, or program using only the results of a standardized device. A standardized test always should be used along with a number of *informal devices, most important, that of teacher observation.*

In any case, almost all students have been given a number of standardized survey reading/achievement tests during their school careers. Although such a test can be given alone, more often it is given as part of an achievement test battery that also includes tests in other curricular areas such as language arts, social studies, and arithmetic. Although the major purpose of such a device is to attempt to evaluate a student's general or overall reading ability in word meaning (vocabulary) and sentence or paragraph comprehension, it also may evaluate ability in literacy-study skills in such content areas as social studies, science, and mathematics.

Any standardized survey reading/achievement test is a group-administered, norm-referenced test (you can compare the results achieved by your group of students with the results achieved by a similar group of students in the standardization sample). Usually these are students of the same grade level, sex, socio-economic group, and geographic location. Norms can then be reported in *grade equivalent scores, percentile ranks, stanines,* or *standard scores.*

- Although they are not valid and are not recommended by the International Reading Association, *grade equivalents* are still probably the most commonly used way to report a student's scores. Grade equivalent scores often *overestimate* a student's actual performance on a test. The grade equivalent score is the grade level for which a raw score is the median score.

- A *percentile rank* indicates how a student compares in performance with other students of his or her age or grade and is based on a percentage score of 1% to 100%.

- *Stanines* are normalized standard scores that range from a low of 1 through a high of 9, with 5 being the average performance.

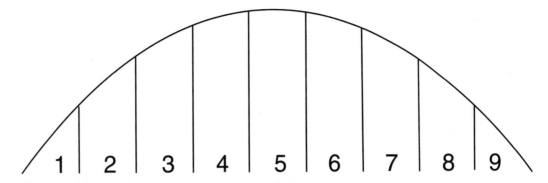

- A *standard score* is a normalized score that allows you to compare a student's performance on a number of different tests. It is the only type of score that can be averaged from test to test.

Any standardized test should be reliable and valid to be useful. *Reliability* refers to the degree to which a test provides consistent results, while *validity* indicates the truthfulness or accuracy with which a test measures what it is supposed to measure.

Any standardized survey reading/achievement test has these major advantages:

- It serves as a valuable screening device to determine which students need additional individual testing using various kinds of informal devices.
- It normally is easy to administer and score. Often this type of device can be given in about 45 to 90 minutes, and the scoring can be done entirely by computer.
- It normally is both reliable and valid.
- It is formulated by test experts and experts in the content areas that the test evaluates and therefore is theoretically valid and useful.
- It can be given by a virtually untrained examiner since the directions for administration are so complete and easy to follow.

However, *all* of these tests have the following important limitations:

- They often *overestimate* the student's actual instructional reading level and true abilities in the other skills being evaluated due to the guessing factor and the difficulty of obtaining a true estimate of a student's grade equivalents at the upper and lower ends of the scale.
- They have considerable difficulty in evaluating a student's ability in implicit (higher-level) thinking skills since only one answer is normally possible for any question.
- They often are not passage dependent. A student, for example, may well be able to answer the comprehension questions without ever reading the material.
- They use only short excerpts to evaluate reading comprehension or competency in any of the literacy-study skills. This is unlike the reading-study skills required in actual school reading and study.

These limitations indicate why a student's score on any type of standardized device should *always be thought of as only a tentative indicator of what that device is trying to evaluate.*

A Partial List of Standardized Survey Reading/Achievement Tests That Have Subtests Devoted to the Literacy-Study Skills

Here is a partial list of the most common standardized survey reading/achievement tests that have subtests devoted to assessing strengths and weaknesses in the various literacy-study skills. Keep in mind that these are only a few of the more useful tests. It is not a comprehensive list.

Canadian Test of Basic Skills (1981). Levels 5 and 6 (K–1) are readiness tests. Levels 5–8 assess listening, word analysis, vocabulary, reading, oral and written reading, work-study skills, and mathematics. Levels 9–14 (grades 4–8) evaluate vocabulary, reading, writing mechanics, study skills, and mathematics. Levels 15–18 (grades 9–12) have the following four subtests: reading, mathematics, written expression, and using sources of information. It is available in two forms for grades K1–2 and can be from the following source:

Nelson Canada
1120 Birchmount Road
Scarborough, ON M1K 5T4
Canada

Iowa Silent Reading Tests (1973). These tests measure the ability to apply reading strategies to different types of tasks. The Reading Efficiency Index shows the relative effectiveness of reading rate and comprehension. Level 1 (grades 6–9) and Level 2 (grades 9–14) contain subtests of vocabulary, comprehension, and directed reading (work-study skills including locational skills, skimming, scanning, and reading efficiency). The tests are available from the following source:

Psychological Corporation
555 Academic Court
San Antonio, TX 78204

Iowa Tests of Basic Skills (1986). Levels 5 (K.8–1.5), 6 (K.8–1.9), 7 (1.7–2.6), and 8 (2.5–3.5) evaluate listening, word analysis, and vocabulary. Levels 6–8 also evaluate reading comprehension. Levels 9–14 (grades 3, 4, 5, 6, 7, and 8–9) have vocabulary, comprehension, and reference subtests. They also list behavioral objectives to which the test items were written.

Iowa Tests of Educational Development (1978). This test is available in two forms and is designed for use in grades 9–12. It evaluates performance in vocabulary, comprehension, language arts, and mathematics. It takes approximately 2½ hours to administer. It is available from the following source:

Science Research Associates
155 North Wacker Drive
Chicago, IL 60606

Library Skills Test (1980). This test consists of 45 items designed to locate strengths and weaknesses in working with library materials including terminology, a card catalog classification system, filing, parts of a book, reference tools, and bibliographic forms. It is designed for use in grades 7–13 and is available from the following source:

Scholastic Testing Service
555 Broadway
New York, NY 10012

Performance Assessment in Reading (PAIR) (1978). This test is designed for use at the junior high school level and evaluates ability in vocabulary, comprehension, and study skills. It is available in one form from the following source:

California Test Bureau
Del Monte Research Park
Monterey, CA 93940

Stanford Diagnostic Reading Tests (1984). Although these tests are called "diagnostic reading tests," all of them can be given on a group basis and can serve the function of survey tests in the various literacy-study skills. This test battery consists of four levels: Red (grades 1.5–4.5), Green (grades 3.5–6.5), Brown (grades 5.5–8.5), and Blue (grades 1.5–6.5). The following subtests are included in this test battery: phonic analysis, grades 1.5–8.5; auditory vocabulary (meanings of spoken words), grades 1.5–8.5; literal (explicit) and interpretive (implicit) reading comprehension, all grade levels; structural analysis, grades 3.5–13.0; reading rate, grades 5.5–13.0; knowledge of affixes and base words, vocabulary, skimming, and scanning, grades 7.5–13. Each level is available in the forms, and the four levels cover grades 1–13. The tests are available from the following source:

Psychological Corporation
555 Academic Court
San Antonio, TX 78204

Tests of Achievement and Proficiency (1986). The reading comprehension subtest measures ability to define words from context and comprehend prose, poetry, newspaper articles, advertisements, and subject-matter content. The sources-of-information subtest evaluates the reading of maps, graphs, tables, charts, and reference materials. The tests are available in Levels 15–18 for grades 9–12. The tests also contain an optional listening test. They are available from the following source:

Riverside Publishing Company
8420 Bryn Mawr Avenue
Chicago, IL 60631

The 3-R's Test: Reading (1982). This test evaluates reading comprehension ability at all levels. Levels 8–18 are designed for grades 2–12 and measure main ideas, explicit and implicit details, and logical relationships/inferences. Levels 9–18 also evaluate words in context, literary analysis, and author's purpose. Vocabulary (word meaning in sentences) is evaluated at Levels 8–18, and synonyms are also evaluated at Levels 8–18 (grades 1–12).

Visual discrimination and sound-symbol association are measured at Levels 6 and 7 (grades K–1). Study skills are also evaluated at Levels 8–18 (grades 2–12). Abilities tests (Levels 9–18) measure verbal and quantitative reasoning. A grade-development score (GDS) provides an estimate of a student's level of reading ability. The test is designed for use in grades K–12 and is available from the following source:

Riverside Publishing Company
8420 Bryn Mawr Avenue
Chicago, IL 60631

DESCRIPTION, ADVANTAGES, AND LIMITATIONS OF STANDARDIZED CRITERION-REFERENCED TESTS THAT ASSESS COMPETENCIES AND WEAKNESSES IN THE LITERACY-STUDY SKILLS

Although criterion-referenced tests are not so popular as they were a number of years of ago, they may still have some usefulness in the assessment of competencies and weaknesses in the content areas of literature (language arts or English), social studies, science, and mathematics. Therefore, they are mentioned very briefly at this point.

Criterion-referenced tests are also called *mastery tests* because they deal with one or more of the reading, writing, spelling, or study subskills and specify the point at which the student *may* have mastered that subskill. They are not norm-referenced, but they may be used to evaluate a student's strengths and weaknesses in all of the word identification, comprehension, and study skills. The major purpose of their use is to help a teacher determine which subskills a student already knows and therefore does not have to learn and which subskills still need to be taught and/or practiced. Thus, the major purpose of their use is to help the literacy or content teacher *individualize instruction* more effectively.

Here are the major advantage of these standardized devices:

- They may help a literacy or content teacher be sure that a student has truly mastered important reading, writing, spelling, or study skills.
- The student need not learn nor practice a reading, writing, spelling, or study skill he or she already knows.

However, here are the major limitations of these tests:

- They fragment the entire literacy process. This is not in keeping with contemporary language theory nor with the whole language philosophy.
- The *80%* criterion level is an arbitrary and often inaccurate cutoff point.
- It is difficult for such a test to evaluate ability in higher-level (implicit) comprehension and the higher-level study skills. Therefore, such tests often overemphasize lower-level (explicit) comprehension and lower-level study skills—the skills that generally are relatively unimportant in comparison with the higher-level skills.

A PARTIAL LIST OF STANDARDIZED CRITERION-REFERENCED TESTS

Here is a list and very brief description of a few of the more commonly used standardized criterion-referenced tests. Remember that these are only a few of the tests of this type. It is not a comprehensive list.

Analysis of Skills (ASK) (1974). Each of 4 levels (grades 1–2, 3–4, 5–6, 7–8) measures 43 to 48 objectives of the total of 60 covered by the series. Each skill is sampled by three items; mastery equals all 3 correct, or 2 of 3 including most difficult item. Three main areas are evaluated: word analysis, comprehension, and study skills. The test is designed for use in grades 1–8 and is available from the following source:

> Scholastic Testing Service
> 555 Broadway
> New York, NY 10012

Brigance Diagnostic Comprehensive Inventory of Basic Skills (1983). This is an informal, *individual* battery of criterion-referenced tests covering a wide range of literacy skills. The reading subtests include word recognition, word analysis, vocabulary, and oral reading. Spelling and study skills are evaluated by other tests. It is designed for use in grades K–6 and is available from the following source:

> Curriculum Associates, Inc.
> 6620 Robin Willow Court
> Dallas, TX 75248

Fountain Valley Reading Skills Tests (1977). The first group of tests are designed for use in grades 1–6. They include a series of 77 one-page tests covering 367 objectives (number of objectives per test level range from 33 to 125 with 2 to 12 items per objective). The skill areas evaluated are phonic and structural analysis, vocabulary, comprehension, and study skills. For grades 7–12 there are 61 specific objective subtests usually with 4 to 6 items each. This part of the test evaluates vocabulary, comprehension, and study skills. The tests are available from the following source:

> Richard L. Zweig Associates, Inc.
> 20800 Beach Boulevard
> Huntington Beach, CA 92648

Individual Pupil Monitoring System—Reading (1974). This test has separate test booklets for word attack, vocabulary and comprehension, and discrimination/study skills for each grade level (1–6). Each of 343 overlapping objectives is evaluated by a 5-item test. The entire test is available from the following source:

> Riverside Publishing Company
> 8420 Bryn Mawr Avenue
> Chicago, IL 60631

IOX Basic Skills Competency in Reading (1984). This criterion-referenced test contains two forms. The competencies assessed are decoding, word meaning, comprehension of main ideas and details, drawing conclusions, and using references. It is available from the following source:

Instructional Objectives Incorporated
2750 Old St. Augustine Road S191
Tallahassee, FL 32301

MULTI SCORE (1984). These criterion-referenced tests are customized to match local school programs. The tests evaluate reading readiness, sound-symbol associations, word meaning, comprehension skills, study skills, and classifying forms of literature. The tests are designed for use in grades K–12 and are available from the following source:

Riverside Publishing Company
8420 Bryn Mawr Avenue
Chicago, IL 60631

Prescriptive Reading Inventory (PRI) (1977). These tests cover 30 objectives for Levels 1 (grades K.0–1.0) and 2 (grades K.5–2.0) and 90 objectives for Levels A (1.5–2.5), B (2.0–3.5), C (3.0–4.5), and D (4.0–6.5). Readiness skills are evaluated at Levels 1 and 2. The other four levels evaluate phonic and structural analysis, translation (vocabulary), and literal, interpretive, and critical comprehension. Over *80%* of the pretest objectives are measured by 3 to 4 items, and mastery is defined as not more than one error. The test is available from the following source:

California Test Bureau
Del Monte Research Park
Monterey, CA 93940

PRISM: READING I (1982). This test is found on computer software, and the item bank contains over 2,000 items in three skills areas: word identification, comprehension, and study skills. It is available in Levels C, D, and E for grades 3, 4, and 5 from the following source:

Psychological Corporation
555 Academic Court
San Antonio, TX 78204

Wisconsin Design Tests of Reading Skills Development (1972). These tests evaluate a wide range of word attack at 5 levels: A (grades K–2), Transition (grade 1), B (1–3), C (2–4), and D (3–6). Comprehension and study skills are evaluated at 7 levels (K–6). Number of items per subtest is greater than is found on most criterion-referenced tests, and the mastery criterion is *80%*. At various levels the test is available in either one or two forms. The entire tests are designed for use in grades K–6 and are available from the following source:

Learning Multi-Systems
340 Coyier Lane
Madison, WI 53713

VARIOUS TYPES OF GROUP READING INVENTORIES IN LITERATURE (LANGUAGE ARTS OR ENGLISH), SOCIAL STUDIES, SCIENCE, AND MATHEMATICS

As has been stated earlier, a number of students in the intermediate grades and beyond simply are not able to successfully read and study the required content textbooks in literature (language arts or English), social studies, science, and mathematics. Although theme (unit) teaching using lower-level content textbooks, trade books, computer software, newspapers, and magazines, among other resources, should be provided for the disabled readers and learning-handicapped students, many of the above-average, average, *and* disabled readers need to be taught the specialized literacy-study skills required for effective comprehension and retention of their selected content textbooks. However, you should determine which of these reading, writing, spelling, and study skills a group of students does not possess so that you can present and/or reinforce them. It obviously is a waste of time to focus on literacy-study skills a group of students already knows. A group informal test can help you determine which specialized literacy-study skills you should emphasize in content classes.

Three major types of *group reading inventories* are described in this section. The first is a group informal reading test that can help you determine *if your students can effectively use the aids found in their content textbooks*. This informal assessment device usually is given at the beginning of a course or semester. You may be surprised at how many students in the intermediate grades and beyond cannot use such textbook aids as the table of contents, the index, the glossary, italicized words, subheadings, maps, graphs, diagrams, tables, and pictures. This is an open-book assessment technique in which each student demonstrates his or her competency in using these different textbook aids.

The second type of informal reading test is sometimes called an *informal reading inventory*. It is designed to see if your students can successfully read and study a required content textbook in areas such as literature, social studies, science, and mathematics and it can be given near the beginning of a course or semester. In this inventory, each student reads a passage of approximately 1,000 to 2,000 words from near the middle of the required textbook. When the students have finished reading the passage, each student responds in writing to the selection by answering an open-ended question. The student's response not only indicates his or her comprehension and retention of the material, it also indicates his or her competency in sentence structure and spelling. Each student also answers a number of objective questions about the passage. These questions can evaluate a student's ability in such reading-study skills as literal (explicit) comprehension, interpretive (implicit) comprehension, critical reading, creative (applied or schema implicit) reading, locating the directly stated main idea, locating significant details, and locating the implied main idea.

The third type of group informal reading assessment technique *is based on a specific chapter of a required content textbook*. This is an open-book test that is given near the beginning of the course or semester. It is designed to determine if your students possess the specialized reading skills required to comprehend a selected content textbook effectively. This informal reading test can include a matching vocabulary exercise composed of the specialized vocabulary terms included in the chapter. It also can contain several literal (explicit), interpretive (implicit), critical, and creative comprehension questions from the chapter as well as objective questions about the main ideas and significant details found in that specific chapter.

Obviously it is a waste of time to give students any of these informal assessment devices if the results from them are not followed up by providing instruction and/or practice in the specific skills in which a group of students or an individual student lacks competence, using the appropriate materials.

Sample Group Reading Inventories in Social Studies, Science, and Mathematics

The next part of this chapter contains one example of each of the three types of group reading inventories described above. You can use them for models for inventories that you formulate from your own content textbooks. You will find each of the three types of inventories easy to construct and evaluate.

Name _____ Grade _____ Teacher _____ Date _____

EXAMPLE OF AN INFORMAL INVENTORY BASED ON USING TEXTBOOK AIDS*

1. On what page does the chapter "The Spanish and Portuguese in the Americas" begin?

2. On what page does Unit 4 "Mexico" begin?

3. According to the "Gazetteer" in the book, what is "Baja California"?

4. According to the glossary in the book, what is the definition of the term "guerrilla"?

5. According to the index of the book, on what pages does the "War of 1812" appear?

6. What is the title of the map on page 457?

7. How many units does the book contain?

8. According to the glossary in the book, what is the definition of the term "criollo"?

9. What is the title of Chapter 22?

10. What man is pictured on page 415 of the book?

11. What is the title of the subheading on page 344 of the book?

12. What does the color *yellow* represent on the map on page 319 of the book?

13. According to the "Gazetteer" in the book, what is "Hispaniola"?

14. What are the names of the two people who are pictured on page 460 of the book?

15. What are the names of the three subheadings on page 434 of the book?

16. What word is printed in bold print in the section entitled "Looking Ahead" on page 360 of the book?

17. According to the key of the map on page 301, what does the color *purple* represent?

18. According to the review of Chapter 13 on page 284, on what page is the term "immigrant" mentioned?

19. According to the circle graph on page 233, what percentage (%) of Canada's total *exports* are "mining products"?

20. According to the timeline on page 169, when was the Dominion of Canada established?

*Formulated from a sixth-grade social studies textbook. Use only as a model of this type of inventory.

EXAMPLE OF A GROUP READING INVENTORY

Source of Reading Selection

Jay K. Hackett and Richard H. Moyer, "The Nervous System," *Science in Your World.* New York: Macmillan/McGraw Hill School Publishing Company, 1991, pp. 366-371.

Length of Reading Selection

About 1,000 words

Subject Area

Science

Grade Level

Fifth Grade

Brief Summary

This selection discussed the parts of the human body that comprise the nervous system.

Part One

What did the authors say are the three parts of the nervous system?

Part Two

A. It is important to select the significant details in what you read. Here are statements of details in the selection that you have read. If the statement is **true,** put a **T** on the line before the statement. If the statement is **false,** put an **F** on the line before the statement.

_____ 1. The medulla is the largest part of the human brain.

_____ 2. The spinal cord is a thick cord like bundle of nerve cells.

_____ 3. A reflex is a special action that happens without being controlled by the brain.

B. It is important to get main ideas from your reading. Put an **X** in front of each statement below that represents a **main idea** in this selection.

_____ 1. A human brain is the main control center of the body.

_____ 2. The brain and spinal cord must work as a complete unit to control a human body.

_____ 3. A single nerve cell may have one end in the spinal cord and the other end in an ankle.

C. It is important for you to draw conclusions and generalizations from what you have read. Put an **X** in front of each of the **conclusions and generalizations** that can be correctly drawn from the selection.

_____ 1. Damage to the cerebellum of the human brain may result in a person's feeling dizzy.

_____ 2. It is not helpful for human beings to have reflexes.

_____ 3. The human brain is much more complex than any computer yet made.

EXAMPLE OF A GROUP READING INVENTORY

(cont.)

D. It is important to know the exact meaning of words that you read. Below are sentences with a word *italicized* in each. Under each sentence are four choices. Put the **correct letter** on the line in front of the sentence.

_____ 1. The cerebellum is the part of the brain that *coordinates* movement.

     a. discourages   c. directs

     b. prevents   d. isolates

_____ 2. Your nervous system *responds* to sending impulses from your brain and spinal cord to muscles, and an action occurs.

     a. reacts   c. repels

     b. directions   d. attempts

_____ 3. A reflex is an *involuntary* response.

     a. moves on its own   c. frightening

     b. special   d. tendon

_____ 4. The muscles *contract* and the leg bones move.

     a. become smaller   c. break

     b. become larger   d. become loose

EXAMPLE OF AN INFORMAL READING INVENTORY BASED ON A SPECIFIC CHAPTER*

A. *Matching Vocabulary Exercise*

_____ 1. face
_____ 2. vertex
_____ 3. hexagon
_____ 4. pentagon
_____ 5. ray
_____ 6. congruent figures
_____ 7. line of symmetry
_____ 8. radius
_____ 9. diameter
_____ 10. perimeter

a. the point at which the edges of a figure meet
b. a figure containing six sides and six vertices
c. part of a line with one endpoint
d. line segment with one endpoint on a circle
e. flat surface of a cube
f. closed plane figure with straight sides
g. a figure containing five sides and five vertices
h. figures that have the same size and shape
i. line segment with both endpoints on the circle
j. the distance around a polygon

B. Put an **X** in front of the following statements that are **true.**

_____ 1. A sphere has no flat surfaces.

_____ 2. A triangle is one example of a closed figure with straight sides.

_____ 3. A line segment has no endpoints.

C. Put an **X** in front of the following generalizations that are **true.**

_____ 1. Heptagons, octagons, and hexagons are all examples of polygons.

_____ 2. A circle is an example of a plane figure.

_____ 3. Congruent figures always must look exactly the same.

*Formulated from a fourth-grade mathematics textbook. Use only as a model of this type of inventory.

A CONTENT-ORIENTED INDIVIDUAL READING-THINKING INVENTORY

As you undoubtedly know, the *Individual Reading Inventory* is an informal assessment device designed to determine a student's approximate *independent, low independent, high instructional, instructional, low instructional,* and *frustration reading levels.* It also can be useful for determining a student's specific reading skill strengths and weaknesses. Although it can be given to all students in an elementary or middle school, it most typically is given only to disabled readers or learning-disabled students.

However, a contemporary version of the traditional Individual Reading Inventory probably may be more useful than the traditional version. After considerable reading and classroom testing, I have formulated my own variation of a *Content-Oriented Individual Reading-Thinking Inventory.* This differs from the traditional Content Individual Reading Inventory in several important ways.

As one example, *it assesses a student's prior knowledge before he or she reads a passage* either orally or silently. This assessment or activation of prior knowledge is extremely important before a student reads either narrative or content material. It gives the student purposes for reading and helps the student use his or her prior knowledge in the reading, which adds greatly to effective comprehension of the material.

In addition, after reading the material either orally or silently, each of the student's explicit (literal), implicit (interpretive), and applied (creative) *responses is evaluated in terms of its accuracy, inaccuracy, or excellence.* Last, *the student self-monitors his or her comprehension after completing the reading.* Students should learn to self-monitor their reading comprehension as this is extremely important in improving comprehension ability. Research has shown that good readers continually self-monitor their comprehension, while poor readers usually do not.

Since a detailed explanation of a Content-Oriented Individual Reading-Thinking Inventory is beyond the scope of this book, literacy teachers who are interested in learning more about how to give such an inventory are encouraged to consult my book *Alternative Assessment Techniques for Reading & Writing.* In addition to a detailed explanation of this type of inventory, this resource also contains complete, reproducible examples of an Individual Reading-Thinking Inventory for use from the primer reading level through the twelfth-grade reading level. The passages contained in this contemporary inventory, a number of which are subject-matter related, should be very useful for reading teachers in determining a student's ability in activation of prior knowledge, comprehension abilities, and self-monitoring abilities as well as accurate reading levels and specific reading skill strengths and weaknesses. All of this information is found in the following resource:

Wilma H. Miller, *Alternative Assessment Techniques for Reading & Writing. West Nyack, New York: The Center for Applied Research in Education, 1995, Chapter 5, pp. 141-215.*

Reproducible Example of a Content-Oriented Reading-Thinking Inventory

The following is a reproducible example of a contemporary Content Reading-Thinking Inventory from social studies at about the sixth-grade reading level.

Although you can reproduce and use this inventory in its present form if it seems applicable, more important, it can serve as a model of this type of inventory you can construct from appropriate content material in literature (language arts or English), social studies, science, or mathematics. It also illustrates the type of reproducible assessment materials that are found in my above-mentioned resource book for teachers.

CONTENT-ORIENTED INDIVIDUAL
READING-THINKING INVENTORY
(Approximately Sixth-Grade Reading Level)*

WHY SHOULD ENDANGERED SPECIES BE PROTECTED?

Do you think that humans have the right to endanger any of the species with which we share our earth? If humans have endangered a species either deliberately or accidentally, do we have the right not to do everything that we can to save that species from extinction? Indeed, humans are the only living creature with the ability both to foresee extinctions and then try to prevent them. However, some people argue that the direct interests of the human race such as developing new lands for farming, manufacturing, or housing should take precedence over the survival of other animal or plant species.

Certainly there are a number of important reasons why we should be concerned with endangered species of animals and plants. Because human beings are *omnivores*— creatures that eat both meat and vegetables—we eat both plants which trap the sun's energy in carbohydrates and animals which in turn eat the plants that trap the sun's energy. Besides providing food, plants also protect the landscape from wear and tear. Grass and trees on a hillside effectively protect the hillside from erosion.

In addition, one-fourth of all medicines prescribed in the United States are derived in some form from plants. For example, the opium poppy supplies such painkillers as *morphine* and *codeine*; other plants are the source of *strychnine* and *curare* which are muscle relaxants used in surgery; and the wild foxglove plant is the source of *digitalis,* a medicine used with heart patients. New medical uses for wild plants are being found all the time. As one example, the rosy periwinkle plant of Madagascar produces a chemical which is useful in treating childhood leukemia and other types of cancers. However, the native plants of Madagascar are disappearing very rapidly, and if the usefulness of the periwinkle had not been discovered in time, it might have become extinct, and the cancer and leukemia treatments using the chemicals derived from it never would have been developed. In addition, animals can be the source of medically valuable treatments. For example, the venom from a deadly snake called the Malayan pit viper prevents life-threatening clots from forming in the human blood, venom from bee stings can help the pain of arthritis, and poisons from sea anemones are useful in the fight against cancer.

Thus, for all of these reasons and many others, it is important to protect all the animals and plants with which we share the earth. Their survival also may help to ensure the survival of the human race.

*The readability level of this passage was computed by the Dale-Chall Readability Formula.

CONTENT-ORIENTED INDIVIDUAL
READING-THINKING INVENTORY
(Approximately Sixth-Grade Reading Level)*

(cont.)

WHY SHOULD ENDANGERED SPECIES BE PROTECTED?

BEFORE READING

Assessing Prior Knowledge and Reading

1. What do you know about the importance of saving endangered species of animals and plants?

2. Do you think you will like reading this story ? Why? Why not?

AFTER READING

Number of words in this selection __418__

Number of word identification miscues _____

Word Identification Miscues

Independent reading level __0-6__

Low independent reading level __7-15__

High instructional reading level __16-25__

Instructional reading level __26-36__

Low instructional reading level __37-45__

Frustration reading level __46+__

Assessing Comprehension

Score *1* for a correct response and *0* for an incorrect response in the appropriate column. Score ✓ for any answers that are clearly illogical or + for any answers that are very good, detailed, or insightful.

	Score	Appropriateness

Reading the Lines

1. What is an omnivore? _____ _____

an animal that eats both plants and animals

2. What two painkillers are derived from opium poppies? _____ _____

morphine and codeine

3. What disease can be treated by using the poisons from sea anemones? _____ _____

cancer

CONTENT-ORIENTED INDIVIDUAL
READING-THINKING INVENTORY
(Approximately Sixth-Grade Reading Level)*

(cont.)

4. What might be some reasons that some people would want   _____   _____
   to cut down portions of a tropical rain forest?

   **they might want to clear the rain forest and grow
   crops on the land**

   **they might want to build a town in that part of the
   rain forest**

   **they might want to build a house in that part of the
   rain forest**

5. How do you think that grass and trees on a hillside can   _____   _____
   prevent soil from eroding?

   the roots might help to hold the soil in place

   **the soil can't be washed away because the rain
   would soak into the grass instead of making
   gullies in the soil**

   **the grass and trees would prevent the soil from
   running away**

6. What other diseases can you think of that might be   _____   _____
   prevented by or cured by plants or animals?

   AIDS

   other forms of cancer

   Alzheimer's disease

   Multiple Sclerosis

   Muscular Dystrophy

Reading Beyond the Lines

7. How could you be involved in protecting some endangered   _____   _____
   species?

   any logical response; some examples:

   write letters to the editor of the local newspaper

   **join an organization devoted to protecting
   endangered species**

   **study much more about endangered species so that
   I could be a scientist in that field when I grow up**

CONTENT-ORIENTED INDIVIDUAL
READING-THINKING INVENTORY
(Approximately Sixth-Grade Reading Level)*

(cont.)

8. Would you want to become a scientist to attempt to
   protect endangered species? Why? Why not?   _____   _____

   any logical response; some examples:

   yes

   **I think being involved in protecting endangered species
   is very important and would also protect human beings
   in the long run**

   I like to study about scientific topics

   I like all animals and plants

   no

   I don't like to study science

   reading and studying science is very hard for me

   I don't like to study about either animals or plants

Number of comprehension questions correct _____

Comprehension Score

   Independent reading level ___8___

   Instructional reading level ___5-7___

   Frustration reading level 4 or fewer

SELF-MONITORING OF COMPREHENSION

   How well do you think you answered these questions?

   very well _____

   all right _____

   not so well _____

A TEACHER-CONSTRUCTED ASSESSMENT DEVICE WITH SELF-RATING INCLUDED BOTH BEFORE AND AFTER TAKING THE TEST

Literacy and content teachers can formulate informal tests with three levels of self-assessment included in the administration and evaluation of the test.

Before a student takes any teacher-constructed test, he or she can respond to the following open-ended questions:

- How did you go about studying for this test?
- How much time did you spend studying for this test?
- How well do you think you will do on this test?
- In what ways do you feel confident about taking this test?

The student then takes the teacher-constructed test in the content areas of literature (language arts or English), social studies, science, or mathematics. This test can be objective with multiple choice, true-false, or matching items. It also can be a short-answer or essay test. After the test is completed, the teacher grades it in his or her usual manner.

However, before returning the test to the student, the student should be given the following questions to answer to assess his or her skill in self-monitoring, test-preparation, and test-taking skills:

- Now that you have taken the test and will be getting it back soon, was this test about what you expected and what you studied for?
- What grade do you expect to receive on this test?

The teacher then returns the graded test to the student for examination. After the teacher has gone over the test with the student in the usual way, the student then responds to these questions:

- Now that you have gone over your test, do you think you studied in the right way and long enough for the test?
- Do you think your grade was a fairly good reflection of what you actually learned about this subject?
- What did you learn about taking tests that can help you in the future?

From using these three sets of questions, students will learn to do effective self-monitoring about their preparation for and taking of tests. Both literacy and content teachers also can learn a great deal about students' views of studying and taking tests from using this strategy. Such information can greatly help teachers both in teaching and in constructing tests.

However, for this assessment strategy to work effectively, teachers should grade and return tests as soon as possible. Class discussion should be held so students can use taking the test as a learning experience for subsequent tests. In addition, previous tests should be used as the basis for constructing subsequent tests. Teachers should consider students' test-studying and test-taking styles carefully when constructing tests; for example, if the test directions were clear and if the students had sufficient time to study for the test.

Reproducible Example of an Assessment Device with Self-Rating Included Both Before and After Taking the Test

The following is a reproducible example of the type of content assessment device that was just described. This example was constructed from the content area of science about the subject of *dolphins*. It is designed to be used at about the fifth-grade reading level. You can duplicate and use it in its present form if it seems applicable. However, more important, it should serve as a model of this type of device that you can construct yourself from any appropriate topic in any of the content fields.

ASSESSMENT DEVICE WITH SELF-RATING INCLUDED
BEFORE AND AFTER TAKING THE TEST
(Approximately Fifth-Grade Reading Level)

Here is a passage about *dolphins*. Read this passage silently and be prepared to take an informal test about the passage after you have finished reading it.

DOLPHINS—OUR INTELLIGENT FRIENDS

Although dolphins look just like fish and are completely at home in the water, they actually are warm-blooded, air-breathing mammals just like humans, dogs, and cats. Since they are mammals, they have to come to the surface of the water regularly in order to breathe.

Since a baby dolphin is a mammal, the first thing that it does after being born is to swim to the surface of the sea, sometimes with the help of its mother or another dolphin, even though it is born with the ability to see and to swim well. A baby dolphin, called a *calf,* must learn to drink its mother's milk. Almost right after birth, the calf finds one of its mother's two nipples which are located on the underside near her tail. Since dolphins have solid, beak-like snouts and lips that are not flexible, the calf wraps its tongue around a nipple. Then the mother tightens the muscles over her milk glands and squirts milk into its mouth, and the calf gets a big drink of milk quickly. The young dolphin begins to eat fish when the dolphin is between the ages of five and fifteen months.

Dolphins become very active when they are tracking schools of fish. They may jump out of the water and slap their bodies down hard. This frightens the fish and causes them to move closer together. Some of the dolphins then circle the fish, while other dolphins dive in and eat. Later the circlers and the divers trade places.

Although dolphins are air-breathing mammals, their bodies are well designed to glide through the sea at speeds up to thirty miles an hour. A dolphin's body looks rather like a submarine, and some designers of submarines and torpedoes have studied the bodies of dolphins to find ways of improving their own designs. A large fin on the dolphin's back helps it to keep its balance, while its flippers help it to steer and brake. A powerful tail is the dolphin's built-in propeller. While swimming, a dolphin moves its tail fins, called *flukes,* up and down which is different from the side-to-side motion of fish while swimming. Dolphins, like whales, breathe through a blowhole in the top of their head.

Dolphins are highly intelligent creatures who have been trained since the 1940s. Today dolphins perform many crowd-pleasing stunts in aquariums such as leaping high and doing flips, jumping over hurdles, playing with balls, walking on their tails, carrying their trainers on fast rides, and performing water ballets in unison. Dolphins truly enjoy performing for people and even playing with them since they are rewarded with food or praise and always treated very kindly by their trainers. When a dolphin does something wrong, the mistake is just ignored and never punished.

Dolphins seem to have little sense of smell but probably have some sense of taste. However, their sense of **touch** is very well developed and their skin is smooth like the inner tube of a tire and very sensitive. Members of dolphin family groups often touch and rub against each other. In addition, the sense of **hearing** is very well developed in dolphins. To communicate, navigate, and find food in the ocean, dolphins use a system of sound waves called *echolocation.* To echolocate dolphins send out as many as 1,200 high-pitched clicking sounds per second. The clicks may be seven or eight times higher than the sounds that humans can hear. Scientists believe that dolphins make these sounds from air

ASSESSMENT DEVICE WITH SELF-RATING INCLUDED
BEFORE AND AFTER TAKING THE TEST
(Approximately Fifth-Grade Reading Level)

(cont.)

cavities beneath their blowholes. Then the sounds travel to the melon, a fatty organ on the forehead of dolphins. The melon focuses the sounds and sends them forward in a pattern resembling the travel beam of a flashlight.

As a dolphin swims through the water, it moves its head back and forth to scan for objects ahead. When the clicking sounds hit an object such as a rock or a fish, the sounds bounce back as echoes. Scientists believe that these echoes travel through the dolphin's lower jaw to the inner ear. Then they are transmitted to the brain. Much like a computer, the brain analyzes the echoes and tells the dolphin the location, size, and shape of the object.

Dolphins are truly intelligent, friendly, and interesting creatures. Perhaps one day you will be able to see them perform at an aquarium if you have not already done so.

Now that you have finished reading the passage about dolphins, write your answer for each of these questions before you take the test on the material.

1. Just how did you go about studying for this test? _____

2. How much time did you spend studying for this test? _____

3. How well do you think you will do on this test? _____

4. In what ways do you feel confident about taking this test? _____

_____

_____

_____

TEST ON THE PASSAGE
"DOLPHINS—OUR INTELLIGENT FRIENDS"
(TOTAL—25 POINTS)

Multiple Choice (10 points)

There are one, two, or three correct answers for each question. Be sure to read each question very carefully and circle the letter in front of each right answer.

1. Dolphins are

   a. a kind of fish

   b. a kind of mammal

   c. highly intelligent

   d. very trainable

2. A baby dolphin

   a. drinks its mother's milk

   b. can eat solid food at birth

   c. is called a calf

   d. is able to swim well

3. When tracking fish, dolphins

   a. slap their bodies down hard in the water

   b. are not very successful

   c. are not very intelligent

   d. are unable to do it

4. A dolphin's body resembles a

   a. torpedo

   b. rifle

   c. submarine

   d. cannon ball

5. The tail fins of dolphins are called

   a. propellers

   b. flukes

   c. flippers

   d. blowholes

6. Dolphins can be trained to

   a. walk on their tails

   b. dig for food

   c. give their trainer a ride

   d. do flips in the air

7. Dolphins have an excellent sense of

   a. sight

   b. smell

   c. hearing

   d. touch

8. The clicks which a dolphin sends out cannot be heard by

   a. other dolphins

   b. people

   c. horses

   d. fish

TEST ON THE PASSAGE
"DOLPHINS—OUR INTELLIGENT FRIENDS"
(TOTAL—25 POINTS)

(cont.)

9. Dolphins probably make the clicking sounds from

    a. air cavities between their blowholes   c. the blowhole

    b. the melon   d. their teeth

10. The dolphin's brain analyzes the sound echoes much like a

    a. computer game   c. telephone

    b. machine   d. computer

True-False (10 points)

Put a *T* for *True* or an *F* for *False* on the line in front of each item.

_____ 11. Dolphins are not fish, but warm-blooded mammals.

_____ 12. A baby dolphin is born with its eyes closed like a puppy.

_____ 13. A baby dolphin is called a cub like a young lion.

_____ 14. Dolphins have inflexible lips unlike the lips of a human.

_____ 15. Young dolphins begin to eat solid food between the ages of five to fifteen months.

_____ 16. Dolphins are highly intelligent, adaptable mammals that like humans.

_____ 17. A dolphin moves its tail from side to side like a fish while swimming.

_____ 18. It is most helpful to train dolphins through kindness rather than through punishment.

_____ 19. Dolphins have a very good sense of smell.

_____ 20. Echolocation is a system of using sound waves to help dolphins locate food, among other uses.

Open-Ended Questions (5 points)

Write the correct answer to each question on the line.

21. A dolphin must come to the _____ of the sea often in order to breathe.

22. A young dolphin is called a _____.

23. Dolphins can be taught to perform water _____ in unison.

TEST ON THE PASSAGE
"DOLPHINS—OUR INTELLIGENT FRIENDS"
(TOTAL—25 POINTS)

(cont.)

24. Dolphins have _____ skin somewhat like the inner tube of a tire.

25. A dolphin's brain analyzes echoes much like a

_____.

AFTER TAKING THE TEST ABOUT
"DOLPHINS—OUR INTELLIGENT FRIENDS"

Now that you have finished taking the test about "Dolphins—Our Intelligent Friends," write an answer to each of these questions.

1. Now that you have taken the test and will soon be getting it back graded, was this test about what you expected? _____

2. What grade do you expect to receive on this test? _____

Answer Key for "Dolphins—Our Intelligent Friends"

1. b, c, d		14. T	
2. a, c, d		15. T	
3. a		16. T	
4. a, c		17. F	
5. b		18. T	
6. a, d		19. F	
7. c, d		20. T	
8. b, c, d		21. surface (top)	
9. a		22. calf	
10. d		23. ballets	
11. T		24. smooth	
12. F		25. computer	
13. F			

If you want to give a letter grade, here is one possible system to use for doing it. Of course, any grading system that is relevant with your students is equally acceptable.

A—0 to 3 incorrect

B—4 to 5 incorrect

C—6 to 7 incorrect

D—8 to 10 incorrect

F—11 or more incorrect

Note: This grading scale is based on the following percentages:

A—90% to 100%

B—80% to 89%

C—70% to 79%

D—60% to 69%

F—59% or below

AFTER THE TEST HAS BEEN GRADED AND RETURNED TO THE STUDENTS

Now that the test has been graded and returned to you, write an answer to each of these questions.

1. Now that you have gone over your test, do you think you studied in the right way and long enough? _____

_____

2. Do you think your grade was a fairly good reflection of what you actually learned about dolphins? _____

_____

3. What did you learn from this experience about taking tests that can help you take tests in the future? _____

_____

_____

USING MISCUE ANALYSIS IN ASSESSING CONTENT READING SKILLS

Miscue analysis is one of the assessment strategies that can be used with content material to see if students can effectively comprehend and study literature (language arts or English), social studies, science, or the expository reading material of mathematics. Every literacy and content teacher should be adept in at least one system of miscue analysis although there are considerable differences between the various systems.

The concept of *miscue analysis* is mainly credited to the work of Kenneth and Yetta Goodman of The University of Arizona and to some of their associates. Miscue analysis is based upon the study of *psycholinguistics*. It is a method of analyzing how a student approaches the reading process and for determining how he or she views it. Very simply, this theory states that deviations from the printed material are not really *errors* but instead are *miscues* that may or may not interfere with comprehension.

Miscues are usually classified into some variation of the following:

- *graphophonic (graphonic, graphic, or visual) miscues*—those deviations in which there is a graphic change in the deviation (the substitution of *tall* for *talk*)

- *semantic (meaning) miscues*—those deviations in which there is a meaning change in the deviation (the substitution of *mad* for *made*)

- *syntactic (structure) miscues*—those deviations in which there is a substitution in the grammatical structure of the sentence; for example, turning a question into a statement

Graphophonic cues are concerned with whether a student's miscues are mainly found in the knowledge of sight words or with graphophonic (phonic) analysis which deals with the beginnings, middles, or endings of words. The semantic miscues are concerned with whether or not the miscue interferes significantly with comprehension. The syntactic miscues deal with whether the student's responses correctly reflect the grammar of a language.

Miscues that significantly change the meaning of the material often are called *major miscues,* while those that do not may be called *minor miscues.* Miscue analysis also considers the degree to which a student self-corrects while reading either orally or silently. Obviously, a student should be concerned with understanding what he or she reads and should monitor his or her reading and self-correct when this is appropriate.

Thus, the use of miscue analysis should help a reading or content teacher to better understand the characteristics of a student's reading which may impact upon his or her comprehension. The reading instruction for that student subsequently should be improved in the light of the findings from miscue analysis.

The Advantages and Limitations of Using Miscue Analysis

Very briefly, here are some of the *major advantages* of using miscue analysis while a student is reading either narrative or content material:

- the teacher can learn much about how a student understands or views the purpose and content of the reading process

- the teacher can learn whether or not a student's miscues interfere significantly with comprehension

- the reading teacher can learn if the student has the most difficulty with graphophonic (visual), semantic (meaning), or syntactic (structure) cues
- miscue analysis is a fairly accurate way to determine reading strengths and weaknesses

However, here are some of the *major limitations* of using miscue analysis when a student is reading either narrative or content material:

- it requires an experienced, well-trained teacher to use it effectively
- it can be time-consuming to implement successfully
- it always must be done on *an individual basis* which may make it somewhat impractical in a content classroom especially if the teacher has a fairly large class; however, having a reading specialist serve as a resource teacher in a content classroom may well overcome this limitation
- the teacher must use considerable judgment when using miscue analysis; therefore, the results may not always be entirely accurate and should not be thought of in that way

Despite its inherent limitations, every literacy teacher and content teacher should be competent in at least one, if not several, systems of miscue analysis. This chapter now will briefly mention three different systems and will provide references and one example so that the interested literacy or content teacher can learn more about any or all of these systems.

The Miscue Analysis Used in the Author's Individual Reading Inventory

Chapter 5 of the following resource contains two forms of a complete Individual Reading Inventory that encompasses preprimer through twelfth-grade reading levels:

Wilma H. Miller, *Alternative Assessment Techniques for Reading & Writing.* West Nyack, New York: The Center for Applied Research in Education, 1995, pp. 157-215.

This resource describes this kind of miscue analysis in detail and provides a concrete example of exactly how to implement it on pages 124-134. You are encouraged to consult this teacher's resource for ready-to-use help in implementing this type of miscue analysis. However, this chapter now very briefly summarizes a few of the most important elements of this kind of miscue analysis.

Here are the major guidelines you should consider when using this system of miscue analysis:

1. Count as a *major oral reading miscue* and deduct *one point* for any error that interferes with comprehension. Some examples are *ran* for *rain, pretty* for *party,* or *horse* for *house.*

2. Count as a *minor oral reading miscue* and deduct *one-half point* for any deviation from the printed material that does *not* seem to interfere significantly with comprehension. Some examples are *lovely* for *beautiful, large* for *big,* or *home* for *house.*

3. Count an *addition* as *half an oral reading miscue* if it does not change the meaning of the material significantly. Often an addition or insertion is a minor oral reading miscue since it does not alter the meaning of the material significantly.

4. Do *not* count a *self-correction* as a miscue if it occurs within a short period of time such as five seconds. A self-correction usually indicates that a student is *monitoring* his or her own reading and attempting to read for meaning.

5. Count a *repetition* as *half an oral reading miscue* if it occurs on *two or more words*. A repetition of a single word may indicate that the student is trying to monitor his or her own reading or trying to correct the miscue.

6. Do not count more than *one oral reading miscue* on the same word in any one passage. For example, if the student mispronounces the same word more than once while reading the passage, count it as a miscue only once.

7. Do not count an oral reading miscue on any *proper noun* found in a passage.

8. Deduct *one point* for any word that a student cannot pronounce after about five seconds *if that word interferes with comprehension*. Deduct *one-half point* for any word that a student cannot pronounce after about five seconds *if that word does not seem to interfere with comprehension*.

9. Do not count oral reading miscues that seem to exemplify a student's *cultural and regional dialect*. To consider this point, you must be familiar with the basic characteristics of the student's speech patterns such as in the African-American dialect, the Hispanic dialect, or the Vietnamese dialect.

When you have marked all of the miscues from the material that the student has read orally, you then determine the student's appropriate *independent, low independent, high instructional, instructional, low instructional,* and *frustration reading levels*. The teacher's resource *Alternative Assessment Techniques for Reading & Writing* explains in detail how to do this accurately.

THE BASIC CHARACTERISTICS OF ANY RUNNING RECORD

Some variation of a *running record* is a very useful classroom (informal) assessment tool with which every experienced literacy and content teacher should be familiar. The variations of the running record range from very simple (as will be described shortly) to much more complex (as is referenced later in this section).

A running record can be used to informally determine if a student can read a selected content passage effectively. It also may be used to determine what type of literacy program a student has been exposed to and what type of reading instruction a student needs. It can help to ascertain if the student makes effective use of *visual, meaning, and structure clues*. In addition, running records can be used to indicate and document a student's reading progress over time.

Perhaps one of the main differences between an Individual Reading Inventory and any type of running record is that the latter requires only a blank sheet of paper and a pen (quieter to use) or a pencil. Running records, therefore, are more flexible because any type of reading material the student is going to read—including all types of materials in literature (language arts or English), social studies, science, and mathematics—can be analyzed by using a running record.

Like learning a system of shorthand, learning any type of running record requires much motivated practice on the teacher's part. A tape recorder only should be used when the literacy or content teacher is first learning this assessment tool to avoid his or her becoming overdependent on it. A running record can determine such areas of reading as the following: words read correctly, omitted words, substitutions, insertions, self-corrections, repetitions, and teacher help (intervention).

Perhaps the simplest type of running record and the only one that is described here is that of simply placing a check mark ✓ above each word that the student pronounces correctly. You can select a 100-word passage from the appropriate content material and have the student read it aloud. Place a check mark on your piece of paper for each word that the student pronounces correctly. You can use the following rough guidelines to estimate the student's ability to read orally (*but not necessarily comprehend*) the selected content passage:

Words Correctly Pronounced	Approximate Reading Level
98-100	Independent
90-97	Instructional
89 or fewer	Frustration

Here is how a *112-word passage* from science at the ninth-grade level might look if a literacy or content teacher made a running record of a student reading it aloud. Although for sake of clarity, the check marks are placed above each word in the passage, more typically they are placed on a blank piece of paper that the teacher uses while the student is reading orally. However, theoretically, the teacher also can have a copy of the selected material if this makes the recording of the running record easier.

It is a certainty that while <u>fire</u> is the greatest <u>discovery</u> ever made by humans, the <u>wheel</u> is the greatest <u>invention</u> ever made. The invention of the wheel has been credited to people who lived in the Tigris-Euphrates River Valley at least 5,000 years ago.

Humans became civilized by finding simpler means of doing tasks; for example, people realized after a time that oxen and horses could carry burdens that people could not. After the Spaniards brought horses to America, Native Americans began dragging heavy objects with long poles lashed together across a horse's back at one end and trailing the ground on the other in what was called a <u>travois</u>.*

*Reproduced from Wilma H. Miller, *Alternative Assessment Techniques for Reading & Writing*. West Nyack, New York: The Center for Applied Research in Education, 1995, p. 212.

Since the student did not pronounce 19 words correctly, it can be *estimated* that this passage is at his or her *approximate* frustration (difficult) reading level and ordinarily should not be read.

However, if you want to learn about how to record a more complicated running record that will help you analyze a student's ability in the various cueing systems of visual, meaning, and structure cues, one valuable resource you can consult is the following:

Marie M. Clay, *An Observation Survey of Early Literacy Achievement,* Portsmouth, NH: Heinemann, 1993.

A USEFUL SYSTEM OF MISCUE ANALYSIS CODING

One useful, fairly simple system for coding reading miscues described and illustrated in some detail in this resource was developed by Susan B. Argyle (adapted from "Miscue Analysis for Classroom Use," *Reading Horizons,* 29, Winter 1989, pp. 93-102). Very simply, this coding system attempts to determine if the miscue caused *a meaning change, a graphic change, or was a self-correction.* If the student's miscues resulted in few meaning changes, they normally are not very significant since they probably would not interfere with comprehension. If the student made a number of miscues that resulted in graphic changes, he or she may need additional instruction or practice in graphophonic (phonic) analysis or word structure depending upon their frequency or whether they interfered significantly with comprehension. If the student made a number of self-corrections, he or she probably does not have a very significant reading problem in comparison to a student who does not recognize his or her miscues and, therefore, does not attempt to correct them.

Here is an adaptation of the steps Argyle recommends for using this system of miscue analysis:

1. Select narrative or content material that is unfamiliar to your students. This may be part of a basal reader story, a trade book, a passage from a content textbook, or a passage from some other type of content material. Usually even adept readers make some miscues with completely unfamiliar material.

2. Copy the reading or content selection.

3. If you want to administer this material on an individual basis, tell the student that it is not a test in order to reduce his or her nervousness about reading it.

4. Have the student read the passage orally without any preparation. Tape recording helps you to code all of the miscues but may not be completely practical in a noisy setting. It is possible to code the miscues while the student reads aloud, but it is fairly difficult.

5. Place the miscues on a summary sheet so that they can be analyzed.

Here is a very brief example of Argyle's coding system:

- **Omission**　　　　　　　　　in a (tropical) rain forest

- **Addition**　　　　　　　　　in a ^hot^ tropical rain forest

- **Pause**   in a//tropical rain forest

- **Substitution**   in a ~~tropical~~ rain forest
                                                        tragic

- **Repetition**   in a tropical <u>rain</u> forest

- **Reversal**   in a tropical rain forest

- **Self-Correction**   in a <u>tropical</u> rain forest
                                                        T
- **Word Supplied by Teacher**   in a tropical rain forest

TROPICAL RAIN FORESTS OF THE WORLD*

A tropical rain forest is a beautiful, emerald-green forest that is warm, moist, and quiet. It essentially looks like it did millions of years ago. In a rain forest the trees grow tall and close together blocking out the sunshine to the forest floor below. It is so quiet since the wind cannot move the dense top leaves.

Over two hundred million people live in the world's tropical rain forests. People in a tropical rain forest live mainly by hunting, fishing, and eating wild fruits. In some rain forests the people live in houses made of poles and palm leaves, while in other forests the houses may be built of wood. Some children who live there do not go to school but instead learn what they need to survive from their parents and other adults. They may learn to hunt deer, wild pigs, and other animals. They also may learn to grow vegetables.

Many of the foods that you eat were first grown in a rain forest. Some of these foods are corn, sweet potatoes, rice, oranges, and chocolate. Today coffee beans, vanilla, and cinnamon are only grown in tropical rain forests. These forests also are very important to doctors and medical research. Many of the drugs that are now sold in drug stores first came from plants in a rain forest. Many waxes, flavorings, and dyes also come from the tropical rain forests of the world.

However, the tropical rain forests of the world are now in danger. People are cutting down the trees for firewood or lumber. More than *40%* of the world's tropical rain forests have already been destroyed. The clearing and burning of the forests is called *deforestation,* and many scientists believe that it must be stopped.

Number of words in this selection __291__

*The readability level of this passage was computed by the Dale-Chall Readability Formula.

Illustration of This Type of Miscue Analysis Coding System

An oral reading passage entitled "Tropical Rain Forests of the World" was written on the fifth-grade level and was taken from Wilma H. Miller's *Alternative Assessment Techniques for Reading & Writing* (West Nyack, New York: The Center for Applied Research in Education, 1995, p. 174). It was given to Melvin, a fifth-grade student who had evidenced reading problems especially in the areas of comprehension in content reading materials, pronouncing words that are not semantically acceptable while reading, and self-monitoring of his reading. The passage was tape recorded, and Melvin's teacher coded his miscues using the system just described. The coded copy of this social studies passage is included on page 82.

Melvin's teacher then transferred his miscues to a summary sheet he had constructed. The summary sheet contains a list of all of Melvin's oral reading miscues. For each miscue the correct word is written first. Then as close a representation as possible of the student's response is written in each instance. If the miscue resulted in a *complete meaning change,* the word *yes* is written, while if only a partial meaning change occurred, the word *partial* is written. If no meaning change resulted from the miscue, the word *no* is written. Next, each miscue is analyzed in terms of a graphic change in either the *beginning, middle,* or *end of the word.* In each case, a — usually is recorded *for a miscue* in that part of the word, while a ✓ is recorded *for a correct response* in that part of the word. (Notice the similarity to the check marks typically used in a running record as was explained earlier.) If the student *self-corrects a miscue,* the self-correction, which is very significant in self-monitoring, also is noted.

After coding all of Melvin's responses on the summary sheet, his teacher attempted to determine some of Melvin's reading strengths and weaknesses *in terms of patterns* that can be discovered. You will learn that it takes considerable time and practice to become adept in the interpretation of oral reading miscues and to develop an in-depth understanding of the complex reading process. You must use your own judgment in making such an analysis, and you will find considerable variation among teachers in their interpretation of this type of miscue analysis. That does *not* indicate that it is not a valuable assessment strategy to use, but rather that it is a fairly complicated one.

You will notice that Melvin made a total of **24 miscues** that are counted in this system of miscue analysis. **Twelve** of these miscues interfered *significantly* with comprehension, while **6** of them interfered only *partially* with comprehension. **Six** additional miscues did not seem to interfere with comprehension significantly. Thus, out of the total 24 miscues, **50%** of them had a significant effect on comprehension, **25%** of them had only a partial effect on comprehension, and **25%** of them had no significant effect on comprehension.

The percentages of different types of *graphic miscues* that Melvin made also were coded by his teacher. From this analysis Melvin's teacher tried to ascertain if Melvin appeared to be more competent in identifying the *beginnings, middle,* or *endings* of the miscued words. Melvin's teacher noticed that he had the most difficulty with *word middles* that usually involved the vowel sounds, a little less difficulty with *word endings,* and the least difficulty with *word beginnings.* This is a very typical pattern of graphic miscues for a disabled reader. It is quite common for a student to have the most difficulty with word middles because they typically contain the vowel sounds that are the most difficult for nearly all students to discriminate and identify.

Melvin's teacher also noticed that he made **6** *self-corrections* out of the 30 miscues that are coded on the summary sheet that is included on page 86. Although 30 words are listed on this summary sheet of oral reading miscues, I consider only **24** of them are *actual miscues* since the remaining **6** are *self-corrections*. Melvin self-corrected **20%** of the 30 total miscues listed on the summary sheet, showing a fair degree of self-monitoring. However, his self-monitoring skills certainly should be improved to ensure his improved comprehension ability.

You will also notice from the summary sheet that Melvin made **24** actual miscues on this passage out of a total of **291** words. This indicates that he mispronounced about **8%** of the words, while pronouncing about **92%** of them correctly. This percentage is in the low instructional range since the instructional reading level encompasses about **90%** to **99%** accuracy in word identification. Notice that the self-corrections are not included in this analysis, since self-corrections should be encouraged and are not considered as true miscues.

Melvin had **11** *pauses* in the reading of this passage that indicates although he may not have complete oral reading fluency, there are not so many pauses as are typical of students who truly read in a word-by-word manner. In addition, Melvin had **7** *repetitions* which is not an excessive number of repetitions while reading this passage.

> **Note:** Comprehension is not evaluated in this system of miscue analysis except in the area of *word identification*. However, comprehension always should be evaluated by some means such as retelling, questioning strategies, or the use of other strategies to gain a complete understanding of a student's reading strengths and weaknesses.

In summary, here are some of Melvin's reading strengths:

- fairly good attempt at self-correction ability
- fairly good oral reading fluency
- quite good knowledge of word beginnings
- not an excessive number of repetitions

Here are some of his reading weaknesses:

- substituting words that do not have *meaning acceptability* (do not make sense in context) which then undoubtedly interferes significantly with comprehension
- not using continual self-correction or self-monitoring
- inability to identify word middles
- inability to identify word endings

Melvin's program of reading improvement should contain several different elements to ensure his optimum reading progress. He should be given reading materials that are on his independent reading level so that he will be more likely to substitute meaningful words than he would if the material were more difficult. In addition, he needs additional encouragement to *monitor* his silent and oral reading at all times and to use *self-correction* whenever a word does not make sense. Metacognition (monitoring his own reading to ensure that he is understanding) is very crucial for Melvin. These two areas should receive the most emphasis while Melvin reads either content or narrative material. However, in addition, he may need minimal additional instruction and reinforcement in *only the most important graphophonic (phonic) elements,* especially word middles and word endings. Only these very important phonic elements should be emphasized in the middle school.

In summary, the preceding is just one way in which a variation of oral reading miscue analysis can be used to determine a student's reading strengths and weaknesses. You will notice that although it is fairly easy to implement and modify—since it is an *informal assessment device*—it requires considerable experience and knowledge of the reading process to correctly analyze. This technique, therefore, should be used very carefully by an inexperienced literacy teacher. It is much easier for an experienced literacy teacher to use it effectively. You may, in either case, wish to used another system of miscue analysis as a supplement to this one at least sometimes.

Sample Summary Sheet of Oral Reading Miscues

Page 86 is a sample completed summary sheet of this type of oral reading miscue analysis that is based on Melvin's performance on the passage "Tropical Rain Forests of the World." It should prove helpful in understanding the material just included.

It is followed on page 87 by a ready-to-duplicate summary sheet you can use to record a student's performance using this miscue analysis system. This summary sheet can be copied as many times as needed or modified to fit your particular needs.

Name _____ Melvin Hayes _____   Date _ September 14, 1997 _

SUMMARY SHEET OF ORAL READING MISCUES

TEXT	MISCUE	MEANING CHANGE	B	GRAPHIC M	E	SELF-CORR.
1. tropical	_____	partial	—	—	—	
2. rain	✓	✓	✓	✓	✓	yes
3. emerald-green	_____	no	—	—	—	
4. quiet	quite	yes	✓	✓	—	
5. essentially	really	no	—	—	—	
6. millions	many	partial	✓	—	—	
7. blocking	_____	yes	—	—	—	
8. sunshine	sun	no	✓	—	—	
9. dense	_____	partial	—	—	—	
10. tropical	_____	partial	—	—	—	
11. tropical	✓	✓	✓	✓	✓	yes
12. fruits	fries	yes	✓	—	✓	
13. palm	_____	partial	—	—	—	
14. _____	new	no	—	—	—	
15. instead	inside	yes	—	—	—	
16. survive	_____	yes	—	—	—	
17. _____	old	no	—	—	—	
18. wild	✓	✓	✓	✓	✓	yes
19. vegetables	_____	yes	—	—	—	
20. vanilla	_____	yes	—	—	—	
21. and	_____	yes	—	—	—	
22. cinnamon	_____	yes	—	—	—	
23. tropical	✓	✓	✓	✓	✓	yes
24. research	reach	yes	✓	—	✓	
25. flavorings	flavors	partial	✓	✓	—	
26. dyes	_____	yes	—	—	—	
27. tropical	✓	✓	✓	✓	✓	yes
28. firewood	✓	✓	✓	✓	✓	yes
29. deforestation	_____	yes	—	—	—	
30. believe	think	no	—	—	—	

24 miscues
6 self-correction
Total *100%/ 54%/ 33%/ 38%*

Name _____ Grade _____ Teacher _____ Date _____

Name _____ Date _____

SUMMARY SHEET OF ORAL READING MISCUES

TEXT	MISCUE	MEANING CHANGE	B	GRAPHIC M	E	SELF-CORR.

Using Writing to Assess Competency in Content Literacy Skills

There are several ways in which writing can be used as a product to assess competency in literacy skills. Several of these are as follows: a holistic writing evaluation system for assessing expository writing, reading response journals, summaries of various types, the Guided Writing Procedure, and essay questions. Any of these can give the literacy teacher an indication of a student's reading and writing strengths and weaknesses in the content areas.

Holistic Scoring of Expository Writing

When one of your students has written an expository composition from the content areas of literature, social studies, or science, you may wonder what the most effective way is for you to evaluate this composition. At the present time, there is no way to assess writing skills with complete precision. However, the *holistic scoring of writing* probably is one of the more promising and effective ways of doing this despite the great amount of subjectivity a teacher must use in making the assessment. At the present time the state of Illinois uses holistic scoring with trained evaluators of writing to evaluate the Illinois Goal Assessment Program— Writing (IGAP—Writing) which is given to all students in the state at various grade levels. Therefore, in spite of its inherent limitations, holistic scoring can be very helpful.

Since a detailed description of holistic scoring is beyond the scope of this *Handbook,* you are encouraged to consult the following teacher's resource for a complete description with actual students' compositions to help you learn how to use holistic scoring effectively:

Wilma H. Miller, *Alternative Assessment Techniques for Reading & Writing.* West Nyack, New York: The Center for Applied Research in Education, 1995, pp. 389-421.

However, this book now gives a brief description of the holistic scoring of expository writing of content material so that you may have at least a general idea about it.

The holistic scoring I recommend has five main elements: clarity, supporting details, organization, mechanics, and the overall rating.

Clarity. A well-executed composition has a topic that is clear and well-defined. The composition has a unified opening and summary. The rating scale for evaluating the clarity of a piece of writing ranges from **5** as the highest to **1** as the lowest.

Supporting Details. A good composition contains details that support the main idea and subpoints. Additional information can be provided through the use of *explanations, examples, reasons,* and *descriptions.* The rating scale for evaluating the support of a composition ranges from **5** as the highest to **1** as the lowest.

Organization. A well-organized composition exhibits a well-thought-out plan of development. The ideas are logically sequenced and related and are in correctly constructed paragraphs. The length of the composition should be appropriate for the grade level and the expository writing style. The rating scale for organization ranges from **5** as the highest through **1** as the lowest.

Mechanics. A good composition has correct spelling, sentence structure, paragraphing, grammatical usage, punctuation, and capitalization. Mechanics develop through the grade level of the student who is writing the expository composition. *Major errors* are those errors that interfere with communication and include mechanics that a student should have mastered by a specific grade level. On the other hand, *minor errors* do not interfere with communication. They include errors in which a student is not supposed to have mastery at a specific age. The rating scale ranges from **5** as the highest through **1** as the lowest.

Overall Rating. The purpose of the holistic rating is to form an overall assessment of how adequately the student performed the specific writing task. The teacher should rate the paper from beginning to end to make an assessment of how the student met the requirements of the previously mentioned features. The ratings for the holistic component are a **5** for the highest through **1** the lowest.

Overall Rating	Clarity, Supporting Details, Organization	Mechanics
5	Two features must be a 5; one may be a 4	Must be 4 or 5
4	Two features must be a 4; one may be a 3	Must be 3, 4, or 5
3	Two features must be a 3; one may be a 2	Must be 3, 4, or 5
2	Two features must be a 2; one may be a 1	Must be 2, 3, 4, or 5
1	Two features must be a 1; one may be a 2	Usually will be no higher than a 2

Reading Response Journals

Reading response journals are a very effective way to assess a student's understanding of content material in literature, social studies, or science. It is also an effective strategy for integrating reading and writing instruction.

When a student keeps a reading response journal, he or she simply writes a personal response to an entire book or story from literature or to a chapter or part of a chapter from social studies or science. The response usually should emphasize higher-level comprehension skills such as interpretive responses, critical responses, and especially creative (applied) responses. A student can keep all of his or her entries in the same reading response journal, and the journal then serves as a very good record of a student's content reading and his or her written responses to it.

Writing Summaries to Assess Content Reading

Many different kinds of summaries can be used to assess comprehension of content reading and to integrate reading and writing instruction. Obviously, a traditional summary simply consists of having a middle–upper level student read a narrative or expository passage and then write a summary in one or more paragraphs. To be used most effectively as a technique both for assessing and improving comprehension ability, the student first should be given instruction in the proper techniques of writing a summary. Usually the traditional summary contains the main ideas from the material written in a cohesive, concise manner.

There also are several unique variations of traditional summaries that can be used both to assess and improve comprehension. One variation is an activity requiring the selection of a good summary; a reproducible example of this variation is found in the following resource:

Wilma H. Miller, *Reading Comprehension Activities Kit.* West Nyack, New York: The Center for Applied Research in Education, 1990, pp. 256-257.

Another variation is called the *GIST Procedure (Generating Interactions Between Schemata and Text)* (James W. Cunningham, "Generating Interactions Between Schemata and Text," in *New Inquiries in Reading Research and Instruction,* edited by J. A. Niles and L. A. Harris. Thirty-First Yearbook of the National Reading Conference, pp. 42-47). This procedure contains the following basic steps:

1. Select an appropriate passage. This probably should be a short subsection of a book or chapter that contains only a few paragraphs.

2. Have the student read the *first paragraph* of the passage and write a *20-word summary of it.*

3. Have the student read the *next paragraph* of the passage and then write a *20-word summary of both paragraphs.*

4. Have the student read the *next paragraph* of the passage and then write a *20-word summary of the three paragraphs.*

5. Have the student read the *next paragraph* of the passage and then write a *20-word summary of the four paragraphs.*

6. Have the student continue in the same manner with the rest of the material. The final *20-word summary should encompass all of the paragraphs in the short content selection.* Thus, the GIST Procedure is a *cumulative summary strategy.*

If you want to read about the GIST Procedure in detail and also locate a ready-to-duplicate example of this reading/writing strategy, you can consult the following teachers' resource:

Wilma H. Miller, *Reading Comprehension Activities Kit.* West Nyack, New York: The Center for Applied Research in Education, 1990, pp. 258-264.

The Guided Writing Procedure

Another strategy for both assessing and improving ability in content literacy skills is called the *Guided Writing Procedure* (Carl Smith and T. W. Bean, "Integrating Content and Writing Improvement," *Reading World,* 19, January 1980, pp. 290-298). This strategy is an attempt to use the *process of writing* as a way of helping students learn from textbook material. However, it also can be an informal assessment tool in content literacy. Writing fluency (the processes of writing) can be assessed and taught concurrently with the content material itself. This is an extension of the concept that the processes of listening and reading can be assessed and taught along with content material.

This strategy contains the following two main steps:

1. Informal assessment of prior content knowledge and written expression.
2. Teaching content and written expression.

The following teachers' resource contains a complete description of this strategy along with a reproducible example of it:

Wilma H. Miller, *Reading Comprehension Activities Kit.* West Nyack, New York: The Center for Applied Research in Education, 1990, pp. 265-270.

Essay Questions

As every teacher knows, essay questions are a useful strategy for assessing understanding and retention in the content fields of literature (language arts or English), social studies, and science. In some ways essay questions are more useful than objective questions and may give the teacher a better view of a student's actual knowledge of the important content material. The use of essay questions especially benefits the student who writes well but may read too much into objective questions such as multiple-choice and true-false questions.

However, essay questions must be well designed to be successful in determining students' comprehension and retention. As much as possible, essay questions should motivate higher-level thinking such as interpretive, critical, and creative thinking. Essay questions that require application of what was learned to real-life situations may be especially valuable.

In addition, essay questions always should be structured in an open-ended manner so that students can respond in a number of different correct ways. This is one of their main advantages over objective questions that usually permit only one correct response. Much more detail about constructing valid essay questions is found in Chapter 7.

USING PORTFOLIOS TO ASSESS COMPETENCIES AND WEAKNESSES IN THE LITERACY-STUDY SKILLS

A portfolio is a collection of a student's work in such areas as reading, writing, and spelling among other content subjects. The use of a portfolio is part of what can be called *authentic assessment.* The use of portfolios should not entirely replace traditional assessment such as the use of standardized and informal tests of various kinds. Instead, portfolios should be an important part of a *comprehensive assessment program.*

Any portfolio is usually kept in some type of holder. Perhaps the most common type of holder for a portfolio is an accordion-type with compartments or sections. However, the holder also can be a folder, a box, a brown envelope, or even a paper bag. The holder should be large enough to keep many papers, tapes, and drawings, and the student also can design and illustrate its cover. It is essential that students be able to take them out, look through them, organize them, and add or delete material when they need or want to do so.

Although the use of portfolios in instruction and assessment is not completely new, portfolios are now being used much more often because they are compatible with the increased understanding of how language develops and the more widespread use of the whole language philosophy and the thematic (unit) teaching of literature (language arts or English), social studies, and science. As you know, the whole language philosophy and thematic (unit) teaching emphasize instruction that stresses the teaching of all content together, the use of *authentic* reading and writing materials and activities, and the integration of all of the literacy skills.

The idea of using portfolios in instruction and assessment probably stems from their use by other professionals such as artists, photographers, models, and architects. When portfolios are used in such professions as these, they usually are *show portfolios* that display a range of the very best work done by the professional. However, most of these professionals also have a *working portfolio* from which the material for the show portfolio is taken.

Both *working portfolios* and *show portfolios* can be used in the assessment of content literacy instruction. However, *working portfolios* are much more relevant for students in the elementary and middle schools. A working portfolio contains all of the materials with which the student is currently engaged. On the other hand, a *show portfolio* can be derived by choosing certain materials from the working portfolio (preferably by the student him- or herself and once in a while by the teacher) to be shown at parent-teacher conferences, to administrators, to school board members, or to various parent groups. A teacher can learn a great deal about a student's abilities and interests by carefully examining his or her portfolio on a regular basis and by having regularly scheduled conferences of about ten to fifteen minutes with the student about the portfolio at least four times a year.

Certainly, however, *working portfolios* are more relevant and useful for students in the elementary and middle schools. Here are some of the elements that can comprise a working portfolio:

- a table of contents to show the organization of the portfolio
- a reading/writing log
- various drafts of all types of writing that a student might do
- examples of all types of informal teaching and assessment devices in the content fields of literature (language arts or English), social studies, and science that the student has completed
- reading response journals
- dialogue journals
- examples of all types of activities and materials that the student is currently working on or has completed from the content fields of literature (language arts or English), social studies, and science
- examples of writing done outside of class
- teacher-completed and student-completed checklists and surveys of various types
- tape-recorded oral reading protocols
- audiotapes
- videotapes
- student-teacher conference notes

- various types of self-assessment devices
- the results of various kinds of standardized and informal tests
- teacher anecdotes and observations
- graphs of progress

It always should be remembered that the **major purpose of using a portfolio is the opportunity for a student to self-assess his or her work in the content fields.** Without allowing the student the opportunity and time to make such a self-assessment, portfolios have very little meaning, making them merely a collection of a student's work. It also is important that both the student and teacher have input in selecting what is going to be placed in the student's working portfolio with **the student always having the major input in the selection process.** However, each student should understand that his or her portfolio is going to be available for inspection by his or her teacher, classmates, and parents, among others. Some material from a student's working portfolio can be gathered together and sent home after the student has decided with or without teacher input that it is no longer relevant for inclusion in his or her portfolio.

Parents must be thoroughly informed before a teacher implements portfolio assessment in any classroom. Such information should be given to them by using a letter to parents, newsletters, a back-to-school meeting at the start of the school year, or some other means. It is essential that parents understand the purpose and content of portfolios before any literacy or content teacher attempts to implement their use in any classroom. **It also is very beneficial for literacy teachers and content teachers to work cooperatively in implementing portfolio assessment in any type of classroom except a completely self-contained classroom.** Such cooperation can much more readily ensure successful portfolio assessment.

In summary, *portfolios can be an important part of total assessment in any literacy or content program.* Their use has many advantages for students, teachers, and parents. I urge you to consider implementing portfolios as one important part of your assessment program. If you wish more concrete information about how to use portfolios in *any literacy or content classroom* as well as access to many ready-to-duplicate materials that can make portfolio assessment much easier and more successful for you to implement, you can consult the following teachers' resource among many other helpful professional books about using portfolios:

Wilma H. Miller, *Alternative Assessment Techniques for Reading & Writing.* West Nyack, New York: The Center for Applied Research in Education, 1995, pp. 443-470.

USING THE CLOZE TECHNIQUE AS A GROUP TECHNIQUE FOR ASSESSING READING LEVELS AND TEXTBOOK READABILITY

The *cloze procedure* can be used as an alternative technique for determining a student's independent, instructional, and frustration reading levels as well as for assessing textbook readability. The cloze procedure was developed by Wilson L. Taylor in 1953 and is based upon the psychological theory of *closure* (Wilson L. Taylor, "Cloze Procedure: A New Tool for Measuring Readability," *Journalism*

Quarterly, 30, Fall 1953, pp. 415-433). Briefly, this theory states that a person attempts to complete any pattern that is not complete. Therefore, the cloze procedure makes use of both semantic (word meaning) and syntactic (word order or grammatical) clues to help a person deduce unknown words.

The cloze procedure has been researched extensively for many years. It has been studied in relation to its usefulness as a way of determining a student's reading levels, an alternative way of judging textbook readability (whether or not a student can effectively comprehend and study the selected content textbooks), and as a way of improving a student's comprehension ability. In general, research has determined that the traditional cloze procedure may be used as an *alternative or supplementary way* of determining a student's instructional reading level or if a selected textbook in literature (language arts or English), social studies, or science is acceptable. However, any cloze procedure usually provides only a *rough estimate* of either a student's actual instructional reading level or his or her ability to read a selected content textbook, and the results of a traditional cloze procedure are best used as a *supplement* to other standardized and informal assessment devices such as survey reading/achievement tests, an Individual Reading-Thinking Inventory, structured checklists, or other types of informal assessment devices described in this chapter, among other sources. Although the cloze procedure has many variations, only the traditional cloze procedure is described and illustrated in this *Handbook*.

You can construct a traditional cloze procedure from any narrative or content material at either the elementary, middle, or secondary school level. In constructing a traditional cloze procedure, you select a passage of about *250 words* at the appropriate reading level or from the content textbook that you have selected for a class or a group to use. The first and last sentences of the passage are usually typed in their entirety. Every fifth word is then deleted from the remainder of the passage and is replaced by a typewritten line fifteen spaces long. However, a proper noun is not deleted if it is the fifth word; instead, the following word is deleted.

The traditional cloze procedure usually is given to a group of students at the same time, although it also can be given to an individual student. Each student should be encouraged to complete the exact deleted word in each case. The student should have all the time he or she needs to complete the cloze procedure. When the traditional cloze procedure is used to determine a student's approximate instructional reading level, you must count as correct only those completed blanks that are identical to the original passage.

In evaluating the traditional cloze procedure to ascertain a rough estimate of a student's instructional reading level or to see if he or she can comprehend a selected content textbook, you follow this procedure:

1. Count the total number of blanks in the passage.
2. Count the number of blanks that were completed with the *exact deleted word.*
3. Divide the total number of blanks into the number of blanks completed with the exact omitted word to get a percentage. For example, let us suppose that a traditional cloze procedure contained *50* blanks, and the student completed *30* of the blanks with the exact omitted word. *Divide 50 into 30 to get a percentage.* The student completed *60%* of the blanks correctly. Then you can use the following percentages as a *rough estimate* of the student's reading levels and his or her ability to comprehend the content passage:

- *60% or more of the blanks completed with the exact omitted word—independent reading level*
- *40%-60% of the blanks completed with the exact omitted word—instructional reading level*
- *less than 40% of the blanks completed with the exact omitted word—frustration reading level*

When the traditional cloze procedure is used to determine if an entire class or a group of students will be able to effectively read, comprehend, and study the selected content textbook in literature (language arts or English), social studies, or science, the procedure the literacy or content teacher follows is slightly different.

1. Construct a traditional cloze procedure from a *250-word passage* near the *beginning* of the selected content textbook; construct another traditional cloze procedure from a *250-word passage* near the *middle* of the selected content textbook; and construct a third traditional cloze procedure from a *250-word passage* near the *end* of the chosen content textbook.

2. Then give each student in the class or group the three traditional cloze procedures. Although theoretically he or she can complete all three procedures on the same day, due to the difficulty of completing a traditional cloze procedure—especially if a student does not possess much prior knowledge in the content field—it probably is much better to administer only one traditional cloze procedure a day.

3. Then score each student's three completed cloze procedures following the procedures described earlier to obtain a percentage of blanks completed with the correct omitted word in each case. Add the three percentages together and divide by *3* to obtain an average percentage for each student. You then use the same criteria to determine the student's *independent, instructional,* and *frustration reading levels* that were given earlier. If the selected textbook is on the student's independent reading level, you may want to consider choosing a more difficult book for him or her. If the chosen textbook is on his or her instructional reading level, it probably is a good choice for that student. On the other hand, if the book is on the student's frustration reading level, you should try to choose an easier textbook that covers the same general material. You also should use thematic (unit) teaching of the content material, cooperative learning groups, partner reading, and other ways that enable the student to be successful in comprehending and studying the textbook. Many students are consistently required to read content textbooks that are much too difficult for them, causing them great frustration and anxiety.

   Note: The following provides a concrete example of how to use traditional cloze procedures in this way.

Sixth-Grade Science Textbook

Benny's percentage score from a traditional cloze procedure from the first passage:

45%

Benny's percentage score from a traditional cloze procedure from the second passage:

39%

Benny's percentage score from a traditional cloze procedure from the third passage:

47%

Benny's *average* percentage score from the three traditional cloze procedures from the selected sixth-grade science textbook:

44%

It therefore appears that Benny should be able to comprehend and study this sixth-grade science textbook *with considerable teacher support.* However, certainly many of the strategies that appear in this *Handbook* should be used to ensure his success with this textbook as well as thematic (unit) teaching, cooperative learning groups, and partner reading.

Reproducible Traditional Cloze Procedure from Social Studies at the Fifth-Grade Level

The following is a reproducible traditional cloze procedure from a social studies textbook at the fifth-grade level. You can duplicate and use this cloze procedure in its present form if it seems applicable for your students. More important, it should serve as a model for you in constructing traditional cloze procedures from your own content textbooks in literature (language arts, English), social studies, and science.

TRADITIONAL CLOZE PROCEDURE
(Fifth-Grade Level)

THE OREGON TRAIL

Starting in 1842 wagon trains of pioneers traveled from Independence, Missouri, to the Oregon Territory on the Oregon Trail. The Oregon Trail was _____ two thousand miles long, _____ it wound through prairies, _____, and deserts. So many _____ traveled on the Oregon Trail _____ even today places can _____ seen where the wagon _____ made deep ruts in the _____.

The pioneers who attempted _____ make the trip had _____ be determined and courageous _____ the very difficult trip _____ took six months. The _____ west always began at Independence _____ the spring. While the _____ were waiting for the _____ to start, they waited _____ of town in their _____ and tents. When enough _____ had gathered there to _____ a wagon train, they _____ a scout who knew _____ way west. They also _____ one person to be _____ leader. Every day the _____ train moved out just _____ dawn, and the train _____ seven days a week. _____ this way, a wagon _____ could cover 15 to 20 _____ a day. At night _____ pioneers brought their wagons _____ a circle for protection. _____ pioneers faced many dangers _____ making their journey. The Native Americans _____ did not want settlers _____ their lands often attacked _____ wagon trains. Any delays _____ the trail because of _____ might mean that the _____ could be trapped in _____ snowstorms. Indeed, only the very fortunate pioneers successfully made the trip to the Oregon territory by wagon train.

Answer Key for "The Oregon Trail"

248 Words—*41* blanks

- 60% or more of the blanks completed with the exact deleted word—*independent reading level*
- 40%-60% of the blanks completed with the exact deleted word—*instructional reading level*
- less than 40% of the blanks completed with the exact deleted word—*frustration reading level*

about

and

mountains

wagons

that

be

wheels

trail

to

to

since

west

trip

in

pioneers

trip

outside

wagons

pioneers

form

hired

the

elected

their

wagon

after

traveled

Traveling

train

miles

the

into

The

while

who

crossing

the

on

weather

pioneers

mountain

USING THE MAZE TECHNIQUE FOR ASSESSING CONTENT READING

The *maze technique* can be used as a *supplementary way* of determining a student's ability to comprehend the selected content material. I especially recommend it for this purpose in second, third, and fourth grades.

A maze technique can be constructed from any type of narrative or content material such as literature (language arts), social studies, or science. A maze technique usually is constructed from a passage of about *120-150 words.* The passage is then modified *by separating it into sentences* with approximately every *fifth word* being replaced with alternatives. One alternative obviously should be the *correct word,* another alternative should be an *incorrect word that is the same part of speech,* while the third alternative should be an *incorrect word that also is another part of speech.* Then type or print the maze technique so that it can be duplicated in some way.

A maze technique usually is given to a group of students although it also is possible to give it on an individual basis. Have the student read each of the choices silently and circle the one alternative that is correct in each choice. Since this technique may well be new to your students, you may wish to provide an example that you will complete with the students before having them complete the technique independently. Since this technique is not timed, each student can have all the time he or she needs to complete it.

Since the research on the maze technique is very limited, the findings from the use of this assessment device should be interpreted cautiously. However, after having my teacher-trainees use it with hundreds of students over the years, I am confident that the following criteria for determining a student's *approximate reading level* and thus his or her ability to comprehend a selected content selection are fairly accurate:

- *80% or more* of the words correctly circled—*independent reading level*
- *60%-80%* of the words correctly circled—*instructional reading level*
- *less than 60%* of the words correctly circled—*frustration reading level*

Reproducible Maze Technique for Assessing Comprehension Ability

The following is a ready-to-use maze technique from science at the third-grade level. You can duplicate and use it in its present form if it seems applicable or, more important, use it as a model for maze techniques that you construct from the content material that your students must read.

MAZE TECHNIQUE
(Third-Grade Level)

KEEPING YOUR BONES AND MUSCLES HEALTHY

Read each sentence silently. Then *circle* the one word in each group that makes that sentence correct.

1. If a person does   now / not / no   have healthy bones and   muscles / manage / mothers,   he or she cannot   do / be / door   even the easiest jobs

2. One / Eight / Open   way to keep bones   but / and / aunt   muscles healthy is to   eat / each / itch   the right foods.

3. Everyone   been / showed / should   have dairy products, fruit,   ant / but / and   vegetables every day.

4. It   also / and / a   is important to eat   meat / met / mole,   fish, and eggs as   will / well / also   as bread and cereals   each / eat / lovely   day.

5. Another important way   to / two / at   keep bones and muscles   or / harm / healthy   is to exercise often.

6. Exercise / Extra / Exit   helps bones and muscles   at / to / two   become stronger.

7. Exercise even   makes / rakes / many   the heart muscle healthy.

8. A / An / Under   third important way to   deep / keep / kept   bones and muscles healthy   is / are / army   to rest and sleep.

9. When / Why / Wonder   a person exercises, muscles   use / under / run   energy that is released   front / under / from   the food.

10. Once this   energy / over / each   is released, waste materials   are / is / ant   made.

11. When a person   rode / rests / ready   or sleeps, the wastes   are / army / is   carried away from the   muscles / mussels / make   by the blood.

12. Rest   also / a / am   helps the body make   and / but / under   fix bone and muscle   tissue / trouble / take.

Answer Key for "Keeping Your Bones and Muscles Healthy"
152 Words—*31 blanks*

not
muscles
do
One
and
eat
should
and
also
meat
well
each
to
healthy
Exercise
to
makes
A
keep
is
When
use
from
energy
are
rests
are
muscles
also
and
tissue

A THREE-LEVEL STUDY GUIDE FOR ASSESSING CONTENT READING

Three-level study guides have been used for assessing and improving content reading skills for a number of years. They remain one of the more useful tools for doing both. Three-level study guides were first developed by Harold Herber

(Harold Herber, *Teaching Reading in the Content Areas*. Englewood Cliffs, New Jersey: Prentice-Hall, 1978). Such a guide connects and integrates the three levels of comprehension with a series of statements to which students must respond. Since three-level study guides demonstrate the hierarchical interaction of the three levels of comprehension and call for student response to a series of statements at these levels, they are a comprehensive tool for assessing comprehension. However, they should only be used occasionally to avoid students becoming bored with them.

Here are some general guidelines for constructing a three-level study guide:

1. Select the **organizing concept or theme** for the guide. This should be a concept or theme with details that support it.

2. Then determine the content objectives. What exactly should the students learn about this material? This content should be the main ideas and the implications of the main ideas that are the most important.

3. Then take these content objectives and formulate a series of statements about them. It may be helpful to construct the statements in the form of questions. **The first level of the guide that you construct is the actual second level of the guide—the interpretive (implicit) level.** It is easier to construct the guide in this way since the details that comprise the first level of the guide should be formulated from the interpretive statements.

4. Then take the statements and the passage and **construct the first level of the guide—the literal (explicit) level.** Write the important facts either as exact replications or paraphrases in which no real thinking is involved in responding. You should have about two literal (explicit) statements to support each major inference.

5. Next you **construct the third or applied level** of the guide. Statements in this level should apply to the major ideas but also should use the students' prior knowledge. Usually there should be about four applied statements on a typical three-level study guide.

6. Then formulate the directions and decide if you want to add some distracters, usually only at the first and second levels of the guide. Be sure that the directions to the students for completing the guide are clear and complete.

When introducing three-level study guides to students, teachers should at first use them as a whole-class activity, as is the case with almost any new assessment or teaching strategy. All students should have their own copy of the guide and also be able to see the guide on the chalkboard or an overhead transparency. Discussion is promoted in a whole-class setting, and students are less likely to feel threatened than if this strategy is presented only to individuals. Since the value of the three-level study guide is mainly in the understanding of the three levels of comprehension and in then talking about this understanding, discussion is a very important part of the activity. Students begin to realize how the facts, interpretations, and applications are interdependent.

After some experience with the guides, students can complete them in small groups or independently. Usually **distracters** should not be added to the guides until students have had some experience with completing them. Three-level study guides can give students opportunities to do meaningful writing, especially at the applied level where students can be asked to connect their prior knowledge with the new information learned in the content material.

Reproducible Three-Level Study Guide

The following is a passage from science about genetic engineering that is designed for use at about the sixth-grade level. It also contains a ready-to-duplicate three-level study guide that was constructed from this passage. If it seems applicable, you can have your students read the passage silently and then complete the guide either with a partner(s) or independently. However, more important, it can serve as a model for you in constructing three-level study guides from your own content materials in literature (language arts or English), social studies, or science.

THREE-LEVEL STUDY GUIDE
(Approximately Sixth-Grade Level)

THE BIOTECHNICAL REVOLUTION
AND GENETIC ENGINEERING

Biotechnology includes all of the techniques that use living cells to produce commercial products. Many scientists consider the biotechnical revolution the most important revolution in science since the discovery four hundred years ago that the earth revolves around the sun instead of the other way around.

One of the more significant discoveries in this area took place in 1982 when scientists took the gene that produces human insulin and inserted it into *E. Coli,* a microorganism that lives in the intestines. Today insulin produced in this way is used by diabetics around the world. Using bacteria to eat up oil spills is a part of biotechnology. Beer- and wine-making is another part of it since the microorganisms are used to transform sugar into alcohol in both processes.

Microorganisms are the workhorses and unsung heroes of the biotechnical revolution. In medicine they help to produce antibiotics, vaccines, and hormones. In industry they make chemicals, fuels, and gases, while in agriculture they produce new plant varieties and medicine for cattle.

Although biotechnology has existed for thousands of years in that microorganisms have been used for such purposes as fermenting grape juice into wine, turning milk into cheese, and helping bread dough to rise, the application of the techniques of genetic engineering is the heart of the biotechnical revolution. Genetic engineering involves the manipulation of the molecules that make up the innermost structure of living matter. These molecules control the hereditary information carried by cells. Genetic engineering is a totally new process and is based on the science of molecular biology which came into being just forty years ago.

The concept of scientists manipulating organisms in the interest of either research or industry has both positive and negative aspects. For example, the new technology represents a significant advance in our ability to use microorganisms to improve life. On the other hand, the new technology can change the very forms of life as they are now known, possibly harming the environment.

Many companies have already invested billions of dollars in research and development in the various areas of biotechnology. Let us hope that all the decisions that scientists make about genetic engineering are correct so that it may realize its potential for great good without doing great harm.

THREE-LEVEL STUDY GUIDE
(Approximately Sixth-Grade Level)

(cont.)

STUDY GUIDE TO "THE BIOTECHNICAL REVOLUTION AND GENETIC ENGINEERING"

I. *Directions:* Put an **X** on the line beside each item you believe says what the author said. Sometimes the exact words are used, while other times somewhat different words may be used.

_____ 1. Biotechnology uses living cells to produce different kinds of commercial products.

_____ 2. The biotechnical revolution probably will not be of much importance in the future.

_____ 3. Insulin can be made by inserting the human gene that manufactures insulin into the microorganism *E. Coli.*

_____ 4. Microorganisms can be used to help clean up oil spills in oceans.

_____ 5. Biotechnology has no real usefulness in agriculture.

_____ 6. Biotechnology is a new phenomenon.

_____ 7. Fermenting grape juice into wine is one example of how microorganisms are used.

_____ 8. Genetic engineering can be used for either good or evil.

_____ 9. Biotechnology has the potential for harming the environment.

_____ 10. Companies have not shown much interest in investing money in biotechnological research.

II. *Directions:* Put an **X** on the line beside any of the statements that are acceptable interpretations of the author's meaning.

_____ 1. Insulin probably is much more readily available now than it was before researchers discovered how to use a gene and microorganisms to produce it.

_____ 2. Microorganisms are fairly hard to locate on our earth.

_____ 3. It may be possible to develop two humans who are identical—"clones"—by using genetic engineering.

_____ 4. Many of the companies that have invested large sums of money are probably very interested in making large amounts of money from their investment.

_____ 5. Genetic engineering probably has been used to develop tastier and more attractive-looking fruits and vegetables.

THREE-LEVEL STUDY GUIDE
(Approximately Sixth-Grade Level)

(cont.)

III. *Directions:* Using the information that you read or already knew, put an **X** on the line beside any of the statements below with which you and the author would agree.

_____ 1. Biotechnology already has improved life in a number of important ways.

_____ 2. Scientists usually are very intelligent, creative men and women.

_____ 3. Genetic engineering in which scientists can create "human clones" will always be a good thing.

_____ 4. Companies investing in biotechnological research *always* are managed by completely honest, sincere men and women who are not concerned about the money that their company may make.

Answer Key for "The Biotechnical Revolution and Genetic Engineering"

375 words
Part I

1. X

3. X

4. X

7. X

8. X

9. X

Part II

1. X

3. X

5. X

Part III

1. X

2. X

Using Graphic Organizers in Content Reading

Graphic organizers, which sometimes are called *advance organizers* or *structured overviews,* help a reader prepare for reading a content assignment by graphically organizing the important concepts. The graphic organizer is a hierarchical overview that demonstrates how the important concepts in the material fit together. It is the teacher's view of the schema found in the material. A graphic organizer can be effective because a teacher can prepare readers with a concise, comprehensive, and compact visual aid. In a sense a graphic organizer is a *visual representation* of the content in the chapter.

Graphic organizers are effective because they are designed to show relationships among the concepts in the content assignment. To construct a graphic organizer, a literacy or content teacher follows these steps:

- Write an important *organizing concept* and then identify all the supporting concepts in the material.
- List all the key terms from the material that reflect the identified concepts.
- Connect the terms to show the relationships between the concepts.
- Construct a diagram based on these connections, and then use it to introduce the content reading material.

It is not necessary to use every word that might be new to the students in a graphic organizer. Some new words may not contribute significantly to the diagram or be very important to the comprehension or retention of the reading material.

The literacy or content teacher should explain to the students why he or she made the graphic organizer in the way in which it was made, showing the relationships. This presentation can include a discussion to which students can contribute what they already know about the terms as well as what they predict they will be learning in the content assignment based on the graphic organizer. Students also should have the graphic organizer available to refer to while they are reading the material.

A graphic organizer can effectively be used as an *assessment tool* as well as an aid to comprehension and retention. One way of doing this is to present the *completed graphic organizer before* the student is to read the content material. Then present the same graphic organizer with *some items missing after* the student has finished reading the material.

The student then tries to determine the missing items and to complete the incomplete graphic organizer correctly.

A new graphic organizer that the teacher has constructed can be a very effective nontraditional assessment tool in content reading. Although no traditional comprehension questions are asked in this type of assessment, comprehension skills can be determined, and the product can be evaluated.

The test item might be as follows:

Study the graphic organizer that I have drawn for you. It is similar to the ones that you have studied in class, but in this one there are several blank spaces. Using the list of terms that is attached, fill in the term that fits best in each space (1 point each—explicit [literal] level of comprehension). Now write one sentence beside each term listed. This sentence should explain why you think that the term belongs where you put it on the graphic organizer (2 points each—implicit [interpretive] level of comprehension). Next write an essay which uses the information found on this graphic organizer. Your first paragraph should mention the main idea; your second paragraph should provide four (4) details; your third paragraph should summarize by telling what new information you have learned from reading this chapter (25 points—applied level of comprehension). (Adapted from: Judy S. Richardson and Raymond F. Morgan, *Reading to Learn in the Content Areas.* Belmont, California: Wadsworth Publishing Company, 1990, pp. 408-409.)

Reproducible Passage with Graphic Organizers

The following is a passage about a famous mathematician that is designed for use at about the seventh- or eighth-grade level. It also contains two ready-to-duplicate graphic organizers, one to be used before students read the passage and the other to be used after students have finished reading it. If this passage seems applicable, you can have your students read the passage silently and then complete the advance organizer found at the end of the passage either with a partner(s) or independently. However, more important, it can serve as a helpful model for you in constructing your own graphic organizers from content materials in literature (language arts or English), social studies, science, or mathematics.

PASSAGE WITH GRAPHIC ORGANIZERS
(Approximately Seventh- or Eighth-Grade Level)

Study this *graphic organizer* before you read the passage "Sir Isaac Newton—Mathematician and Scientist." It should help you know what to look for while you are reading the passage. After you have finished reading it, you will have to finish an incomplete graphic organizer just like this one.

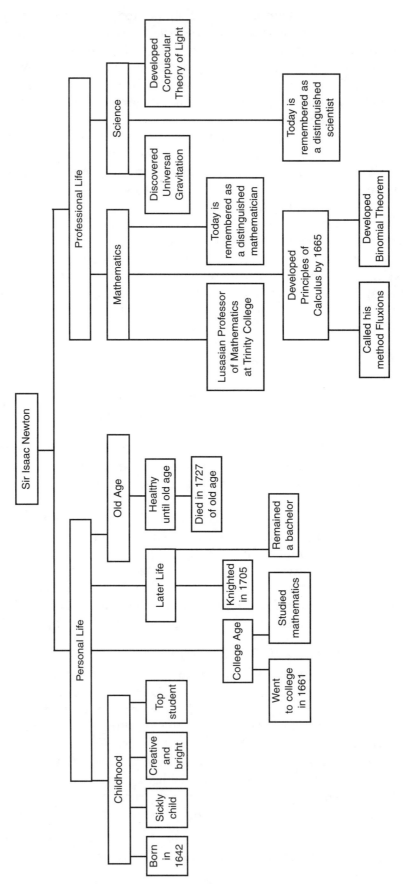

PASSAGE WITH GRAPHIC ORGANIZERS
(Approximately Seventh- or Eighth-Grade Level)

(cont.)

SIR ISAAC NEWTON— MATHEMATICIAN AND SCIENTIST

Now read this passage about Sir Isaac Newton, silently focusing on the items that were included in the *graphic organizer*. You will be asked to finish an incomplete graphic organizer after you have finished reading the passage.

Sir Isaac Newton is considered by many mathematicians and scientists to be one of the most superior intellects the world has ever known. He was born on Christmas Day in 1642 to a farm family living in Lincoln County, England. Isaac's father died before he was born, and Isaac was a premature baby who seemed very frail and sickly. After her husband's death, Mrs. Newton remarried and had three more children, none of whom were extraordinary in any way.

Because of his poor health, Isaac could not play the typical boys' games of childhood, but instead invented his own diversions in which his genius first appeared. He invented perfectly constructed toys such as waterwheels, a mill, and a wooden clock. He attended Grantham Grammar School where he at first was not a superior student but later became the top student in his class. Before he went to college he became engaged but never married his first sweetheart or anyone else since his career soon became his only real interest.

In June, 1661, Newton entered Trinity College in Cambridge, England and was a student who earned his own expenses. Newton's mathematics teacher soon recognized a student who was a more gifted mathematician than even he. His first two years at Trinity College were spent mastering elementary mathematics. During the three years from 1664 through 1666 (when he was 21 to 24), Newton laid the foundation for all of his subsequent work in mathematics and science.

A manuscript dated May 20, 1665, shows that Newton—at the age of 22—had sufficiently developed the principles of the mathematical subject *calculus* to be able to find the tangent and curvature at any point of a continuous curve. He called his method *fluxions,* from the idea of "flowing" or variable quantities and the rates of "flow" or growth. He also discovered the *binomial theorem,* an essential step toward calculus as it is known today.

Newton probably is most famous for his discovery of the scientific theory of *universal gravitation.* The very well-known story of his being hit on the head by an apple falling from a tree helped him to discover that objects of different weights that are dropped at the same time land at the same time.

In 1669 at the age of 26 Newton succeeded his own mathematics professor as Lusasian (distinguished) Professor of Mathematics at Trinity College. His first lectures were on *optics,* and he developed his corpuscular theory of light, according to which light consists of an emission of corpuscles. Even today, Newton's theory contains some elements of truth.

Newton did not always accept criticism well from his fellow mathematicians and scientists, but he always retained their respect and admiration. In 1705 he was knighted by Queen Anne of England. Newton remained healthy and creative well into his eighties. He never wore glasses and lost only one tooth throughout his long life. He died in his sleep on March 20, 1727, at the age of 84. He is buried in Westminster Abbey in London and today remains one of the greatest mathematicians and scientists of all time.

PASSAGE WITH GRAPHIC ORGANIZERS
(Approximately Seventh- or Eighth-Grade Level)

(cont.)

Now complete this unfinished *graphic organizer:* **It is the same one that you studied before you read the passage about Sir Isaac Newton. Do not refer back to either the first graphic organizer or the passage as you complete this graphic organizer.**

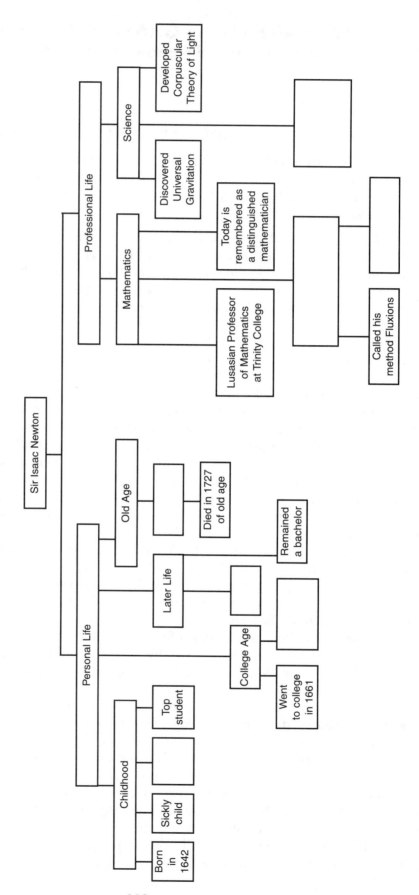

THE PRE-READING PLAN (PReP)

A student's prior knowledge is very important to the degree of success he or she has in effectively understanding a content passage. If a student lacks prior knowledge about the topic he or she is to read, the student usually will have great difficulty in comprehending the material.

The *Pre-Reading Plan* (PReP) is a very good strategy for assessing and activating a student's prior knowledge before reading a selection. It is most effective with an expository (content) selection. Very briefly, here is how it can be used to assess or activate prior knowledge:

1. The teacher chooses **three major concepts** from a 700- to 900-word content passage from literature, social studies, or science. For example, from a passage about Australia, the teacher might select the concepts: *sheep stations, outback,* and *gold coast.*

2. The teacher then tells the students that they will be using what they already know about important ideas that will appear in the passage that they are going to read. The students are told this prereading discussion will help the teacher to determine if any additional background discussion is needed before they read the material. They also are told that this discussion will help them to activate (access) their own prior knowledge of the material because readers comprehend new information by relating it to what they already know.

3. The students then make associations with the first important concept. "Tell anything that comes to your mind when you hear the words *sheep stations.*" The teacher then writes the students' responses in the form of a semantic map as illustrated:

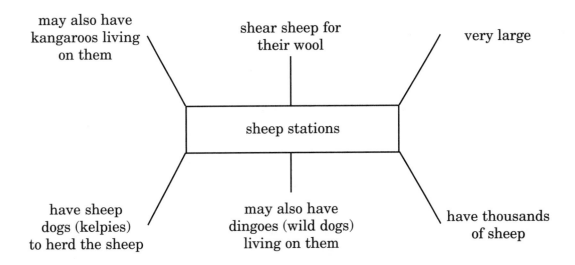

4. The next step is for the teacher to ask the students to think about their initial associations. "What made you think about _____?" This helps the students to better develop their associations with the concept being discussed.

5. The final step is to ask the students to rethink their knowledge about the concepts being discussed. The teacher can say: "Considering our discussion, do

you have any new ideas about _____?" This step helps students to understand any new or modified associations formulated from the discussion. The procedure is repeated for each major concept. (Adapted from Judith A. Langer, "From Theory to Practice: A Prereading Plan," *Journal of Reading,* Volume 25, November 1981, pp. 152-156.)

This prereading discussion helps the teacher to learn how much prior knowledge the student or students have about the topic to be read. If they have much prior knowledge, the responses will be in the form of a *superordinate concept. (Sheep stations are very important to the economy of Australia.)* On the other hand, if the students lack prior knowledge about the topic, the responses usually are in the form of *examples. (A sheep station has a lot of sheep on it.)*

Reproducible Pre-Reading Plan

The following is a model Pre-Reading Plan (PReP) from the colonial period of social studies designed for use at about the fifth-grade level. One of the concepts selected was that of the *Salem Witch Trials.* First you will find a reproducible partially completed Pre-Reading Plan that can serve to assess students' prior knowledge and serve as a basis for a pre-reading discussion about the material that is going to be read. Each student can have his or her own copy of the map if you want, or it can be placed on a transparency or the chalkboard. You should follow the above-mentioned steps in helping your students to complete the semantic map. Then the chapter includes a passage about the Salem Witch Trials. More important, this entire example should serve as a model for you in constructing Pre-Reading Plans (PRePs) from the content materials your students are going to read.

SEMANTIC MAP FOR THE
PRE-READING PLAN (PREP)

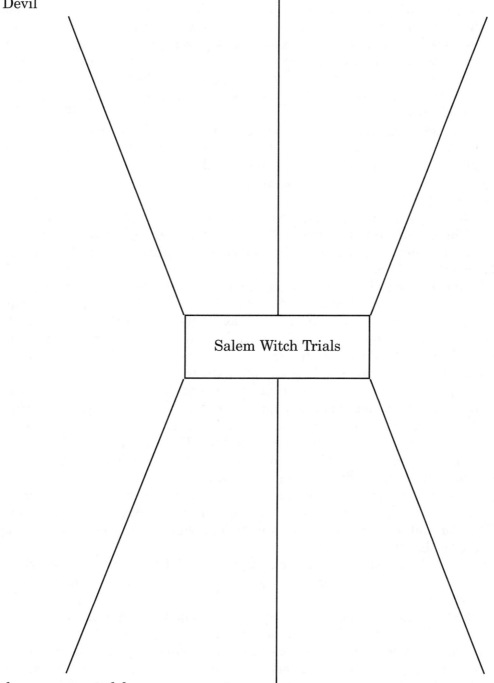

"Witches" sold their souls to
the Devil

Salem Witch Trials

People were executed for
being "witches"

SEMANTIC MAP FOR THE
PRE-READING PLAN (PREP)

(cont.)

THE SALEM WITCH TRIALS

The Salem Witch Trials were one of the most terrible events of the Colonial Period in America. They were held from May, 1692, until September, 1692, and were the result of a general belief in the seventeenth century of the existence of **witches.** Witches were thought to be people who sold their souls to the Devil in exchange for money or certain evil powers over other people.

During the Salem Witch Trials fourteen women and six men were executed in various ways for being "witches." More women than men probably were executed because people unfortunately thought that a woman was just more likely to be a witch than a man. Their accusers were mostly children, some of whom probably had epilepsy. The epileptic convulsions they suffered from may have been taken as a sign that they had been bewitched by a "witch."

The fear of witches reached panic proportions in the Massachusetts village of Salem after a teenage girl had an argument with a washerwoman. The following day the girl had convulsions and supposedly had pains all over her body. When her younger brother and sister also said that they had pains, the washerwoman had to stand trial on the suspicion of being a "witch." Although she said she was completely innocent, she was convicted and hanged for being a "witch."

Within a few days a similar incident occurred that involved a West Indian slave named Tituba. Although she did not immediately confess to being a witch, she was beaten until she had no choice but to confess. She then identified nine other "witches" and later was executed for being a "witch" herself.

Much of the mass hysteria about witches was greatly increased by sermons preached by Reverend Cotton Mather and other ministers. Mather was one of the leading preachers of New England at that time and truly believed in the existence of witches and that people actually could be possessed by the Devil. Although he did not protest the execution of the "witches" at that time, he did denounce the injustices of the witchcraft trials in 1702. His popularity as a preacher had diminished greatly after the trials.

William Phips, the governor of Massachusetts at that time, set up a special court for the Salem Witch Trials and appointed nine judges to deal with the mass hysteria. From the beginning the trials were not really fair since the public demanded convictions and harsh penalties for all of the people who were tried as "witches." The nine judges based their convictions almost entirely on "spectral" evidence—unconfirmed testimony based only on dreams or hallucinations of allegedly bewitched witnesses.

The hysteria about witches became so extreme that even two **dogs** were actually convicted and executed for being "witches." Only after Salem's most important citizens, including Reverend Cotton Mather's own relatives and Phips's wife, were accused did the court begin to doubt the truthfulness of "spectral" evidence.

When the special court was dissolved during the fall of 1692, 150 prisoners who were going to be tried for being "witches" were released, and charges against 200 more suspected "witches" were fortunately dropped.

In 1771 the General Court of Massachusetts gave money to all of the families of the executed victims. The Salem Witch Trials are a terrible example of what can happen when people let their fears overcome their good judgment and common sense. The Salem Witch Trials also have been a popular theme in American literature over the years. As one example, Arthur Miller's play *The Crucible,* which was first shown on Broadway in New York in 1953, is all about the Salem Witch Trials.

THE ANTICIPATION GUIDE

An *anticipation guide* can be used to **assess** a student's prior knowledge in a subject area and to increase his or her comprehension ability in that area. An anticipation guide activates a student's prior knowledge **before** reading and sets purposes for reading.

An anticipation guide uses **statements** instead of questions before reading as an initial way to get students more involved in their reading. As a result of this process students should be better able to generate their own questions and statements. Although a start toward these goals can be made in the primary grades, they can be better refined at the middle school level.

Here is a brief description of how an anticipation guide can be used:

1. *Identify the Major Concepts*—The teacher first identifies the major concepts in the content reading material by carefully reading both it and the teacher's guide for the content material, if one is available.

2. *Determine the Students' Knowledge of These Concepts*—The teacher should try to determine how the main concepts in the material support or refute what the students already know about the material.

3. *Create Statements*—The teacher should write three to five statements about the content material. These statements are those in which the students have enough knowledge to understand what the statements say, but not enough to make any of them completely known to them.

4. *Decide Statement Order and Presentation Style*—The order of the statements ordinarily should follow the order of the statements presented in the material. The guide can be duplicated or written on the chalkboard or an overhead transparency. The directions and blanks for students' responses should be included.

5. *Present Guide*—When giving the guide to students, the literacy or content teacher may read the directions and statements orally if he or she wishes. Students should be told they will share their thoughts and opinions about each statement by defending their agreement or disagreement with the statements. Students can work individually, with a partner, or in a small group while making the responses.

6. *Discuss Each Statement Briefly*—The teacher should first ask for a show of hands from students to indicate their agreement or disagreement with each statement. The teacher then tallies the different responses. Students should be encouraged to judge their own view in terms of the views of the other students.

7. *Have Students Read the Material*—The students then are told to read the material with the purpose of deciding what the author may say about each statement. As they read, students should keep two things in mind: their own thoughts and beliefs as well as those provided by other students and how what they are reading is related to what was discussed earlier.

8. *Conduct Follow-Up Discussions*—After reading the material, the students can respond again to the statements. Then the anticipation guide serves as a basis for the post-reading discussion in which students share the new information gained from the reading and how their previous thoughts may have been mod-

ified by what they believe the reading said. They should understand they do not have to agree with the author depending on what type of material is read. (Adapted from J. E. Readence, T. W. Bean, and R. S. Baldwin, *Content Area Reading: An Integrated Approach.* Dubuque, Iowa: Kendall/Hunt Publishing Company, 1981).

Reproducible Anticipation Guide

The following is a sample anticipation guide at about the third-grade level from the content area of social studies. If it seems relevant, you can duplicate and use it in its present form. However, more important, it should serve as a model for you in constructing your own anticipation guides from the content materials your students read and study.

ANTICIPATION GUIDE
(Approximately Third-Grade Level)

Directions: **Here are four statements about the** *life of cowboys in the Old West.* **Read each statement to yourself and put an X on the line beside each statement you agree with. Be sure to be able to defend your ideas when we talk about the statements later.**

_____ 1. Cowboys in the Old West had one <u>roundup</u> each year.

_____ 2. A typical cowboy in the Old West had a "<u>catch rope</u>."

_____ 3. A cattle drive in the Old West was very hard work for the cowboys.

_____ 4. On a cattle drive in the Old West it was not very important for the cowboys to watch the <u>flanks</u> of the herd.

_____ 5. A cowboy's life in the Old West was a safe, pleasant life.

Now read the story for yourself. Remember what you should look for as you read the story so that we can later discuss what you learned from reading the story.

COWBOYS OF THE OLD WEST

Almost everybody has heard about the cowboys who lived in the Old West. Although a cowboy's life may sound exciting, it often was boring and lonely. However, even today it is interesting to read about the cowboys who lived at that time.

Cowboys in the Old West had two *roundups* each year. The spring roundup was to find the cattle that had wandered away during the winter and to brand new calves. The fall roundup was to gather the cattle that had to go to market, to find lost calves, and to brand more new calves.

A typical cowboy in the Old West had some very interesting equipment . Some of them were a rifle and rifle holder, a broad-brimmed (cowboy) hat, a catch rope or lariat, branding irons, a six-shooter (pistol) and holder, spurs, and a leather saddle. All of these things helped a cowboy do his job easier and better.

A *cattle drive* was one of the most difficult of a cowboy's jobs. Cowboys had to move cattle from the ranch on which they were raised to a railroad line where they could be shipped to market. On a cattle drive cowboys rode behind a herd of cattle as well as on its *flanks* (sides) to guide it. They also had to be on the alert for stray cattle which easily could start a *stampede.* Then, too, outlaws were a big danger to cowboys since they often would try to rustle (steal) the cattle. Besides, on a cattle drive cowboys had to live and work outside in all kinds of weather as well as eat their meals outside. However, the meals were cooked in a *chuck wagon* and were often quite good.

Yes, a cowboy's life in the Old West is fun to read about, but it often was a hard life.

Answer Key for "Cowboys of the Old West"

2. X

3. X

A SELF-MONITORING COMPREHENSION RATING SHEET

As you know, it is very important that students learn to *monitor or assess* their own comprehension ability. They should know when they do and do not understand what they are reading. They also should be able to find the sources of their comprehension difficulty when they do not understand what they are reading. In addition, they should know how to correct the comprehension difficulties they are experiencing.

One technique for assessing a student's self-monitoring skills of reading comprehension is to ask him or her to rate a number of paragraphs in a reading selection in terms of his or her ability to comprehend them. The student can use a three-point rating system. In this system the student rates each paragraph of a longer selection in terms of whether he or she understands it very well, fairly well, or not very well at all. The reading material should be copied with blanks placed at the end of each paragraph and at the end of the selection for the student's ratings. Then a number of different types of vocabulary, explicit (literal), and implicit (interpretive) comprehension questions should be provided that assess the student's actual comprehension of the material. Obviously, the student's own assessment of his or her comprehension ability should closely match his or her actual performance following the selection. If it does not, the student needs to have instruction in the importance and application of self-monitoring of reading comprehension. (Adapted from Beth Davey and Sarah M. Porter, "Comprehension Rating: A Procedure to Assist Poor Comprehenders," *Journal of Reading,* 26, December 1982, pp. 197-202.)

Reproducible Example of a Self-Monitoring Comprehension Rating Sheet

The following is an example of a self-monitoring comprehension rating sheet from social studies at about the sixth-grade level. You can duplicate and use this example if it seems applicable. However, more important, it should serve as a model for you in constructing self-monitoring comprehension rating sheets from the content materials that your students must read and comprehend.

SELF-MONITORING COMPREHENSION RATING SHEET
(Approximately Sixth-Grade Level)

On each blank line at the end of each paragraph, put a *1* if you understood the paragraph *very well,* a *2* if you understood the paragraph *fairly well,* or a *3* if you did *not* understand that paragraph *very well at all.* You also can put a *1, 2,* or *3* to show your understanding of the *entire passage* in the *box* at the end of the passage. Then you should answer the comprehension questions found at the end of the passage.

LIFE IN THE CONCENTRATION CAMPS DURING THE HOLOCAUST

1. Although the Holocaust was a very terrible time in the history of the world, it is important to remember what happened then so that it will never happen again. As you may know, the Holocaust occurred from 1933 to 1945 when the Germans killed 6 million Jews in Europe simply because they *were Jews.* They killed men, women, and children. The Holocaust is an important event to understand, although it unfortunately does not have a happy ending. _____

2. One of the worst parts of the Holocaust was the infamous *concentration camps.* When a person arrived at a concentration camp, he or she was told to undress, and all of his or her clothes and possessions were taken away. Then prisoner barbers shaved the men's heads and beards and clipped the women's hair very close to their skulls. After that, the prisoners had to take ice-cold showers, and then were disinfected with a sticky, bad-smelling liquid. _____

3. The prisoners were given the clothes of others who had been killed recently. They then had a number tattooed in blue on their left upper arm. In a concentration camp, a prisoner had no identity except his or her number. _____

4. The typical prisoner in a concentration camp was not expected to live longer than six weeks. If a prisoner did not starve to death, he or she might die of a disease. If the person still was able to survive, he or she might be murdered in some way by the guards. A concentration camp was not a place to live but was deliberately established as a place to die. Those who managed to survive the starvation diet, the many diseases, and the extremely hard work usually were taken to a gas chamber to be put to death. _____

5. However, some Jews miraculously managed to survive the concentration camps. Those who did were *organized.* That meant to steal, buy, exchange, or in some way get hold of those things necessary for survival. Many of the survivors today tell about the close attachments they made with their fellow prisoners. However, to survive in a concentration camp, a person had to think of himself or herself first. Some survivors wanted to live so that they could later tell the world what life had been like in a concentration camp. Indeed, most of the survivors have done just that, and they are the reason we know now of the horrific conditions in the concentration camps. _____

6. You now know the truth of life during the Holocaust. It is now your duty as a future adult to be sure that no such event ever occurs again anywhere in the world. _____

SELF-MONITORING COMPREHENSION RATING SHEET
(Approximately Sixth-Grade Level)

(cont.)

Comprehension Questions

1. The Holocaust occurred during the

    a. 1940s

    b. 1930s and 1940s

    c. 1950s

    d. 1960s

2. Although this passage does not tell you directly, it makes you believe that the German people who were involved in the Holocaust were

    a. inhumane and without any conscience

    b. unaware of what was occurring

    c. concerned about people of all races and religions

    d. thoughtful

3. The word in paragraph **2** that means *wicked* is

    _____.

4. The men in the concentration camps had their heads and beards shaved to help remove their

    a. dignity

    b. sorrow

    c. similarity in appearance

    d. friendliness

5. The word in paragraph **3** that means *marked* is

    _____.

6. The average life span in a concentration camp was expected to be

    a. one year

    b. 6 months

    c. 6 weeks

    d. 4 weeks

SELF-MONITORING COMPREHENSION RATING SHEET
(Approximately Sixth-Grade Level)

(cont.)

7. Many prisoners at the concentration camps were put to death in a gas chamber.

   Yes   No   It doesn't say

8. The Jews who survived in a concentration camp did so by being

   a. loners

   b. organized

   c. foolish

   d. cowardly

9. Most of the survivors of the concentration camps have never talked about the conditions that existed there.

   Yes   No   It doesn't say

10. The word in paragraph **5** that means *terrible* is

   _____.

Answer Key for "Life in the Concentration Camps During the Holocaust"

  1. a

  2. a

  3. infamous

  4. a

  5. tattooed

  6. c

  7. Yes

  8. b

  9. No

10. horrific

A QUESTIONNAIRE–INVENTORY FOR ASSESSING PRIOR KNOWLEDGE

There are a number of useful, indirect ways of assessing students' prior knowledge. Very briefly, here are several of them:

1. *Simple Questionnaires and Inventories*—The teacher may have students complete a 20- to 30-item duplicated activity sheet of questions that contain some true-false items, fill-in-the-blank items, and incomplete sentence items (only the first part of the statement is given).

2. *Open-Ended Inventories*—The students must write responses to such questions as: *What do you now know about loons?* or *Loons* _____.

3. *Informal Content Checks*—These pretests help to determine how much students already know about a subject before they have to study it.

4. *Informal Concept Tests*—The students list words on the chalkboard or a transparency that label the concept or the sentences containing the concepts. This technique helps the teacher locate students who have inaccurate schemata (prior knowledge) in a subject matter area.

5. *Synonym and Definition Tests*—In these tests the teacher lists words and concepts on the chalkboard, a transparency, or an activity sheet with a parallel list of synonyms placed in incorrect order. The student must draw a line from each word to the correct synonym. (All of these assessment strategies were adapted from Thomas V. Devine, *Teaching Reading Comprehension: From Theory to Practice.* Boston, Massachusetts: Allyn and Bacon, Inc., 1986, pp. 79-81.)

Sample Questionnaire–Inventory to Assess Prior Knowledge

The following is a model questionnaire–inventory for assessing prior knowledge at about the fourth-grade level from the content area of science on the topic of common loons. This questionnaire–inventory is followed by a brief passage about loons that students can read after completing the questionnaire–inventory. This preceding device incorporates both structured and open-ended forms. Although the literacy or content teacher can duplicate and use it in its present form if it seems applicable, it is mainly designed to serve as a model so that literacy and content teachers can construct their own devices using the content materials their students have to read.

Name _____ Grade _____ Teacher _____ Date _____

QUESTIONNAIRE–INVENTORY FOR
ASSESSING PRIOR KNOWLEDGE
(Approximately Fourth-Grade Level)

In a few minutes you are going to read a story about *loons*. The following part of this activity is trying to find out just how much you know about loons *before* you read the story about them. Complete all of the items the best that you can and *then* read the story to yourself. Then see how well you did on the items that you marked.

1. **T F** A common loon makes a sound that is something like a yodel.

2. **T F** A common loon is a fairly small bird like a gull.

3. **T F** A common loon has red eyes that help it to see under water better.

4. **T F** A common loon needs a fairly large body of water to serve as a "runway" before it can fly.

5. **T F** A common loon can dive under water for as long as ten minutes or more.

6. A common loon is a large water _____ that weighs between eight and eleven pounds.

7. A common loon has a wingspan of nearly _____ feet.

8. A common loon has a strong, pointed, dark _____ that is about four inches long.

9. A baby common loon is called a _____.

10. A common loon likes to eat _____ very much.

11. A common loon has large webbed _____ that are placed near the back of its body.

12. Many of a common loon's bones are _____ instead of air-filled like those of many other birds.

13. A common loon has a white _____ in contrast to its dark back that is splashed with white bands and speckles.

14. _____ are an endangered species.

15. Loons are often disturbed on lakes by people riding in _____.

LEARNING ABOUT COMMON LOONS

I spend my summers in a house beside Birch Lake in northern Wisconsin. I especially enjoy hearing the sounds made by the *common loons* that live by the lake. If you have never heard the sound of loons, it is hard to describe, but it is a strange sound that is like a *wail* or a *yodel*.

Common loons are very commonly found nesting by the lakes in Wisconsin, Minnesota, and Michigan. The common loon is a large water bird that averages about twenty-eight to thirty-six inches from bill to tail and weighs about eight to eleven pounds. It also has a wingspan of nearly five feet. Although it is nearly the size of a Canada goose, it has a short neck in relation to its body size.

A common loon is a superb diver looking somewhat like a streamlined torpedo. Its beak (bill) is strong, pointed, dark, and about four inches long. Used to grab fish during dives, the beak also can be an effective defense weapon against enemies that want to hurt it or its chicks. Amazingly, I think, a common loon has red eyes that look very strange in contrast to its greenish, black head. The red color of its eyes' retinas filter light, much improving the loon's vision underwater where it has to look for fish.

A common loon's tapered body helps it to move through water easily. A loon has large webbed feet that are placed near the back of its body. A loon's legs almost work like oars helping it to swim easily. Although a loon is a good flier, it needs a fairly large body of water to "take off" from the water's surface into the air. That is the reason that loons rarely are found nesting near very small lakes. A loon's tail is short and has only eighteen to twenty very stiff feathers.

Common loons also are very well suited for their swimming and diving lifestyle in other ways. Since many of their bones are solid instead of air-filled like those other birds, it makes diving is much easier for them. Interestingly, a loon can dive underwater looking for fish from one to five minutes. Loons can stay underwater for so long partly because their blood is rich in *hemoglobin,* helping it to retain more oxygen than the blood of most other birds.

A common loon also is a very beautiful bird. It has a velvety, dark greenish-black head, a dark beak (bill), a white stomach, and a dark back that is splashed with white *cross-banding* and white *speckles.* As stated earlier, it has unique-looking red eyes.

Common loons are endangered birds. Unfortunately, although the law does not allow people to disturb either them or their nests, they often are bothered by people in motorboats who want to see them. This has resulted in a small loon population near many northern lakes. For example, Birch Lake now has only one pair of loons living near it. Let us hope that the common loon population does not get smaller yet. That would be very sad indeed.

Answer Key for "Learning About Common Loons"

1. T
2. F
3. T
4. T
5. F
6. bird
7. five
8. beak (bill)

9. chick
10. fish
11. feet
12. solid
13. stomach
14. Loons (Common loons)
15. motorboats

Ready-to-Use Strategies and Activity Sheets for Improving Vocabulary in the Content Areas

Jeff was a student who was recommended for tutoring under my supervision several years ago. Although Jeff was a fifth-grade student who had adequate word identification and comprehension skills while reading the narrative material contained in basal readers and tradebooks, he had great difficulty understanding his social studies and science textbooks. He had the most difficulty in understanding his science textbook. His tutor determined from observation and informal assessment that his main problem in effectively comprehending both of these textbooks resulted from his inability to understand the specialized vocabulary they contained. Although he often could decode these specialized vocabulary terms either structurally or phonetically, he simply was unable to determine their meaning in context. He was a disabled reader in the content fields and needed to learn some of the strategies he could use to determine the meaning of these terms in the context of content reading.

Literacy and content teachers will find the strategies and ready-to-use materials contained in this chapter very effective in helping *all students* to improve their comprehension of the vocabulary included in all kinds of content materials.

THE DIFFERENT TYPES OF MEANING VOCABULARIES

It may be helpful to first define *meaning vocabulary*. This can be defined as the number of words to which an individual can attach one or more meanings. Literacy and content teachers also should understand that there are several different types of meaning vocabularies. For example, the *listening vocabulary* is the first type of vocabulary the child must acquire. It is learned primarily in the home by hearing parents and other family members speak. Of course, if a very young child attends a day care center, the adults there also are very important in the acquisition of his or her listening vocabulary. Next the young child learns the *speaking vocabulary* from the imitation and modeling of family members and other adults with whom he or she comes in contact. That is why it is important for the child's speech models to use correct grammar and as interesting, precise vocabulary as possible. It also is why the child may learn a dialect such as the African-American dialect or the Hispanic dialect.

Next the child may learn the *reading vocabulary,* although his or her *writing vocabulary* may develop simultaneously. In any case, the reading vocabulary is primarily developed in school unless the child is an early reader in which case it could be learned in the home or in some kind of child-care facility. By the time the child is in the intermediate grades, his or her reading vocabulary usually exceeds the speaking vocabulary unless the child is a disabled reader. The fourth type of vocabulary is the *writing vocabulary* which also is primarily learned in school although a beginning may be made before school especially if the child is encouraged to use *invented spelling* as should be the case. Normally the writing vocabulary is the smallest because a person may not use a number of words in his or her writing that would be used in speaking or met while reading.

The fifth type of vocabulary is the *potential or marginal vocabulary*. This type of meaning vocabulary is made up of all the words the child can determine the meaning of on a specific occasion while reading by using context clues; the meaning of prefixes, suffixes, or word roots; or by understanding derivatives. It is impossible to determine the size of this vocabulary since the context in which a word is located may determine whether or not it would be known. As stated earlier, it is important that a reader have a very good understanding of context and know the meaning of many word parts so that he or she will have a large and useful potential or marginal vocabulary.

Vocabulary knowledge has been found by significant research studies to be very highly related to reading comprehension. This certainly is true about the knowledge of specialized vocabulary terms and a student's comprehension in the content fields of literature (language arts or English), social studies, and science. In any case, in a classic study conducted in 1944 that was replicated in 1968, Frederick B. Davis researched the reading process and by factor analysis of reading comprehension subskills found that comprehension was composed of two primary skills—*knowledge of word meanings (vocabulary)* and *reasoning ability* which probably can be equated with reading comprehension (Frederick B. Davis, "Fundamental Factors in Comprehension in Reading," *Psychometrika,* 9, September, 1944, pp. 185-197); and Frederick B. Davis, "Research in Comprehension in Reading," *Reading Research Quarterly,* 3, Summer 1968, pp. 449-545).

In another research study, R. L. Thorndike found correlations between vocabulary knowledge and reading comprehension that ranged from .66 to .75 for 10-, 14-, and 17-year-old students in fifteen countries. These are fairly high correlations indicating that vocabulary knowledge indeed is important to effective reading comprehension (R. L. Thorndike, *Reading Comprehension Education in Fifteen Countries.* New York: Wiley and Company, 1973).

John D. McNeil has offered three hypotheses or reasons why he thinks there is a powerful relationship between vocabulary knowledge and reading comprehension. The *aptitude hypothesis* states that individuals with larger vocabularies comprehend better mainly because they have better innate verbal ability. The *instrumental hypothesis* states that specific vocabulary knowledge contributes to comprehension mainly because the prospective reader knows more words. However, the *knowledge hypothesis* states that the more knowledge in the form of concepts or schemata (prior knowledge) that a reader has about a topic, the more words he or she knows that are related to that topic (John D. McNeil, *Reading Comprehension: New Directions for Classroom Practice.* Glenview, Illinois: Scott, Foresman and Company, 1984, pp. 96-97). Undoubtedly none of these hypotheses is really a complete explanation for the relationship between vocabulary and reading comprehension. Any single one or more of them may apply in any given situation.

The traditional view of meaning vocabulary states that the *words* or *terms* are of primary importance in reading comprehension both in narrative and content materials, and without adequate comprehension of individual words there can be no adequate comprehension. Although this seems logical and may be more accurate in content reading than in narrative reading since the specialized terms in the former may be crucial to understanding, there is more to the comprehension of any printed material than the meaning of the individual words taken together. Many contemporary reading specialists believe that because of the redundancy in language, cues within written material provide the information needed for comprehension, and that knowledge of individual word meanings really is not that important. However, as stated earlier, that may not be the case with some specialized vocabulary terms in content reading since a reader must know their exact meaning to completely understand the material.

While it is accurate that the redundancy (word order clues) in language provides very important clues to word meanings, the following example may show you that the reader also sometimes must know the meanings of the individual words to ensure comprehension of what is read.

That talkative young woman has made me very nervous since she talks so much that none of her friends ever has a chance to talk. She always becomes a nuisance when she talks to us no matter where we are.

That loquacious juvenile gentlelady has rendered me exceedingly agitated since she converses so extensively that none of her acquaintances ever has an opportunity to participate in the conversation. She consistently becomes obnoxious whenever she converses with us irrespective of our location.

Obviously, although the sentence structure and content of the second passage is about the same as that of the first one, the vocabulary in the second passage makes it more difficult for most people to understand. The same could be said for many content passages because of their specialized vocabulary and not necessarily because of either their subject matter or sentence structure.

Another research study that may have relevance to the relation between specialized vocabulary knowledge and comprehension in content materials was conducted by P. L. Roelke. He found the following to be important in comprehension, which are listed in order of importance:

1. The number of words that a student knows the meaning of.

2. The knowledge of *multiple meanings* of words; for example, knowing that the word *cut* may mean: slicing a loaf of bread, an injury involving bleeding, removal from a football team, dividing a deck of cards, ignoring a person, or requesting that action be stopped, among many others.

3. Ability to select the correct meaning of a word having multiple meanings in order to fit a specific context. This often is especially relevant while reading content materials. For example, the term *cabinet* has a totally different meaning when reading social studies material than it does when reading narrative material. (P. L. Roelke, "Reading Comprehension as a Function of Three Dimensions of Word Meaning," *Dissertation Abstracts International,* 30, 5300A-5301A. University Microfilms, No. 70-10, p. 275)

CONE OF EXPERIENCES THAT CAN BE USED FOR VOCABULARY IMPROVEMENT IN THE CONTENT AREAS

Edgar Dale has proposed a *cone of experiences* that has great relevance for the teaching of vocabulary both in narrative and content materials. This cone of experiences demonstrates the importance of what are called "activities of action" through which students learn concepts by direct experience whenever possible. When hands-on experiences are not possible, students need "activities of observation" such as field trips, experiments, demonstrations, interactive computer software, graphics, and visuals. Dale stated that learning concepts and vocabulary by starting with written language—the "products"—is very difficult for disabled readers and learning handicapped students (Edgar Dale, *Audio Visual Methods in Teaching.* Orlando, Florida: Holt, Rinehart and Winston, 1969).

Dale has constructed a visual representation of his beliefs that he has called a *Cone of Experiences Model for Vocabulary Building.* Figure 3-1 shows Dale's "Cone of Experiences," and it is used with the permission of Holt, Rinehart and Winston.

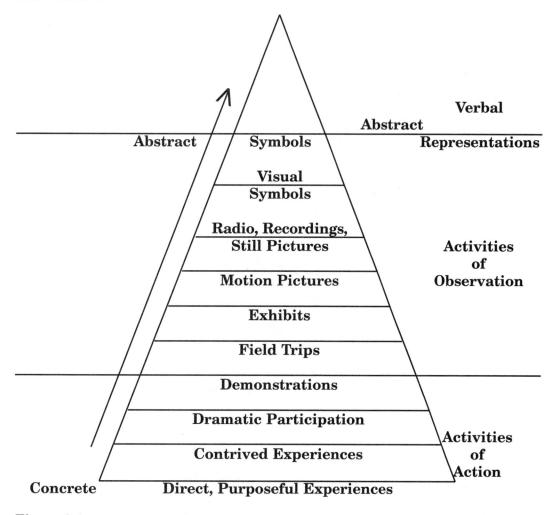

Figure 3-1

Strategies and ready-to-use activity sheets for improving competency in many of the items included in Dale's Cone of Experiences are included in this chapter.

DIRECT AND VICARIOUS EXPERIENCES FOR VOCABULARY IMPROVEMENT IN THE CONTENT AREAS

As Dale has effectively illustrated in his *Cone of Experiences for Vocabulary Building,* direct or first-hand experiences (*activities of action*) are the most effective way for a student of any grade level to learn vocabulary terms in a meaningful way. As one example, a trip to a local planetarium may be the most effective way for a student to learn the following scientific terms: *astronomy, solar system, planet, rotation, revolution, universe, light years, orbit, space, galaxy, meteor, comet,* among many others. Each of these specialized vocabulary terms is the most relevant for students and is the most likely to be remembered after such a direct experience. The following are a few representative examples of direct or first-hand experiences that students at various grade levels may engage in to build vocabulary in the content fields of social studies and science:

Social Studies
- trip to a police station
- trip to a fire station
- trip to a post office
- trip to a television station
- trip to a radio station
- trip to a local court
- trip to historical museums of all types
- visit to an international festival
- visit to a cultural event such as an African-American celebration
- visit to a Native-American (or any other culture) museum
- trip to a local jail or prison

Science
- trip to a zoo
- trip to a wildlife preserve
- trip to a forest preserve
- trip to a natural science museum
- trip to a planetarium
- trip to an aquarium
- visit a hospital
- visit a nursery or greenhouse
- conduct a scientific experiment (demonstration) either independently or with classmates
- conduct a scientific model either independently or with classmates
- use scientific equipment of various kinds
- gardening

Vicarious or second-hand experiences (*activities of observation*) are also very useful in vocabulary development, although they generally are not so effective as are direct or first-hand experiences. However, they may be much more practical in many instances. For example, a student obviously cannot take a trip on the Oregon Trail in a wagon pulled by oxen although the student may be able to "travel" on the Oregon Trail by using the interesting computer software program "The Oregon Trail" (MECC).

Some examples of vicarious or second-hand experiences that can be used for vocabulary development in the content fields of literature (language arts or English), social studies, science, and mathematics are the following:

- using *interactive* computer software (especially useful)
- using other types of computer software
- observing scientific experiments (demonstrations)
- observing demonstrations of other kinds
- looking at models
- looking at pictures
- looking at dioramas
- watching videotapes
- watching filmstrips
- looking at slides
- handling realia (actual items)
- listening to cassette recordings
- listening to records

In summary, both direct and vicarious experiences are very useful for improving the specialized vocabulary required for effective comprehension in the content fields. Both types of experiences should be used whenever possible to improve students' meaning vocabulary knowledge.

WIDE READING FOR VOCABULARY IMPROVEMENT IN THE CONTENT AREAS

Wide reading of relevant, interesting narrative and expository (content) materials at the *independent and low instructional reading levels* is one of the most effective ways both for building vocabulary of specialized vocabulary terms in the contents fields *and* improving reading comprehension. Students often can learn the meaning of many unique terms in the content areas by reading easy, interesting trade books related to the topic under study. For example, when students are studying the *pioneer era* in history, the Laura Ingalls Wilder trade books may be both motivational and beneficial for improving meaning vocabulary knowledge and comprehension.

The more a student reads with the purpose of understanding what is read, the more effective his or her vocabulary and comprehension skills will become since reading is a skill that best improves with motivated practice. In that respect it is like many other skills such as playing a sport. This also is why good readers who enjoy reading for pleasure and information usually become better readers who enjoy reading even more and find it even more fulfilling.

USING WORD STRUCTURE SUCH AS PREFIXES, SUFFIXES, AND WORD ROOTS FOR VOCABULARY DEVELOPMENT IN THE CONTENT AREAS

The use of word structure or word parts (structural analysis or morphemic analysis) can be very useful in vocabulary development in the content fields, especially in *science*. The meaning of word roots, prefixes, and suffixes can be extremely useful in helping students to determine the meaning of unknown, difficult specialized vocabulary terms. For example, in science if a student knows that the meaning of the prefix *hypo* is *under,* he or she probably can deduce the approximate meaning of such scientific terms as the following: *hypothyroidism, hypoglycemia, hypoallergenic, hypodermic,* and *hypochrondria.*

The use of word parts for vocabulary development is probably the most effective when the student meets the unknown specialized vocabulary term while reading a content textbook or other content material. The student can then refer to a list of prefixes, suffixes, or word roots and their meanings to try to determine an approximate meaning of the word. If you wish, you also can have the student learn the meanings of the most relevant prefixes, suffixes, or word roots as an aid to vocabulary improvement. However, this activity rarely should involve just memorization of word parts or looking up their meanings. It is much more useful if the activity can be made meaningful and directly related to the student's actual content reading. Thus, the study of word parts can add many words to a student's meaning vocabulary, consequently improving his or her comprehension ability while reading content materials.

Here is a partial list of prefixes and their meanings that may be relevant in content reading:

Prefix	Meaning	Example
ab-	from, away	abnormal
ambi-	both, around	ambidextrous
amphi-	both, around	amphibian
ante-	before	antebellum
anti-	against	antislavery
auto-	self	autobiography
be-	make	becalm
bene-	good	benediction
bi-	two	binocular
circu-	around	circumference
counter-	opposite	counteroffensive
contra-	against	contraband
de-	from, down	debate
deci-	ten	decimal
dys-	bad	dysentery
e-	out, away	emigrate
en-	in	enclose
epi-	after	epitaph
equi-	equal	equidistant
ex-	out	exalt

Prefix	Meaning	Example
hecto-	hundred	hectometer
hex-	six	hexagon
homo-	same	homogenous
hyper-	excessive	hyperglycemia
il-	not	illegitimate
im-	not	immobilize
inter-	among, between	international
kilo-	thousand	kilogram
macro-	large, long	macrobiotic
magni-	great	magnanimous
mega-	large	megaton
micro-	small, short	microscope
mis-	bad	misanthrope
neo-	new	neonatal
pent-	five	pentagon
post-	after	posterior
pre-	before	preamble
pro-	before	prognosis
quadr-	four	quadrant
re-	again	reappear
semi-	half	semiconscious
sub-	under	subterranean
super-	over	superimpose
tele-	distant	telescope
trans-	across	transatlantic
ultra-	beyond	ultraconservative
uni-	one	universe

Here is a partial list of noun suffixes and their meanings that may be relevant in content reading:

Noun Suffix	Meaning	Example
-ade	action or process	blockage
-ance	state or quality of	repentance
-arium	place for	aquarium
-ation	action or process	emancipation
-cle	small	molecule
-ectomy	surgical removal of	appendectomy
-ery, -ry	trade or occupation	surgery
-ics	scientific or social system	physics
-ide	chemical compound	fluoride
-ine	chemical or basic substance	chlorine
-ism	doctrine of	capitalism
-ite	mineral or rock	granite
-ization	state or quality of	civilization
-ment	action or process	embezzlement
-mony	product or thing	alimony
-ol	alcohols	methanol
-ology	study or science of	geology

Here is a partial list of adjective suffixes and their meanings that may be relevant in content reading:

Adjective Suffix	Meaning	Example
-ant	inclined to	vigilant
-etic	relating to	dietetic
-ious	state or quality of	ambitious
-oid	resembling	asteroid
-ose	full of	comatose
-ulent	full of	corpulent
-uous	state or quality of	contemptuous

Here is a partial list of word roots and their meanings that may be relevant in content reading:

Word Root	Meaning	Example
aero	air	aerodynamics
alt	high	altimeter
ambul	walk, go	ambulatory
anthr	man	anthropoid
aud	hear	auditorium
baro	weight	barometer
bio	life	biochemistry
cardi	heart	cardiologist
chron	time	chronology
corp	body	corpse
dem	people	demography
fac	make, do	benefactor
fid	faith	infidel
fract	break	fracture
geo	earth	geophysical
gram	letter, written	monogram
iatr	medical care	psychiatry
ject	throw	inject
jur	law	jurisprudence
lab	work	collaborate
lum	light	luminous
mar	sea	mariner
nat	born	natal
neo	new	neophyte
paleo	old	paleontology
phob	fear	xenophobia
photo	light	photosynthesis
phys	nature	physique
poli	city	metropolis
rad	ray, spoke	radiology
rect	straight	rectangle
sci	know	scientific
sect	cut	dissect
soph	wise	philosopher
spir	breathe	respiration
stell	star	constellation

Word Root	Meaning	Example
terr	land	terrain
therm	heat	thermal
urb	city	urbane
vid	see	video
vor	eat	herbivorous

USING QUESTIONING STRATEGIES FOR VOCABULARY DEVELOPMENT IN THE CONTENT AREAS

Questioning strategies can be used both to improve meaning vocabulary knowledge and comprehension skills while reading content materials. Questioning for vocabulary development can occur both before and after reading content materials. Prediction strategies can be used to help students predict certain specialized vocabulary terms that may occur in the content materials, while questions after reading can determine if students were able to deduce an approximate meaning for important, unknown vocabulary terms.

As is the case with comprehension, students should be asked only about the meanings of unknown, specialized vocabulary terms that are important to the comprehension of the content material. Most students at all grade levels are asked far too many unimportant questions both during and after reading.

WHOLE-GROUP MINI-LESSON FOR VOCABULARY DEVELOPMENT IN THE CONTENT AREAS

The whole-group mini-lesson is another strategy that literacy and content teachers can use for developing vocabulary in the content fields. This strategy is designed to involve the entire class or a group of students in an activity that demonstrates the meaning of some new specialized vocabulary terms. Whole-group vocabulary mini-lessons obviously will not be effective in presenting all vocabulary terms but may be useful and motivational if used once in a while. The idea is to provide concrete understandings for abstract concepts. (Adapted from D. Ray Reutzel and Robert B. Cooter, Jr., *Teaching Children to Read: From Basals to Books.* New York: Merrill, an imprint of Macmillan Publishing Company, 1992, p. 449.) Here is an example of this strategy for fifth-grade students who are learning about the *solar system*:

Step One—The teacher introduces important information and specialized vocabulary terms about the solar system emphasizing the *sun* and the *planets* (Mercury, Venus, Earth, Mars, Jupiter, Saturn, Uranus, Neptune, and Pluto) that *revolve* around it. The *moons* that revolve around the various planets also can be discussed. In addition, the concept of *rotation* can be mentioned.

Step Two—The teacher then takes the class out to the play area and assigns students to a role-playing situation in which they will take turns being various planets and moons demonstrating revolution and possibly rotation. Props can be made that help to identify the various kinds of planets and moons.

Step Three—Circles are then drawn with chalk on the playground surface that demonstrate the *orbits,* or oval-shaped paths, of each of the planets around the sun. A student portraying the sun will stand in the middle of the orbits. The children who will portray moons also take their places to demonstrate the orbit of each moon around its planet.

Step Four—The students then demonstrate the orbit of each planet around the sun at the approximate correct rate of movement. The students representing the moons also demonstrate the orbit of each moon around its respective planet trying to coordinate their movement with that of their planet if this is not too confusing. Later each of the planets can demonstrate rotation as well as revolution around the sun if the teacher does not think this would produce too much confusion. A teacher aide or parent volunteer can videotape the entire mini-lesson while standing on a ladder if the teacher would like to have the class watch the video for a review of what happened and just "for fun."

THE FIVE-STEP GUIDE TO VOCABULARY INDEPENDENCE IN THE CONTENT AREAS

Although many helpful strategies for improving specialized vocabulary in content reading are found later in this chapter, there are five basic steps that can be used as a *general guide to vocabulary independence.* Here are these five basic steps:

1. Trigger background knowledge. Have the student ask himself or herself: "What do I already know about these words?"
2. Preview the reading material for clues as to what the words might mean.
3. Read the material.
4. Refine and reformulate predicted meanings of the vocabulary based upon information gained from reading the material.
5. To make the new word permanent, the student must read and use it. Have him or her use new vocabulary in writing and be alert to the word in future reading and writing.

DIRECT AND INCIDENTAL INSTRUCTION FOR VOCABULARY IMPROVEMENT IN THE CONTENT AREAS

Literacy and content teachers always should determine whether vocabulary instruction in content fields should be *explicit (direct)* or *incidental.* Although most reading specialists believe that both kinds of vocabulary instruction are helpful for students, a number of them think explicit (direct) vocabulary instruction in the content fields is the more useful and will result in the better achievement by students.

Direct instruction in vocabulary is needed for optimum vocabulary growth since the process of learning new words incidentally through repeated exposures is slow and often not particularly effective. Direct strategies that include *active student involvement* are needed for the best vocabulary development. The typical student needs many repeated exposures to new vocabulary terms in different contexts before they really are part of his or her meaning vocabulary. For good vocabulary development, students also need to have many opportunities to relate target words to known concepts or prior knowledge.

However, at the present time target vocabulary words in content reading often are *wrongly* presented by the literacy or content teacher in isolation or in sentences before a selection is read, the words decoded by the students, and their meanings determined either from the sentence context or by looking them up in the glossary or dictionary. Sometimes students are asked to use the target words in sentences of their own after reading the selection in which the words are found. Sometimes the words are not discussed at all or are only listed on the chalkboard, pronounced, and their meanings briefly discussed. Vocabulary instruction traditionally has focused on *drill and memorization* instead of on activities that require active student involvement and the opportunity to relate the new terms to students' own concepts and prior knowledge. Students have not been asked to apply their own skills in semantic (meaning) analysis, structural analysis, and prior knowledge effectively in vocabulary development.

To summarize, the best vocabulary instruction in the content fields *combines passage-specific (content-oriented) direct instruction* with active student involvement and extensive use of prior knowledge with *incidental vocabulary instruction* stressing the use of sentence context, use of structural analysis such as the meanings of prefixes, suffixes, and word roots, and especially wide reading of relatively easy, high-interest content material. This material often should be in the form of supplementary materials to content textbooks such as trade books, magazines, newspapers, and other related materials.

OTHER STRATEGIES FOR VOCABULARY IMPROVEMENT IN THE CONTENT AREAS

The chapter now contains a number of useful, classroom-tested strategies that literacy and content teachers can use for developing specialized vocabulary in literature (language arts or English), social studies, science, and mathematics.

Cinquains

A *cinquain* (pronounced sĭng-kān) is a five-line poem with the following pattern: the first line is a noun or the subject of the poem; the second line consists of two words that describe the first line (adjectives); the third line contains three action words (verbs); the fourth line contains four words that convey a feeling; and the fifth line is a single word that refers to the first line.

Students enjoy writing cinquains after they have been given some large- or small-group instruction and practice in this strategy, and it can be very helpful in improving specialized vocabulary in content fields. A cinquain can be written that uses specialized vocabulary found in any of the content fields. The following four cinquains were composed by middle school students from the content areas of literature (language arts or English), social studies, science, and mathematics. They are included in this chapter mainly for illustration of how cinquains can be related to the various content areas.

Literature (Language Arts or English)
(very loosely based on *Little House in the Big Woods* by Laura Ingalls Wilder)
Woods
Beautiful, peaceful
Growing, Blowing, Logging
Source of great peace
Majestic

Social Studies
The First Olympic Games
Exciting, Inspiring
Honoring, Running, Winning
True test of courage
Festival

Science
Earthquakes
Terrifying, Destructive
Shaking, Trembling, Shifting
May cause much damage
Disaster

Mathematics
Fractions
Difficult, Confusing
Adding, Multiplying, Dividing
A very important subject
Calculations

What, Why, When, and How Strategy

Sometimes precise semantic (meaning) clues for unfamiliar specialized vocabulary terms may not be provided in content textbooks or other content materials. However, even when semantic clues are included, students have been found to have difficulty determining the meaning of unknown terms. As an example, several researchers found that sixth-grade students were able to determine the meaning of unfamiliar words through the use of semantic clues only *40%* of the time. Students had the greatest difficulty when semantic information was separated from unfamiliar terms. However, these researchers also stated that students can be taught to improve their skill in using semantic clues to determine the word meanings of both general and specialized vocabulary terms. A modification of the instructional technique that these researchers developed is as follows:

What, Why, and When—First the literacy or content teacher explains to students what they will be working on and why this is important. They should learn how to look for meaning clues for unfamiliar words that will help them better understand what they are reading. Semantic analysis is useful because if students are able to generate an approximate meaning for an unfamiliar word, they will not have to stop and consult a textbook glossary or dictionary.

How—Next the teacher models semantic analysis using the content reading material that the students currently are using. The teacher may read a paragraph aloud containing an unfamiliar word (such as *enzyme*) and discuss how other words in the same sentence or in nearby sentences may provide clues to the meaning of the term. The teacher then helps the students to deduce an approximate meaning for the word. After modeling the process a few times, the teacher and student together locate clue words and derive approximate meanings for unfamiliar words. The student then continues to read independently and stops to write down clue words and approximate meanings for unfamiliar specialized vocabulary terms that have been targeted by the literacy or content teacher. (Adapted from Douglas Carnine, Edward J. Kameenui, and Gayle Coyle, "Utilization of Contextual Information in Determining the Meaning of Unfamiliar Words," *Reading Research Quarterly,* 19, Winter 1984, pp. 188-204).

Semantic Association

Another strategy that can be used for expanding the specialized vocabulary in content fields is *semantic association*. This strategy is especially useful at the middle school level and above. The purpose of semantic association is to extend vocabulary by involving students with terms that share some common feature. Although this can be begun as a group (preferable) or independent activity, *it must end with a group discussion to be useful*. The following are the basic steps in this procedure. They can be varied if you would like to do so.

1. Select any vocabulary term or terms of interest to the class or to you. These can be words from any material from literature (language arts or English), social studies, science, or mathematics.

2. Write the term(s) on the chalkboard. For example, the literacy or science teacher might write the terms *teeth* and *intestines* before reading a chapter in a science textbook about *digestion.*

3. Have half the class write as many things as they can think of related to *teeth*. Have the other half write as many words as they can think of related to *intestines*. Have the students think and write both in small groups (preferable) or independently.

4. Compile lists on the chalkboard of all the terms that the students thought of. For example:

		Teeth			
mouth	molars	incisors	canine	brush	toothbrush
abscess	toothpaste	cavity	decay	crown	filling
drill	dentist	silver	gold	porcelain	enamel
root	orthodontist	braces	floss	gum	periodontal
root canal	dam	dental hygienist	gloves	mask	disease

		Intestines			
small	large	tube	muscles	villi	duodenum
peptic ulcer	cancer	digestive juice	food	blood	waste
nutrients	absorption	fecal matter	length	storehouse	reabsorbed
erosions	enzymes	acid			

5. If you wish, you may have the students use several of these vocabulary terms in sentences.

6. Lead a discussion on the meanings and uses of any of these terms that were unknown to the students. For example, although they may know the meanings of the terms *cavity, decay, silver, root, floss,* and *braces,* they may not know the meanings of the terms *incisors, abscess, porcelain, orthodontist, periodontal disease,* and *dam* (as is used in dentistry). The new terms can be learned by classifying them with terms already known. Besides learning new terms, new meanings or connotations for known words probably will develop. *Discussion is crucial to the expansion of vocabulary because it helps students to expand categories.*

Motor Imagery

Ula Price Casale found that *motor imagery* is helpful for vocabulary development in the content fields. Casale discovered that when students attempted to remember word meanings, they made slight hand gestures similar to the ones she used in teaching those same words. Her other observations confirmed her belief that most people use subtle hand or body gestures when they look for a word from memory. From her observations Casale developed the following six-step procedure for teaching a word through the use of motor imagery:

1. The teacher writes the term on the chalkboard or overhead projector, pronounces it, then tells the class its meaning.

2. The teacher tells the students to imagine how they might pantomime the term to show its meaning.

3. The teacher has the class pantomime the word. Upon being given a specific clue, all of the students begin.

4. The teacher watches the students to determine the most common pantomime, and then explains it to the class. The students then pantomime the term while saying it.

5. The teacher repeats each new term and has the class pantomime it and give a brief meaning or synonym.

6. The students then read the selection that contains the new terms.

Casale stated that fairly abstract terms can be defined for students in language that translates easily into motor imagery. As an example, the term *domicile* can be defined as a "place in which a person lives." Several examples of the language meaning and motor meaning for this and several other words are as follows:

New Term	Language Meaning	Motor Meaning
domicile	place in which a person lives	hands meeting above the head in a triangular roof shape
exultation	great happiness or joy	large smile on one's face and arms stretched upward
affliction	sadness or trouble	one or both hands over the eyes, and the head slanted forward

(Adapted from Ula Price Casale, "Motor Imagery: A Reading-Vocabulary Strategy," *Journal of Reading,* 28, April 1985, pp. 619-621).

Vocabulary Bingo

Bingo is one of the most popular of all games. My teacher-trainees use it on a regular basis with their tutees to reinforce both sight-word identification and graphophonic (phonic) analysis. However, bingo can also be used to reinforce the specialized vocabulary contained in the various content fields. It is a very relaxing, "fun" activity for students and gives them a change of pace.

Here are the steps to follow in playing *vocabulary bingo* with your students:

1. Have each student make a "bingo" card with a list of at least twenty specialized vocabulary terms you want them to review. They should be encouraged to choose terms from those that are to be reviewed at random to fill each square.

2. The teacher (or student reader) then reads definitions of the terms aloud, and each student covers the terms he or she believes matches the definition. It is helpful to have the definitions on 3″ × 5″ cards and to shuffle them between bingo games. The winner is the first student to cover a vertical, horizontal, or diagonal row.

3. Then check the winner by rereading the definitions used. This step not only keeps students honest but also serves as review and provides an opportunity for students to ask questions if they like.

A bingo game on *weather,* for example, can be constructed using the following vocabulary terms and definitions:

Term	Definition
troposphere	layer of the atmosphere closest to the earth's surface
relative humidity	the amount of water vapor in the air compared with the total amount that the air can hold
air mass	a large body of air having about the same temperature and moisture throughout
front	the boundary between two air masses
thunderstorm	a small local storm with tall clouds, heavy rain, thunder, and lightning
storm	a weather disturbance caused by unusual weather conditions
hurricane	a large tropical storm that has very high winds and heavy rainfall
tornado	a small funnel of rapidly spinning air
weather forecast	a prediction of what future weather conditions will be
meteorologist	a scientist who studies weather
isobars	lines on a weather map that connect places that have the same barometric pressure
wind	occurs as a result of the differences in air pressure
millibars	the units for measuring air pressure
National Weather Service	the agency of the federal government that prepares weather forecasts
barometer	an instrument for determining the pressure of the atmosphere

Term	Definition
isotherm	a line on a weather map that connects places that have the same temperature
hail	precipitation in the form of small balls or lumps of layers of clear ice
cloud	a visible mass of particles of water found high in the sky
monsoon	a season in a country like India that has very, very heavy rainfall
date of the spring equinox	March 21

Sample Bingo Card:

National Weather Service	wind	tornado	spring equinox
meteorologist	cloud	monsoon	isotherm
hail	front	air mass	thunderstorm
relative humidity	hurricane	storm	isobars
millibars	barometer	March 21	weather forecast

Suggestions for Modification of Vocabulary Bingo:

Periodic table bingo—Have students make bingo cards with symbols of the elements. The names of the elements are called out or the caller could use other characteristics of the elements such as atomic number of a description.

Math using geometric shapes—The student bingo cards could be made using the names of shapes such as the triangle, rectangle, square, octagon, trapezoid, parallelogram, etc. The callers gives the definition of each of the geometric shapes.

In summary, bingo is an excellent game for reinforcing the specialized vocabulary contained in the content fields. The constant repetition of the definitions is very helpful for some students. (Loosely adapted from Judy S. Richardson and Raymond F. Morgan, *Reading to Learn in the Content Areas*. Belmont, California: Wadsworth Publishing Company, 1990, pp. 384-385.)

Word Connections

Camille Blanchowicz has suggested another interesting strategy for vocabulary expansion called *word connections*. Given a list of specialized vocabulary terms from a content textbook, she stated the students should use the word connection procedure to broaden word meaning knowledge. Students can pick any two words from the list of terms and tell how they might be related. For example, an instructional word list for a chapter "The Geography of the South" from a middle school social studies textbook might be the following:

river	delta	tributary
bay	barges	bays

A student might be able to connect the terms *river* and *tributary* since a tributary is a river or stream that joins a larger river. A student might also be able to connect the terms *river* and *barges* since *barges* travel on *rivers* carrying their loads. A student also may possibly be able to connect the terms *river* and *delta* since the soil that is left when a river empties into an ocean or gulf is called a *delta*. Word connection is simply a form of *classification*. It is important to remember that only through group discussion with students about how the vocabulary terms relate to each other can this strategy be used in the best way for vocabulary expansion. Students always should be encouraged to develop independence in the use of word connections by having them make connections between and among vocabulary terms that are presented in content units. (Adapted from Camille Blanchowicz, "Making Connections: Alternatives to Vocabulary Notebooks," *Journal of Reading,* 29, April 1986, pp. 643-649.)

"Talk Through" Procedure

The *Talk Through* procedure is another strategy that can be used successfully for the development of specialized vocabulary in the content areas. This strategy incorporates the following features that contribute to student success in vocabulary development:

- *Talk Through* is grounded in the psychological principle of *paired association,* the process of connecting new ideas with old ones.

- *Talk Through* minimizes teacher direction and increases student involvement. Engaging the class or a group in *Talk Through,* literacy or content teachers use a particular type of question to attempt to elicit the meaning of vocabulary terms from students instead of imposing the meaning on them.

- *Talk Through* builds on students' strengths to overcome their weaknesses. As an example, when the unknown term is related to something students already know, almost all students can give relevant responses. This strategy encourages all students to speak out, even those who don't ordinarily do so.

Before the *Talk Through* strategy is used with selected vocabulary terms, the teacher identifies *key concepts or terms* in the content assignment that are likely to give the students difficulty. Here is an actual example of the *Talk Through* procedure from a fifth-grade social studies textbook.

Write the following sentence on the chalkboard:

> **In 1862 Congress decided to let two companies begin building a *transcontinental* railroad which was then completed in 1869.**

It is important for the word under discussion to be *in writing* so that students can see it as the *Talk Through* procedure is used. One of the objectives is to have students recognize this word when they meet it again in printed form. Second, the word should be in *context,* not isolation, giving students the benefit of semantic (contextual) clues.

Then the processing begins of relating the vocabulary terms to students' everyday lives. At this point, the teacher *asks, not tells.*

"Brent, didn't your grandparents recently fly from New York where they live to California to spend the winter?" Brent responds that they made this trip this past January.

"Have any of your families ever driven all the way across the country or taken a plane or train all the way across the country?" One student raises her hand in positive response to this question.

Sammy then volunteers that he saw a show on Public Television that showed how some men tried to lay railroad tracks that would go all the way across the country.

At the end of the discussion, the teacher makes his or her first input. The teacher takes the vocabulary term out of the sentence and writes:

transcontinental

and then erases "trans" and "al." He or she says: "The prefix 'trans' means *across* and the suffix 'al' means *relating to*. Thus, the term 'transcontinental' means 're-lated to across the continent.' What do you think is a synonym for the word 'continent'?" Response: country. "So, what does the term 'transcontinental' mean?" Response: "It means related to across the country."

The teacher then asks if the students can think of any other words that begin with the prefix "trans" which mean across, and the students respond with the following vocabulary terms: *transatlantic, transpacific,* and *transcend*.

Many specialized vocabulary terms also have a word root that helps students to determine the meaning of the term. Prefixes, suffixes, and word roots all should be used when appropriate in the *Talk Through* procedure.

In this procedure the literacy or content teacher has tried to establish meaning for the term *transcontinental* by relating it to students' everyday lives as much as possible. He or she also has helped students to use prefixes and suffixes to help students deduce the meaning of the unknown specialized vocabulary term. Hopefully the meaning for the word as it is used in the example has been *discovered* by the students, and someone other than the brightest students in the class will be able to discuss what the term means in the context of the sentence of the chalkboard. Finally, it is necessary for the teacher to take the discussion back to the term in the context of the sentence for closure. (Loosely adapted from Dorothy Piercey, *Reading Activities in the Content Areas*. Boston: Allyn and Bacon, 1976, pp. 6-8.)

USING COMPUTER SOFTWARE FOR VOCABULARY IMPROVEMENT IN THE CONTENT FIELDS

Although the use of the computer obviously offers many useful opportunities for the future of content literacy instruction, at this time truly creative and beneficial software programs for teaching content vocabulary are limited. Indeed, many available programs tend to be computerized workbook exercises that may be more motivational for students than a traditional workbook.

A review of vocabulary software in the content fields indicates that the present possibilities are fairly limited. Some are of a drill-and-practice nature such as crossword puzzles (which literacy or content teachers also can construct themselves from specialized vocabulary by using a computer program), "Hangman," and "Scrabble." In addition, other drill-and-practice programs provide practice with word meanings that the teacher has already taught, while some tutorial programs focus on synonyms, antonyms, homonyms, and words with multiple meanings. Others provide work with analogies and classification.

Word-processing programs that have a "find and replace" function may be able to be used profitably in some content vocabulary instruction. A student is given a disk containing files that have in them paragraphs with certain words used repeatedly. The student may use the "find and replace" function to replace all instances of the selected term with a synonym to see if the synonym makes sense in each place that it appears. If it does not, the student can delete the synonym in the inappropriate place and select other more appropriate replacements for the original word or actually put the original word back into the file. Then the student can read the file again to see if the terms chosen convey the correct meanings and if the variation in the word choices makes the paragraph more interesting to read.

You should begin to select software for vocabulary improvement in content fields by examining software catalogs. These are published monthly or yearly by general publishers and by computer software reviewers. These catalogs compile, list, and briefly describe educational software although they usually do not provide an evaluation of the software. Catalogs are available on request, but are usually sent automatically to school libraries, university libraries, and curriculum centers. In addition, computer journals, both those intended for educators as well as the general public, include listings and evaluations of educational software. Literacy and content teachers can check the following journals and review publications under "new product announcement" or "software evaluation" departments.

- *BYTE—The Small Systems Journal*
- *Classroom Computer News*
- *Computers in Reading and Language Arts*
- *Digest of Software Reviews: Education*
- *Educational Technology*
- *Microcomputers in Education*
- *T. H. E. Journal (Technological Horizons in Education)*
- *The Computing Teacher*

However, one of the largest distributors of educational software of all types is:

Minnesota Educational Computing Consortium (MECC)
3490 Lexington Avenue North
St. Paul, MN 55112

MEEC offers a subscription service to school systems and other educational users that automatically provides every piece of software that it distributes as well as updates of new offerings as they appear. Many school districts subscribe to MEEC, keeping the software in a district resource center from which teachers can borrow for use in their classrooms.

Since the available computer programs are changing daily, no specific computer programs are included in this *Handbook.* Indeed, such a list becomes obsolete almost as soon as it is published. However, because computer programs vary greatly in pedagogical soundness, technical accuracy, and ease of use, literacy and content teachers must evaluate them very carefully before choosing to use them with students. You have to judge if the program presents or reinforces specialized vocabulary terms in a more effective and motivational way than could be done using other strategies and reproducibles.

USING A SEMANTIC WEB (MAP) FOR
VOCABULARY IMPROVEMENT IN THE CONTENT FIELDS

Semantic webs or maps can be used both in primary grades and middle school as a very effective way to improve vocabulary in the content fields. This strategy also is an effective way to improve comprehension as well as to motivate writing. Semantic webs or maps for vocabulary improvement can be used both before and after reading any type of content material. Their use enables students to see the relationships between specialized vocabulary, thus hopefully enabling them to remember the terms more effectively because of these relationships. Semantic webs or maps also can be called *story maps, story webs, advance organizers,* and *think-links.* Although there may be slight variations among all of these strategies, they are very similar.

In any case, they are all graphic representations of the relationships among the important vocabulary in the material and therefore are designed to organize schema (prior knowledge) and vocabulary. There are as many variations of semantic maps or webs as there are researchers in the area, and you are encouraged to experiment with your own version of this strategy.

In formulating a semantic map or web, it is useful to first display a completed map on the chalkboard or a transparency using the important, specialized vocabulary from a content topic that your students are going to study in the near future. At the primary-grade level, the map (web) obviously should be a simple one. Illustrate to the students how the map shows the relationship among important vocabulary terms. Then put a partially completed map on the chalkboard or transparency either before or after the students are to read a portion of content material. They then can complete it as a group with your help if necessary.

Only after they have had considerable experience with completing semantic maps or webs should the students be asked to construct one independently or even with a partner. At first a partially completed map or web can be duplicated for each student to complete independently or with a partner. It often is preferable to have a student work with at least one partner in completing or constructing a map or web. If semantic mapping is not presented carefully with much preparation, a student can experience frustration and never wish to use this strategy again. *It also is important that semantic mapping be used as a strategy fairly often instead of just once or twice if it is to be eventually used independently.*

To briefly summarize, semantic maps can be used for vocabulary improvement of specialized vocabulary terms both before and after reading a content assignment. It is one of the more motivational and effective ways of doing this.

Sample Semantic Map to Be Used After Reading

The following is a passage about *rocks* from science at about the fourth-grade level. It then includes a partially completed map that a student(s) can complete after reading this passage. This partially completed map is designed to show the relationships between the specialized vocabulary terms found in the passage. You may duplicate this map and use it in its present form or use it as a model. There are many variations of this technique, and you are encouraged to help students to develop their own versions of semantic maps or webs.

SEMANTIC MAP
(Approximately Fourth-Grade Level)

LEARNING TO BE A ROCK "HOUND"

A rock is a solid that is made up of one or more minerals. Rocks are classified into three groups depending upon how they were formed.

The first group of rocks is called *igneous rocks,* and they are formed from melted rock that has cooled and then hardened. A person can tell what kinds of minerals are found in igneous rocks by looking at their color. These minerals are grouped as either light colored or dark colored. For example, one kind of igneous rock called *granite* is composed of light-colored minerals, while another type called *basalt* has mostly dark minerals in it. Igneous rocks also differ in the kinds and sizes of their mineral crystals. For example, the mineral crystals in granite and *gabbro* are large, while those in *rhyolite* and basalt are small.

Another group of rocks form when sediments become cemented together from broken up rocks by water, wind, and ice. Often streams move the sediments, and they are usually deposited at the bottom of a lake or ocean. These are called *sedimentary rocks* and are formed in layers that are deposited on top of one another. The top layers push down on the lower ones, and this squeezes the sediments closer together until they harden. Sedimentary rocks can be classified by the way they form. *Conglomerate* is made of bits of rock the size of gravel, and the rounded, gravel-sized bits of rock are held together by tiny minerals. *Sandstone* is mainly made up of sand-sized bits of rock. Another sedimentary rock, *shale,* is made of bits so small that you cannot see them. The minerals in shale are usually made of quartz and clay materials.

Sedimentary rocks like *limestone* may contain *fossils.* A fossil is the remains or traces of living things preserved in rocks. When an animal dies, its hard parts such as shells, bones, or teeth become fossils. Sometimes just the print of a plant or animal remains in the rock and these are also called fossils.

Metamorphic rocks form from rocks that are changed by heat and pressure under earth. Sedimentary, igneous, or other metamorphic rocks can be changed to form new metamorphic rocks. The heat and pressure change the rocks but do not melt them. Heat and pressure can change the size and shape of the mineral crystals. They also can change the minerals in the original rock into other minerals. When heat and pressure act on the igneous rock *granite,* it can be changed to a metamorphic rock *gneiss* (nys). The sedimentary rock *shale* can be changed into the metamorphic rock called *slate.* Even though slate is already a metamorphic rock, it can be changed further to another metamorphic rock called *schist.* Finally, the sedimentary rock *limestone* can be changed into the metamorphic rock called *marble* which is often used to make buildings.

Did you learn a number of new facts about rocks from reading this passage? Rocks are indeed a very interesting subject in science.

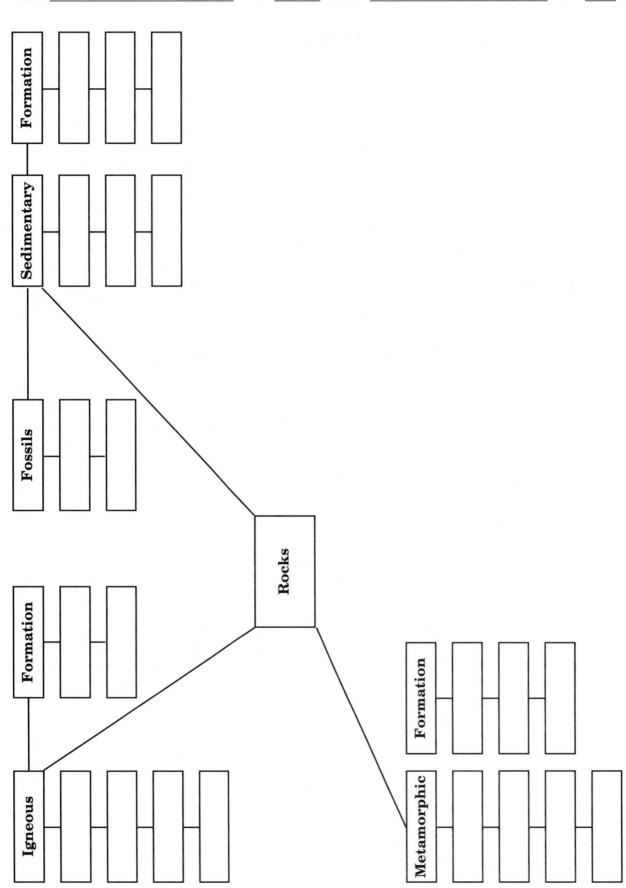

USING THE CLOZE PROCEDURE TO
IMPROVE VOCABULARY KNOWLEDGE IN THE CONTENT AREAS

A variation of the traditional cloze procedure can be used to improve vocabulary knowledge in the content fields. Since the cloze procedure was described in detail in Chapter 2, it is only mentioned here. You are encouraged to refer to Chapter 2 for detailed information on this strategy.

However, when cloze is used for the purpose of improving meaning vocabulary, it is somewhat different from than of traditional cloze. For example, the literacy or content teacher should delete only the targeted vocabulary terms, and they can be deleted in a random way just focusing on the words that the teacher wants to emphasize. Students should be encouraged to complete each blank with the most descriptive word that makes sense in context. They also should be encouraged to use a thesaurus to locate a truly appropriate word if necessary. Any word that makes sense in sentence context should be considered correct although truly unique, but accurate, responses should be encouraged. The formula described in Chapter 2 cannot be used since every fifth word is not necessarily omitted, and any word that can make sense should be considered correct.

Reproducible Modified Cloze Procedure from Literature at the Middle School Level

The following is a reproducible modified cloze procedure from the genre of biography about the life of Nellie Bly, the famous pioneer newspaperwoman. The student should be encouraged to complete each blank with the most descriptive term possible and to use a thesaurus for this purpose if necessary. Any term that makes sense in sentence context should be considered correct, although the most encouragement probably should be given for the most interesting or precise vocabulary terms.

If it seems appropriate, you can duplicate and use it in its present form or modify it in any way you like. More important, this variation of the cloze procedure is designed to serve as a model for you in constructing similar cloze procedures from the content material you use with your students, targeting the most important vocabulary terms.

MODIFIED CLOZE PROCEDURE
FROM LITERATURE
(Middle School Level)

NELLIE BLY—PIONEER NEWSPAPERWOMAN

Read the following passage about Nellie Bly, who was a pioneer newspaperwoman, to yourself. Try to complete each blank with the most *interesting, descriptive* word you can. Use a thesaurus if you need to make each word choice as unique as possible. When you have finished filling in the blanks, read the entire passage again to be sure it all makes sense. You can work with a partner if you want to.

Elizabeth Cochrane, who was later known as Nellie Bly, undoubtedly was a born reporter.

One day in Pittsburgh's _____ newspaper *The Dispatch,*

she read an editorial entitled "What Girls Are Good For." This editorial stated that women

had "_____ brains," and that they should stay home and do

"women's chores" like cleaning, cooking, laundry, and raising children. Since this editorial

made Nellie _____ furious, she wrote an

_____ letter to the newspaper, leaving it unsigned. Her

letter was so _____ that George Madden, who had written

the editorial, thought that a man had written it, and he wanted someone with that much

_____ to work for the newspaper.

In an advertisement Madden offered a job as a reporter to the gentleman who had

written the _____ letter. Naturally, he was shocked when

Elizabeth _____ him and told him that she, a

_____ woman, had written the letter. Through much

_____, she finally convinced Madden to give her a job

although he insisted that she take the _____ name "Nellie

Bly," the name of a _____-_____

song at the time, to protect her and her family.

Almost immediately Nellie, the reporter, fought for the poor and

_____ with her writing. She went into the slums and wrote

about the _____ conditions there—the dirt, illness, and

almost _____ suffering. She even pretended that she

needed a job and went to work in one of the darkest, coldest, and most

_____-_____ factories she

could find. The story that Nellie then wrote for the newspaper about the factory made the

owners extremely _____.

152

Name _____ Grade _____ Teacher _____ Date _____

MODIFIED CLOZE PROCEDURE
FROM LITERATURE
(Middle School Level)

(cont.)

After that Nellie traveled to New York and became a reporter for the New York World, under the most _____ editor of all, Joseph Pulitzer. She told him she wanted to pretend she was _____ so that she could learn about Blackwell's Island, a home for the insane in New York. Nellie found the conditions there completely _____ including dirty, ice-cold water to wash in and _____ bread and stringy meat to eat. She found that the nurses there were _____ and ignorant. After ten days of _____ there, Nellie was rescued by a lawyer, and she rushed home to write a whole series of articles about the _____ conditions there.

Her opening story "Beyond Asylum Bars" was so well _____ that the *World* had to print thousands of extra copies of the newspaper that day. Nellie felt very _____ when the city raised a large sum of money for better food, better clothing, and _____ nurses at Blackwell's Island. Nellie pointed the way for many other _____ and rescued countless people from misery and injustice in _____ factories, jails, and workhouses.

Probably the most _____ feat Nellie attempted was going around the world in eighty days after reading a book entitled *Around the World in Eighty Days.* Nellie took only two dresses on the entire trip, and she even received a _____ proposal from a gentleman whom she met on the trip. Nellie traveled by ship and arrived back in New York Harbor after 72 days, 6 hours, and 11 minutes. Nellie's _____ was the biggest story in the newspapers of that time.

Nellie led the way for women into journalism and became a legend in her own time because she had new ideas and the courage to carry them out.

Answer Key for "Nellie Bly—Pioneer Newspaperwoman"

The answers included here are the words I included in the original. However, any word that makes sense in context should be considered correct, although descriptive, interesting terms should be encouraged if possible.

major

inferior

absolutely

anonymous

outstanding

talent

perceptive

confronted

mere

persuasion

pen

well-known

downtrodden

horrible

unbelievable

rat-infested

angry

famous

insane

unbearable

moldy

cruel

misery

horrible

received

proud

better

reforms

abominable

daring

marriage

adventure

A Semantic Features Analysis Grid

Another strategy that helps students to learn the meanings of specialized vocabulary by relating them to known words is called *semantic features analysis*. This technique involves looking at the similarities and differences of related concepts. Semantic features analysis has proven very useful for improving students' knowledge of specialized vocabulary terms in all of the content fields.

Semantic features analysis involves a literacy or content teacher choosing a category such as *arthropods* and listing in the left-hand column of a semantic features analysis grid some members of this category such as *shrimp, lobster, crab, tick, mite, scorpion, spider, bee, centipede,* and *millipede.* Features that may be common to the category such as *exoskeleton, antennae, two-segments, three-segments, multiple segments, disease-carrying, insect, head, thorax,* and *abdomen* may be listed in a row across the top of the grid. The teacher and student can use a system of *pluses* and *minuses* to determine which members of the category under investigation have which features.

A plus in a semantic features analysis grid means *yes* (that the category members have this feature), a minus means *no* (that it does not have the feature), and a *question mark* means perhaps or maybe it has this feature. If one of the category members is a new vocabulary term, students will be able to see how this new term is similar to, yet different from, the other words the student already knows.

As an example, the teacher puts the new vocabulary terms at the top of the column of category members and asks the students to add other examples of category members to the grid. The students then are asked to add features of the category members to the grid. The students then complete the grid by using pluses and minuses to match members and features as explained earlier.

Reproducible Semantic Features Analysis Grid from Science*

The following is a reproducible semantic features analysis grid from science on the topic of *simple living organisms* at about the fifth-grade level. You may duplicate and use this semantic features analysis grid if it seems applicable for your students. However, more important, it is primarily designed to serve as a model of this type of strategy that you can construct from your own students' content material.

***Note:** This semantic features analysis grid can be presented to a group of students either *before* or *after* (or *both*) they read a chapter from a science textbook or other scientific material on simple living things (organisms).

SEMANTIC FEATURES ANALYSIS GRID
(Approximately Fifth-Grade Level)

SIMPLE LIVING ORGANISMS

Put a + in the proper spaces on this grid if the category member has the feature; put a − in the proper space if the category member does not have the feature; or put a ? if you are not sure whether or not the category member has the feature.

Category Members	Must Be Viewed Through a Microscope	One-Celled	Many-Celled	Grows	Reproduces	Animal-Like	Plant-Like	Has a Nucleus	Helpful to Humans	Harmful to Humans
Protists										
Fungi										
Monerans										
Viruses										

Answer Key for "Simple Living Organisms"

Protists—Must be viewed through a microscope

One-celled

Grows

Reproduces

Animal-like

Plant-like

Has a nucleus

Helpful to humans

Harmful to humans

Fungi—Must be viewed through a microscope

One-celled

Grows

Reproduces

Plant-like

Helpful to humans

Harmful to humans

Monerans—Must be viewed through a microscope

One-celled

Grows

Reproduces

Animal-like

Helpful to humans

Harmful to humans

Viruses—Must be viewed through a microscope

Grows

Reproduces

Harmful to humans

A PREDICT-O-GRAM FOR VOCABULARY DEVELOPMENT IN THE CONTENT FIELDS

Camille Blanchowicz has described the *predict-o-gram* as a strategy that combines vocabulary development and story structure awareness. Thus, it is relevant for improving vocabulary in literature (language arts or English) in the lower intermediate grades and above. Students are encouraged to make predictions about how an author will use vocabulary to tell about the setting, the characters, the problem or goal, the actions, the resolution, or feelings of a character in a trade book or story. (Adapted from Camille Blanchowicz, "Making Connections: Alternatives to the Vocabulary Notebook," *Journal of Reading,* 29, April 1986, pp. 643-649.)

Given the following vocabulary from the trade book *Rufus* by Eleanor Estes, the students would be asked to classify the words according to how they predict the author might use them in the book. Students can learn to use this strategy independently or with a partner when they are given vocabulary lists by predicting how the words relate to the elements of story structure. The following illustrates how this strategy may be used:

Rufus
library card
Sylvie
got library card
home
Rufus
librarian
library
cellar
book
Jane
checked out *Palmer Cox Brownie*
washing hands
Joey
printing name
riding a scooter
mother

The Setting	*The Characters*	*The Goal or Problem*
home	Rufus	library card
library	librarian	book
cellar	mother	
	Joey	
	Jane	
	Sylvie	

The Actions		*The Resolution*
riding a scooter		got library card
printing name		checked out *Palmer Cox Brownie*
washing hands		

Blank Reproducible Predict-o-Gram

The following is a blank reproducible Predict-o-gram form. It is appropriate for use in fourth grade and above. If you use it, you can write the title and author of the trade book or story on the chalkboard and have the student complete them on his or her copy of the form. You also can *choose the key vocabulary terms* in the book or story and *write them on the chalkboard* before giving it to a student. The *student then copies the key vocabulary* on his or her form. The student next writes the key vocabulary terms from the story on the correct lines under *The Setting, The Characters, The Goal or Problem, The Actions,* and *The Resolution.* The form contains more blank lines in each category than may be needed.

PREDICT-O-GRAM
(Appropriate for Fourth Grade and Above)

_____

Title of book or story

_____

Author

Key Vocabulary

_____

_____

_____

_____

_____

_____

_____

_____

_____

_____

_____

PREDICT-O-GRAM
(Appropriate for Fourth Grade and Above)

(cont.)

The Setting

_____

_____

_____

_____

_____

The Characters

_____

_____

_____

_____

_____

The Goal or Problem

_____

_____

_____

_____

The Actions

_____

_____

_____

_____

The Resolution

_____

_____

_____

Using Word Analogies for Vocabulary Improvement

Word analogies are interesting activities that are excellent for structuring higher-level thinking. To effectively complete word analogies, students must be able to perceive relationships between what is similar to two sides of an equation. This is a high level of critical thinking in that the student is encouraged to attempt various combinations of possible answers to solve the problem. Since many students may have difficulty at first with this concept, literacy and content teachers should practice with students and explain the equation used in analogies:

_____ **is to** _____ **as** _____ **is to** _____.
Where, is to =:
as = ::

For elementary students it is usually preferable to spell out "is to" rather than use symbols. In addition, students say that analogies are easier when the blank is always in the *fourth position* as in the following three analogies:

Calf is to cow as child is to _____.
(adult)

Mitten is to hand as shoe is to _____.
(foot)

Sun is to moon as day is to _____.
(night)

More difficult analogies can be constructed by varying the position of the blank as in the following three analogies. This variation probably is the most useful in the upper intermediate grades and above.

_____ is to old as grandchild is to grandparents.
(Young)

City is to _____ as large is to small.
(village)

Black is to white as _____ is to light.
(dark)

Analogies can present a very difficult challenge to older students in the secondary school. Such analogies may be useful in stressing the specialized vocabulary contained in the content fields of literature (English), social studies, science, and mathematics. They also are often included in measures of qualitative (verbal) intelligence on standardized intelligence tests of various types.

Here are four examples of this difficult type of analogy from the content area of science:

mammal: embryo: : reptile: _____
(egg)

sonar: _____: : radar: sight
(sound)

botanist: plants: : _____: animals
                    (zoologist)

_____: meat: : herbivore: plants
(carnivore)

In summary, the different variations of analogies are very useful in emphasizing specialized vocabulary in content fields and can be used effectively for this purpose.

Reproducible Example of Word Analogies

The following is a reproducible example of the first type of word analogies that was illustrated earlier. It was constructed from vocabulary terms that would most often be found in literature at about the fifth-grade level. If it seems applicable, you can duplicate and use it in its present form or modify it in any way you wish in the light of the interests and needs of your own students. If you want, students can complete the analogies with a partner(s).

WORD ANALOGIES
(Approximately Fifth-Grade Level)

Complete each analogy with the correct word. You can use a thesaurus or dictionary to help you if you wish. You also can work with a partner on the analogies if you would like to.

1. Adjective is to noun as adverb is to _____.

2. Sunshine is to moonlight as day is to _____.

3. Praise is to good as complain is to _____.

4. Person is to house as bear is to _____.

5. Food is to person as gasoline is to _____.

6. Miniature is to small as enormous is to _____.

7. Murmur is to soft as shout is to _____.

8. Necklace is to neck as bracelet is to _____.

9. Chicken is to poultry as bluegill is to _____.

10. Remarkable is to unusual as ordinary is to _____.

11. Generous is to selfish as empty is to _____.

12. Shiver is to cold as perspire is to _____.

13. Thaw is to melt as swift is to _____.

14. Daybreak is to twilight as light is to _____.

15. Bashful is to shy as brazen is to _____.

16. Chuckle is to laugh as weep is to _____.

17. Envious is to jealous as unselfish is to _____.

18. Grief is to sorrow as happy is to _____.

19. Author is to book as playwright is to _____.

20. Hamlet is to village as metropolis is to _____.

Answer Key for "Word Analogies"

Note: In most cases only one word best fits each analogy. However, in a few instances, there may be more than one possible answer. Although I have tried to include all of the possible correct answers in the Answer Key, any answer that a student can defend effectively should be considered correct.

1. verb
2. night
3. evil (bad)
4. den (cave)
5. car (automobile, truck)
6. large (big)
7. loud
8. wrist
9. fish
10. common

11. full
12. hot
13. rapid (fast, quick)
14. dark
15. bold (daring, impudent)
16. cry
17. generous
18. joy (delight, gladness)
19. drama (play)
20. city

USING MAGIC SQUARES FOR VOCABULARY IMPROVEMENT IN THE CONTENT FIELDS

Magic squares are an exceedingly motivational way to improve the knowledge of specialized vocabulary terms in the content fields. Magic squares can be used at any level from upper primary through secondary. Magic squares are special arrangements of numbers that *when added across, down, and diagonally always equal the same sum.*

Literacy and content teachers can construct vocabulary exercises by having students match a lettered column of words to a numbered column of definitions. Letters on each square of the grid match the lettered words. Students try to find the magic number by matching the correct word and definition and entering the number in the appropriate square on the grid. A magic square is fairly easy to construct, and some students in the middle school and above even may enjoy constructing their own magic squares either independently or preferably with one or more partners.

Reproducible Magic Square

The following is a reproducible magic square about "Body Systems at Work" from science at about the sixth-grade level. You may duplicate and use it with your students if it seems applicable. However, more important, it can serve as a model for the magic squares that you and your students can construct using the specialized vocabulary from the content materials they read.

MAGIC SQUARE
(Approximately Sixth-Grade Level)

Select from the numbered statements the best match for each vocabulary term. Put the number in the proper space. The total of the numbers will be the same across each row and down each column. Try to find the Magic Number!

BODY SYSTEMS AT WORK

A. excretory system

B. muscular system

C. immune system

D. digestive system

E. nervous system

F. skeletal system

G. circulatory system

H. hormone

I. respiratory system

1. chemical made by an endocrine gland

2. cells and tissues that are involved in fighting disease

3. system that changes food into a form that cells can use

4. system that removes wastes from the body

5. the brain, the spinal cord, and the nerves

6. transport system that brings oxygen into the blood

7. frame of bones that supports the body

8. transport system that carries food and oxygen to the cells

9. organ system made up of muscles that move the parts of the body

A	B	C
D	E	F
G	H	I

Answer Key for ""Body Systems at Work"

The Magic Number is *15*.

A 4	B 9	C 2
D 3	E 5	F 7
G 8	H 1	I 6

USING A CROSSWORD PUZZLE FOR VOCABULARY IMPROVEMENT IN THE CONTENT AREAS

A *traditional crossword puzzle* can be a very effective tool for reviewing the specialized vocabulary words in a content subject that have already been presented and are thoroughly understood by students. As was stated earlier, a literacy or content teacher can easily construct a traditional crossword puzzle using a software program by simply entering the chosen specialized vocabulary terms on the computer keyboard in either the *across or down column*. The computer then prints a completed crossword puzzle using the selected terms. This saves a great deal of time, although a teacher can construct his or her own puzzle if he or she wishes. Two such software programs are *Spelling Puzzles and Tests* and *Spellevator*, MECC, Minneapolis, MN (1-800-685-6322.)

Most students find completing a crossword puzzle to be very motivating. A student may want to work with a partner(s) in completing a puzzle; it usually is easier and more interesting that way. Although I have included the terms that are used in the crossword puzzle along with the definitions, you may or may not want to include them depending upon the ability of your students.

Reproducible Crossword Puzzle

The following is a ready-to-use crossword puzzle that was constructed using specialized vocabulary terms from mathematics at the upper level. If it seems appropriate, your students should find it challenging and interesting to complete. You can include the terms along with the definitions if you wish, but you do not have to do so.

CROSSWORD PUZZLE—MATHEMATICS
(Upper-Grade Level)

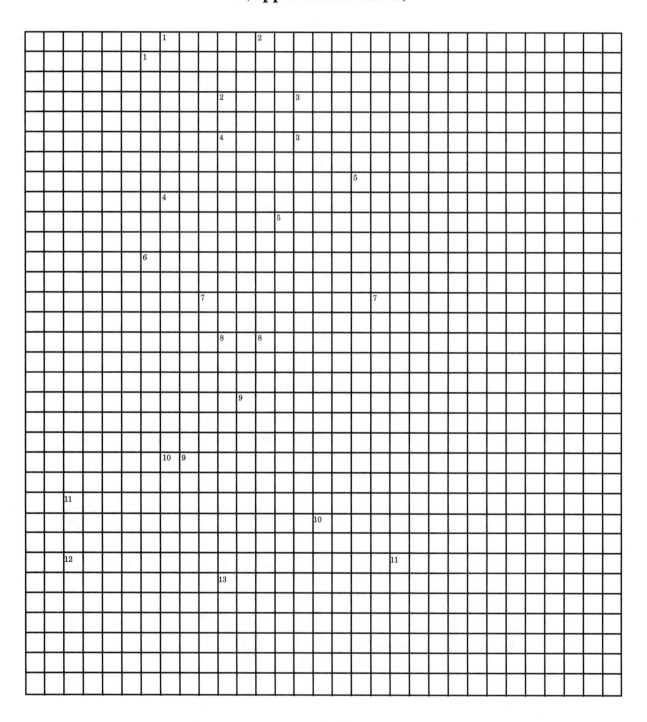

CROSSWORD PUZZLE—MATHEMATICS
(Upper-Grade Level)

(cont.)

TERMS FOR THE CROSSWORD PUZZLE FROM MATHEMATICS

trapezoid	radius	acute	convex
center	rectangle	tangent	mean
sine	square	diameter	octagon
pi	parallelogram	equilateral	rhombus
circumference	isosceles	concentric	diagonal
hexagon	obtuse	median	scalene

CLUES FOR THE CROSSWORD PUZZLE FROM MATHEMATICS

Across

1. ratio between the leg opposite the angle when it is considered part of a right triangle and the hypotenuse
2. an angle extending 90° but less than 180°
3. ending in a sharp point or forming an angle of less than 90°
4. a rectangle with all four sides equal
5. being in the middle or intermediate position
6. curved or rounded like the exterior of a circle or sphere
7. having a common axis
8. a parallelogram with four equal sides and especially one with no right angles
9. line segment extending from the center of a circle or sphere to its circumference
10. a line joining two vertices of a figure that are not adjacent
11. a quadrilateral having only two sides parallel
12. the length of a straight line through the center of a circle or sphere
13. having all sides equal as in a triangle

Down

1. the symbol π denoting the ratio of the circumference of a circle to its diameter
2. a parallelogram all of whose angles are right angles
3. having three sides of unequal length
4. a quadrilateral with opposite sides parallel and equal
5. the average score of a number of scores
6. the point around which a circle or sphere is described
7. the perimeter of a circle
8. a polygon of eight angles and eight sides
9. having two equal sides
10. a polygon of six angles and six sides
11. the ratio between the leg opposite to the angle when it is considered part of a right triangle and the leg adjacent

Answer Key for Crossword Puzzle—Mathematics

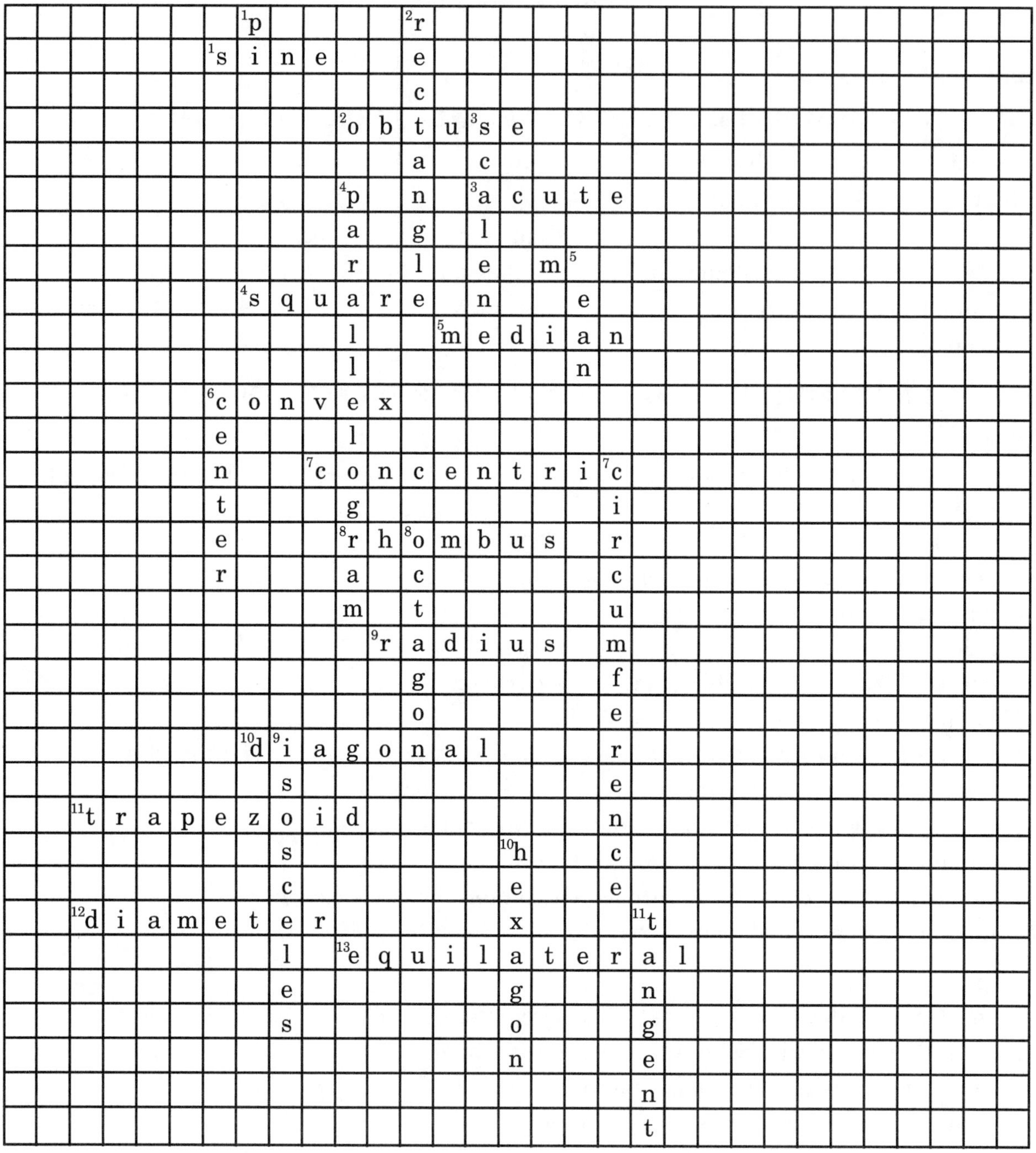

The completed crossword grid reads as follows:

Across and down words:
- ¹sine
- ²obtuse
- ³acute
- ⁴square
- ⁴pan... (parallellll)
- ⁵median
- ⁶convex
- ⁷concentric
- ⁸rhombus
- ⁹radius
- ¹⁰diagonal
- ¹¹trapezoid
- ¹²diameter
- ¹³equilateral

Down words include: prectangle (¹p, ²rectangle), scalene, circumference, circle, center, isosceles, hexagon, tangent, diagonal, rhombus, median, etc.

Grid letters (as arranged):

```
              ¹p       ²r
       ¹s  i  n  e     e
                       c
             ²o  b  t  u ³s  e
                    a  c
             ⁴p     n  ³a c  u  t  e
                    g  l
                    r  e  m ⁵
       ⁴s q  u  a  r  e     n     e
                    l     ⁵m e  d  i  a  n
                    l        n
       ⁶c  o  n  v  e  x
        e          l
        n      ⁷c  o  n  c  e  n  t  r  i ⁷c
        t          g                      i
        e      ⁸r  h ⁸o  m  b  u  s        r
        r          a  c                    c
               m  t                    u
                ⁹r  a  d  i  u  s        m
                    g                    f
                    o                    e
       ¹⁰d ⁹i  a  g  o  n  a  l          r
           s                            e
  ¹¹t r  a  p  e  z  o  i  d            n
           s              ¹⁰h          c
           c              e            e
  ¹²d i  a  m  e  t  e  r  x     ¹¹t
           l    ¹³e q  u  i  l  a  t  e  r  a  l
           e              g            n
           s              o            g
                          n            e
                                       n
                                       t
```

USING A WORD PUZZLE IN THE CONTENT FIELDS

A variation of a word puzzle can be highly motivating for *reviewing* the specialized vocabulary terms that have been presented in a content unit or chapter. It is certainly a more motivating way to reinforce vocabulary terms than is a traditional test or a word matching exercise. A student can complete such a word puzzle independently or preferably with a partner.

Two Reproducible Word Puzzles

The following are two reproducible word puzzles you can duplicate and use in their present forms or modify in any way you like. In addition, they should serve as models for you in constructing your own word puzzles from the specialized vocabulary terms you would like your students to review after completing a content unit or chapter.

WORD PUZZLE FROM SCIENCE
(Sixth-Grade Level)

ELEMENTS AND COMPOUNDS

1. Write a one-syllable word that is a compound that can be formed when an acid is mixed with a base.

s __ __ __

2. Write a three-syllable word that is a particle formed by sharing electrons

m __ __/__/__ __ __ __

3. Write a four-syllable word that is a dye that changes color when mixed with an acid or base.

i__/__ __/__ __/__ __ __

4. Write a one-syllable word that is an atom that has gained or lost electrons.

i__ __

5. Write a two-syllable word that is a substance formed when two or more elements combine chemically.

c__ __/__ __ __ __ __

6. Write a three-syllable word that is a group of symbols that shows the elements in a compound.

f__ __/__ __/__ __

7. Write a four-syllable word that is a compound made of just the two elements hydrogen and carbon.

h__/__ __ __/__ __ __/__ __ __

8. Write a three-syllable word that indicates matter that is made up of just one kind of atom.

e__/__/__ __ __ __

9. Write a one-syllable word that is a compound that turns blue litmus to red.

a__ __ __

10. Write a three-syllable word that is an organic compound that consists mainly of a long chain of carbon atoms.

p__ __/__/__ __ __

11. Write a five-syllable word that is a chemical reaction or change between an acid and a base.

n__ __/__ __ __/__ __/__ __/__ __ __ __

WORD PUZZLE FROM SCIENCE
(Sixth-Grade Level)

(cont.)

12. Write a three-syllable word and a two-syllable word that make up the number of protons in an atom of an element.

a/__ __ __/__ __ n__ __/__ __ __

13. Write a three-syllable word and a one-syllable word that make up a force that holds together the atoms in a compound.

c__ __ __/__/__ __ __ b__ __ __

14. Write a four-syllable word and a two-syllable word that make up a chart that contains many facts about the elements and their atoms.

P__ __/__/__ __/__ __ T__/__ __ __

15. Write a one-syllable word and a two-syllable word that make up a model of the atom that shows electrons moving in orbits around the nucleus of an atom.

B__ __ __ m__ __/__ __

Answer Key for "Elements and Compounds"

1. salt
2. molecule
3. indicator
4. ion
5. compound
6. formula
7. hydrocarbon
8. element

9. acid
10. polymer
11. neutralization
12. atomic number
13. chemical bond
14. Periodic Table
15. Bohr model

WORD PUZZLE FROM SOCIAL STUDIES
(Fourth-Grade Level)

LAND AND WATER TERMS

1. Write a one-syllable word that is part of an ocean or lake extending into land.

   b__ __

2. Write a two-syllable word that is an area of land completely surrounded by water.

   i/__ __ __ __

3. Write a two-syllable word that is a waterway dug across land through which ships can pass.

   c__/__ __ __

4. Write a two-syllable word that is a large body of salt water that covers almost three-fourths of the earth's surface.

   o/__ __ __ __

5. Write a two-syllable word that is a large and flat rolling area high above sea level that may have deep canyons.

   p__ __/__ __ __ __

6. Write a one-syllable word that is the top of a mountain or hill.

   p__ __ __

7. Write a two-syllable word that is a sheltered area where ships can anchor.

   h__ __/__ __ __

8. Write a one-syllable word that is a part of an ocean extending into land usually larger than a bay.

   g__ __ __

9. Write a two-syllable word that is a raised part of the earth's surface with a pointed or rounded top—higher than a hill.

   m__ __ __/__ __ __ __

10. Write a two-syllable word that is low land between hills or mountains.

    v__ __/__ __ __

11. Write a two-syllable word that is a deep, narrow valley with high, steep sides.

    c__ __/__ __ __

12. Write a four-syllable word that is land surrounded by water on all sides but one.

    p__ __/__ __/__ __/__ __

WORD PUZZLE FROM SOCIAL STUDIES
(Fourth-Grade Level)

(cont.)

13. Write a one-syllable word for broad and flat or gently rolling land.

p__ __ __ __

14. Write a one-syllable word for low, wet land on which grass and trees grow.

s__ __ __ __

15. Write a one-syllable word for a narrow body of water separating a large island from the mainland.

s__ __ __ __

Answer Key for "Land and Water Terms"

1. bay
2. island
3. canal
4. ocean
5. plateau
6. peak
7. harbor
8. gulf
9. mountain
10. valley
11. canyon
12. peninsula
13. plain
14. swamp
15. sound

USING SCRAMBLED WORDS IN THE CONTENT FIELDS

Scrambled words are another interesting strategy that can be used to help students *review* the specialized vocabulary terms in the content fields. As was true with word puzzles, scrambled words only should be used after the literacy or content teacher has presented the specialized vocabulary terms. Scrambled word activity sheets can be completed by a student independently or preferably by a student working with a partner.

Two Reproducible Scrambled Word Activity Sheets

The following are two reproducible scrambled word activity sheets you can duplicate and use in their present forms or modify in any way you wish. In addition, they should serve as models for you in constructing your own word puzzles from the specialized vocabulary terms you would like your students to review after they have completed a content unit or chapter.

SCRAMBLED WORD ACTIVITY SHEET FROM ENGLISH
(Sixth-Grade Level)

Read the definition following each word. Then unscramble the letters to form a word that corresponds to the definition and write it in the blank.

1. **gbaniar** _____
   something purchased for a lower price than normal

2. **pedealbend** _____
   something that can be counted on

3. **mebsrsraa** _____
   to make uncomfortable

4. **tusclruep** _____
   the art of carving wood, chiseling stone, working with metal to make statues

5. **tneussmaih** _____
   strong liking or interest

6. **lafat** _____
   causing death

7. **nitipriaosn** _____
   something that brings about a thought or action

8. **elna** _____
   a narrow path

9. **imnertuai** _____
   very tiny

10. **echro** _____
    a job that has to be done regularly

11. **pqeiutenm** _____
    special things needed for an activity

12. **nergsoue** _____
    willing to share

13. **cfnutoin** _____
    the purpose of a thing

14. **sgraociu** _____
    kind or polite

15. **rqueiv** _____
    to shake or tremble

Answer Key for "Scrambled Word Activity Sheet from English"

1. bargain
2. dependable
3. embarrass
4. sculpture
5. enthusiasm
6. fatal
7. inspiration
8. lane
9. miniature
10. chore
11. equipment
12. generous
13. function
14. gracious
15. quiver

Name _____ Grade _____ Teacher _____ Date _____

SCRAMBLED WORD ACTIVITY SHEET
FROM MATHEMATICS
(Intermediate Grade Level)

Read the definition following each word. Then unscramble the letters to form the word that corresponds to the definition and write it in the blank.

1. **gintree** _____
   any of the natural numbers

2. **ndeontaroim** _____
   the part of the fraction below the line that signifies division

3. **dorlain** _____
   a number designating the place

4. **ldmiaec** _____
   based on the number 10

5. **mrga** _____
   a metric unit of weight equal to 1/100 kilogram

6. **rftcoa** _____
   any of the numbers in mathematics that when multiplied together form a product

7. **rdviios** _____
   the number by which a dividend is divided

8. **esba** _____
   a number equal to the number of units in a given digit's space

9. **oocdsetanir** _____
   any of a set of numbers used in specifying the location of a point on a line

10. **dporutc** _____
    a number resulting from multiplying two numbers together

11. **traoi** _____
    the indicated quotient of two mathematical expressions

12. **dmiunen** _____
    a number from which the subtrahend is subtracted

13. **ozer** _____
    the arithmetical term for the absence of any quantity

14. **dddane** _____
    a number to be added to another

15. **qtnuoeia** _____
    a formal statement of the equality of mathematical expressions

Answer Key for "Scrambled Word Activity Sheet from Mathematics"

1. integer
2. denominator
3. ordinal
4. decimal
5. gram
6. factor
7. divisor
8. base
9. coordinates
10. product
11. ratio
12. minuend
13. zero
14. addend
15. equation

USING A HIDDEN WORD PUZZLE (WORD SEARCH) IN THE CONTENT FIELDS

A hidden word puzzle (word search) can be very motivating for *reviewing* the specialized vocabulary terms that have been presented in a content unit or chapter. Hidden word puzzles can be completed by a student independently or preferably by a student working with one or more partners.

Two Reproducible Hidden Word Puzzles (Word Searches)

The following are two reproducible hidden word puzzles (word searches) that you can duplicate and use in their present forms or modify in any way you wish. More important, they can serve as models for constructing your own hidden word puzzles (word searches) from the specialized vocabulary terms you would like your students to review after they have completed a content unit or chapter.

HIDDEN WORD PUZZLE (WORD SEARCH)
FROM SOCIAL STUDIES
(Approximately Fifth-Grade Level)

The Civil War

Here are the clues to the vocabulary terms related to "The Civil War" that are hidden in the Hidden Word Puzzle (Word Search). They may be hidden horizontally, vertically, or diagonally. When you find each term, circle it so that it makes a complete word.

to leave or withdraw from

to block off a place so that no one can enter or leave without permission

a synonym for "freedom" that was used during the Civil War

the name for soldiers from the North

the name for soldiers from the South

the name of the president of the United States during the Civil War

the name of the president of the Confederate States during the Civil War

the name of the Confederate general who surrendered to Grant at Appomattox

the name of the Union ship that fought at sea with the Confederate ship the *Merrimack*

the name of the famous battle that occurred on July 1-3, 1863

the name of the Union general who marched from Atlanta, Georgia, to the sea in 1864

the name of the actor who assassinated President Lincoln

HIDDEN WORD PUZZLE (WORD SEARCH)
FROM SOCIAL STUDIES
(Approximately Fifth-Grade Level)

(cont.)

```
O  H  I  J  B  O  O  T  H  R  V  W  Y  X  C  A  J  V  U  R
C  E  Y  I  O  K  M  B  C  S  W  R  O  D  S  C  R  U  O  F
R  E  Y  G  B  F  E  W  T  X  P  V  U  A  E  R  O  M  M  I
R  W  Q  S  F  G  H  K  U  R  Q  R  I  V  M  A  W  X  P  O
Y  H  P  O  K  L  M  N  O  R  E  C  U  I  A  A  O  J  H  R
T  B  V  Y  A  N  K  E  E  W  O  B  O  S  N  W  R  Z  I  X
B  N  M  U  B  G  T  H  O  P  Z  P  E  U  C  V  N  M  L  A
M  E  N  U  Y  T  M  B  V  C  Z  M  E  L  I  P  Z  M  M  N
O  R  L  I  N  C  O  L  N  C  M  J  U  B  P  A  R  U  V  O
N  B  U  I  S  Y  T  B  M  B  V  U  A  Q  A  W  N  V  C  X
I  X  O  P  R  E  O  P  L  K  J  M  B  A  T  I  O  V  T  U
T  O  R  C  V  X  C  T  Y  P  K  M  B  R  I  O  X  C  V  B
O  B  K  U  Y  R  E  E  B  U  Y  M  O  R  O  U  B  R  E  X
R  U  R  C  X  B  Y  D  D  R  O  M  X  O  N  B  R  Q  E  W
S  H  E  R  M  A  N  O  E  E  R  E  G  H  B  N  M  P  U  Y
R  B  O  U  G  E  T  T  Y  S  B  U  R  G  O  V  M  O  N  P
U  L  B  G  X  V  N  M  V  M  J  U  Y  O  P  A  X  V  B  O
R  O  X  G  H  J  Y  T  R  M  B  J  K  L  P  U  Y  R  M  N
O  C  U  M  B  V  C  X  U  Y  T  R  E  W  Q  A  P  L  K  J
P  K  A  R  M  B  J  Y  T  I  O  U  T  Y  R  M  N  B  X  Z
A  A  O  I  Y  X  P  O  U  Y  T  R  M  N  B  H  U  U  L  R
R  D  O  U  Y  T  R  N  M  K  L  O  P  C  X  Z  U  L  E  A
O  E  V  I  Y  T  R  H  O  P  L  J  H  G  N  M  V  A  E  A
```

Answer Key for "The Civil War"

```
O  H  I  J  B  O  O  T  H  R  V  W  Y  X  C  A  J  V  U  R
C  E  Y  I  O  K  M  B  C  S  W  R  O  D  S  C  R  U  O  F
R  E  Y  G  B  F  E  W  T  X  P  V  U  A  E  R  O  M  M  I
R  W  Q  S  F  G  H  K  U  R  Q  R  I  V  M  A  W  X  P  O
Y  H  P  O  K  L  M  N  O  R  E  C  U  I  A  A  O  J  H  R
T  B  V  Y  A  N  K  E  E  W  O  B  O  S  N  W  R  Z  I  X
B  N  M  U  B  G  T  H  O  P  Z  P  E  U  C  V  N  M  L  A
M  E  N  U  Y  T  M  B  V  C  Z  M  E  L  I  P  Z  M  M  N
O  R  L  I  N  C  O  L  N  C  M  J  U  B  P  A  R  U  V  O
N  B  U  I  S  Y  T  B  M  B  V  U  A  Q  A  W  N  V  C  X
I  X  O  P  R  E  O  P  L  K  J  M  B  A  T  I  O  V  T  U
T  O  R  C  V  X  C  T  Y  P  K  M  B  R  I  O  X  C  V  B
O  B  K  U  Y  R  E  E  B  U  Y  M  O  R  O  U  B  R  E  X
R  U  R  C  X  B  Y  D  D  R  O  M  X  O  N  B  R  Q  E  W
S  H  E  R  M  A  N  O  E  E  R  E  G  H  B  N  M  P  U  Y
R  B  O  U  G  E  T  T  Y  S  B  U  R  G  O  V  M  O  N  P
U  L  B  G  X  V  N  M  V  M  J  U  Y  O  P  A  X  V  B  O
R  O  X  G  H  J  Y  T  R  M  B  J  K  L  P  U  Y  R  M  N
O  C  U  M  B  V  C  X  U  Y  T  R  E  W  Q  A  P  L  K  J
P  K  A  R  M  B  J  Y  T  I  O  U  T  Y  R  M  N  B  X  Z
A  A  O  I  Y  X  P  O  U  Y  T  R  M  N  B  H  U  U  L  R
R  D  O  U  Y  T  R  N  M  K  L  O  P  C  X  Z  U  L  E  A
O  E  V  I  Y  T  R  H  O  P  L  J  H  G  N  M  V  A  E  A
```

HIDDEN WORD PUZZLE (WORD SEARCH) FROM SCIENCE
(Approximately Fourth-Grade Level)

THE ATMOSPHERE

Here are the clues to the vocabulary terms related to "The Atmosphere" that are hidden in the Hidden Word Puzzle (Word Search). They may be hidden horizontally, vertically, or diagonally. When you find each item, circle it so that it makes a complete word.

the blanket that surrounds the earth

an instrument used to measure air pressure

water vapor in the air

energy that travels through space in waves

a scientist who forecasts the weather

an instrument to measure the temperature

a term for moving air

a term for a cloud on or near the ground

a cloud that looks like large fluffy balls of cotton

a term for a light wind

HIDDEN WORD PUZZLE (WORD SEARCH)
FROM SCIENCE
(Approximately Fourth-Grade Level)

(cont.)

```
R  O  V  U  T  R  A  D  I  A  T  I  O  N  T  M  X  Y  V  M
U  M  J  K  L  O  P  U  Y  N  B  M  K  I  H  J  T  R  P  P
O  R  B  M  J  H  G  Y  T  V  C  X  J  Y  R  O  I  P  L  E
X  S  R  E  E  Q  B  N  J  U  Y  T  O  K  K  U  Y  T  P  L
W  O  E  E  R  W  Q  P  O  K  M  V  N  H  Y  G  T  R  K  I
I  B  E  U  H  U  M  I  D  I  T  Y  P  O  L  K  M  N  V  R
N  E  Z  R  N  B  V  C  X  M  L  Y  T  R  E  W  Q  P  O  L
D  Z  E  F  O  G  K  U  H  M  K  J  L  P  U  Y  T  R  H  N
C  R  O  V  N  M  B  A  R  O  M  E  T  E  R  O  R  X  L  M
P  U  O  M  E  T  E  O  R  O  L  O  G  I  S  T  X  X  Y  T
R  O  M  O  R  M  N  J  K  U  Y  T  R  L  K  M  B  N  U  H
P  Y  M  U  X  N  H  G  B  V  N  M  K  U  Y  T  R  O  P  E
O  M  N  G  L  O  A  T  M  O  S  P  H  E  R  E  O  T  X  R
M  N  B  G  J  U  X  Z  A  Q  P  L  M  H  N  B  C  R  O  M
B  M  J  K  Y  T  S  N  J  Y  T  G  B  C  H  J  U  O  P  O
W  T  R  F  E  D  H  K  L  M  B  C  Z  X  S  W  Q  R  T  M
P  K  M  B  N  G  T  R  K  L  P  N  J  K  B  V  C  G  E  E
U  R  E  W  Q  A  S  X  Z  V  B  T  R  O  P  K  L  H  N  T
Y  M  N  K  L  Q  W  W  A  Z  X  V  B  N  J  Y  T  E  W  E
P  M  L  J  H  G  R  P  L  M  N  J  Y  G  V  F  E  W  A  R
```

Answer Key for "The Atmosphere"

```
R   O   V   U   T   R   A   D   I   A   T   I   O   N   T   M   X   Y   V   M
U   M   J   K   L   O   P   U   Y   N   B   M   K   I   H   J   T   R   P   P
O   R   B   M   J   H   G   Y   T   V   C   X   J   Y   R   O   I   P   L   E
X   S   R   E   E   Q   B   N   J   U   Y   T   O   K   K   U   Y   T   P   L
W   O   E   E   R   W   Q   P   O   K   M   V   N   H   Y   G   T   R   K   I
I   B   E   U   H   U   M   I   D   I   T   Y   P   O   L   K   M   N   V   R
N   E   Z   R   N   B   V   C   X   M   L   Y   T   R   E   W   Q   P   O   L
D   Z   E   F   O   G   K   U   H   M   K   J   L   P   U   Y   T   R   H   N
C   R   O   V   N   M   B   A   R   O   M   E   T   E   R   O   R   X   L   M
P   U   O   M   E   T   E   O   R   O   L   O   G   I   S   T   X   X   Y   T
R   O   M   O   R   M   N   J   K   U   Y   T   R   L   K   M   B   N   U   H
P   Y   M   U   X   N   H   G   B   V   N   M   K   U   Y   T   R   O   P   E
O   M   N   G   L   O   A   T   M   O   S   P   H   E   R   E   O   T   X   R
M   N   B   G   J   U   X   Z   A   Q   P   L   M   H   N   B   C   R   O   M
B   M   J   K   Y   T   S   N   J   Y   T   G   B   C   H   J   U   O   P   O
W   T   R   F   E   D   H   K   L   M   B   C   Z   X   S   W   Q   R   T   M
P   K   M   B   N   G   T   R   K   L   P   N   J   K   B   V   C   G   E   E
U   R   E   W   Q   A   S   X   Z   V   B   T   R   O   P   K   L   H   N   T
Y   M   N   K   L   Q   W   W   A   Z   X   V   B   N   J   Y   T   E   W   E
P   M   L   J   H   G   R   P   L   M   N   J   Y   G   V   F   E   W   A   R
```

Ready-to-Use Strategies and Activity Sheets for Improving Comprehension, Critical (Evaluative) Reading, and Creative (Applied) Reading in the Content Areas

Most of the students whom my teacher-trainees tutor in literacy skills have fairly good word identification and lower-level (explicit) comprehension skills. However, they have great difficulty with higher-level (implicit) comprehension especially when they are attempting to read materials in literature, social studies, and science. They also have great difficulty in understanding and solving mathematical verbal problems. These students often find understanding content materials at the higher levels virtually impossible.

This chapter is devoted to helping both literacy and content teachers present and reinforce interpretive comprehension, critical (evaluative) reading, and creative (applied) reading in the content fields. Although a few of the strategies and ready-to-use materials emphasize explicit (literal) comprehension of content materials, most of them are designed to improve students' understanding and retention of implicit (higher-level) skills.

Both literacy and content teachers should find this chapter to be a storehouse of ready-to-use strategies and activity sheets for improving comprehension and retention in content reading.

THE ELEMENTS OF READING COMPREHENSION AND THEIR RELATION TO SUCCESS IN READING IN THE CONTENT AREAS

Since reading comprehension is a very complex process, it is difficult to define in simple terms. Briefly, comprehension is **constructing meaning from the printed material.** It is an *interactive process* that requires the use of *prior knowledge* in combination with the *printed material.* When this definition is used, it is important to consider the characteristics of both the reader and the printed material. In the case of the reader, his or her prior knowledge of the material, interest in reading the material, purpose for reading the material, and ability to pronounce the words found in the material should be considered. In the case of the printed material, the number of difficult words, the syntax or sentence structure, the length of the sentences, and the format should be taken into account.

Although both prior knowledge and features of the printed material are important, in many cases the reader's prior knowledge is of the primary importance. In addition, the more prior knowledge a reader has, the less use he or she needs to make of the printed material. That is the reason a specialist in a particular area (botany, geology, etc.) normally reads material in that area much more rapidly than does a person with less prior knowledge.

Contemporary research in comprehension also focuses on *schema theory*. Schema theory attempts to explain how a person stores information or knowledge in his or her mind, how the knowledge already possessed is used, and how new knowledge is acquired. Another recent focus of comprehension is *metacognition,* which is concerned with the student's awareness of his or her own thinking as he or she is attempting to understand the printed material. It is important for a student to learn how to monitor his or her own comprehension. Research has found that good readers are much better at monitoring their comprehension than are poor readers. This chapter includes some materials that are devoted to improving students' ability in metacognition in content reading.

The Different Levels of Reading Comprehension

In the past comprehension skills usually have been divided into four major categories: literal, interpretive, critical, and creative. However, today comprehension is considered by most researchers to be a *language-based process* that cannot really be divided into arbitrary levels such as these. Instead, reading specialists state there are only two major categories of comprehension: *vocabulary knowledge (word meaning)* and *the understanding of the reading material.*

Some contemporary reading specialists have stated that since comprehension cannot be accurately divided into subskills in research studies, the various levels of comprehension therefore should not be taught to students. However, it is important to try to teach the most important elements of comprehension separately, at least sometimes, to most students, but perhaps especially to disabled readers and learning-handicapped students using the students' own materials in literature, social studies, science, and mathematics. For example, how can a social studies teacher be certain that a student can answer cause-effect questions ("Think and Search") questions effectively if the teacher does not make an effort to ask this type of question sometimes?

In any case, very briefly, here are the various levels of comprehension and the more important subskills that comprise them. You will note from later chapters in the *Handbook* that some levels of comprehension are more relevant in some content fields than in others.

Textually Explicit (Literal or Factual—"Right There") Comprehension

- answering "Right There" questions found in the reading material
- locating directly stated main ideas
- locating significant and irrelevant details
- placing a number of items in correct sequence or order
- reading and carrying out directions

Textually Implicit (Interpretive or Inferential—"Think and Search") Comprehension

- answering "Think and Search" questions (the reader has to *deduce* the answers from reading the material)
- answering questions that call for interpretation (the answer is not found directly in the material)
- drawing conclusions and generalizations
- predicting the outcomes
- summarizing what is read
- sensing the author's mood and purpose
- locating implied main ideas

Critical (Textual Explicit or Evaluative—"Think and Search") Comprehension

- responding to questions in which the reader must *evaluate* the reading material in terms of some criteria
- discriminating between real and make-believe (fact and fiction)
- evaluating the accuracy or truthfulness of the reading material
- sensing an author's biases
- recognizing propaganda techniques such as the bandwagon technique, testimonials, emotionally-toned words, and cardstacking

Scriptally Implicit (Script Implicit, Schema Implicit, Creative, or Applied— "Reading Beyond the Lines") Comprehension

- answering "On My Own" questions (the reader has to combine his or her prior knowledge with the printed material to arrive at new knowledge or actions)
- applying knowledge gained from reading to one's own problem-solving
- bibliotherapy (solving a problem through reading about a similar problem)
- cooking and baking activities after reading simplified recipes
- any art activities that can be used as a follow-up to reading
- creative writing of prose and poetry (including the use of inventive spelling if necessary)
- any construction activities that can be used as a follow-up to reading
- any rhythm activities as a follow-up to reading
- creative dramatics and socio-drama
- puppetry
- scientific experiments (demonstrations)
- *creative* book reports
- any reading that appeals to the emotions (the *affective* aspect of reading)

The Relation Between Reading Comprehension and Success in the Content Fields

It is obvious there is a very high, direct relationship between a student's ability to effectively comprehend what is read especially at the *higher-levels* and his or her success in reading all types of content material. For example, any student who does not possess the ability to successfully read a required social studies or science textbook obviously will have great difficulty in learning the important material contained in that textbook. Of course, the student may be able to obtain enough information to succeed at least to a minimal level by participating in thematic units as is explained shortly or by teacher lecture or demonstration, but there is no really satisfactory substitute for effective comprehension of the content materials.

Even if a student can understand content material at the explicit (literal) level, that normally is not sufficient for effective comprehension. Both literature and social studies require that a student comprehend at the implicit levels of comprehension for a real understanding of the material. Even the content field of science which does emphasize explicit comprehension requires much application of what is read in the form of performing scientific experiments (demonstrations). Mathematics also requires that a student be able to critically read difficult verbal problems that it includes and then to solve them, which is an element of creative or applied comprehension, the highest level of comprehension.

Therefore, any student who is not competent in all the elements of comprehension is certain to have more or less difficulty in reading content materials. The classroom-tested strategies and materials contained in this chapter should enable both literacy and content teachers to present and reinforce these important elements of comprehension in a meaningful, effective way as well as save them much time and effort.

QUESTIONING STRATEGIES AND QARS AS A TEACHING TECHNIQUE IN THE CONTENT AREAS

Questioning strategies or QARs can be both an **assessment strategy** and **teaching strategy** for comprehension in content reading. In several research studies Taffy Raphael and P. David Pearson taught students three kinds of *question-answer relationships or questioning strategies* (QARs). QAR instruction encourages students to consider both the information found in their own prior knowledge and the reading material when answering questions. The relationship for questions with answers directly stated in the material in one sentence was called **"Right There."** The researchers encouraged the students to look for words in the questions and read the sentence containing the answer.

However, the relationship of questions with an answer in the story that required information from a number of sentences or paragraphs was called **"Think and Search."** The relationship of questions for which the answer had to come from the student's own prior knowledge was called **"On My Own."**

In the research studies *modeling the decision* about the kind of QAR that a question constituted was an important part of teaching the students about the concepts of QARs. *Supervised practice* following the teacher's modeling with immediate feedback of students' responses also was very important. The practice involved gradually increasing passage lengths, thus progressing from simpler to more difficult tasks. The students in the study who were taught the three types of QARs were able to answer questions more successfully than were the students in a control group. **Average and below-average students had the greatest improvement after training in the use of QARs.** However, as might be expected, primary-grade students needed more repetition to learn QARs than did intermediate-grade students.

Later Raphael modified QAR instruction to include four categories, clustered under two different headings. Figure 4-1 illustrates her modifications.

In the modified plan, the "In My Head" category is divided into questions that involve both the reader's prior knowledge (**Author and You**) and the text information and those that can be answered from the reader's experience without any information from the material (**On My Own**).

Discussing the use of QAR categorization to plan questioning strategies, Raphael stated:

> Questions asked prior to reading are usually "On My Own" QARs. They are designed to help students think about what they already know and how it relates to the upcoming story or content text. In creating guided reading questions, it is important to balance text-based and inference questions. For these, "Think and Search" QARs should dominate since they require integration of information and should build to the asking of "Author and You" QARs. Finally, for extension activities, teachers will want to create primarily "On My Own" or "Author and You" QARs focusing again on students' background information as it pertains to the text. (Taffy E. Raphael, "Teaching Question-Answer Relationships, Revisited," *The Reading Teacher,* February, 1986, pp. 516-522. Reprinted with permission of Taffy E. Raphael and the International Reading Association.)

It is very important for both literacy and content teachers to be aware of the concept of the three types of QARs or questioning strategies. As stated earlier, reading in literature and social studies should usually emphasize higher-level thinking skills. Therefore, students should be asked mainly "Think and Search" and "On My Own" questions. Even in science and mathematics, the number of

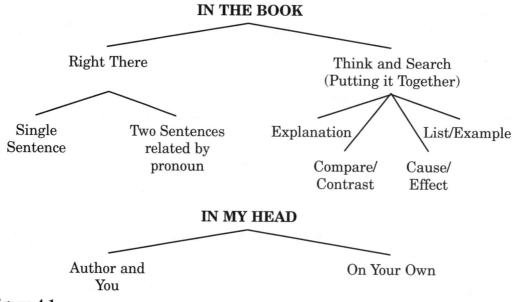

Figure 4-1

"Right There" questions that are asked should be limited as much as possible. In the past far too many reading and content teachers have asked a majority of "Right There" questions that did not allow for any interpretation or the use of the student's prior knowledge. This was even true in middle and secondary schools as well as in a number of college classes. This was because lower-level questions are very easy both to formulate and evaluate.

However, if a student has not been asked many "Think and Search" or "On My Own" questions, it is not logical to assume that he or she ever will become competent in answering these kinds of questions. Although contemporary reading and content teachers probably are asking more higher-level comprehension questions than in the past, we all should be very much aware of the importance of doing so on a regular basis with all students including those with reading and learning disabilities.

TEACHING LITERATURE, SOCIAL STUDIES, SCIENCE, AND MATHEMATICS IN THEMATIC UNITS SUCH AS IN WHOLE LANGUAGE PROGRAMS

Many content teachers are unsure about how to best help the students in their classrooms who simply cannot read the required textbook. As has been explained earlier in this *Handbook,* this can occur for several reasons—such as textbooks being written above the grade level of the students who are to read them, their demanding specialized vocabulary and concept load, and their organizational patterns which may be very different from those in basal readers or tradebooks. Even good students often find content textbooks rather dull and unmotivating.

A good alternative to the use of the traditional content textbooks that many English, social studies, science, and mathematics teachers are now using is *thematic units* for presenting and reinforcing content. Students are generally much more "turned on" by thematic unit teaching than they are by more traditional teaching approaches that mainly emphasize the use of textbooks.

When a content teacher decides to use thematic units to present and practice subject matter, he or she first selects a topic that may be appropriate for the needs and interests of his or her students. Theoretically, the students should select their own topic(s) to study since they therefore should be the most interested in such subjects. However, this may or may not be feasible. Even if a teacher appears to give the students complete freedom in selecting the topics to study, he or she may direct the choices to a greater or lesser degree.

In any case, let us suppose that a fourth-grade class has decided to study the topic "Tropical Rain Forests" in depth. The teacher, with the help of the school librarian or media specialist, brings in many basic resources that are related to this topic. Various content textbooks could be one source of information, but many other resources also are used such as trade books, videotapes, computer software, films, filmstrips, cassette recordings, resource people, pictures, realia, among others. The students then usually divide themselves into *cooperative learning groups,* which are described in the next section of this chapter, to research the topic. Although the teacher may assign each of the cooperative learning groups a specific topic to research, the group leaders usually make this determination among themselves. The teacher should act mainly as a facilitator, not a true "director."

Each group then conducts its own research on the topic "Tropical Rain Forests." Each group can use any of the resources already available or other resources that are not in the classroom nor even in the school. A field trip, for example, to a museum that has a display of tropical rain forests could be part of the unit study. In addition, usually all of the content in literature, social studies, science, and mathematics is related to the theme "Tropical Rain Forests." Each group then presents summaries of what it has learned to the rest of the class in various types of creative ways.

Thus, thematic unit teaching is *integrated teaching with active student involvement* at every stage of the process. Theoretically, in thematic unit teaching each student reads materials that he or she can read successfully, is highly motivated to learn, is actively involved in learning, and is given the opportunity to display much independence in learning. Therefore, the topic of the unit usually becomes much more "alive" and relevant to them than it would through traditional teaching that uses only content textbooks as the main resource. Since all of the content learning is integrated and uses actual reading materials, thematic unit teaching is said to be part of the whole language philosophy.

The following are the *major advantages* of using thematic units to present and reinforce content learning:

- Each student usually reads at his or her own independent or instructional reading level and thus can experience success.
- Many of the strategies for improving vocabulary knowledge and comprehension that are illustrated in this *Handbook* can be taught and practiced effectively in the context of units.
- Students learn to work cooperatively with their peers.
- Students develop independent work habits.
- Students are more likely to see the relevance of what they are learning and its relation to their daily lives.
- It effectively integrates learning in all of the content fields of literature, social studies, science, and mathematics.
- It promotes actual student involvement and *critical and creative thinking skills,* all of which are very important to their later success in our democratic, technological society.
- It enhances each student's self-esteem.

The following are the *main limitations* of using thematic units:

- It requires an *experienced* teacher who also is very knowledgeable, creative, flexible, well organized, and cooperative.
- Although it is fairly easy to implement in a self-contained classroom or in a middle school, it would be more difficult to implement effectively in a departmentalized junior or secondary school since it requires much cooperation on the part of the various subject matter teachers.
- Not all schools have access to the requisite resources of all kinds that are required for its successful implementation.

- Students cannot just be thrust into this type of curriculum without a gradual introduction. This may make it difficult if just one or two teachers in a school want to implement it, while the remainder want to teach content in traditional ways. This also may make it difficult for a transfer student who has had no exposure at all to it.

- A few students may not be independent nor mature enough to handle that degree of freedom well.

In summary, although thematic unit teaching can be a very effective way of teaching content skills, it probably is not practical for every teacher or every student in every circumstance. However, it should be used as much as possible in the light of each teacher's, student's, and school district's needs and interests.

USING COOPERATIVE LEARNING GROUPS IN BOTH THEMATIC UNITS AND TRADITIONAL CONTENT INSTRUCTION

As has been mentioned earlier, *cooperative learning groups* are a very effective strategy in the thematic unit teaching in content areas. However, it is equally effective in more traditional instruction such as content instruction using a single book, the basal reader approach, or a phonic approach. Cooperative learning groups are especially useful in traditional types of instruction since below-average readers or learning-handicapped students often are stigmatized by such instruction. For example, when one required social studies textbook is used for an entire class, a number of the students simply cannot comprehend and study it effectively for all of the reasons stated earlier in this chapter. Therefore, the teacher either has to present much material by lecturing or by having the better readers read aloud the textbook a portion at a time. If and when students with reading problems have to read a portion aloud, they often are virtually unable to do so well and feel an acute sense of embarrassment. Thus, both their oral and silent reading in that class may become even poorer due to their lowered self-esteem.

However, when cooperative learning groups are used even with one required content textbook, students with reading problems usually can be helped inconspicuously by the other students in the group or even encouraged to read simpler materials on the same topic under study by the class. They will thus be able to use their prior knowledge effectively which may be quite good even though they have reading problems. Such students also may have other unique abilities such as a talent in art that is helpful in accomplishing the work of the cooperative learning group. They usually will be able to build a higher self-esteem in this way.

In summary, I highly recommend using cooperative learning groups on a regular basis in both thematic unit content teaching and traditional content teaching. Their use has so many potential advantages that they are a teaching strategy that no literacy or content teacher can afford to ignore. Any cooperative learning group should be composed of above-average readers, average readers, below-average readers, and learning-handicapped students.

SEVERAL PREDICTION AND PURPOSE-SETTING STRATEGIES TO AID EFFECTIVE COMPREHENSION AND RETENTION IN THE CONTENT AREAS

There are several *prediction and purpose-setting strategies* that can be used to improve comprehension and retention in content reading. Some of them are as follows: the PreReading Plan (PReP), the Directed Reading-Thinking Activity (DR-TA), the Mystery Clue Game, the Anticipation Guide, and Advance (Graphic) Organizers. The PreReading Plan (PReP), the Anticipation Guide, and Advance (Graphic) Organizers all were described in detail in Chapter 2 of this *Handbook*. In addition, reproducible examples of each of these three strategies from content reading were included in that chapter. Therefore, due to space limitations, they are not discussed or illustrated again in this chapter. However, you are encouraged to refer to Chapter 2 to refresh your memory about these strategies as they are equally as useful in *improving comprehension and retention in content reading* as they are in *assessing* a student's ability to read and remember content materials effectively. In fact, they are extremely helpful for this purpose because when a student activates (uses) his or her prior knowledge and has a purpose for reading content material, this virtually ensures that his or her comprehension and retention of the material will improve.

However, another very effective reading strategy that is applicable for use in both content and narrative reading beginning in the primary grades is the *Directed Reading-Thinking Activity (DR-TA)*. My teacher-trainees have used it very successfully in the primary grades, the intermediate grades, the middle school, the junior high school, and the secondary school.

Although the Directed Reading-Thinking Activity was first developed many years ago by Russell S. Stauffer, professor emeritus of the University of Delaware, it still is relevant and helpful today. It is a very useful strategy with all kinds of readers since it involves prediction and reading content material for specifically formulated purposes. Briefly, the DR-TA encourages *active involvement* with the reading material by having students generate hypotheses about the material and then checking the accuracy of their predictions. This is why its use can improve reading comprehension and retention so effectively. Very briefly, here are the basic steps of the DR-TA:

1. Have the students read the title of the content chapter or unit they subsequently are going to study. On the basis of this title and their own prior knowledge, have them then formulate predictions about the material. If you wish, each student can write his or her own predictions on a sheet of paper or a group of students or the entire class can write or dictate the predictions on the chalkboard. They also can tell what they already know about the topic (activate their prior knowledge).

2. Tell the students that they should read to see if the content material confirms the predictions that were made. Then have them silently read a portion of the material or the entire chapter or unit.

3. Have the students then discuss each of their predictions, indicating which ones were confirmed and which ones were not. Help the student to determine what criteria should be used in determining whether or not the predictions were confirmed. This portion of the DR-TA also can be written if you wish.

4. If the content material was not read at one time, alternate periods of silent reading and discussion until the entire material has been read. In each case, emphasize the validity of the reasoning that the students are using rather than the correctness of the original hypotheses. (Russell G. Stauffer, *Directing Reading Maturity as a Cognitive Process.* New York: Harper & Row, 1969, pp. 35-36.)

To summarize, you can see that the Directed Reading-Thinking Activity (DR-TA) helps students to predict outcomes, set purposes for reading, and analyze their reading in a meaningful way. Thus, its use can improve critical reading and thinking skills, comprehension, and retention of content material. Most helpful is that it does not require any unique materials or equipment; it uses the students' own content materials. Rather, it just requires a *mind-set* on the part of literacy and content teachers and students.

An additional purpose-setting activity that capitalizes on an organizational pattern of the content material is the *group mystery clue game* which is designed to help students understand sequence. It is especially helpful when students are to understand a sequence of events. Basically it consists of the following steps:

1. To construct a mystery clue game, the literacy or content teacher first studies the sequence of events in the material and then writes clear, specific clue cards to each event. More than one card may be made for each clue.

2. The teacher then divides the class into small groups and gives each group member at least one clue card.

3. No student may show the card to another student in the group, but the card can be read aloud or paraphrased so that all the group members know what is on each card. In this way, students who are poorer readers will still be encouraged to try to read and to share in the group process.

4. Each group of students must use the clues that the teacher provides them to solve the mystery. For example, they must find the equation that will solve a mathematical verbal problem, must find the formula that will make a chemical reaction, or must find the result of an experiment in science, among many other creative possibilities.

5. You should give them a time limit to find the solution to the mystery.

6. A group recorder reports the group's solution to the entire class.

7. Students are instructed to read the material to find out which of the groups came the closest to solving the mystery. (Adapted from Judy S. Richardson and Raymond F. Morgan, *Reading to Learn in the Content Areas.* Belmont, California: Wadsworth Publishing Company, 1990, p. 181.)

This cooperative learning activity promotes *oral language* as well as *comprehension skills*. It also stresses the (explicit) literal level of comprehension in advance of the reading, thus allowing students to concentrate on the interpretation and application of what they read. This activity can be used in different content areas in the following ways: English teachers can write clues for solving of a murder mystery in a novel, social studies teachers can write clues for historical events, science teachers can write clues for solving an experiment, and mathematics teachers can write clues for solving a problem or equation.

Reproducible Mystery Clue Game

The following is a ready-to-use mystery clue game from the topic "The Middle Ages—A Time of War" from the content area of social studies. It is appropriate for use at about the sixth-grade or middle-school level. Complete instructions are included for you on how to construct this game and then have your class play it. You are free to use it in its present form or modify it in any way you like. More important, it should serve as a model for constructing your own mystery clue games from the content material that your students are subsequently going to read.

MYSTERY CLUE GAME
(Approximate Sixth-Grade or Middle-School Level)

Directions for the Teacher—Divide the class into small groups giving each student a clue slip or card. Tell the students they must share their clues with their group members without actually showing the clue slip or card. They are to work with their group to try and solve the mystery questions. Put these mystery questions on the board or a transparency. Give the students a time limit to come up with their guesses. After the time limit has expired, ask students to share their responses with the entire class. Next they need to read the material to see if their predictions were accurate. These clues relate to the social studies topic "The Middle Ages—A Time of Wars" which can be found in any social studies textbook containing material about World History, or in encyclopedia material either on CD-Rom or in printed form about the Middle Ages.

Questions for the Mystery Clue Game:

1. What groups controlled Europe during the early Middle Ages?

2. What person came close to recreating the Roman Empire during the early Middle Ages?

3. What group were the conquerors and plunderers during the middle of the Middle Ages?

4. Who went to war to fight against the "unbelievers" during the last part of the Middle Ages?

Mystery Clues:

1. The Middle Ages lasted from 500 A. D. until 1500 A. D.

2. Five Germanic tribes controlled most of Europe during the early Middle Ages.

3. The Visigoths controlled the Iberian peninsula where Spain is now located during the early Middle Ages.

4. The Vandals controlled North Africa and large Mediterranean islands during the early Middle Ages.

5. The Ostrogoths controlled most of Italy and the Western Balkans during the early Middle Ages.

6. The Saxons controlled the southern part of what is now known as England during the early Middle Ages.

7. The Franks controlled what is now France and western Germany during the early Middle Ages.

8. Each Germanic tribe had a chieftain or leader.

9. Many Germanic people became Christians.

10. Charlemagne, who was very tall and strong, was a king during the early Middle Ages.

MYSTERY CLUE GAME
(Approximate Sixth-Grade or Middle-School Level)

(cont.)

11. Charlemagne defended the Roman Catholic Church and was given the name "Augustus" by Pope Leo III in 800 A.D.

12. Charlemagne tried to rule his kingdom fairly.

13. Charlemagne acted very much like Augustus, the emperor of Rome.

14. Charlemagne's peaceful rule was a positive part of the early Middle Ages.

15. Fierce warriors called the Vikings threatened the security of Charlemagne's empire even before his death.

16. The Vikings came from what is now known as Norway, Sweden, and Denmark.

17. The Vikings were first interested in plunder—goods taken by force.

18. The Vikings wore leather helmets, and they were extremely fearless.

19. When the Vikings arrived at a town, they usually attacked the church first and stole various religious objects.

20. The Vikings made the journey to North America 500 years before Christopher Columbus did.

21. The crusaders went to war for what they believed was a holy cause.

22. The crusaders fought against what they thought were pagans.

23. The crusaders fought in wars that were called Crusades.

24. The volunteers in the Crusades tore strips of cloth from their cloaks and pinned them to their tunics in the shape of a cross.

25. Many of the two armies of children that traveled to the Holy Land in the Children's Crusades either died of hunger or sickness or were sold into slavery before they arrived there.

MARGINAL GLOSSES AS AN AID TO
COMPREHENSION AND RETENTION IN CONTENT READING

Both *marginal glosses* and the *guide-o-rama* can be used to improve students' comprehension and retention in content reading. The guide-o-rama signals the reader to note certain information in a reading passage. Literacy and content teachers will find a reproducible guide-o-rama later in this chapter.

A marginal gloss often can be found in content textbooks. Glosses are comments that authors make to readers as marginal notations or "asides" that are designed to improve their comprehension and retention. Teachers can make their own marginal glosses if their selected content textbooks already do not contain them or if they are not satisfied with those already included. Marginal glosses are designed to be a help for guiding students' reading attention.

Literacy and content teachers can make marginal glosses by following these procedures:

1. Fold a ditto master against the margin of the content textbook.
2. Identify the textbook page at the top of the master and line numbers beside the teacher statements.
3. Write the marginal notes on the ditto master.
4. Duplicate and give students copies of these notes to match with textbook pages and lines as they read.

When using marginal glosses, the teacher should select the beginning portions of the text or the most difficult portions, since making marginal glosses for students to use for the entire textbook would be very time-consuming. However, for providing help in improving comprehension with very difficult reading material, marginal glosses are well worth the teacher's time. (Adapted from Harry Singer and David Donlan, *Reading and Learning from Text.* Hillsdale, New Jersey: Erlbaum, 1985.)

USING RECIPROCAL QUESTIONING (THE REQUEST PROCEDURE) TO
IMPROVE COMPREHENSION AND RETENTION IN CONTENT READING

My teacher-trainees have found *reciprocal questioning (the ReQuest Procedure)* to be an extremely useful strategy in helping students to become *active questioners* at the implicit (higher level) of comprehension. The original ReQuest Procedure was developed by Anthony V. Manzo and since then has been used and revised by many different reading specialists (Anthony V. Manzo, "The ReQuest Procedure," *Journal of Reading,* November 1969, pp. 123-126). However, it remains one of the most useful strategies for improving comprehension and retention in the content fields of literature, social studies, and science.

Here are the basic steps of this strategy:

1. The teacher first tells the students to ask the type of questions about each *sentence* in a content selection they think the teacher might ask.
2. The teacher then answers each question as fairly and completely as possible and tells the students that they must subsequently do the same.

3. Then the teacher and the students both silently read the first sentence.

4. The teacher closes the book, and a student asks questions about that sentence that the teacher is to answer.

5. Next, the student closes the textbook, and the teacher asks questions about the material. The teacher should provide an excellent model for the student's questions. The questions should mainly be of the higher type such as implicit (interpretive and critical) and creative (applied) questions.

6. After a number of additional sentences, the procedure can be modified to use an entire *paragraph* instead of just individual sentences. Questioning should continue until the student can answer the question: "What do you think will happen next in this selection?"

The ReQuest Procedure or reciprocal questioning is so valuable because it clearly shows students just how to formulate and answer implicit comprehension questions instead of just explicit questions. We used reciprocal questioning in tutoring a fourth-grade student named Matt several years ago. Matt's major reading problem was interpretive comprehension of his social studies and science textbooks. Although a tutor had tried to help him during the fall semester using mainly activity sheets to improve his interpretive comprehension, we had been unsuccessful because he just marked any answer that he saw and did not even read the material at all. The following semester I suggested reciprocal questioning as the major strategy to help improve Matt's interpretive comprehension skills, and it proved very successful. Matt truly enjoyed reading his content textbooks so carefully that he could ask his tutor questions about the material that she really was unable to answer! He found "tricking her" to be very motivating, and she really was unable to answer all of the detailed high-level questions that he asked her, especially from the longer reading selections. Therefore, I am convinced that the ReQuest Procedure (reciprocal questioning) can be very valuable in improving higher-level reading skills.

TEACHING THE FIVE-PHASE INSTRUCTIONAL SEQUENCE FOR IMPROVING COMPREHENSION AND RETENTION IN THE CONTENT FIELDS

The *five-phase instructional sequence* also can be useful in helping students to comprehend and retain content information. It consists of the following steps:

1. *Preparation:* Begin this instructional strategy by presenting an overview of the content material and background information. Be sure to activate the students' prior knowledge and clear up any misconceptions they may have about the content material they are going to read.

2. *Exploration:* Help the students explore the topic and become more aware of their prior knowledge. Activities that can be included in this step are science experiments (demonstrations), opportunities for problem-solving, discussions that encourage creative or divergent thinking, open-ended writing, use of computer software, and independent reading. Tell the students that they are to express their own thoughts and ideas. Ask them critical questions with the goal of creating some internal mental conflict in order to stimulate their thinking.

3. *Acquisition:* Discuss the conceptual conflict with the students and help them to change their misconceptions. Present content (expository) material from the content textbook. It may be important to present additional reading material besides the content textbook in this step. Always have the students read for a specific purpose(s) and have a follow-up discussion to the reading. Rereading of the textbook or other materials may also be necessary.

4. *Practice/Application:* To ensure that the students retain new knowledge and concepts, students should be given many opportunities to work with the ideas. Some such activities may be experiments, discussions, and small-group problem-solving sessions.

5. *Synthesis:* Help the students to synthesize the new information for the purpose of ensuring that the new ideas and concepts are related to other concepts and prior knowledge. Some activities to use in this step are answering test questions correctly, applying new concepts, explaining new concepts, and constructing a concept map to indicate the relationships. (Adapted from K. J. Roth, E. L. Smith, and C. W. Anderson, "Verbal Patterns of Teachers: Comprehension Instruction in Content Areas," in Gerald Duffy, Laura Roehler, and Jana Mason [Editors], *Comprehension Instruction: Perspectives and Suggestions.* New York: Longman, Inc., 1984.)

USING A STUDY STRATEGY TO AID COMPREHENSION AND RETENTION IN THE CONTENT FIELDS

There are several different *study techniques* that can be presented to students at the intermediate-grade level and above to aid comprehension and retention of the content material they are going to read. Undoubtedly the most widely known of these is *Survey Q3R—survey, question, read, recite, and review.* Survey Q3R was developed by Francis P. Robinson during World War II to aid in the comprehension and retention of the reading material that military personnel had to try to understand and remember. It is based on an information-processing theory of learning. Each part of Survey Q3R is designed to facilitate the processing of incoming print so that the student can deal with it effectively.

Although Survey Q3R varies somewhat depending upon the content field in which it is used, it contains the following main steps:

1. *Survey or Preview:* The students survey the entire textbook chapter to obtain an overall impression of its content. In this survey or preview, they may read the introduction and summary of the chapter and the first sentence in each of the paragraphs. They may also examine the pictures, maps, graphs, diagrams, tables, and other aids contained in the chapter. **Note:** This survey or preview is the most useful aspect of Survey Q3R. It should always be used in reading content material even when no other part of this study strategy is used. The use of the survey or preview alone will greatly add to the comprehension and retention of content material.

2. *Question:* The students pose questions they want to read to answer in this step of the study technique. They can turn each subheading into a question and formulate additional questions to read to answer.

3. *Read:* The students read the entire chapter on a selective basis to try to answer the questions they have posed. In this selective reading, they attempt to fill in the gaps in their reading by capitalizing on their prior knowledge. This step of the procedure helps them to become actively involved in their reading.

4. *Recite:* This step applies only to one section at a time. After the students have read a section at a time in a purposeful way, they can recite the important information obtained from that section in either an oral or a written form, depending on which is more efficient for them.

5. *Review:* This step applies after the students have completed the chapter. They attempt to review the important concepts, generalizations, and facts gained from the chapter. They often can use the written notes they may have made in the fourth step of this procedure. (Adapted from Francis P. Robinson, *Effective Study.* New York: Harper and Row, 1961.)

There are a number of variations of Survey Q3R that literacy or content teachers can use. Probably the most common variation is called *PQRST (preview, question, read, state, test).* However, a similar study technique also can be called Survey Q4R, POINT, C2R, OK4R, and REAP, among others. In any case, since they are all very similar in purpose and procedure, they are not described further here.

Survey Q3R must be varied depending upon the content area in which it is applied. For example, in literature (English or language arts) the survey step probably can be used effectively in the novel, the short story, the essay, and poetry. Since few of these literary forms contain subheadings, students usually must formulate their own purposes for reading in the light of prior knowledge. The final step of Survey Q3R may be valuable in summarizing what was learned from the reading. Survey Q3R can be used in its original form with most social studies textbooks. As an example, in a middle school history textbook, the student can use the survey, can turn each subheading into a question, can read each section to answer the question, can review the material in that section, and can subsequently summarize the entire chapter. When students use Survey Q3R to study a science textbook, they survey the chapter, turn the subheadings into questions and use this step to understand the author's pattern of writing, read to answer the formulated questions and to recall details and processes, try to remember the main ideas and specific details, and write a brief outline of what was read.

However, Survey Q3R must be modified considerably in solving a verbal problem in mathematics. This is one way in which it can be modified for this purpose:

1. *Survey:* Skim the problem to gain a general impression of it.

2. *Question:* Decide what the question is in the problem, what facts are needed to solve it, and the order of the steps that are needed for solving it.

3. *Read:* Read very carefully to understand the question thoroughly and to determine the steps that are needed for the solution.

4. *Recite:* Decide what facts the answer depends on.

5. *Review:* Estimate the answer and later check the answer after the problem has been solved.

USING OTHER STRATEGIES TO IMPROVE COMPREHENSION AND RETENTION IN CONTENT READING

There are a number of other strategies that can be effectively used by literacy and content teachers to improve comprehension and retention while reading content materials of all types. Some of these strategies are very briefly summarized now:

- **Venn Diagram**—This is a diagram composed of two circles that show the relationship between two entities in a content subject. Figure 4-2 is an example of it.

- **Phase In–Phase Out Strategy**—This is a strategy that is designed to encourage active student questioning. In this strategy the teacher phases in the questioning process by taking the first step in modeling questions that are appropriate to the content. The teacher then offers additional information about the content to be read or explains additional information about the topic. Some knowledge of the material to be read is necessary in order to generate the appropriate type of questions. Once students have an idea of the kinds of questions that can be asked about different types of content, they are placed into groups to ask each other questions regarding the material to be read. Final phasing out occurs when the students ask and answer appropriate questions of various kinds on their own.

- **C/T/Q Strategy**—This strategy helps content teachers to isolate key concepts, key vocabulary terms, and key questions and to present these in advance of content reading assignments. Children should record these points in their notebooks to guide them through later lessons and home-school reading assignments. (For exact information about how to implement this strategy, see the following source: Anthony V. Manzo, "Three Universal Strategies in Content Area Reading and Languaging," *Journal of Reading,* November 1980, pp. 146-149.)

- **Concept-Text-Application (CTA) Approach**

    C—Concept assessment/development phase—This phase consists of a prereading discussion in which the student's prior knowledge about the topic is assessed, and new concepts and terms needed for comprehension of the text may be developed.

    T—Text phase—In this phase the teacher introduces the reading selection and sets purposes for the reading. The class reads the text silently in parts, with guided discussion following the reading of each part.

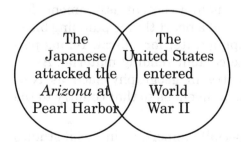

Figure 4-2

A—Application phase—In this phase the teacher plans post-reading activities to encourage the students to use the knowledge they have gained. This phase involves summarizing and synthesizing information and an evaluation of and creative response to the material.

- **SEARCH Procedure**

Set goals—After having read material about Florida, for example, several students may decide they want to learn more about this state. Their teacher helps them classify their goals into "Knowing," "Doing," and "Becoming" categories.

Explore resources—The students then list each "Knowing" and "Doing" goal at the top of a piece of paper on which two columns are provided. The first should be headed "Source," while the second is headed "Information." The "Becoming" goals are placed on a separate sheet of paper. With the help of their teacher if needed, the students decide on the sources of information for each "Knowing" and "Doing" goal.

Analyze and organize information—When the students are ready to record their information, they use the second column on the sheet to match the information to the sources.

Refine and rehearse—Using whatever strategies they prefer, the students survey their information and decide on an audience and on how they wish to present the information.

Communicate with others—In the time decided on for sharing, the students present their SEARCH to the group or the class with the aids they have prepared.

Help yourself to improve—The final step is the creation of a way to assess the SEARCH. Means that can be used are self-evaluation, peer evaluation, checklists, teacher evaluation, visitor evaluation, or analysis of a tape-recorded presentation. (Adapted from Roselmina Indrisano, *Independent Application of SEARCH in the Reading and Language Arts*. Columbus, Ohio: Ginn Occasional Paper, Number 12, 1982.)

- **Directed Reading/Singing Activity**—This strategy uses an informational song as the basis for the reading lesson. The steps of the Directed Reading Activity (DRA) are all incorporated (Activation of Prior Knowledge, Directed Silent and Oral Reading, Strategy or Skill-Building Activities, Follow-up Practice, and Enrichment Activities), but *singing* replaces oral reading. Use of songs may help students remember the words of the selection better. Many songs have content related to literature and social studies. However, teachers need to select the songs carefully in order to promote accurate content concepts.

- **Using Analogies and Personal Anecdotes**—Teachers can use analogies to help give familiar connections to the new ideas in a content assignment. For example, a study in the content area of science of a heart that is pumping blood can be related to a water pump that is pumping water for a farm. Telling personal anecdotes also can help to personalize content reading material. As an example, in studying about a certain country in geography such as New Zealand, the content teacher can bring items indigenous to that country to the class for display.

- **Evaluating an Author's Biases**—It is especially important in social studies for students to be adept at evaluating an author's biases when he or she was writing the material. This evaluation is, of course, an important part of critical thinking and critical reading. It can be done in several different ways. For example, students can be taught to look for emotionally toned words such as *liberal, conservative, radical, reactionary, left-wing, right-wing,* and *bigot,* among countless others. They also can be exposed to many other different kinds of propaganda techniques such as the bandwagon, testimonials, and the halo effect. In addition, students always should be encouraged to locate materials on controversial topics from several different sources. The citizens in a democratic society must be very competent in critical thinking and reading in order for that democracy to survive. Unfortunately, this is not always the case.

- **Teaching the Six Major Paragraph Patterns of Organization**—It is helpful to teach students in the intermediate grades and beyond the characteristics of the major patterns of organization. Here are the six major paragraph patterns of organization that are commonly found in content reading:

  1. *Enumeration*—This is an easy pattern to recognize. It usually consists of a statement and a number of subordinate statements that list subtopics of the major topic.

  2. *Generalization*—This pattern is often called the *main idea pattern.* In this pattern, a broad statement is made and then supporting evidence is provided for this statement. This evidence can take the form of examples, reasons, or explanations.

  3. *Comparison and Contrast*—In this pattern, two related ideas are compared or contrasted.

  4. *Sequence*—In this pattern, the order in which ideas are presented is of great importance. There is no way to rewrite a sequence pattern without changing the author's intended meaning.

  5. *Cause-Effect*—This pattern emphasizes the subordination of one idea to another to show its dependence on the idea.

  6. *Question and Answer*—In this pattern, both parts are needed to complete the idea of the author.

- **Teaching the Clue Words to Help Locate Patterns of Organization in Content Materials**—Different subject matter areas have different patterns of organization. In any case, teachers can discuss how authors use language to signal the type of organization that is being used. Here is one useful list of signal words for the four main types of organizational patterns:

Time Order	Enumeration	Comparison/Contrast	Cause-Effect
on (date)	to begin with	however	because
not long after	first	but	since
now	second	as well as	therefore
as	next	on the other hand	consequently
before	then	not only/but also	as a result
after	finally	either ... or	this led to
when	most important	while	so that
	also	although	nevertheless
	in fact	unless	accordingly
	for instance	similarly	if ... then
	for example	yet	thus

(Richard Vacca, *Content Area Reading*. Boston: Little, Brown and Company, 1981, p. 143)

- **Question Prediction**—This procedure is designed to practice useful, independent questioning strategies. Here is this seven-step procedure:

  1. The teacher presents and explains the common patterns of organization such as enumeration, generalization, comparison and contrast, sequence, cause-effect, and question and answer.

  2. The teacher lists unlabeled groups of key words that signal the patterns. Then the teacher asks students to scan some paragraphs to locate such signal words.

  3. The teacher gives students selected topic sentences and asks students to identify the probable pattern from the clue words in the topic sentence.

  4. The teacher prepares cloze paragraphs from the content area. (See the description of cloze in Chapter 2.) The content-specific information is what should be deleted, but topic and key pattern words should not be deleted. Students are asked to underline the key words and predict the pattern.

  5. The teacher asks students to read several text paragraphs and state the main idea of each paragraph. Then the teacher has students combine the main ideas of the paragraphs into an overall main idea.

  6. The teacher asks students to translate the main idea statements into a possible question the teacher might ask, particularly on a test.

  7. The teacher reminds the students that they will find several patterns within a text reading, but when students can find the main idea and make questions of it, they will become good detectors of organizational patterns. (Adapted from C. D. Finley and M. N. Seaton, "Using Text Patterns and Question Prediction to Study for Tests," *Journal of Reading,* 30, November 1987, pp. 124-132.)

- **Think-Reflect in Pairs (TRIP)**—For this activity, the teacher divides students into pairs. Students share information on TRIP cards, which list propaganda techniques or situational problems. Answers are printed on the back of cards for immediate reinforcement. Points may be given for correct answers, with a designated number of points needed for any certain grade in the class. For a different TRIP experience, students are given problems from the content textbook. They first solve the problem in pairs and then write the problem on the front and the answer on the back of the card. In this way, students can create their own TRIP files for reinforcement or for future use. Figure 4-3 shows the front and back of a model TRIP card for an example.

(FRONT)	(BACK)
A manufacurer of athletic shoes gets a star football quarterback to make a television advertisement praising its product.	*testimonial* This correct answer is worth 5 points.

Figure 4-3

- **Retelling**—One of the oldest techniques for evaluating reading comprehension at the end of a selection is called *retelling or the tellback strategy.* It was first used in the 1920s as the way of assessing comprehension on the first standardized reading tests. However, it has not been very commonly used for many years due to the difficulty of accurately evaluating students' responses on standardized reading tests. Such tests instead usually used the multiple-choice format to assess comprehension skills. However, with the popularity of whole language programs, it is becoming much more commonly used at the present time. Since it is an example of *process comprehension,* it reflects the philosophy of whole language very well.

  To use this technique, simply have the student read the content material and ask: "What was this material about?" or "Can you tell me all that you remember about the material?" This simple strategy can enable literacy and content teachers to effectively assess a student's comprehension of content material in an informal manner.

- **Locate Omitted Steps from a Sequenced Passage**—When a selection has a time-sequenced or numbered, step-by-step organization, develop an ordered list of the steps. Leave out some of the steps in the sequence. (For example, in a six-item sequence, steps 3 and 5 might be omitted.) Give the list to students before they read the selection and discuss the concept of a sequenced organizational pattern. Have students check the steps on the list as they occur during their reading and add those that are missing.

- **Idea Mapping**—This strategy is a way of teaching students to locate important information by analyzing text structure. This technique is designed to help students use the patterns of organization found in content textbooks to improve comprehension. In this strategy the relationships among the important ideas are *mapped.* The goal is to help students understand the key concepts and their interrelationships. This procedure probably is best used with students reading at about the sixth-grade level and above. The procedure requires the student to learn to use mapping symbols such as the following:

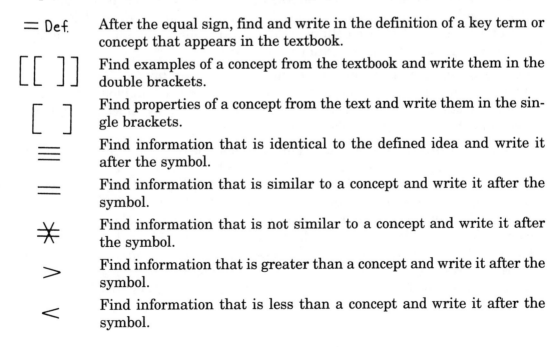

$= \text{Def.}$	After the equal sign, find and write in the definition of a key term or concept that appears in the textbook.
$[[\ \ ]]$	Find examples of a concept from the textbook and write them in the double brackets.
$[\ \ ]$	Find properties of a concept from the text and write them in the single brackets.
$\equiv$	Find information that is identical to the defined idea and write it after the symbol.
$=$	Find information that is similar to a concept and write it after the symbol.
$\not\equiv$	Find information that is not similar to a concept and write it after the symbol.
$>$	Find information that is greater than a concept and write it after the symbol.
$<$	Find information that is less than a concept and write it after the symbol.

$\longrightarrow$ Find information that occurs after an event and write it after the symbol.

$\Longrightarrow$ Find information that is causally related to a concept and write the cause before the symbol and the result after the symbol.

$\rightsquigarrow$ Find information that illustrates a concept and write it before the symbol.

Here is a very brief description of how idea mapping can be used:

1. To teach the students how to recognize the symbols and read an idea map, start with a text they have recently read. Select a passage organized according to only one text structure. A list is a good structure to use at first because it is likely to include information that is easily found and mapped, such as definitions or examples. Read the text and map it before discussing it with students.

2. Show the students a completed idea map. Help them understand how the maps may help them learn and retain important information.

3. Help the students study several completed maps. Have them use increasingly more difficult maps.

4. Construct handouts for the students in which the symbols are included, but the text is missing. Hand these out for the students to complete as a text assignment is read. On completing the maps, it is best to have a group of students discuss the information they located and how they decided where the information belonged in the map. Have them keep their maps to study for tests.

5. More competent students who have learned to complete maps may be taught to construct maps of their own from content assignments. Have them first work on well-organized texts and help them to identify the kind of structure as well as the relationships among others. (Adapted from Bonnie Armbruster and Richard Anderson, "Idea Mapping: The Technique and its Use in the Classroom or Simulating the 'Ups' and 'Downs' of Reading Comprehension." Urbana, Illinois: The Center for the Study of Reading, Reading Education Report, Number 36, 1982.)

- **The Guinness Book of Records**—This resource is an invaluable tool in motivating students to want to comprehend various types of supplementary material. My teacher-trainees have used it successfully many times in tutoring. It is published by Facts on File, 1996.

- **Computer Software**—Computer software may be of some limited value in improving comprehension skills in the content areas. However, it is not so helpful for this purpose as it is for vocabulary development which lends itself somewhat better to the software format. Since any list of computer software for improving comprehension skills undoubtedly would be outdated almost as soon as it were published, none is included in this resource. However, literacy and content teachers are urged to consult all of the sources of computer software that were mentioned in Chapter 3 for help in locating software for improving the various comprehension skills in the content fields.

THE ANTICIPATION GUIDE

The *Anticipation Guide* helps students to *activate their prior knowledge* before reading and also uses *statements* instead of questions before reading as a beginning way to involve students in their reading. Statements require students only to recognize and respond, while questions require students to give an answer. The end result of this process should be the production of the student's own statements and questions. A start can be made in this process in the upper primary grades and it can be refined and extended in the intermediate grades. My teacher-trainees have used the Anticipation Guide very effectively with all kinds of disabled readers and learning-handicapped students especially in the intermediate grades and the middle school.

Here is a very brief description of the Anticipation Guide as adapted from *Content Area Reading* by J. E. Readence, T. B. Bean, and R. S. Baldwin (Dubuque, Iowa: Kendall/Hunt Publishing Company, 1981):

1. *Identify the Major Concepts*—The teacher first reads the material and identifies the most important concepts contained in it.

2. *Determine Student's Knowledge of These Concepts*—The teacher determines how the major concepts in the material support or refute the student's prior knowledge in the area.

3. *Create Statements*—The teacher creates three to five statements about the material. The statements are those in which the students have enough knowledge to understand the statements, but not enough to make any of them completely known.

4. *Decide Statement Order and Presentation Style*—The order of the statements should follow the order of the statements presented in the material. The teacher writes the guide on the chalkboard, a transparency, or a ditto.

5. *Present Guide*—The teacher reads the directions and statements orally or has the students read them silently depending upon their reading ability. Tell the students that they will share their thoughts and opinions and that they must defend them. The guide can be done individually or with a partner. Often it is more effective if a student works with a partner(s).

6. *Discuss Each Statement Briefly*—The teacher asks for a show of hands from students to indicate their agreement or disagreement with each statement.

7. *Have Students Read the Material*—The teacher tells the students to read the material with the purpose of deciding what the author may say about each statement.

8. *Conduct Follow-Up Discussions*—After they have read the material, have the students again respond to the statements. The Anticipation Guide can serve as the basis for a post-reading discussion in which the students can share what they have learned and how their prior knowledge has been influenced by the reading.

Reproducible Anticipation Guide

Here is a reproducible Anticipation Guide from the content area of literature at the upper primary grade level. It is based upon the well-known Caldecott-winning trade book *Yonie Wondernose* by Marguerite de Angeli (New York: Doubleday and Company, 1944). You should have your students complete this Anticipation Guide *before* they read this charming trade book if it seems applicable for them. More important, it can serve as a model as you construct your own Anticipation Guide from material from any of the content fields at the appropriate reading level.

ANTICIPATION GUIDE
(Approximately Second- or Third-Grade Level)

Here are some sentences about the interesting trade book *Yonie Wondernose* by Marguerite de Angeli. Read each sentence to yourself and put an X next to each sentence you agree with. Be sure to be able to talk about your answers later when we talk about the sentences and the book.

Yonie Wondernose by Marguerite de Angeli

_____ 1. Yonie's father gave him the name Wondernose because he was so curious.

_____ 2. Yonie lived in a big city that had many cars and trucks.

_____ 3. Yonie liked to go swimming in the cool Conestoga Creek.

_____ 4. Dunder was the name of Yonie's best friend.

_____ 5. Yonie was smart and brave when there was a fire in the barn.

Now read the trade book *Yonie Wondernose* to yourself. Remember what you should look for as you read the book so that we can discuss later what this book is all about.

Answer Key for *Yonie Wondernose*

1. X

3. X

5. X

A USEFUL PREDICTION STRATEGY

Another interesting *prediction strategy* involves the cyclical steps of *activation, prediction, reading,* and *verifying.* Here is a very brief description of these steps:

1. *Activation*—The students should be given a section of content material that is relevant to the passage in order to activate the prediction process. The teacher has to decide which part of the text passage might be the most appropriate for generating good predictions. It could be the title of the selection, a picture or another graphic presentation, or maybe a paragraph from the material.

2. *Prediction*—The students then make predictions about what will happen based upon the content material and their prior knowledge about the content. The students should understand that there are no incorrect predictions. To make a good prediction, students should use prior knowledge in combination with the passage information. The teacher can model such *prediction questions as these:*

   What do I think this passage material might be about?

   What could I learn from reading this passage?

   What do I think may happen next in this passage?

   The teacher should stress that students must compare the content information with prior knowledge in order to make valid, text-relevant predictions.

3. *Reading*—The students read the content material to determine how accurate their predictions were.

4. *Verifying*—The students should compare the predictions made with what information was gained from the reading. Students should give evidence that the predictions were:

   A. *True*—If there is support in the material for the prediction.

   B. *False*—If there is support in the material that indicates that the prediction was not true.

   C. *Questionable*—If there is not information to support either the accuracy or inaccuracy of the prediction.

Sometimes the students must do additional reading or other research to determine if a prediction was relevant or not. The teacher can record each prediction on the chalkboard or a transparency as the students discuss their findings. Predictions that are verified as being accurate can be starred, while those that are inaccurate or unimportant can just be crossed out. The predictions that were found to be questionable can have a question mark placed next to them.

New predictions about the remaining text material can be generated, and the entire process then continues. The teacher may say something similar to this to help the students generate more accurate predictions:

Now that you have learned _____, can you make some good predictions about what will happen next?

(Adapted from Robert M. Wilson and Linda B. Gambrell, *Reading Comprehension in the Elementary School.* Boston; Allyn and Bacon, 1988, pp. 32-36.)

Reproducible Activity Sheet Based Upon This Prediction Strategy

The following is a reproducible activity sheet based on the prediction strategy just described. It was constructed from a social studies passage at about the sixth-grade level. You can duplicate and use it in its present form if it seems applicable or modify it in any way you wish depending upon the interests and needs of your students. In addition, it can serve as a useful model for you in constructing this type of activity sheet using the content materials that your students need to understand.

ACTIVITY SHEET USING THE PREDICTION STRATEGY
(Approximately Sixth-Grade Level)

Teacher: **Let me show you how the *prediction strategy* can help you read with much better understanding. The name of the story that you are going to read is "Robin Lee Graham—the True Story of a Boy Who Sailed Alone Around the World." You are going to read this story and try to understand it very well. One thing you can do to help you better understand what you read is to make some *predictions* about what you think may happen in the material. Making predictions helps you know what to look for as you read any type of material. You know what the title of the story is. You are now going to make some predictions of what the material might be about from the title and your own knowledge of sailing and world geography.**

I. Now write down as many predictions as you can based on the title of the story.

_____

_____

_____

_____

ROBIN LEE GRAHAM—THE TRUE STORY OF A BOY WHO SAILED ALONE AROUND THE WORLD

In 1965 at the age of sixteen Robin Lee Graham left the port of Long Beach, California, to try to sail around the world alone in his sailboat, the *Dove.* Since no sailor that young had ever sailed totally around the world at the time, Robin was not sure that he could do it, but he was determined to try. To the dismay of some people he had obtained his parents' permission to try to do this although it obviously was very dangerous.

Teacher: **Now that you have read the first paragraph of the story you know which of the predictions that you made from the title probably were correct. You probably predicted that a boy tried to sail all the way around the world in his sailboat. You probably also predicted that this trip would be very dangerous. You may have predicted that this trip could be very exciting, but very difficult.**

II. Write as many predictions as you can about the rest of the story. Then read the rest of the story to see if your predictions are right.

_____

_____

_____

_____

ACTIVITY SHEET USING THE PREDICTION STRATEGY
(Approximately Sixth-Grade Level)

(cont.)

Robin first sailed with two kittens toward Hawaii and was extremely happy when he landed at the Hawaiian island of Oahu after twenty-two days, the youngest sailor ever to sail from mainland America to Hawaii. However, leaving Hawaii and sailing across the endless Pacific Ocean was an awesome experience for Robin. He battled loneliness although he did enjoy seeing the porpoises jumping and splashing. He reached the islands of Fanning, Pago Pago (pronounced Pango Pango), and the Fijian islands after having many dangerous experiences such as hidden reefs, pounding surf, a mast that fell into the ocean, a sting from a poisonous stonefish, and a hurricane on Pago Pago where he stayed for a while. Robin found that the native people on all of the islands were friendly, helpful, and honest. He met a girl from California named Patti at Fiji, and they became very good friends.

Since one of his cats had died and one had run away by this time, Patti gave Robin a new kitten before he left for Guadalcanal and Australia. During this time Robin suffered from extreme loneliness and talked to himself often to hear the sound of a human voice. Before he arrived in Darwin, Australia, a freighter ran down the *Dove* and did some damage to it. Patti met Robin in Darwin, and he especially enjoyed seeing the aborigines—the native people of Australia.

On the voyage across the Indian Ocean Robin fell overboard while trying to fix the twice-broken mast. He was later able to get a new mast, but he was in a terrible storm by Malagasy, and the *Dove* was barely able to sail to Africa. When Robin arrived at Durbin, South Africa, he married Patti at the age of only eighteen. She had been waiting for him there. On their honeymoon they explored Africa on an old motorcycle, and they liked Africa very much.

Robin then began sailing alone across the Atlantic Ocean with two new kittens. Robin was so lonely during this time that he even crocheted a woolen cap for himself. When he arrived in Surinam, South America, Patti was again waiting for him. At this time the *National Geographic* magazine, which had been paying Robin for telling his story, bought him a new sailboat named the *Big Dove* to finish his sailing voyage around the world. Before finishing the voyage, Robin and Patti spent months exploring the Caribbean islands. Robin then went alone through the Panama Canal, traveled to the Galapagos Islands, and finally left for California where Patti was waiting for him while expecting their baby. On the boring trip home, porpoises came to visit Robin often. Robin found the last few days of his voyage especially tedious as he was anxious to arrive home. He had not seen anyone for thirty-eight long days by then.

He finally arrived safely in Long Beach, California, after five years and 30,600 miles. He was given a warm welcome and was even interviewed for television. He had met and overcome incredible obstacles and had been *very, very lucky*. This is the true story of Robin Lee Graham, the youngest person at that time ever to sail alone around the world—1965 to 1971. Perhaps you would like to read more about his many adventures some time since his trip was certainly very exciting.

III. Now write all of your predictions that you think were right.

_____

_____

_____

_____

ACTIVITY SHEET USING THE PREDICTION STRATEGY
(Approximately Sixth-Grade Level)

(cont.)

IV. Now write all of your predictions that you think were wrong.

_____

_____

_____

_____

K-W-L, K-W-H-L, AND K-W-L PLUS

K-W-L is an acronym for *What Do I Know—What Do I Want to Learn—What Have I Learned?* Developed by Donna Ogle, a Professor at National-Louis University in Evanston, Illinois, K-W-L stresses a student's prior knowledge, encourages him or her to formulate questions to read to answer, directs him or her to look for answers to their questions, and enables him or her to effectively summarize what was learned. This strategy is only applicable with *expository (content) material.* This strategy is extremely effective in helping students understand and remember content material because it helps them to use their prior knowledge the entire time they are reading. My teacher-trainees have used K-W-L successfully with intermediate-grade and junior high school students many times in helping them comprehend and retain content both their social studies and science textbooks.

To begin K-W-L with "What Do I Know," identify the most important concepts in the content material and ask students to tell what they already know about this concept. As the students provide the information, ask questions so that they can link their knowledge to that of the author. At this time your role should be to focus and guide students' thinking so that they better understand what they already know. As students identify the information they already know, have them write it on the K-W-L worksheet (see the reproducible sample sheet) under the column labeled "What I Know."

In the second step "What Do I Want to Know," provide motivation by focusing on what the students want to learn. Encourage them to formulate their own questions about the topic they are studying and give them time to write their questions under the column labeled "What I Want to Find Out." Once the students have written their questions, have them read the material looking for answers.

In the final part of K-W-L, have the students report what they have learned from reading the material. Have them write down what they have learned in the column of the worksheet "What I Have Learned." Have them do this without referring to the text. However, if there is disagreement, have the students reread the passage to check their statements for accuracy.

Note: If a student cannot write his or her own questions and answers on the K-W-L worksheet, you may have the student dictate them to you. In addition, it may be very helpful to have students work with partners if you wish.

K-W-H-L

In another variation of traditional K-W-L that I have recently seen being used, a third step is added before the final step. This step can be called *"How Can I Find Out."* In this step students brainstorm for resources they can use to locate the needed information. In addition to their content textbooks, other resources they can use may be as follows: other content textbooks, trade books, newspapers, magazines, encyclopedias, the *INTERNET,* computer software, computer software on a CD-ROM disk, videotapes, and films. This third step can be very useful in motivating students to think of additional useful resources to use in addition to their textbook, a concept they might not otherwise consider.

K-W-L Plus

Ellen Carr and Donna Ogle have added a *writing component* to K-W-L that my teacher-trainees also have found very effective. It is called *K-W-L Plus.* (See their article "A Strategy for Comprehension and Summarization" in *Journal of Reading,* 30, April 1987, pp. 626-631.) K-W-L Plus helps students to organize information they have learned from using the K-W-L worksheet to write a *summary or report.* When students have finished reporting what they learned and the "L" section of the worksheet is finished, the students then organize their learning by using a *mapping or webbing technique.* (See the description presented later in this chapter.)

The material in the "L" section of the worksheet can help students to identify appropriate categories and the specific information learned can be attached to the appropriate categories. The webbing technique used in K-W-L Plus can replace the traditional outline that commonly is used in writing a report. Students often can construct a semantic map (web) much more easily than a traditional outline, and we have found that they like doing it much better. In addition, it seems to be a more effective technique to use to motivate the writing of a summary or report.

Reproducible K-W-L and K-W-H-L Worksheets

Here is a blank sample K-W-L worksheet you can duplicate and use with your students. It undoubtedly is most effective in the intermediate grades and above, although it probably could be used as early as third grade. It always should be used with content (expository) material.

Following that sample worksheet is a reproducible K-W-H-L worksheet you can duplicate and use with your students. It also probably is most effective in the intermediate grades and above, and should always be used only with content (expository) material.

K-W-L WORKSHEET

K	W	L
What I Know	**What I Want to Find Out**	**What I Have Learned**

K-W-H-L WORKSHEET

K What I Know	W What I Want to Find Out	H How Can I Find Out	L What I Have Learned

A JOT CHART

The *jot chart* is a good purpose-setting strategy that can demonstrate *organizational patterns* for students. A jot chart can effectively present such organizational patterns as cause-effect, comparison-contrast, enumeration, and description.

Literacy or content teachers can use the information found in a content reading assignment to create a jot chart, leaving several blank spaces in it. Students then fill in the chart's blank spaces as they read. Since students are writing important information, a jot chart can give them practice in writing; by the time the content reading assignment is finished, it has helped them to develop a study guide. Thus, the use of jot charts should help to improve students' comprehension and retention of the content assignments they must read. (Adapted from Richard Vacca and Joanne Vacca, *Content Area Reading.* Glenview, Illinois: Scott, Foresman and Company, 1989.)

Reproducible Example of a Jot Chart

The following is a reproducible passage about the waves in seas and oceans from science at about the fifth-grade level. You will then find a ready-to-use partially completed jot chart students can complete by using the material in the preceding passage. A student can work with a partner in completing this chart if you wish.

You can duplicate and use the passage and the jot chart if they seem applicable for your students. More important, it can serve as a model of this type of chart that you may want to have your students construct from the content material they must read.

JOT CHART
(Approximately Fifth-Grade Level)

LEARNING ABOUT WAVES

Have you ever seen the waves on an ocean? If you have, you know how waves sound as they break upon the shore. However, waves also are interesting to learn about.

As you have noticed if you ever have seen an ocean, seas and oceans are never still as the water in them is always moving either below the surface or at the surface. Moving air stirs up the surface waters, and even a gentle breeze forms patches of tiny ripples called *catspaws*. A stronger wind creates waves, and waves are parallel rows of watery ridges with valleys in between. The ridges are called *wave crests,* while the valleys are called *troughs.* Crests and troughs follow one another through the seas.

In the open ocean, although waves appear to carry water with them, each wave crest starts water particles circling. As each crest passes, particles are lifted and moved briefly forward, but then sink down and back. That is why a gull bobs up and down on the sea instead of moving with the waves.

By the shore, however, waves behave differently. When a wave reaches shallow water, some of its circling water particles hit the sea bed so that the bottom of the wave slows down. However, the wave crest keeps on moving until it topples forward and breaks upon the shore.

As you might suppose, the stronger the wind, the larger the waves become. Waves are measured by their height and length. *Wave height* is the height from a wave trough to the next wave crest. *Wave length* is the distance between two crests. The longest waves form where strong winds blow for a long time across a great stretch of open ocean. Here, rounded waves called *swells* can reach a wave length of over half a mile. Where storm waves come near a coast, they can be as high as 110 feet.

However, some of the highest waves are not caused by winds but by underwater earthquakes or volcanoes. These waves are called *tsunamis.* Tsunamis travel across the Pacific Ocean at up to 500 miles an hour. Where they reach shallow bays, their wave height can reach 220 feet. They sometimes come ashore and destroy entire towns, drowning many people.

JOT CHART
(Approximately Fifth-Grade Level)

(cont.)

PARTIALLY COMPLETED JOT CHART
LEARNING ABOUT WAVES

	Name	General Characteristics	What Happens at the Shore	Possible Consequences
Breeze	catspaws	tiny ripples		insignificant
Wind	wave crests troughs		some noise when waves break on the shoreline	usually insignificant unless poor swimmer or in a very small boat
Strong Wind	wave crests	long distance between	may cause severe shore erosion	can capsize small and even larger boats
Earthquakes or Volcanoes	tsunamis	travel as fast as 500 miles an hour	may cause very severe shore erosion	

Answer Key for "Learning About Waves"

Note: The answers included here are only for illustrative purposes. Any statements a student uses to complete the unfinished jot chart that seem logical should be considered correct.

	Name	General Characteristics	What Happens at the Shore	Possible Consequences
Breeze	catspaws	tiny ripples	insignificant shore erosion	insignificant
Wind	wave crests troughs	parallel rows of watery ridges that do not have excessive length or height	may cause slight shore erosion some noise when waves break on the shoreline	usually insignificant unless poor swimmer or in a small boat may cause seasickness
Strong Wind	wave crests troughs swells	long distances between wave crests tall height from a wave crest to the next wave	may cause severe shore erosion loud noise of waves breaking on the shore	can capsize small and even larger boats can even cause ships difficulty may cause seasickness
Earthquakes or Volcanoes	tsunamis	travel as fast as 500 miles an hour wave height up to 220 feet	may cause very severe shore erosion crashing noise at the shore	can capsize boats and ships can swamp an entire town can drown many people extremely dangerous

USING THE CLOZE PROCEDURE AND MAZE TECHNIQUE FOR IMPROVING COMPREHENSION IN THE CONTENT AREAS

Both the *cloze procedure* and the *maze technique* were explained in detail in Chapter 2 as examples of strategies for assessing competencies and weaknesses in comprehension in the content fields. However, both of these strategies are equally good ways of improving comprehension skills in content materials. Chapter 2 also contained reproducible examples of a traditional cloze procedure and a maze technique. You should refer to that chapter for detailed information on how to construct both of these techniques.

Reproducible Example of a Variation of the Cloze Procedure

This chapter will not describe either of these strategies further. However, the following is a reproducible example of a variation of the cloze procedure that can be used at about the first-grade, second-semester level. You can duplicate and use this example of cloze in its present form if it seems applicable or modify it in any way you like. It also can serve as a model for you of this type of cloze procedure that you may construct from any appropriate content material. You may want to have a pupil complete this cloze procedure with a partner(s). This variation of cloze is most appropriate for students in the primary grades or for older disabled readers.

VARIATION OF THE CLOZE PROCEDURE
(Approximately First-Grade, Second-Semester Level)

Read this story about *turtles*. It has some *blank spaces* in it. Find the *one word* in each sentence that will make the story right. Then print that word on the line. You should use all of the words below the story.

TURTLES

In the summer I live in the big woods. I always _____ turtles on the roads then. The turtles go across the road to lay _____ in the sand by the side of the road. I have seen many _____ laying their eggs. When the turtles _____ done laying their eggs, they leave. When the _____ turtles are born, they have to take care of themselves. One mother turtle even _____ her eggs in my driveway. I never _____ any baby turtles.

When people drive on the roads _____, they must watch out for the turtles. They may _____ just like a big rock. One day this _____ I helped a turtle get off the road so it didn't get hit by a car. I pushed it with my foot, but _____ didn't hurt it. I like to see _____ turtles in the summer. They are fun to watch.

here	*turtles*	*saw*
see	*look*	*are*
laid	*eggs*	*I*
baby	*summer*	*the*

Answer Key for "Turtles"

see

eggs

turtles

are

baby

laid

saw

here

look

summer

I

the

A THREE-LEVEL GUIDE FOR
IMPROVING COMPREHENSION IN CONTENT READING

Three-level guides are explained in detail by Harold Herber in the book *Teaching Reading in the Content Areas* (Englewood Cliffs, New Jersey: Prentice-Hall, 1978). Such a guide connects and integrates the *three levels of comprehension— explicit (literal), implicit (interpretive), and applied (creative)*—with a series of statements to which students must respond. Since three-level guides demonstrate the hierarchical interaction of the three levels of comprehension and call for student reaction to a series of statements, they are a valuable way to improve comprehension and retention of content material. As with any other strategy for improving comprehension, they should only be used occasionally instead of regularly to avoid becoming tedious.

Here are some guidelines for constructing a three-level guide:

1. Determine the organizing concept. This usually should be the most important concept in the content assignment with a number of significant details that support it.

2. Determine the content objectives. For example, what do you want students to understand and remember about this material? This probably should be the most important ideas and their interpretation.

3. Take these ideas and make a series of statements from them. If you wish, you can write the main ideas as questions and then rephrase them as statements until you feel competent in writing the statements. If it helps, you can think *"The author means"* in front of each statement to be sure the statements are at the implicit (second) level of comprehension. You probably should construct about five or six statements at the implicit level.

4. By studying these statements and referring to the passage, next identify the most important facts that support the major ideas you have made into *level-two statements*. Then write these facts either as replications or paraphrases of

the material. You may want to think *"The author says"* in front of these statements to ensure they are on the explicit (first) level. You can have about two explicit statements to support each major inference. These statements then become *level one* of the guide.

5. Next you are ready to construct the third or applied level. Statements in this level should apply to the major ideas but also should capitalize on the students' prior knowledge. If you wish, you can insert a mental *"We can use"* before each statement to be sure the statements are on the applied level of comprehension. You should probably have about four or five of these statements for this level of the guide.

6. Finally, write the directions and decide if you want to add some *distracting statements* at levels one and two. Both of these tasks will depend upon your students' ages, abilities, and the difficulty of the content material. Be sure the directions are clear and complete. If you include distracters, be sure to tell your students that the guide may contain them.

When three-level study guides are used in a class for the first time, teachers should introduce them as a whole-class activity. All students probably should have their own copy of the guide. In this way, students are introduced to this strategy in a nonthreatening manner with their peers. Since the value of three-level guides is that they stress the three levels of comprehension so effectively, class discussion is an important part of the activity. Students can begin to understand how interdependent the facts, interpretations, and applications are to the complete understanding of a content topic.

After the initial exposure to three-level guides, students should be able to complete them either independently or with a partner(s) depending upon their abilities and your wishes. Distracters probably should not be used until students are fairly familiar with the use of three-level guides.

Once literacy and content teachers have had some practice in constructing three-level guides, they are not difficult to construct. Since content teachers are very familiar with the most important concepts in the topics in their own content area, they usually find them fairly easy to construct after some trial-and-error. Students even can construct their own three-level guides after they have completed a number of them. They may well enjoy making them with a partner(s) after awhile.

Reproducible Passage and Three-Level Guide

The following is a passage entitled "How Plants Make Food" from the content area of science at about the sixth-grade level. It then includes a three-level guide that was constructed from this passage. You can duplicate and use both the passage and the three-level guide if they seem appropriate for your students or modify either of them in any way you want. More important, this three-level guide can serve as a model for you in constructing your own three-level guides from the content material your students are to read and remember.

THREE-LEVEL GUIDE
(Approximately Sixth-Grade Level)

Read this passage silently about how plants make food. After you have finished reading the passage, complete the three-level guide that follows it. You can refer back to the passage while completing the guide if you want.

HOW PLANTS MAKE FOOD

Of course, you know that people eat and then digest the food to make the energy they need to have in order to live. However, you may not be aware how plants are able to make their food.

The term *photosynthesis* can be defined as "put together with light." It is the process by which plants make food. In this process, carbon dioxide and water combine in the presence of light to form sugar, which is a food. Most photosynthesis in plants occurs in the cells of the leaves. A waxy covering coats the surfaces of leaves. Beneath both the top and bottom waxy surfaces of the leaf is a tissue made up of a single layer of cells. *Stomates,* which are small openings, are found in the layers of protective cells on the surfaces of the leaf. Gases move into and out of the leaf through the stomates. These openings connect to large air spaces in the middle layer of the leaf. Carbon dioxide in this layer is available to the food-making cells of the leaf.

Most photosynthesis takes place within cells in the middle layer of the leaf. These cells contain many *chloroplasts* which is a green structure in plant cells where food is made. A chloroplast is green because it contains a pigment, or coloring material, that is called *chlorophyll.* This is a green pigment that absorbs energy from sunlight. This energy is then used in the process of making food for the plant. In a way *chloroplast is a food factory.* Carbon dioxide and water are the raw materials that go into the food factory. Sunlight is the energy that changes the raw material into the product—food that is in the form of sugar. Oxygen is then given off as another product of the process.

As you may have understood by this time, photosynthesis is a very complex process. A series of chemical reactions change the raw materials into the food product the plant can use. However, the process can be shown in a simple manner by the starting materials and the end products:

water + carbon dioxide + energy → sugar + oxygen

Here are the main steps in the process of photosynthesis:

- Water is taken in by the roots and moves through the *xylem,* a kind of tissue made up of tubes, to the food-making cells.

- Sunlight touches the leaf, passes through the top layer of cells, and is captured by the chlorophyll, which is found in the chloroplast. Energy from sunlight is stored in the chloroplast.

- Stored energy in the chloroplast breaks water down into two gases—hydrogen and oxygen. Oxygen is given off and moves out of the leaf through the stomates.

- Air enters the leaf through the stomates. Carbon dioxide from the air combines with hydrogen, forming a kind of sugar.

THREE-LEVEL GUIDE
(Approximately Sixth-Grade Level)

(cont.)

- The sugar moves through the *phloem,* a type of tissue made of tubes, to other parts of the plant. Some of the sugar is used by the plant as soon as it is made, while some of the sugar is stored in the plant. The rest of the sugar may be changed into such other foods as starches, proteins, or fats.

Although you can see by now that the entire process of how plants make food is very complicated, at least you now may have some idea what happens. Perhaps you would like to learn more about this process. If you would, there are many different resources you can refer to for additional information.

Name _____ Grade _____ Teacher _____ Date _____

THREE-LEVEL GUIDE FOR THE PASSAGE "HOW PLANTS MAKE FOOD"

I. Check ✓ the items below that you believe say what the author said. Sometimes the exact words are used, while at other times other words may be used.

_____ 1. The scientific term for the way in which plants make food is called photosynthesis.

_____ 2. In the process of photosynthesis, oxygen and water combine in the presence of sunlight to make sugar.

_____ 3. Stomates, which are small openings, are found in the middle of leaves.

_____ 4. A chloroplast is green because it contains chlorophyll.

_____ 5. Chloroplast could be compared to a food factory.

_____ 6. At the end of a plant's food-making process, it gives off carbon dioxide.

II. Put a check ✓ on the line beside any of the statements below that you think are reasonable interpretations of the author's meaning.

_____ 1. To understand photosynthesis, it is probable that scientists have studied the leaves of a plant under a microscope.

_____ 2. A plant cannot grow properly in a completely dark environment.

_____ 3. A plant can be completely black and still live.

_____ 4. Plants will not grow well during a drought such as sometimes happens in the Midwest.

_____ 5. Since plants release carbon dioxide as a result of photosynthesis, they probably should not be given to patients in the hospital.

III. Using information that you have read or already knew, put a check ✓ in the blank beside any statements below that you and the author would agree with.

_____ 1. If you are given a plant, it is helpful to place it near a window at least some of the time.

_____ 2. If you are given a plant, it should only be watered about one time every two or three weeks.

_____ 3. If your plant's leaves all begin to turn yellow, photosynthesis probably is not occurring properly.

_____ 4. If a person raises plants in a greenhouse, he or she probably is trying to improve photosynthesis.

Answer Key for "How Plants Make Food"

I.

    1. X

    4. X

    5. X

II.

    1. X

    2. X

    4. X

III.

    1. X

    3. X

A SELECTIVE GUIDE-O-RAMA FOR IMPROVING COMPREHENSION IN CONTENT READING

A useful strategy for improving comprehension and retention with students at the middle and upper level reading levels is called the *Selective Guide-o-Rama* and was developed in its present form by Cunningham and Shablak. (Adapted from Dick Cunningham and S. L. Shablak, "Selective Guide-o-Rama: The Content Teacher's Best Friend," *Journal of Reading,* February 1975, pp. 380-382.) In some ways it is a modification of a traditional *content study guide.*

This technique is designed to help students locate the main ideas and important details in a content textbook chapter and to teach them flexibility in their reading. This strategy assumes that most students are not "experts" in the subject matter material they are reading, and that they cannot select the most important information in the textbook material as if everything in the chapter were equally important. The content instruction, however, should guide students through a content reading assignment by giving them clues as to which information is important and which material they can read rapidly.

Therefore, a Selective Guide-o-Rama is designed for students in middle school and above who need additional help in understanding and studying their content material. Before the content teacher formulates such a guide, he or she must decide what students should know and what they should be able to do when they finish reading the chapter.

The content teacher can follow approximately these six steps in using this strategy:

1. The content teacher first must identify the important information in the textbook chapter he or she wants the students to understand and remember.

2. The teacher then goes through the content textbook and selects those portions of the text that provide students with the previously selected important information. The teacher marks the margin with the letter **M** for *main ideas* and **D** for *important details.*

3. Then the teacher should imagine he or she has already completed the introduction to the lesson (such as with the Directed Reading Activity or the Directed Reading-Thinking Activity—see an earlier portion of this chapter for a description of DR-TA).

4. The teacher then constructs the guide in a way in which the students will recognize the important information in the content reading assignment.

5. The teacher should point out unimportant as well as important information to show students they must be flexible in their reading.

6. The completed guide should be in logical order and should move the students from the beginning of the chapter through the end.

Note: The Selective Guide-o-Rama strategy can be used for several months and then removed gradually. It may work best with those students who need extra help and who can profit from a very structured approach used to teach these skills. *If you wish, the instructor can design a cassette tape-recorded version of this technique if the student cannot read a printed copy.* For example, the teacher can tell the student: "Turn the recorder off and read the first two paragraphs on page 35 very carefully. When you have finished, turn the recorder on again, and I will discuss the material that you have read."

Reproducible Selective Guide-o-Rama

Here is a sample Selective Guide-o-Rama from the content area of science at about the fifth-grade level. The teacher can duplicate and use this guide in its present form if the appropriate content textbook is available. However, much more important, it can serve as a model for constructing your own Guide-o-Ramas from your own content textbooks at the appropriate reading level.

Name _____ Grade _____ Teacher _____ Date _____

SELECTIVE GUIDE-O-RAMA
(Fifth-Grade Level)

(Mallinson, George G., Jacqueline B. Mallinson, Linda Froschauer, James A. Harris, Melanie C. Lewis, and Catherine Valentino, Chapter 4, "Biomes," *Science Horizons,* Grade 5. Morristown, NJ: Silver Burdett & Ginn, 1991, pp. 120-155.)

Now that we already have briefly discussed what you now know about *biomes* and what you want to learn about this topic in science, read the chapter. If you use this Guide-o-Rama, it should help you better understand and remember what is the important information in this chapter.

Page 124—You should remember the definition of the term *climate.*

Page 125—You should remember the definition of the term *biome.*

Page 125—Look at the *biomes map* at the top of this page. In which *biome* do you live?

Page 126—You should study the chart entitled *Average Precipitation and Temperature of Land Biomes* very carefully.

Page 127—The chart on this page can be skimmed for a general impression.

Page 128—You should remember the definition of the term *tundra.*

Pages 129-130—You should remember the definition of the term *permafrost.* The rest of this section should be read fairly carefully.

Page 131—You should remember the definition of the term *deciduous forest.* You also should learn the meaning of the term *taiga.*

Pages 132-133—Read this section for a general impression.

Page 134—You should remember the definition of the term *deciduous forest.* You also should learn the meaning of the term *temperate.*

Pages 135-137—Read this section for a general impression.

Page 138—You should remember the definition of the term *tropical rain forest.*

Pages 139-141—You should read this section fairly carefully.

Pages 142-143—You should read this section carefully. Why do you think the tropical rain forests are so important to all the people in the world?

Page 144—You should remember the definition of the term *grassland.*

Pages 145-146—You should read this section for a general impression.

Page 148—You should remember the definition of the term *desert.*

Pages 149-150—You should read this section for a general impression.

Page 151—You should study this chart very carefully. Can you remember the **main** features of each of the *biomes* found on the earth? You should be able to do this.

Pages 152-153—You should be able to complete the end of Chapter 4 activities very well. Are you able to do this successfully?

SEMANTIC WEBS (MAPS) FOR IMPROVING COMPREHENSION IN CONTENT READING

As was described in detail in Chapter 3, *semantic webs* also have a number of other names. They are sometimes called *semantic maps, story maps, think-links,* or *advance organizers.* There is very little difference among all of them although usually a semantic web means that the vocabulary or concepts included in the web are written inside of circles, while a semantic or story map indicates that the vocabulary or concepts are written in boxes or in some other way.

Since this strategy is very helpful for improving vocabulary in content reading as well as improving comprehension in content reading, it was described in some detail in Chapter 3. Therefore, you are encouraged to refer to that chapter to refresh your memory on how to construct semantic webs (maps) and then to use this strategy if you need to do so. In addition, semantic webs and maps can be used to motivate writing both *before and after* reading content material.

However, since the *story map* was not described in detail in Chapter 3, it is mentioned now. A story map is very useful in *literature,* and it must be modified slightly to teach *story grammar.* A story grammar or story structure can involve helping students to recognize the setting, the plot, and the resolution of a story. The more formal story map can include the following elements.

STORY MAP

The Setting

> Characters

> Place

The Problem

The Goal

> Event 1

> Event 2

> Event 3

> Event 4

> Event 5

The Resolution

A Series of Questions That Are Related to the Story

Adapted from *Reading Comprehension: New Directions for Classroom Practice,* 2nd Edition by John D. McNeil. Copyright 1987, 1984, by Scott, Foresman and Company.

To summarize, semantic webs (maps) can be used as a pre-reading device—a way of eliciting from students the prior knowledge they have about a topic. Instead of randomly writing all of the concepts and vocabulary terms before reading, the teacher attempts to organize them under the appropriate headings as the discussion continues. Semantic maps also can be used as guides during reading as students add to their own personal webs (maps) while they read a selection silently. In addition, they can be used as post-reading guides for review. Semantic webs (maps) also can be used to motivate writing as in *K-W-L Plus* which was described earlier in this chapter.

Reproducible Semantic Map for Improving Content in Social Studies

The chapter now includes a passage at about the fifth-grade level on the topic of the voyage of Christopher Columbus to the "New World" from the content area of social studies. It then contains a partially completed semantic web that was constructed from this passage. If you wish, several students can work together to complete it. You may duplicate this web and use it in its present form or use it as a model in constructing semantic webs (maps) from the content material your students read. No answer key is included as the items that can be used to complete the semantic web may vary somewhat among students.

You also are encouraged to help students formulate their own versions of semantic webs (maps) from their content materials. It often is most effective if several students can work together on constructing a semantic web (map).

SEMANTIC WEB
(Approximately Fifth-Grade Level)

Read this passage about the voyage of Christopher Columbus to the "New World" silently. After you have read the passage carefully, you should finish the partially completed *semantic web* that is found after the passage. You can refer back to the passage as you are completing the semantic web if you want.

THE VOYAGE OF CHRISTOPHER COLUMBUS
TO THE "NEW WORLD" IN 1492-1493

What was the perilous, exciting voyage that Christopher Columbus and his men made to the "New World" really like? You will learn about it by reading this passage.

Columbus was born in Genoa, Italy, the son of a wool merchant. While still a young man, he sailed to Africa and England. When he lived in Portugal, he was a *cartographer*, or map maker, and he also made many other voyages. During that time he started thinking about reaching China and Japan by sailing **westward** to them. Although Columbus understood that the world is round, he was unaware that the continents of North and South America were located between Europe and the Orient. Columbus wanted to be able to sail to the Orient to find gold, silk, precious gems, and spices. All of these things had been brought to Europe overland by long, exhausting caravan journeys.

By early August, 1492, Columbus had finally convinced Queen Isabella and King Ferdinand of Spain to finance his expedition to the "New World." Columbus and his men would sail on the *Santa María,* the flagship, and the *Niña* and the *Pinta, caravels,* which were fast and easy to sail. Columbus was the captain of the *Santa María,* while Martín Alonso Pinzón, a famous navigator, was captain of the *Pinta,* and Vicente Yañez Pinzón was captain of the *Niña.* The sailors were all experienced and in good health. On the voyage they ate vegetable soup, salted meat, soaked hardtack, cheese, and pickled sardines. They also caught some fresh fish. The sailors slept in the open between their watches.

Finally, after a voyage of nearly three months, the three ships landed at San Salvador, a small island inhabited by peaceful, naked people. Later Columbus and his men landed at what is now Cuba and explored it. Still later, the *Pinta* disappeared, and the *Santa María* ran aground on a reef and had to be abandoned. On January 16, 1493, having located the *Pinta,* Columbus set sail for Europe on the *Niña.*

On April 20, 1493, Columbus had arrived back in Spain and was honored as a "hero" by King Ferdinand and Queen Isabella in Barcelona, Spain. Columbus showed them proof of his exploration of the "New World"—parrots in cages, pieces of pure gold, skeins of cotton, amber, multicolored feather headdresses, and many unknown plants. The king and queen then held a banquet in Columbus's honor. By this time all of the hardships he and his men had endured were all but forgotten—rough seas, violent storms, a wrecked ship, poor food, and sleeping out in the open. All of these hardships were forgotten in the satisfaction of having successfully sailed to the "New World." Columbus and his men were considered to be true heroes in all of Spain.

SEMANTIC WEB
(Approximately Fifth-Grade Level)

(cont.)

SEMANTIC WEB
THE VOYAGE OF CHRISTOPHER COLUMBUS
TO THE "NEW WORLD" IN 1492-1493

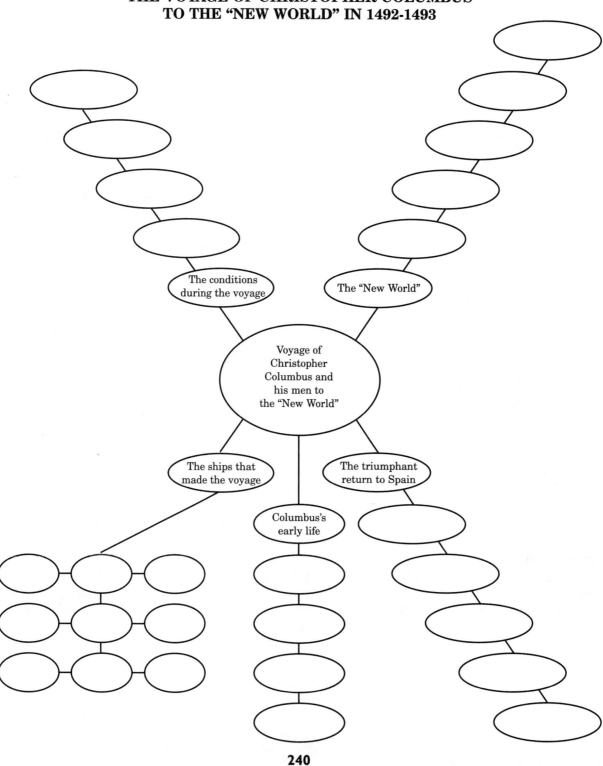

© 1997 by John Wiley & Sons, Inc.

USING THE GUIDED READING PROCEDURE FOR IMPROVING COMPREHENSION AND RETENTION OF CONTENT MATERIAL

The *Guided Reading Procedure* is most appropriate to use while students are reading content assignments at the middle and upper levels. It can improve students' ability to formulate their own implicit (interpretive and critical) questions, develop their use of self-correction while reading, and improve their ability to organize information.

Briefly here are the steps of this procedure and how you can implement it:

1. *Prepare the Students to Read the Assignment*—The teacher should use some kind of prereading activity such as the *Directed Reading-Thinking Activity (DR-TA)* before the the students read the content material. The students should understand why they are to read the material.

2. *Students Read and Remember the Information*—Remembering their purposes for reading, the students should be directed to read the material silently and then turn the material face down when they have completed the reading. When most of the students are finished, the teacher asks the students to retell (tell back) what they remember, and writes what is given using abbreviations if possible.

3. *Return to the Material for Additional Facts and Corrections*—When the students cannot remember additional information, they are allowed to look at the material again, and the teacher writes the additional information on the chalkboard.

4. *Organize the Remembered Information*—The students are now to organize the material into a modified outline form. The outline should show the main ideas and supporting details. Questions such as these can be used: "What happened first in this material?" "What happened next?"

5. *Give Students Thought-Provoking Questions*—The teacher next helps the students see how the new information relates to material they already have learned (prior knowledge). In a gradual manner the teacher gives the students more independence in finding out how the new material relates to previously learned material such as by saying: "Do you see how this information and what we learned last week are related?"

6. *Test Students on Their Knowledge of the Material*—Since this strategy is very intense and demanding, the teacher should check students' recall of the concepts that were presented by providing a short quiz to show how much they have learned by using this procedure. Any type of test format can be used for this purpose. (Adapted from Anthony V. Manzo, "Guided Reading Procedure," *Journal of Reading,* 18, January 1975, pp. 287-291.)

Reproducible Example of the Guided Reading Procedure

The following is a reproducible example of the guided reading procedure from social studies on the topic of Omaha Beach during the D-Day Invasion in World War II. You can duplicate and use it in its present form or modify it in any way you wish in light of your own students' interests and needs if it seems applicable. However, it also can serve as a model for you in using this strategy with your own students in reading content assignments, especially in social studies and science.

THE GUIDED READING PROCEDURE
(Approximately Seventh- or Eighth-Grade Level)

I. Preparation for the Reading Assignment:

1. What do you know about "D-Day" which happened near the end of World War II?

2. What do you know about Omaha Beach on the Normandy coast of northern France during D-Day?

3. What do you think are some of the important concepts (ideas) you might need to learn about D-Day and Omaha Beach?

4. What is your major purpose for reading this passage about D-Day and Omaha Beach?

II. Silent Reading

Now think about the questions that you posed and your purposes for reading and then read this passage about Omaha Beach to yourself. *When you are finished, turn the material face down on your desk.*

OMAHA BEACH

No one likes to think about any kind of war as it has been said that "War Is Hell," and that statement is certainly true. However, it is important to remember past wars in which the United States has participated to understand the great sacrifices that American men and women have made to preserve our freedom. The surviving men and women who served so bravely in World War II are now getting older and will all be gone sometime in the not-too-distant future. Therefore, it is important to honor the contributions of World War II veterans, both living and dead.

The Allied force participated in the enormous invasion of the Normandy coast of northern France in early June, 1944, to liberate the French people whose country had been invaded and held by German forces. The liberation force was the largest number of men and equipment ever assembled for such a purpose in the history of the world.

One of the heaviest losses of American troops occurred at a section of the Normandy coast called *Omaha Beach* where countless American men lost their lives. These men crossed the English Channel to the Normandy coast on June 6, 1944. The seas were very rough and the weather was terrible, adding to the difficulty of the operation. Another great difficulty was the weight of all the equipment the men had to carry—some of which weighed as much as 68 pounds. Then, too, because of the miserable weather, the aircraft did not bomb the German forces high on the bluffs as they were supposed to do.

Some of the men drowned in the rough seas even before they could wade ashore after leaving their landing crafts several hundred yards off shore. Even if a man reached the shore successfully, most of the time his rifle, gun, or machine gun was damaged by the salt water of the English Channel and would not fire. Thus, he had no real defense against the artillery, mortar-fire, and machine gun fire of the Germans who were high up in the bluffs.

When the men who were able to do so finally reached Omaha Beach, they were perfect targets for the German soldiers who were high above them. Many, many Americans were killed on Omaha Beach without ever having a chance to climb up the bluffs.

THE GUIDED READING PROCEDURE
(Approximately Seventh- or Eighth-Grade Level)

(cont.)

However, the Germans lost Omaha Beach by failing to come down from the bluffs to the beach to kill the remaining Americans, many of whom were unarmed. Instead, they never left their bunkers in the bluffs, and a few brave men were able to crawl to the top of the bluffs without getting killed.

Finally, Omaha Beach and the bluffs above it were taken for the Allies, and later Normandy and all of France were liberated from the Germans by the Allied Forces. The D-Day Invasion was a major turning point for the Allies in World War II. However, the casualties were very great. Although almost everything that could go wrong during the invasion had gone wrong, the Allied invasion had been successful due to the bravery and perseverance of the troops and some good luck.

Let us never forget the horror of war in the hope that wars will cease to exist. What could be more terrible than what happened at Omaha Beach on June 6, 1944? I can't imagine anything else much worse, can you?

III. The teacher should now say, *"Now tell me everything that you can remember about the passage about Omaha Beach."*

IV. The teacher then says: *"Now look at the article again and see what additional information you can learn about Omaha Beach and notice anything on the chalkboard that is not correct."*

V. The teacher now adds the new information to the chalkboard.

VI. *Outline of the Omaha Beach Passage*

    I. Importance of Remembering What Happened at Omaha Beach

        A. _____

        B. _____

        C. _____

    II. Purpose of the D-Day Invasion

        A. _____

        B. _____

        C. _____

    III. Beginning of the Invasion at Omaha Beach

        A. _____

        B. _____

        C. _____

        D. _____

        E. _____

THE GUIDED READING PROCEDURE
(Approximately Seventh- or Eighth-Grade Level)

(cont.)

IV. As the Troops Neared Omaha Beach

    A. _____

    B. _____

    C. _____

V. After the Troops Reached Omaha Beach

    A. _____

    B. _____

VI. Reasons the Germans Lost Omaha Beach

    A. _____

    B. _____

    C. _____

VII. Result of the Invasion at Omaha Beach

    A. _____

    B. _____

    C. _____

    D. _____

    E. _____

VIII. Conclusion

    A. _____

VII. *Thought-Provoking Questions*

"How does this information compare with what you already knew about Omaha Beach?"

"What have you learned about the truth of the statement 'War Is Hell'?"

"What have you learned from reading this passage that you can apply to your own life?"

"Tell me how this material compares with or is different from the material you have read about the Civil War."

THE GUIDED READING PROCEDURE
(Approximately Seventh- or Eighth-Grade Level)

(cont.)

VIII. True-False

T   F   1. The invasion at Omaha Beach during D-Day occurred on June 6, 1946.

T   F   2. One major purpose of the invasion at Omaha Beach was to liberate the French people at Normandy.

T   F   3. The weather conditions for the invasion at Omaha Beach were fairly good.

T   F   4. Many of the guns refused to fire because they had been immersed in salt water.

T   F   5. The German forces lost Normandy because they didn't come down from the bluffs.

Multiple Choice

6. Many Americans lost their lives at Omaha Beach because

    a. the weather was miserable

    b. their rifles and guns would not fire

    c. the aircraft did not bomb the German troops as had been planned

    d. all of the above

7. Because the German troops were in the bluffs above Omaha Beach

    a. the Americans could defend themselves well

    b. they had a difficult time firing at the Americans

    c. the Americans on the beach were easy targets

    d. they could not see Omaha Beach very well

8. The Germans lost Omaha Beach because

    a. they did not come down from the bluffs

    b. they did come down from the bluffs

    c. they could not shoot very well

    d. they were not very committed to their cause

9. The result of the invasion of Omaha Beach was

    a. Normandy was liberated

    b. the Germans were victorious

    c. the Americans retreated back to England

    d. Germany was liberated

THE GUIDED READING PROCEDURE
(Approximately Seventh- or Eighth-Grade Level)

(cont.)

10. The main thesis of this passage is

    a. the American troops were brave

    b. the German troops were foolhardy

    c. Omaha Beach was a terrible event in American history

    d. war should be avoided if at all possible

Answer Key for "Omaha Beach"

Outline of the Omaha Beach Passage

(The answers on the outline are included only for illustrative purposes. A student's answers can vary somewhat from these and be correct.)

I. Importance of Remembering What Happened at Omaha Beach

    A. People should learn that "War Is Hell"

    B. People should remember the sacrifices that were made to preserve our freedom

    C. Most World War II veterans are nearing the end of their lives

II. Purpose of the D-Day Invasion

    A. Liberate France from German control

    B. Try to turn the tide of World War II to the Allies

III. Beginning of the Invasion at Omaha Beach

    A. Omaha Beach was a part of the Normandy coast

    B. Crossed the English Channel on June 6, 1944

    C. Rough seas

    D. Terrible weather

    E. Weight of the equipment

IV. As the Troops Neared Omaha Beach

    A. Men drowned in the rough seas

    B. Men and equipment got soaked

    C. Rifles and guns would not fire

V. After the Troops Reached Omaha Beach

    A. Perfect targets

    B. Many Americans were killed or wounded

VI. Reasons the Germans Lost Omaha Beach

    A. Didn't come down from the bluffs

    B. Some Americans were able to crawl up the bluffs

    C. Some Americans were extremely brave

VII. Result of the Invasion at Omaha Beach

    A. It was taken for the Allied Forces

    B. Normandy was liberated

    C. Later all of France was liberated

    D. A turning point in World War II

    E. Successful due to the perseverance and bravery of the troops and good luck

VIII. Conclusion

    A. The hope that wars will never again exist

True-False

1. F
2. T
3. F
4. T
5. T

Multiple Choice

6. d
7. c
8. a
9. a
10. d

USING VISUAL IMAGERY TO IMPROVE COMPREHENSION AND RETENTION OF CONTENT MATERIALS

Although *visual imagery,* also known as *mental imagery,* has often been presented in school as a way of appreciating literature, it usually has not been taught as a strategy for improving comprehension and retention. However, it can be very effective for these purposes if the content material lends itself to making mental images of what is read. In many instances, students do not use this strategy unless they have instruction and practice in doing so.

Although the use of visual imagery can be extended in the intermediate grades and above, it usually should begin in the primary grades. As an example, G. M. Pressley taught eight-year-old children to construct mental images for the sentences and paragraphs they read. When he compared these children with a control group whose members merely read the story, the imagery group remembered more of the story's events (G. M. Pressley, "Mental Imagery Helps Eight-Year-Olds Remember What They Read" in *Journal of Educational Psychology,* 68, January 1976, pp. 355-359).

John D. McNeil illustrated one useful strategy for helping students find out what is important in reading material and change this material into mental images. This procedure is called *Mind's Eye* and consists of the following parts:

1. *Key Words*—Students should be taught to recognize important words in sentences and passages. Have students first underline *key words,* and then form mental images only from these key words. Later have students select key words on their own and immediately create mental images for them.

2. *Discussion of Imageries*—After silent reading of key words, ask students questions that help them make clear mental images. *What type of pictures do you see about these words?* The discussion also can focus on prediction: *What do you think might happen next?*

3. *Oral Reading*—After discussing their mental images, have students read orally to verify that their images reflect the material.

   If you want to evaluate the possible value of visual imagery in improving the comprehension and retention skills as students read various types of content materials, first discuss its usefulness and model how it can be helpful to your students. You may want to use an adaptation of the following strategy that is somewhat based on the one described by McNeil:

1. Select content reading material that is unfamiliar to the students and is very good for stimulating visual imagery.

2. Divide the large group into two random groups.

3. Read the entire passage to both groups. Ask the members of one group to draw several pictures that depict what is described in the passage. Ask the members of the other group to draw several pictures of anything that interests them.

4. Several days later ask the students in both groups to write a short summary of what was found in the passage.

5. Evaluate the summaries in terms of main ideas and significant details.

6. Determine whether the group that formulated visual images seemed to remember more of the passage that the group than did not.

   According to McNeil, this strategy probably can be begun at about the third-grade level and may be effective from that level on. (Adapted from John D. McNeil, *Reading Comprehension: New Directions for Classroom Practice.* Glenview, Illinois: Scott, Foresman and Company, 1984.)

Reproducible Activity Sheet Using Visual Imagery to Improve Comprehension and Retention

The following is a reproducible activity sheet about lizards from the content area of science on about the fifth-grade level that uses visual or mental imagery to improve comprehension and retention. You can duplicate and use this activity sheet in its present form if it seems applicable or modify it in any way you wish. However, perhaps more important, it can serve as a model for constructing your own activity sheets for improving the comprehension and retention of content materials by using the strategy of visual or mental imagery.

Name _____ Grade _____ Teacher _____ Date _____

USING VISUAL IMAGERY AS AN AID TO
READING COMPREHENSION AND RETENTION
(Approximately Fifth-Grade Level)

Read this passage about *lizards* to yourself. Then follow the directions to complete the rest of the activity sheet.

LEARNING ABOUT LIZARDS

Do you think you would like to be a lizard? Certainly, if you were a lizard, your life would be very, very different. In what ways do you think it would be different? You will learn some of the ways in which it would be different by reading this passage.

For one thing, a lizard is a cold-blooded animal, or *ectotherm*. However, this does not mean that a lizard's blood is cold. Rather, it means that lizards must depend on heat absorbed from their environment to keep their bodies at the correct temperature. Thus, when a lizard needs to adjust its body temperature, it must move to a cooler or warmer spot. As soon as a lizard gets up in the morning, for example, it has to find a place to warm up. After it has warmed up its body, it must then find a shady spot. That is why lizards are often seen constantly moving from sun to shade and back again—quite a lot of trouble, don't you think?

Most lizards have good eyesight and mainly use vision to spot prey and predators. They have two primary eyes, one on each side of their face and a third eye which is in the middle of the lizard's forehead. This third eye is used as a light meter to determine when the lizard has been out in the sun too long. Although lizards also can hear fairly well, they are essentially voiceless animals. Lizards also have a chemical sense that is called the *vomeronasal system* that is a little like smell and taste but different from both of them. A lizard uses its vomeronasal system when it sticks out its tongue. For some lizards this sense is important in finding food and locating a mate.

Various kinds of lizards live in different types of places on the land. Different types of lizards live in deserts, jungles, the banks of rivers, the edges of oceans, in caves, and in the tops of trees. Various kinds of lizards have adapted to their particular environment in ways such as by having a crest, spiny scales on each toe, a prehensile tail, and ribbed foot pads. Each of the adaptations helps lizards to live successfully in their particular environment.

Many lizards also can change color for various reasons. Some lizards change color according to the temperature or the amount of light they are exposed to. The *chameleon,* for example, changes its color depending upon the light around it from very pale yellowish green to olive green marked with black to very dark brownish green with no spots at all. A lizard's emotions also sometimes can cause it to change its colors. For example, the Indian bloodsucker turns red when victorious in a fight or remains brownish or grayish when it has lost a fight.

If you were a lizard, it is likely that insects would be your favorite food. Most lizards are *insectivorous* and eat spiders, grasshoppers, beetles, or any other available insect. Many lizards don't stalk their prey but instead remain motionless in one place until a potential meal walks by. Then the lizard grabs the insect with its jaws. A lizard's jaws and teeth usually are very strong. A few of the larger lizards—such as the *gila monster* that lives in the desert—eat eggs of reptiles and birds, baby animals, and nesting birds. Huge *monitor lizards*—which sometimes can reach five or six feet in length—eat rats, eggs, fish, crabs, frogs, and birds.

Yes, your life would be very different if you were a lizard, wouldn't it? I'm very happy that I'm a warm-blooded human, aren't you?

USING VISUAL IMAGERY AS AN AID TO READING COMPREHENSION AND RETENTION
(Approximately Fifth-Grade Level)

(cont.)

Now think about the passage you have just read about lizards. Make several pictures in your mind about the passage and then draw one of the pictures on the back of this sheet.

Using Self-Questioning About the Main Idea for Improving Comprehension and Retention of Content Materials

M. E. D. A. Andre and T. H. Anderson have written about a *self-questioning study strategy* that may improve comprehension and retention of content materials at the middle-grade level and above. In this strategy students are taught to identify the *main idea* of each paragraph as they are reading and then are shown how to *formulate and answer a question* about the main idea. They then repeat this procedure with the next paragraph.

Briefly, here are the main steps to follow in using the self-questioning study strategy:

What—Students are told they will be learning how to ask and answer questions about main ideas of the paragraphs as they read content material.

Why—Students are told this is important because they then will have better comprehension and retention of the content material they are studying.

How—The teacher first models how to identify main ideas in a paragraph. The teacher next decides on one or two words that state the topic of the paragraph. Next, a main idea sentence about the topic is formulated. The teacher then provides several examples of possible main idea sentences for a particular paragraph as well as several unacceptable main idea sentences. Then the students should be shown how to generate and answer a question about the main idea and are provided with several examples of possible questions that could have been formulated for a particular paragraph. Several unacceptable questions also are discussed.

When—Students can be told to employ the self-questioning strategy whenever they are reading content material that seems very difficult to understand and remember. They should then begin again identifying main ideas for the paragraphs and formulating and answering questions about these main ideas. (Adapted from M. E. D. A. Andre and T. H. Anderson, "The Development and Evaluation of a Self-Questioning Study Strategy," *Reading Research Quarterly,* 14, pp. 605-623.)

Reproducible Activity Sheet Using the Strategy of Self-Questioning About the Main Idea

The following is a ready-to-duplicate activity sheet on the topic of the sense of touch from the content area of science at about the middle-school level that illustrates the strategy of self-questioning about the main idea. If it seems applicable in the light of the needs and interests of your students, you can duplicate and use it in its present form. However, more important, it also can serve as a model in constructing your own activity sheets using this helpful strategy from the content material that your students must use. It often is helpful for a student to work with a partner(s) in completing this activity sheet as this strategy can be fairly challenging and thought-provoking.

ACTIVITY SHEET FOR SELF-QUESTIONING ABOUT MAIN IDEAS
(Approximately Middle-School Level)

Read the following passage about the *sense of touch*. Next make a statement of the topic of each paragraph on the line below it. On the next line, write the main idea of the paragraph. Then make up a possible question for that paragraph. You may work with one or several partners in completing this activity sheet. The *first paragraph has been done for you as a model.*

THE SENSE OF TOUCH—MESSAGES OF FEELING

The sense of touch brings you an endless flow of information from the world around you. There are many thousands of tiny sense receptors scattered all over your body. A nerve fiber links each receptor to the spinal cord or brain stem. From there, other nerve cells transmit the messages to your brain. Every time you touch something, the receptors send messages that tell the brain you are feeling something. Then your brain figures out what the sensation actually is and what action you should take, if any.

Topic of paragraph 1: touch is a source of important information _____

Main idea of paragraph 1: There are thousands of tiny sense receptors that tell the brain

what various sensations are and what should be done. _____

Possible question for paragraph 1: How does the sense of touch transmit various sensations to the brain? _____

Touch-pressure, temperature, and injury receptors are located all over your body. Any part of your skin can detect touch pressure, temperature, or injury. However, the different kinds of receptors are not spread evenly over your body. The hands, the feet, and the face contain the most sense receptors. Scientists have determined this fact by placing an instrument that looks somewhat like a drawing compass on different areas of the skin. At first they set the two points of the instrument together and then gradually open the points until the person feels *two sensations* instead of one. The skin of the fingertips can detect the two points when they are only *2/25* of an inch apart, while in some areas of the back the two points can be as much as *three* inches apart before they are detected.

Topic of paragraph 2: _____

Main idea of paragraph 2: _____

_____

Possible question for paragraph 2: _____

_____

ACTIVITY SHEET FOR SELF-QUESTIONING ABOUT MAIN IDEAS
(Approximately Middle-School Level)

(cont.)

Since sense receptors are found all over the body, many of them have to send their messages long distances. While the nerve pathways from your nose to your brain may be only a few inches, the nerve pathways between the receptors in your toes and your brain may be several feet long. If you stub your toe, receptors in your toe create nerve impulses that travel along nerve fibers in the foot and leg. Then the impulses reach the nerve cells of the spinal cord or brain stem and then finally reach the *somatosensory cortex* of the brain. This part of the brain automatically tells you what you should do if any action is necessary.

Topic of paragraph 3: _____

Main idea of paragraph 3: _____

_____

Possible question for paragraph 3: _____

_____

Sense receptors often get used to the feel of an object over a period of time. This is called *adapting*. While some touch-pressure receptors adapt quickly, others adapt quite slowly. For example, if you hold a pet hamster in your hand, you can feel the pressure against your skin. When you first pick up the hamster, all of the touch-pressure receptors in your hand will respond, but some stop responding as long as the hamster remains still. However, when the hamster starts to move, the receptors respond quickly. However, one sensation that you do not get used to is *pain*. Pain tells your brain that something harmful is happening to your body and that you should protect yourself in some way.

Topic of paragraph 4: _____

Main idea of paragraph 4: _____

_____

Possible question for paragraph 4: _____

_____

Answer Key for "The Sense of Touch—Messages of Feelings"

Note: These answers are only for illustrative purposes. Other answers can be equally acceptable.

Topic of paragraph 2: Sense receptors are located in different amounts all over a person's body.

Main idea of paragraph 2: Although touch-pressure, temperature, and injury receptors are located all over a person's body, some areas of the body have more than do others.

Possible question for paragraph 2: What parts of the body have the most touch-pressure, temperature, and injury receptors?

Topic of paragraph 3: how sense receptors send messages to the brain

Main idea of paragraph 3: The way in which sense receptors transmit messages to the brain.

Possible question for paragraph 3: How do sense receptors transmit messages to the brain?

Topic of paragraph 4: Some sense receptors adapt more than others.

Main idea of paragraph 4: Although some sense receptors adapt more than others to the feel of an object, a person does not get used to the sensation of pain.

Possible question for paragraph 4: For what reasons do some touch-pressure receptors adapt more quickly than do others?

USING THE HERRINGBONE TECHNIQUE TO IMPROVE COMPREHENSION AND RETENTION OF CONTENT MATERIALS

One useful study strategy that my teacher-trainees have used very successfully for improving comprehension and retention of content materials is the *herringbone technique.* This strategy helps students locate the important information in content material by asking the six basic comprehension questions—*Who? What? When? Where? How?* and *Why?* An outline is then provided to record this information and thus provide the structure for note taking. The herringbone technique can be used as early as in the second grade although it is used more commonly from the fourth-grade level and above.

A herringbone diagram can be used with either the *fish outline* or in its *traditional form.* In either case, the main idea of the material is written on the center horizontal line, while the diagonal lines contain the answers to the following questions: *Who? What? When? Where? How?* and *Why?* The following questions (or an appropriate variation of them) may be used to motivate students to provide answers to these questions on the herringbone diagram:

Who was involved? (This answer is the name of one or more persons or groups of persons.)

What did this person or group do?

When was it done?

Where was the action accomplished?

How was it accomplished?

Why did it happen?

Note: Students in the upper primary and lower intermediate grades usually enjoy having the herringbone diagram in the fish outline since it seems to be more motivating for them than the traditional outline.

Show either (or both) variation of the herringbone diagram on the chalkboard or a transparency and demonstrate its use to the students. They should *not* be asked to use this strategy until is has been explained and demonstrated to them. They also need some directed practice with it before they are asked to complete it independently. Even then it may be helpful for them to work with a partner in completing the form. Depending upon the material, they can complete a herringbone form as they are reading or after they have finished reading. It usually is more effective to have them complete the form *as* they are reading content material.

As with any content reading assignment, the teacher should first prepare for the instruction by determining what are the most important concepts and vocabulary terms found in that content assignment. Students then can be prepared to read the assignment by using any of the prereading strategies that have been described and illustrated either in Chapter 3 or in this chapter.

The herringbone technique helps students to find the important relationships within the content assignment. After the students have completed this technique, a follow-up group discussion often is valuable. Students can be helped to note that the content textbook does not always provide all of the information that is required to complete the herringbone outline or that some of the information required on the outline is not very important to the comprehension and retention of the material. If students think some of the missing information is important, they may be encouraged to locate it by using a variety of research resources. If the teacher considers some of the answers provided on the form to be rather superficial, additional questioning may help students to understand the material better. Since the herringbone technique asks students to write a statement of the main idea of the chapter on the horizontal line, this is an important step in helping them to understand and remember the most important concept in the content chapter.

Reproducible Herringbone Diagrams

The chapter now contains a passage about Oskar Schindler from the content area of social studies at about the sixth-grade level. It then contains two reproducible herringbone outlines—one in the traditional outline form and one using the fish diagram. You are encouraged to have your students read the passage and complete either herringbone diagram with the information contained in that passage if you think it is applicable to your students. However, more important, the chapter contains the two reproducible herringbone outlines that can be duplicated and then completed by your students using any content material they must understand and remember.

THE HERRINGBONE TECHNIQUE
(Approximately Sixth-Grade Level)

Read this passage silently about Oskar Schindler, a Gentile who helped many Jews during the Holocaust during World War II. Then complete either herringbone outline that follows the passage with the necessary information. You may refer back to the article if you wish.

OSKAR SCHINDLER—THE GENTILE WHO SAVED MANY JEWS

Oskar Schindler was a man who seemed to have many less than desirable qualities. He was a drinker, gambler, wheeler-dealer, briber, and profiteer. Yet he managed to save 1,200 Jews from death during the Holocaust that occurred during World War II by using all of his many "talents."

Oskar became a Nazi when he was a sales manager of an electrical company since his Nazi badge helped him, to get orders when he visited German companies. However, Oskar was not pleased about being a Nazi when Hitler's troops began invading other European countries in the late 1930s. In fact, he was appalled at how the Nazis treated the Jewish people. Even so, when a Nazi intelligence officer suggested that Oskar obtain military and industrial information in Poland while he traveled for his company and then supply it to the Nazis, he agreed.

In Poland Oskar took charge of a factory that made mess kits and field kitchenware for the German Army and became wealthy and influential. After the Nazis started to persecute the Jews in the area, Oskar became disgusted with the Nazis and began to hire Jews for his factory, soon employing 150 of them. By 1941 those Jews who worked for Oskar received a blue sticker that allowed them to go in and out of the Jewish ghetto where they lived so that they could go to work. Later Oskar added a night shift and hired even more Jews. He told them that as long as they continued to work for him, they would be safe.

In addition to hiring more and more Jews, he continued to make more deals with the Germans. After he heard that the Jews who lived in the Jewish ghetto might be killed, he even allowed the Jews who worked for him to sleep in his plant on cots.

Although Oskar was arrested by the Nazis several times for protecting Jews, each time his influential friends managed to get him out of prison. He then still went on helping his Jewish employees. When he heard that all of the Jews who lived in the ghetto probably would be executed, he decided to build a camp right in his own factory yard where his Jewish employees could live. Because of his persuasiveness, the Nazis allowed him to do just that. At that time 1,200 Jews lived under fairly good conditions at this camp.

Finally, in 1944 Oskar received word that his camp would be closed and that his Jewish employees probably would be executed. So he decided to move his plant to Czechoslovakia with as many Jewish employees as possible. At that time 800 men and 300 women were placed on *Schindler's List.* First the men boarded freight trains to go to their new life and work. Unfortunately, the women were not allowed to leave and were instead put into the Auschwitz Camp, where they were scheduled to die. However, Schindler was able to get them out of this camp although even today no one knows exactly how he managed this unbelievable feat. It probably involved many bribes to the officers at the camp.

Schindler's new factory produced virtually nothing, but Schindler wined and dined the Nazi inspectors so much that he was never reported to the head Nazis. At the end of the war, Oskar was penniless but "Schindler's Jews" took care of him for the rest of his life. He and his wife farmed in Argentina for ten years but finally went back to Germany. He went to Israel in 1961 and was recognized as a hero. In 1974 Oskar died in Germany, but at his request is buried in Latin Cemetery in Jerusalem. Oskar was a true hero although a rather improbable one.

THE HERRINGBONE TECHNIQUE
(Approximately Sixth-Grade Level)

TRADITIONAL HERRINGBONE OUTLINE

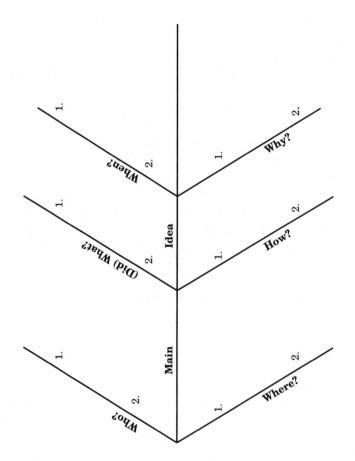

(cont.)

Name _____ Grade _____ Teacher _____ Date _____

THE HERRINGBONE TECHNIQUE
(Approximately Sixth-Grade Level)

HERRINGBONE OUTLINE USING THE FISH DIAGRAM

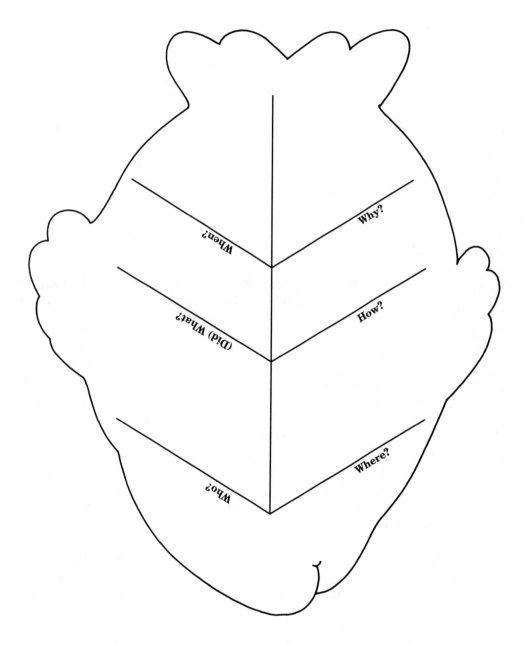

(cont.)

Answer Key for "Oskar Schindler"

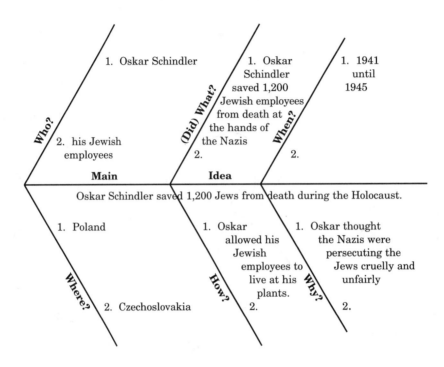

Using Expository Paragraph Frames for Improving Comprehension and Retention of Content Reading

Expository story frames can be used as sentence starters that include *signal words* or *phrases* to fit the paragraph organization. The *sequential pattern of organization* probably is the easiest one for young students to recognize and use.

The teacher can write a paragraph about content material that uses such *cue words* for sequences as *first, next, then, after that, later,* and *finally.* Then copy the sentences on sentence strips, discuss the sequential nature of the material in a group setting, and ask students to arrange the sentences in sequential order in a pocket chart. The students then can read the arranged sentences together. They then can have the opportunity to arrange the sentences individually and copy the paragraph on their papers in paragraph form. Finally, if you wish, they can illustrate the information that was found in the paragraph.

After this procedure has been used several times, this strategy can be *adapted* to the form of an activity sheet that uses a *passage* containing sequentially ordered paragraphs. The teacher can select a content passage that has a definite sequential pattern of organization. Have the students read the passage silently. Then provide them with an activity sheet that provides an expository passage frame that shows sequence for them to complete. This paragraph frame should emphasize the sequential nature of the content passage the students just read. This expository passage frame then provides students with a summary of the content passage, which should help them to understand and remember it better.

Reproducible Example of an Activity Sheet that Uses an Expository Passage Frame

The chapter now includes a reproducible passage about dinosaurs from the content area of science that is written at about the fourth-grade level. Following this passage is a ready-to-use example of an expository passage frame that is based on this passage. You can use this passage and expository passage frame if they seem applicable for your students. More important, the model expository passage frame should serve as a model for constructing such a passage frame from the content materials your students are to read and remember.

ACTIVITY SHEET USING
AN EXPOSITORY PASSAGE FRAME
(Approximately Fourth-Grade Level)

Read this passage about *dinosaurs* to yourself. Then you will have to complete the *expository passage frame* that is found after the passage. You can look back at the passage while you are completing the frame if you want.

LEARNING ABOUT DINOSAURS

Many thousands of years ago, there lived an extraordinary group of animals called *dinosaurs*. They lived for nearly 50 million years and then disappeared from the face of the earth in the most mysterious extinction ever.

Although dinosaur remains have been around for millions of years, people only learned about these extraordinary creatures during the nineteenth century. One of the first people to discover dinosaur bones was an English doctor named Gideon Mantell who collected rocks and fossils as a hobby. In 1820, Dr. Mantell and his wife Ann discovered some large teeth embedded in stone. After a lot of work, Dr. Mantell decided that the teeth and bones had belonged to some kind of giant reptile. However, it was not until 1841 that Dr. Richard Owen, a well-known scientist of the time, decided they should be called *dinosaurs* which means *terrible lizards*.

Dinosaurs, like the reptiles and birds of today, laid hard-shelled eggs. Baby dinosaurs, like baby birds, apparently stayed in their nests no matter what happened to their mother. Dinosaur mothers laid their eggs in hollowed-out nests in the ground, and the mother dinosaur probably brought food back to the nest.

Although many of the dinosaurs were huge, there were some tiny ones that were no bigger than a chicken. The largest dinosaurs that we know about were all plant-eaters, and the biggest dinosaur of all was *brachiosaurus* which weighed 70 tons, was 70 feet long, and stood 39 feet tall—which is about as tall as a four-story building. In contrast, the tiny dinosaurs like *compsognathus* were mainly agile, crafty meat-eaters no heavier than a cat.

Dinosaurs were reptiles that had scaly skin and in some cases armor-plated skin for extra protection. Dinosaur skin was well suited to life on land. Just like reptile skin, it was waterproof, tough, and horny. Waterproof skin prevents an animal from drying out quickly in the air, sun, or wind. Dinosaurs also had very useful tails. Some dinosaurs had long, thin tails that they used like whips for their main form of defense. Others had sharp tail spikes that they used on attackers. All of the dinosaurs that used their tails for defense were four-footed and plant-eating.

Scientists still do not know exactly why dinosaurs disappeared from the earth suddenly about 65 million years ago—perhaps in a matter of months. However, a whole range of swimming and flying reptiles disappeared at about the same time so no one really knows for sure what caused the extinction of all these creatures.

ACTIVITY SHEET USING
AN EXPOSITORY PASSAGE FRAME
(Approximately Fourth-Grade Level)

(cont.)

LEARNING ABOUT DINOSAURS

First this passage _____

_____

_____

_____

Next this passage _____

_____

_____

_____

Then this passage _____

_____

_____

_____

After that this passage _____

_____

_____

_____

Later this passage _____

_____

_____

_____

Finally this passage _____

_____

_____

_____

Answer Key for "Learning About Dinosaurs"

The answers included here are only for illustrative purposes. Other answers can be equally correct.

First this passage *discusses the life and then extinction of dinosaurs.*

Next this passage *describes how the existence of dinosaurs was discovered.*

Then this passage *describes how dinosaur babies were born and lived their early lives.*

After that this passage *describes the size, weight, and eating habits of various kinds of dinosaurs.*

Later this passage *discusses the type of skin and tails that dinosaurs had.*

Finally this passage *says that scientists still do not really know why dinosaurs and other kinds of reptiles became extinct.*

USING TEXT LOOKBACKS TO IMPROVE COMPREHENSION AND RETENTION IN THE CONTENT AREAS

A very obvious but often overlooked way of improving a student's comprehension and retention after he or she has read a content selection is a strategy called a *text lookback*. Obviously, any student should look back in the content textbook or other content material for an answer when he or she is uncertain about it. However, students who do not comprehend well are also not so adept in using text lookbacks to answer questions as are students who are more effective comprehenders.

A strategy has been developed by Ruth Garner and others to improve middle-grade students' use of text lookbacks. The reading or content teacher uses or prepares short, 200-word passages that are printed on two pages. *Two text-based questions* (the answers are found in the material) and *one reader-based question* (the answers are found in the student's prior knowledge) are written on the third page.

Very briefly, the main steps in this procedure are as follows:

What—Students are told they will be learning to *look back* in the content text or other content material to help them answer questions.

Why—Students are told this strategy is important because looking back can help them find the answers to questions. As elementary as this may sound to teachers, a number of students do not use text lookbacks when they would benefit from doing so.

How—The teacher models the text lookback strategy by looking back to the first or second page of the prepared passage to answer the two text-based questions. The teacher then explains that it will not help to look back for the reader-based question as it must be answered from their prior knowledge.

When—Students are told to use this strategy whenever they cannot answer questions about what they have read.

To practice this extremely important strategy, the teacher and students first use several of the short *three-page passage and question sets*. Then they use the procedure with questions written for a two- or three-page segment in their content textbook or some other relevant content material. For independent practice, students first work with several more three-page passage and question sets and then work with questions written for two- or three-page segments in one of their content textbooks. The students can keep a progress chart indicating how many questions they answered correctly and how many times they used the lookback strategy to help them answer questions. (Adapted from Ruth Garner, Victoria C. Hare, Patricia Alexander, Jacqueline Haynes, and Peter Winograd, "Inducing Use of a Text Lookback Strategy Among Unsuccessful Readers," *American Educational Research Journal,* 21, Winter 1984, pp. 789-798.)

A Reproducible Example of a Text Lookback Strategy Sheet

The following is a reproducible example of a text lookback strategy sheet from the content area of arithmetic at about the fourth-grade level. Due to space limitations, it has been printed all on one page, although you can alter it and print it on the three pages that were suggested earlier if you wish. You may duplicate it and use it in its present form if it seems applicable for the needs and interests of your students or modify it in any way you would like. However, more important, it should serve as a model for you of using this type of strategy.

TEXT LOOKBACK STRATEGY SHEET
(Approximately Fourth-Grade Level)

Read the two short passages silently. Then look back at the passages to find the answers to the *text-based questions* and answer them. Write an answer to the *reader-based question* based on your own experience.

(*Page 1*)   Although the origin of numbers as we know them today is not very clear, it is probable that *pebbles* were used to make sure that animal herders brought all of their animals back home. Even today a tribe in Africa checks its animals by putting pebbles into a pouch. If the pebbles and the animals don't match when the animals are back home, the herder knows that there are either too few or too many animals. *Thus, **matching** probably was the first important step in the story of numbers.*

   The second most important step in the story of numbers probably came about from matching. This was the concept of *as many as* (the pebbles and animals matched exactly); *less than* (there were not enough pebbles to match the animals); and *more than* (there were too many animals to match the pebbles).

(*Page 2*)   The third step in the story of numbers also probably came from matching, and this step is the *naming of numbers.* If the people of long ago did match sets of objects like pebbles and animals, they probably noticed that two pebbles always matched two eyes, two ears, two hands, or two feet. Someone may have pointed to his eyes to mean *"as many animals as I have eyes."* After awhile the word for *eyes* was enough to mean *two.* For example, in parts of China the word for *two* is the same as the word for *eyes* and in Tibet the word for *two* is the same as the word for *ears.*

   In trying to trace how numbers were named, *five* is the only other number that we are sure of. Most people of long ago named *five* for the fingers they have on one hand. There are some languages in which the word for *five* and the word for *hand* is the same. A long time ago in our West in Native American picture writing, a hand drawn next to a picture of a tree meant five trees.

(*Page 3*)   Text-Based Question: *What skill probably was the first important step in the history of numbers?*

_____

_____

   Text-Based Question: What probably was the third important step in the history of numbers?

_____

_____

   Reader-Based Question: What things can you think of that you did today that are somehow connected to numbers?

_____

_____

Using Self-Monitoring of Comprehension for Improving Understanding and Retention of Content Materials

Self-monitoring strategies are an extremely effective way to help students improve both comprehension and retention of the content reading they must do. Often students with reading problems cannot monitor or evaluate their own reading comprehension nearly so well as can students who are adequate or above-average readers. Yet the consistent use of *self-monitoring* can greatly improve a student's understanding and remembering of important content material.

Beth Davey and Sarah Porter have developed a four-step instructional procedure they found to be especially effective in improving disabled readers' comprehension monitoring ability. This procedure is designed to help students do the following: understand the purpose of print, focus their attention on meaning while reading, evaluate their comprehension while reading, and develop fix-up strategies to improve both comprehension and retention.

Very briefly, here are the main steps in this procedure:

1. *How*

    a. *The first step involves teacher demonstration and modeling.* Through the use of the cloze procedure (see Chapter 2) the reading teacher can show students that they can understand what they read even if they do not read every word in that passage. *Fix-up strategies* such as rereading, the use of semantic (meaning) clues, or the use of a glossary or dictionary also can be introduced. The reading or content teacher also should model comprehension monitoring while reading aloud to his or her students.

    b. *The second step involves focusing attention during reading on comprehension and consists of a comprehension-rating task.* The students are given simple sentences to read and then rate for comprehension. Some should make sense, while others should not because of incorrect words or faulty logic. Two examples may be the following: *My older brother is much younger than me.* Or *I watched television while I was sleeping and having a nightmare last night.* Working first in small groups and later independently or with a partner, students rate their comprehension of each *sentence* using a + for sentences that they understand and a – or **0** for sentences that they do not understand.

    Later students are given *paragraphs* to read and rate for understanding. Some paragraphs should make sense, while some should not due to sentences that are out of sequence, concepts that do not make sense, or faulty logic. Students in groups and then independently or with a partner rate paragraphs as being sensible by the use of a + or not making sense by the use of a – or a **0.**

    c. *The third step is to help students establish their criteria for understanding which involves a three-point rating task.* First working in groups and then working independently or with a partner, students rate sentences, paragraphs, and longer print material in the following manner. *I understand this very well; I sort of understand it;* or *I don't understand this at all.* The teacher and student then share their ratings for various sentences, paragraphs, and longer passages and discuss their reasons for the ratings. Students then are shown how to locate sources of difficulty in content material. An example of an activity sheet that is somewhat based on this concept is contained later in this section.

d. *The fourth step is devoted to developing fix-up strategies and is implemented when students have developed a competence with the first three steps.* The students should be shown and have practice with both *word fix-up* and *concept fix-up strategies.* Some of the word fix-up strategies may be as follows:

- *Skip the word* if you believe it will not interfere with comprehension significantly.
- *Use context clues* to predict or decode the word. Often an approximate meaning and pronunciation is fine.
- *Use word structure* such as base or root words, prefixes, suffixes, and syllables or meaning units within the word to help determine its approximate meaning.
- *Use graphophonic (phonic) clues* to sound out the word.
- *Use a textbook glossary or a dictionary* to locate the meaning and pronunciation of the word.
- *Ask your teacher, parent, or a classmate for help.*

Some concept-level fix-up strategies are as follows:

- Read on in the content passage.
- Reread just the part you did not understand.
- Ask yourself questions about the material as you read.
- Examine the titles, headings, pictures, and graphic aids carefully.
- Visualize the ideas in your mind as you read.
- Relate the ideas in the material to your own prior knowledge.
- Ask someone to help you understand the passage.
- Change your rate of reading by slowing down for difficult parts and speeding up if the material is easy.
- Hypothesize by saying to yourself: I think the author is trying to say this _____.
- Suspend judgment in the hope that the author will add more information later.

2. ***What, Why, and When***—To be sure that middle- and upper-level students will actually use this method of monitoring their comprehension while reading content materials and then employ appropriate fix-up strategies, it is important for reading and content teachers to do the following:

a. *What*—Tell the students they will be learning how to monitor or evaluate their own reading comprehension.

Why—Tell them this is important because the *only purpose of reading is understanding and sometimes remembering what is read.*

When—Tell students they should monitor their own comprehension every time they read. They should pause at various intervals and ask themselves if they are really understanding what they are reading. If they are not, they should use the appropriate fix-up strategies.

(Adapted from Beth Davey and Sarah H. Porter, "Comprehension-Rating: A Procedure to Assist Poor Comprehenders," *Journal of Reading,* 30, December 1982, pp. 197-202.)

Reproducible Example of a Passage to Use with a Variation of a Comprehension Rating Model for Understanding and Remembering Content Material

The following is a ready-to-duplicate activity sheet that is somewhat based on the previously described model of comprehension monitoring and rating. It is from the content area of science and is on about the fifth-grade level. If it seems appropriate for your students, you can duplicate and use it in its present form. However, more important, it should serve as a model for reading and content teachers in constructing this type of strategy sheet from the content materials that your students must understand and remember.

SAMPLE PASSAGE TO USE WITH A COMPREHENSION RATING MODEL FOR SELF-MONITORING
(Approximately Fifth-Grade Level)

Read the following passage about *giraffes* to yourself. There are some sentences that are not accurate in this passage. Rate each paragraph by placing a + on the line beside it if it makes sense and a − on the line beside it if it does not seem accurate to you.

GIRAFFES

At birth a giraffe calf (baby giraffe) is about six feet tall and weighs between 100 and 150 pounds. During the first few days of the calf's life, its horns actually move around on its skull to which they are attached only by connective tissue. However, very soon the horns become erect as bone begins to replace cartilage. The spots on a giraffe calf are usually paler than those on older giraffes, and the spots may change shape as the calf grows. Although a calf's background color tends to be lighter than its mother's, it darkens with age. A young giraffe is a charming, curious animal. Giraffe herds often have "nurseries" where several older female giraffes watch over all of the giraffe calves while the mother giraffes "browse" some distance away.

_____

Giraffes have buff or tan-colored hides covered with spots of darker brown. These markings can be true spots, *reticulated,* jagged, leafy, or blotched. The spot color ranges from pale yellowish-brown to nearly black. The *reticulated giraffe* is dark chestnut colored and has a network of narrow light-colored lines instead of the much wider light-colored spaces found on all other giraffes. Interestingly, all giraffes look exactly alike. There are many theories as to why giraffes and other animals have spots. Most probably the spots allow them to blend in well with their environment. However, a giraffe does not stand completely still as it should do to blend in effectively with its environment. Its head often projects inquisitively above a tree's leafy top, and it flicks its ears and handsome tail back and forth.

_____

A giraffe has a flexible, columnar neck that is five or more feet long. Since many of a giraffe's neck muscles and tendons alternate, the neck has great force and flexibility. A stiff, brush-like mane runs down the giraffe's neck. A giraffe also has a highly specialized skull that is fairly lightweight for its size because of many sinus cavities that are filled with air. A male giraffe's skull may weigh about twenty-two pounds while a female giraffe's skull averages only about seven and a half pounds. A male giraffe's tendency to engage in sparring matches accounts for the differences in the weight of the skull. These bouts are called *head-slamming* and are very common; they cause an increase in the skull weight since bony humps develop all over the skull. Giraffes have eighty-five teeth, some of which are designed to tear flesh apart as when they attack lions and tigers.

_____

SAMPLE PASSAGE TO USE WITH A COMPREHENSION
RATING MODEL FOR SELF-MONITORING
(Approximately Fifth-Grade Level)

(cont.)

Giraffes spend much of their time *browsing* or feeding on leaves, buds, or twigs of trees and shrubs. They are *ruminants* which means that they chew the browsed food again in a similar way to that of cattle. Ruminants have four-part stomachs, each of which has a unique digestive function. Somehow a giraffe's blood pressure is regulated so that the animal does not black out when it lowers its head between bent or *splayed* forelegs to drink at a water hole. For an animal of its size, a giraffe has a rapid heartbeat which ranges from ninety beats a minute when it is lying down to 170 beats a minute when it is galloping. When injured, giraffes have been found to often bleed to death because they have few superficial blood vessels while the main blood vessels of their limbs lie deep beneath the tendons.

_____

Giraffes are often found in herds although individual giraffes also can sometimes be seen. The area over which an animal roams for feeding, mating, and rearing its young is called the *home range*. A giraffe's home range is estimated to be an area of forty to fifty miles. As can be imagined, giraffes spend most of their time *browsing* especially during early morning and late afternoon. When droughts occur, giraffes can go without water for three to eight days or even much longer. However, when it has the opportunity, a giraffe drinks a great deal of water ranging from two and a half gallons on a cool day to as much as ten gallons on a hot day. In midday, giraffes seem to drowse standing up, but giraffes also do lie down. However, they lie down only when they feel completely safe.

_____

There is much more interesting information that you may want to learn about giraffes. If you do, there are trade books, magazines, and computer software that you can use. Giraffes really are unique, fascinating creatures.

_____

Answer Key for "Giraffes"

+ The paragraph is totally correct.

− The following sentence is incorrect: *Interestingly, all giraffes look exactly alike.* The sentence should be as follows: *Interestingly, no two giraffes have identical patterns.*

− The following sentence is incorrect: *Giraffes have eighty-five teeth, some of which are designed to tear flesh apart as when they attack lions or tigers.* The sentence should be as follows: *Giraffes have thirty-two teeth, some of which are designed to comb leaves from branches.*

− The following sentence is incorrect: *When injured, giraffes have been found to often bleed to death because they have very few superficial blood vessels while the main blood vessels of their limbs lie deep beneath the tendons.* The sentence should be as follows: *When injured, giraffes have been found to bleed very little because they have few superficial blood vessels while the main blood vessels of their limbs lie deep beneath the tendons.*

+ The paragraph is totally correct.

+ The paragraph is totally correct.

THE RELIABILITY OF THE AUTHOR

Students are not often asked to examine the background of an author to determine whether or not he or she may have a particular bias that is demonstrated in his or her writing. However, this is an important aspect of *critical or evaluative reading* which is an extremely important comprehension skill for students to master especially in a democratic society such as ours. Therefore, as students evaluate textbook information, they should always note the source of that information. Most important, they should ask who the writer is and what his or her qualifications are. James Baumann and Dale Johnson suggest that students read with the following questions in mind:

1. What is the source? Is anything known about the author's qualifications, the reputation of the publisher, and the date of publication?

2. What is the primary purpose of the author—information, instruction, or persuasion?

3. Are the statements in the material mainly facts, inferences, or opinions?

4. Does the author rely heavily on connotative words that may indicate some kind of bias?

5. Does the author use negative propaganda techniques? (Adapted from James Baumann and Dale Johnson, *Reading Instruction and the Beginning Teacher: A Practical Guide.* Minneapolis: Burgess Publishing Company, 1984.)

Students should be given these questions to think about and discuss in groups as they read any content selection. In addition, students can be supplied with multiple-choice items that will help them to learn to determine an author's qualifications for writing accurate and unbiased statements on a subject. Such an activity sheet can be used as a motivation for class discussion on a content reading assignment and a debate about the material after reading it.

Reproducible Reliability of Information Activity Sheet

The following is a reproducible reliability of information activity sheet such as was just described. It probably is most applicable at about the sixth-grade reading level. If you wish, a student can complete this activity sheet with a partner. If it seems relevant for use with your students, you may duplicate and use it in its present form or you may modify it in any way you wish. More important, it should serve as a model for constructing your own activity sheet of this type based upon the needs and interests of your students.

RELIABILITY OF INFORMATION ACTIVITY SHEET
(Approximately Sixth-Grade Level)

Read each of the following statements to yourself or with a partner. Then check the source that you believe is the *most reliable* of the three that are included for each of the statements.

1. Colorado is a state that is very rich in natural resources and beauty.

   _____ a. Dr. Barry Jones, a physician who spent his summer vacation in Colorado

   _____ b. James Bartlett, a television producer and director

   _____ c. Dr. Beverly Klaus, a geography professor at the University of Iowa

2. Gorillas are a very intelligent group of animals that are similar to humans in a number of ways.

   _____ a. Sarah Moss, Assistant Director of the San Diego Zoo

   _____ b. Michelle Dement, a kindergarten teacher

   _____ c. Jason Lane, a fishing and hunting guide in northern Wisconsin

3. Harry Truman today is considered one of the better presidents of the United States in this century.

   _____ a. Ed McCowan, an avid reader of books about World War II

   _____ b. Kate O'Hara, a student at Parkside High School

   _____ c. Brad Goodman, an anchorman at KCOZ in Salt Lake City, Utah

4. Even today most women in the work force do not earn nearly so much as most men.

   _____ a. Dr. Pearl Walch, a chiropractor

   _____ b. Dr. Anita Contreras, an economist at the Carnegie Foundation

   _____ c. Dr. Ted Laskowski, a neurologist

5. The cure for many diseases may well be found in plants growing in the tropical rain forests of the world.

   _____ a. George Bentley, a pharmacist

   _____ b. Jane Markham, a researcher at the Simmons Drug Company

   _____ c. Sam Wright, a Certified Public Accountant

6. More people are likely to vote Democratic than Republican in Cook County, Illinois.

   _____ a. Reverend Tom Nelson, a Methodist minister in Chicago

   _____ b. Kevin Rather, a political analyst for the Democratic party

   _____ c. Ellen Goeldi, a homemaker and freelance writer in Chicago

RELIABILITY OF INFORMATION ACTIVITY SHEET
(Approximately Sixth-Grade Level)

(cont.)

7. The Golden Retriever is one of the most docile, trainable dogs.

    _____ a. Ralph Swanson, an American Kennel Club judge

    _____ b. Penny Jensen, a breeder of Golden Retrievers

    _____ c. Craig Kolwicz, a middle school teacher who owns a Golden Retriever

8. If a person wants to travel in some parts of Africa, he or she must get a yellow fever shot.

    _____ a. Mark Garabaldi of the Centers for Disease Control

    _____ b. Marybeth Swenson, a school nurse

    _____ c. Father Harry Boylan of Holy Cross Catholic Church

9. One out of nine women in the United States will get breast cancer sometime during their lifetime.

    _____ a. Jerry Crabtree, a junior high school principal

    _____ b. Meg Anderson, an executive secretary at an insurance company

    _____ c. Dr. Sharon Weaver, an obstetrician/gynecologist

10. Cigarette smoking is a leading cause of death due to lung cancer.

    _____ a. Dr. Susan Mellan, an audiologist

    _____ b. Barry Slakski of the American Lung Association

    _____ c. Sam McClintock, a superintendent of schools

11. On the average women live significantly longer than men do.

    _____ a. Don Leonard, college professor of English

    _____ b. Gabe Jackson, an insurance actuary

    _____ c. Kathy Monaco, a learning disabilities teacher

12. Every adult should engage in some form of exercise on a regular basis.

    _____ a. Reverend Jeffrey Henricks, a Lutheran minister

    _____ b. Sandy Foster, a specialist in sports medicine

    _____ c. Marsha Adams, an assembly line supervisor at an automobile plant

RELIABILITY OF INFORMATION ACTIVITY SHEET
(Approximately Sixth-Grade Level)

(cont.)

13. Having a college degree greatly increases a person's lifetime earning ability.

_____ a. Mary Denny, an attorney

_____ b. Frank Carlock, a newspaper reporter

_____ c. Ed Jefferson, a high school counselor

14. Australia is one of the most interesting countries in the world to visit.

_____ a. Flint Grinnell, a travel agent

_____ b. Perry James, a marketing expert

_____ c. Edith Bellott, a surgical nurse

15. A microwave oven is one of the most useful appliances that a family can own.

_____ a. John Fisher, a high school driver's education teacher

_____ b. Ann Fairbanks, a homemaker and second-grade teacher

_____ c. Bill Porter, an attorney

16. Every person who walks should have well-constructed walking shoes.

_____ a. Dr. Ann Stroink, a college professor

_____ b. Dr. Al Callans, a podiatrist

_____ c. Dr. Ben Goldman, a neurosurgeon

17. Every woman over the age of 50 should have an annual mammogram.

_____ a. Dr. Elaine Maxim, a pediatrician

_____ b. Dr. Paul Kasbeer, an optometrist

_____ c. Sylvia Brenner of the American Cancer Society

18. It is very important for someone to read to a preschool child on a daily basis.

_____ a. Gil McGrath, a kindergarten teacher

_____ b. Lou Deprin, a loan officer at a bank

_____ c. Bob Collander, the owner of an automobile dealership

RELIABILITY OF INFORMATION ACTIVITY SHEET
(Approximately Sixth-Grade Level)

(cont.)

19. It is important for a house, an apartment, a condominium, or a mobile home to have an operating smoke detector.

    _____ a. Dave Rasmussen, a security officer

    _____ b. Jill Miller, a lieutenant with a fire department

    _____ c. Theresa Palmquist, a politician

20. The abuse of alcohol can lead to cirrhosis of the liver.

    _____ a. Dr. Jeffrey Nehring, a dentist

    _____ b. Dr. John Bertsche, an internist

    _____ c. Dr. Karen Frinsko, an orthopedist

Answer Key for "Reliability of Information Activity Sheet"

Note: Although the following answers are the most nearly correct, any answer a student(s) can defend should probably be considered correct.

1. c	**6.** b	**11.** b	**16.** b
2. a	**7.** a	**12.** b	**17.** c
3. a	**8.** a	**13.** c	**18.** a
4. b	**9.** c	**14.** a	**19.** b
5. b	**10.** b	**15.** b	**20.** b

USING CAUSE-EFFECT STORY MAPS AND CAUSE-EFFECT STUDY GUIDES FOR IMPROVING COMPREHENSION AND RETENTION IN THE CONTENT AREAS

Another extremely important critical reading skill students need to learn is the ability to distinguish between *cause-effect relationships* when reading content material, especially in social studies and science. It normally is not productive to ask students to look for causes of events since *without direct instruction and practice,* students often simply neglect this critical reading skill or do not understand it completely.

In addition, locating cause-effect relationships is often difficult because the cause of an event or situation may not be known or may not easily be determined. However, students should practice distinguishing cause and effect because of the importance these relationships have to critical reading and critical thinking. At the elementary level this practice can be achieved through the use of *cause-effect story maps* that show the interrelationships between a series of events. At the middle-school and upper levels *cause-effect study guides* can be very effective for this purpose.

Figure 4-4 is an example of a cause-effect story map that you can examine to determine how one can be constructed. It is from the content area of social studies and is on about the fifth-grade level.

ROSE FITZGERALD KENNEDY

List of Events

1. Rose Fitzgerald Kennedy was born on July 21, 1890, in a humble tenement in Boston, Massachusetts.

2. Rose's father, John F. Fitzgerald ("Honey Fitz"), became mayor of Boston in 1906.

3. After being raised as a devout Roman Catholic and receiving her education, Rose married Joseph P. Kennedy on October 7, 1914, at the age of twenty-four.

4. During the next eight years Rose and Joe had nine children—five girls and four boys.

5. During World War II Rose and Joe's oldest son, Joe Junior, was tragically killed in an air crash while flying on a secret mission.

6. In 1948 Rose and Joe's daughter Kathleen ("Kick") also was killed in an air crash.

7. Since one of Rose and Joe's daughters Rosemary was born mentally retarded, Rose became very active in the cause of mental retardation.

8. Two of Rose and Joe's sons—John, then President of the United States, and Robert—were assassinated in 1963 and 1968, respectively.

9. In spite of all the tragedies that Rose endured during her life, she remained optimistic and strong because of great inner strength and devout religious faith.

10. After several strokes and many years of poor health, Rose Fitzgerald Kennedy, matriarch of the powerful and wealthy Kennedy family—a truly remarkable woman—died on January 22, 1995, at the age of 104.

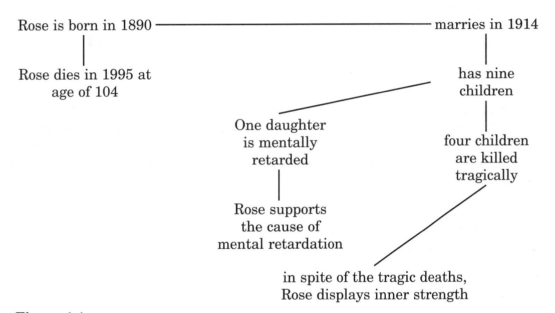

Figure 4-4

Reproducible Example of a Cause-Effect Story Map

The chapter now includes a ready-to-use cause-effect story map from the content area of social studies at about the fifth-grade level. This part of the chapter first contains a passage about Rosa Parks, the African-American Civil Rights pioneer and her struggle for equality. Then the chapter includes a *List of Events* in her life and the beginning of a cause-effect story map that a student can finish independently or perhaps much better with a partner(s). You can duplicate and use the passage and beginning cause-effect story map in their present form if they seem applicable for your students or modify either of them in any way you want. However, what is more important, the cause-effect story map should serve as a model for one that can be constructed from the content materials your students need to comprehend and remember.

 Note: Since any student's cause-effect story map can vary greatly, it is not possible to include an answer key for this activity.

CAUSE-EFFECT STORY MAP
(Approximately Fifth-Grade Level)

Read this passage about *Rosa Parks*, the Civil Rights Pioneer, to yourself. Then independently or *with a partner* read the *List of Events* about her life that follows the passage. Then you can finish the *Cause-Effect Story Map* that has been begun for you. You can refer to the one your teacher showed you earlier to use as a model if you wish.

ROSA PARKS, CIVIL RIGHTS PIONEER

Many young people today have heard the story of Rosa Parks, the 42-year-old African-American woman who refused to ride in the back of a city bus in Montgomery, Alabama, on December 1, 1955, and was quickly arrested. Although Rosa did not plan it, her case became a *court test case* against segregation in the South and led the way to a later almost year-long boycott of the Montgomery city buses by the black people who lived there. All of her life Rosa had thought that segregation was very unfair, and she never could understand why she could not be treated the same as white people.

However, you may not know much about Rosa's childhood or her life before and after the day when she refused to move to the back of the bus. Rosa was born on February 4, 1913, in Tuskegee, Alabama, but spent much of her childhood in Pine Level, Alabama, being raised in her grandparents' home. Her father, James McCauley, was a carpenter and builder, and her mother, Leona, was a teacher. Unfortunately, her parents often were separated since her father worked in other places. In fact, she did not see her father after she was five years old until she was an adult.

Rosa's family always taught her that everyone deserves respect, and that no one should put up with bad treatment from anyone. When she was grown up, Rosa went to all-black schools that were much inferior to those that white children attended. The black schools were small and crowded, and there weren't even any desks for the children to write on. Then, too, the black children went to school for only five months each year, while the white children attended school for nine months a year.

In addition, black people could not drink at the same water fountains as white people or even use the same public restrooms. Neither could they stay in white hotels or live in white neighborhoods. In all these ways, African-Americans were very much *discriminated against*.

In December, 1932, Rosa married Raymond Parks who was just called "Parks." He already was an activist for equal rights for black people, and Rosa supported him in this cause. Rosa became active in the National Association for the Advancement of Colored People (NAACP) in the 1940s and also tried to register to vote, a right that often was denied to blacks. She met Dr. Martin Luther King in 1955 and was very much impressed with his view that minorities should try to gain equal rights in *nonviolent ways*.

After Rosa was arrested on December 1, 1955, for not moving to the back of the city bus, the African-Americans in Montgomery boycotted riding the city buses for almost a year before the United States Supreme Court declared on November 13, 1956 that segregation on public transportation was illegal. This was merely the beginning in the African-Americans' fight for equality in this country, a struggle still going on today.

In 1957 Rosa moved to Detroit where her younger brother Sylvester lived. In 1963 she participated in the huge Civil Rights March on Washington, D.C. with Dr. King, his wife Coretta Scott King, and Reverend Ralph Abernathy among many thousands of others. In 1991 a bust of Rosa Parks was unveiled at the Smithsonian Institution in Washington, D.C.. However, she has never completely gotten used to being a "public person" and does not really like it very much. She still remains in favor of nonviolence for the most part, and she is now called the "Mother of the Civil Rights Movement."

CAUSE-EFFECT STORY MAP
(Approximately Fifth-Grade Level)

(cont.)

ROSA PARKS, CIVIL RIGHTS PIONEER
List of Events

1. Rosa Parks was the first African-American who refused to sit in the back of a city bus in Montgomery, Alabama, in 1955.

2. Rosa was born in 1913 in Tuskegee, Alabama.

3. Rosa's family always taught her that everyone deserves respect regardless of their race.

4. Rosa attended all-black schools that were far inferior to those attended by white children.

5. African-Americans were victims of segregation in many unfair ways during Rosa's childhood and young adulthood.

6. In 1932 Rosa married Raymond Parks who also was an activist for equal rights for blacks.

7. Rosa became active in the NAACP in the 1940s.

8. Rosa's arrest for not moving to the back of the city bus in 1955 became a court test case and resulted in a nearly year-long bus boycott by black people in Montgomery.

9. Rosa continued to be active in the Civil Rights Movement and even today is remembered as the "Mother of the Civil Rights Movement."

CAUSE-EFFECT STORY MAP
(Approximately Fifth-Grade Level)

(cont.)

CAUSE-EFFECT STORY MAP

Now complete this *beginning cause-effect story map* in any way you wish. You can work with a partner(s) if you wish.

Rosa Parks, an African-American, was born in 1913 _____ often faced discrimination as a child and young adult

Reproducible Cause-Effect Study Guide

The chapter now contains a reproducible passage from social studies about the Maya of Central America which is designed for use at about the sixth-grade level. It is followed by a reproducible cause-effect study guide that a student can complete either independently or with a partner. You can duplicate and use both the passage and the cause-effect study guide in their present form if they seem applicable or modify them in any way you would like in the light of the needs and interests of your students.

CAUSE-EFFECT STUDY GUIDE
(Approximately Sixth-Grade Level)

Read this passage about *The Maya, the Native People of Central America,* silently. Then complete the *cause-effect study guide* that follows it either independently or with a partner. You can refer back to the passage while you are completing the study guide if you need to.

THE MAYA, THE NATIVE PEOPLE OF CENTRAL AMERICA

The Maya, the Native American people of Central America, had one of the most amazing civilizations of ancient times. They were an extremely intelligent, innovative people who made significant advances in mathematics, architecture, astronomy, and calendar making. However, they also engaged in human sacrifice and various kinds of blood sacrifice to appease their gods.

The ancient Mayan civilization was mainly found in what are now known as Mexico, Guatemala, Honduras, and Belize. It probably dates from antiquity but may have reached its zenith during the Classic Period that occurred from about 250 A.D. until 900 A.D. During that time many urban centers of commerce, ceremony, and royal rule flourished in the lowlands of the Peten-Yucatan peninsula.

The Maya are usually considered to be the most brilliant mathematicians of early times. They operated a sophisticated number system with only three symbols, a *bar* for *five,* a *dot* for *one,* and a *shell* for *zero.* Amazingly, most of the world's early civilizations had no way to symbolize the concept of *nothing.* The Maya were unique in their ability to symbolize the concept of *zero* with a *shell.* The Maya used the shell, the bar, and the dot in different combinations to indicate the numbers between *0* and *19* and indicated the numbers above *19* by position. Here are several numbers as the Maya represented them:

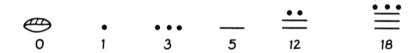

Mayan priests also used mathematics to interpret calendars for marking events in rulers' lives, guiding the agricultural year, determining uses for ceremonials, and recording celestial movements. The Maya recorded their history including dates in *hieroglyphic (picture) writing.* Hundreds of hieroglyphic inscriptions appear on wall panels, *lintels (horizontal pieces of timber or stone over a door, window, or other opening),* and other monuments. The ancient Maya also made flint tools, imported obsidian, and traded in quartzite.

Unfortunately, the Maya of that time also practiced human torture and sacrifice to their gods in the hope that such sacrifices would please them, and the gods would give them such favors as rain or good crops. They even practiced blood sacrifice such as piercing their own tongues in a slanting direction from side to side and passing bits of straw through the holes, which produced terrible suffering.

Today all of those practices have long since stopped although the Christian religion that was brought by the Spaniards to the Maya during the 16th century has been blended with Mayan beliefs. For example, according to the Maya even today the Sun/Christ and Moon/Virgin Mary live in the sky, and the Sun is called *"Our Father"* while the moon is called *"Our Mother."*

CAUSE-EFFECT STUDY GUIDE
(Approximately Sixth-Grade Level)

(cont.)

    The modern Maya living in what is now known as Mexico, Guatemala, Honduras, and Belize have reached somewhat different standards of living because of the different governmental policies in these countries. Today the Maya in the Yucatan Peninsula of Mexico suffer from overpopulation, underemployment, political unrest, and violence. Unfortunately, the Mexican government is now trying to increase industrialization and tourism. However, the Maya in Guatemala have fared even worse by having to work for extremely low wages and having to farm on the steep, infertile mountain slopes. Although the population of Guatemala is one-half Maya, entire Mayan villages have been slaughtered by the Guatemalan Army.

    Many Mayan women today use the art of *weaving* to identify the members of their community. Modern Maya are able to read these traditional codes and contemporary Mayan women rework ancient patterns, slightly varying form, size, and color combinations. Line-by-line sacred symbols such as the movement of the sun (personified as Jesus Christ) are woven into the Mayan cloth. Today rural Mayan men raise *milpa* (maize or corn) while the Mayan women weave, cook, and raise the children. The urban Maya run computers, sewing machines, and other technological equipment. However, all of the Maya of today share an illustrious heritage and a unique inner spirit.

CAUSE-EFFECT STUDY GUIDE
(Approximately Sixth-Grade Level)

(cont.)

Match the *cause* in Column A with the *effect* or result in Column B.

A/Causes

_____ 1. The ancient Maya were a very intelligent, creative people who were very adept at designing architecture.

_____ 2. The early Maya are considered to be the most brilliant mathematicians of early times.

_____ 3. The early Maya developed their own interpretation of a calendar.

_____ 4. The early Maya were adept at hieroglyphics.

_____ 5. It was very difficult to be a captive of the Maya.

_____ 6. The Spaniards brought the Christian religion to the Maya in the 16th century.

_____ 7. The early Maya revered the sun and its rising and setting.

_____ 8. The Maya in Mexico suffer from underemployment.

_____ 9. The Guatemalan Army often discriminates against the Maya.

_____ 10. The contemporary Mayan culture has very traditional gender roles.

B/Effects

A. People today have good records about how the ancient Mayan people lived.

B. The early Maya practiced human torture and sacrifice.

C. Even today the Maya call the Sun, "Our Father."

D. Many of the Maya in Mexico are poor as are a number of other Mexicans.

E. The ancient Maya built beautiful temples to their gods.

F. Entire villages of Guatemalan Maya have been killed.

G. The Maya developed the concept of zero.

H. The events in the Mayan rulers' lives could be documented.

I. Today the Mayan religion combines elements of both earlier beliefs and the Christian religion.

J. The typical Mayan woman of today weaves, cooks, and raises children.

Answer Key for "The Maya"

1. E
2. G
3. H
4. A
5. B

6. I
7. C
8. D
9. F
10. J

EXPLICIT TEACHING APPLIED TO THE CRITICAL READING SKILL OF DISCRIMINATING BETWEEN FACT AND OPINION

The following briefly illustrates how to apply explicit teaching to the higher-level comprehension skill of discriminating between *fact and opinion*. The procedure described also can serve as a *model* for the reading or content teacher to use in constructing his or her own *explicit teaching lesson* about any aspect of comprehension or study in the content fields which are emphasized at either the primary-grade or intermediate-grade level. A few examples might be locating directly stated main ideas, locating implied main ideas, locating significant details, reading and following directions, placing a number of items in correct sequence, and using visual imagery.

I. *Introduction to Skill or Strategy*

The teacher can discuss with the students television advertising and newspaper advertisements that may contain biased statements. The teacher should ask the students how such statements can be evaluated or judged. The teacher can say the following to activate the students' prior knowledge: *"Tell me what you know about statements of fact and about statements of opinion. How are they alike and how are they different?"*

Here are some possible answers:

A fact is always true.

You can prove that a fact is true.

Although an opinion can be true, it isn't always true.

Some people have opinions that are wrong.

A fact is better than an opinion.

The teacher can write all of these answers on the chalkboard or an overhead transparency.

II. *Labeling, Defining, Modeling, and Explaining the Skill or Strategy*

The teacher can say something like this: *"Can any of you give a statement of fact?"*

The teacher then writes examples such as these on the chalkboard or on the overhead transparency. The teacher can provide some of his or her own examples if necessary.

A dog is one kind of animal.

The United States consists of fifty different states.

Abraham Lincoln is buried in Oak Ridge Cemetery in Springfield, Illinois.

I have a yellow cat named Muffin.

It is possible to see lions in some parts of Africa.

The teacher then can say something like this to the students: *"How can you tell whether all of the statements that you made are statements of fact or not?"* The following possible answers then can be written on the chalkboard or on a transparency:

You can read about it in a book.

You can find out about it by using a computer program.

You can see if it is true for yourself.

You can ask someone who knows all about it.

It is important that the students understand that some proof *is required for the statement to be evaluated as true.*

The teacher then can have the students provide some examples of statements of opinion such as the following which are then written on the chalkboard or on a transparency:

The Golden Retriever is the best breed of dog for a family to have.

Colorado has more pretty scenery than Minnesota.

My teacher is the best teacher in our whole school.

Jenny's grandmother bakes the best apple pies in the world.

A tornado is a worse natural disaster than a flood.

Then the teacher attempts to help the students arrive at the generalization that *statements of opinion normally cannot be proven to be true.* At this point the students probably can be given some key words for both statements of fact and statements of opinion. Here are some key words for statements of *fact*: age, location, dates, temperature, and actual physical characteristics such as eyes, nose, and mouth. Here are some key words for statements of *opinion*: beauty, "bestness," goodness, meanness, happiness, sadness, and think.

III. *Guided Practice of the Skill or Strategy*

Next the teacher can say the following: *"If I read that 'The temperature is 88 degrees today,' you can ask yourself if that is a statement of fact. Is it a statement of fact or not?"* Possible Answer: "It's a statement of fact because it's true."

The teacher can say: *"How do you know that it's a statement of fact?"* Possible Answer: "I looked at the thermometer right outside the classroom window."

Next the teacher can say: *"You can prove that the statement is correct. Since we decided that statements of fact contain things that can be proved, even if it is proven to be wrong, it is still a statement of fact. For example, the following statements of fact are still false:"*

Minneapolis, Minnesota, is farther south than Chicago, Illinois.

The White House is in the state of Washington.

Pearl Harbor is near the state of California.

In winter Illinois is warmer than Louisiana.

Omaha is the capital of the state of Nebraska.

The teacher then provides some kind of review such as the following: *"Statements of fact can be proven.* **They can be proven either true or false.** *However, statements of opinion are very difficult or impossible to prove."*

Reproducible Activity Sheet for Discriminating Between Fact and Opinion

The chapter now includes a ready-to-use activity sheet about animals from the content area of science which is designed to be used at about the third-grade level. If it seems applicable for your students, you can duplicate and use it in its present form or you can modify it in any way you wish. However, even more important, it should serve as a model for constructing your own activity sheet of this kind.

ACTIVITY SHEET FOR DISCRIMINATING BETWEEN FACT AND OPINION
(Approximately Third-Grade Level)

Read each of these sentences. Some sentences are *statements of true facts,* some sentences are *statements of false facts,* and some sentences are *statements of opinion.* In the blank before each sentence: write the letters *TF* if it is a statement of *true fact,* write the letters *FF* if the sentence is a statement of *false fact,* or write the letter *O* if the sentence is a *statement of opinion.* Then try to write a place or person that you could use to check your answer such as a science textbook, a library book, a computer program, the encyclopedia, an encyclopedia on CD-ROM, a person, the zoo, or your teacher.

_____   1. A big dog makes the best kind of pet for any child.

_____

_____

_____   2. A chimpanzee is a very intelligent animal.

_____

_____

_____   3. A parrot knows how to talk when it is born.

_____

_____

_____   4. I think a deer is the most beautiful animal there is.

_____

_____

_____   5. A raccoon usually hunts for food at night.

_____

_____

_____   6. Most owls build their nests in trees where their colors make them hard to be seen.

_____

_____

_____   7. A baby kangaroo is born after coming out of an egg.

_____

_____

ACTIVITY SHEET FOR DISCRIMINATING BETWEEN FACT AND OPINION
(Approximately Third-Grade Level)

(cont.)

_____ 8. Baby ducklings usually follow their mother by walking in a row behind her.

_____

_____

_____ 9. The most interesting animal a person can see in Africa is a giraffe.

_____

_____

_____ 10. A baby zebra can stand and run within an hour of its birth.

_____

_____

_____ 11. A roadrunner is a type of bird that lives in the desert.

_____

_____

_____ 12. A lizard makes an excellent pet for any family.

_____

_____

_____ 13. A few farmers are now raising ostriches instead of cattle, sheep, or pigs.

_____

_____

_____ 14. A dolphin usually is a mean mammal.

_____

_____

_____ 15. At birth a baby elephant is quite small.

_____

_____

Answer Key for "Discriminating Between Fact and Opinion"

1. O	9. O
2. TF	10. TF
3. FF	11. TF
4. O	12. O
5. TF	13. TF
6. TT	14. FF
7. FF	15. FF
8. TF	

Ready-to-Use Strategies and Activity Sheets for Improving Writing Skills in the Content Areas

Do you believe that if a student participates in writing activities in the content fields he or she probably also will make simultaneous improvement in reading content materials? Interestingly, the answer to that question usually is "Yes." Research and experience both indicate that when a student practices writing skills, he or she also usually makes improvement in reading and remembering that type of content material. Therefore, most of the strategies and materials contained in this chapter are designed to result in both improved reading and writing ability.

This chapter contains a wide variety of classroom-tested strategies and activity sheets that are useful for improving writing skills in the content fields. However, many of the strategies and materials are equally useful for improving the comprehension and retention of content materials. In addition, they are highly motivating and interesting.

THE IMPORTANCE OF RELATING THE TEACHING OF READING AND WRITING IN THE CONTENT AREAS

The role that writing has in helping students to evaluate their content reading is perhaps best summarized in this statement attributed to E. M. Forster: *"How can I tell what I think until I see what I say?"* As stated earlier, content-area writing activities are especially valuable in helping students simultaneously learn content information and increase language abilities. When students write about what they have read, they become engaged with the ideas and facts that were presented. They then decide what content information is important and which relationships among ideas are worth writing about. They have to make such decisions whether they are just to paraphrase a content passage that they have read or to respond to it through some creative, innovative writing assignment. For example, your students may read about life in the South in the antebellum days just before the Civil War for the purpose of contrasting life at that time with life in the South shortly after the end of the Civil War. With this purpose as a guide, your students could ask themselves questions such as these: "If slavery was important to the economy of the South before the Civil War, what should be said about it? Should its usefulness to the economy receive more emphasis than the terrible suffering and injustice that occurred among the slaves of that time?

On the other hand, it probably is much more important to stress the evils of slavery than it is to stress its contributions to the economy of the South before the Civil War." These examples indicate that even when a teacher provides clear purposes for writing, the students are required to engage in active thinking and decision-making about a topic.

In addition, content writing provides students with opportunities to examine and evaluate their own thinking about the topic they are reading. Reviewing their own writing allows students to confirm their knowledge about a topic. Finally, writing helps students to generate new insights about a topic. As students attempt to compose a passage about a topic—either individually, in a small group, or in the whole class—they frequently discuss relationships among ideas that had never occurred to them before. Indeed, as students write or dictate a passage about something in their own words, they are reorganizing their past experiences. This reorganization is an important part of effective content comprehension and retention.

However, in spite of the inherent importance of relating content reading and writing instruction, reading and writing usually have been taught as separate entities with the most emphasis being placed on *content reading instruction.* It is somewhat shocking to note that "for every $3,000 spent on children's ability to receive information, $1.00 was spent on their power to send it in writing" (Donald H. Graves, "A New Look at Writing Research," *Language Arts* 57, November/December 1980, p. 914). However, content reading and writing instruction always should be related as much as possible. Writing is a *process* that should be integrated with reading and the content areas. For example, *writing is a way to learn social studies and science,* not merely a way to report on what has been learned in those content fields. Instead, writing itself is a useful mode of learning that always should be emphasized in the teaching of content skills both for competent and below-average readers including learning disabled students.

As stated earlier, this chapter contains many useful classroom-tested strategies and materials that can be used very effectively to present and reinforce content writing, comprehension, and retention skills. Most of the strategies and materials contained in this chapter are equally helpful for all of these purposes.

THE VALUE OF TEACHING WRITING AS A PROCESS DURING THEMATIC UNITS IN SOCIAL STUDIES AND SCIENCE

Although writing certainly can and should be related to the comprehension and retention of content materials in any traditional classroom, it perhaps is especially relevant in whole language classrooms that attempt to present all or most of the literacy and content skills together in *thematic units.* Appropriate thematic units can be presented as early as kindergarten and as late as the middle-upper level.

Thematic units from social studies or science can effectively incorporate fiction and content materials as well as *related writing activities* of various types. Such integration helps students to obtain a more complete understanding of the topic. Content reading and writing activities often are simply much more meaningful to students when presented or practiced in the context of relevant units than when presented only in isolation. Therefore, many of the content writing strategies that are explained later in this chapter can be very effectively integrated into appropriate social studies and science thematic units.

You may be able to better understand the types of fiction and content material that lend themselves to thematic units by examining the semantic map at the end of this chapter. You can construct a similar web of reading and writing activities to be used in a thematic unit. The web can serve as a helpful reference since a web is only a reference, not a complete plan. Teachers then must decide on goals and objectives for their units, choose instructional procedures and related activities, gather appropriate materials, schedule unit activities, and decide how to assess the outcomes.

Thematic units integrate information from language arts, social studies, science, mathematics, art, music, and drama. Sets of texts (sets of books on one topic, by the same author, or of the same genre) are helpful in unit instruction. After students read the related texts, they can share or respond to the unit topic in a way that is much more comprehensive than would be the case if only text had been used. Of course, appropriate writing activities also should be included whenever possible.

THE IMPORTANCE OF WRITING NARRATIVE, DESCRIPTIVE, PERSUASIVE OR EXPOSITORY ESSAYS ON CONTENT TOPICS

It is important that students have practice in writing narrative, descriptive, persuasive, or expository essays on a regular basis. Some of these essays can relate to content materials the students are studying. It may be helpful at this point to very briefly describe the basic characteristics of these different types of essays.

Narration. In narrative writing the students tell a story, recount personal experiences, or report observed events. Usually the narrative structure is a chronological account of events. The story assignment requires students to develop a plot and use specific details to elaborate the context, characters, and actions.

Description. In descriptive writing the main purpose is to help the reader visualize what is being described. The students may describe a person, place, or object by using details that appeal to the senses to support and elaborate the essay. Such writing requires the student to observe and organize and also to sometimes analyze, compare, contrast, and imagine. Therefore, a descriptive essay may be relevant in content instruction such as when a student writes a descriptive essay about an historical character or location.

Persuasion. A persuasive composition is written to convince, influence, or motivate an individual or group to act in a certain way. The methods of developing this kind of composition vary according to the intent of the writer and the response to be obtained from the reader. The student should select from among the devices of persuasion the method or methods that best support an argument or point of view. Among these methods are the position approach and the problem-and-solution approach. It is obvious that persuasive essays may be relevant in content writing such as when a student writes a persuasive essay encouraging his or her peers to recycle various kinds of products.

Exposition. In expository writing the aim is to inform or explain. The student must select the best method to present factual information. A student can use a variety of strategies to develop an expository composition. Among them are enumeration, directions, comparison and contrast, and cause and effect. An expository composition focuses on a topic. A well-written expository composition presents a clear thesis statement with supporting details that may include description, examples, explanations, and conclusions. Writing reports in the content areas is a form of exposition. Such an assignment may require a student to analyze, compare or contrast, and infer. It is obvious that expository writing is very relevant in the content fields and should be used often in meaningful ways.

If you want detailed information about how to score each of these types of essays *by holistic scoring* using the criteria of *clarity, support, organization, mechanics,* and *overall rating* on a 1-5 rating scale, you can consult the following source:

Wilma H. Miller, *Alternative Assessment Techniques for Reading & Writing.* West Nyack, New York: The Center for Applied Research in Education, 1995, pp. 389-421.

AUTHOR'S CHAIR

"Author's Chair" is a concept that can be adapted to content writing especially in the primary grades and perhaps in the lower elementary grades. It involves having the child engage in some variation of *process writing* and then sharing it. The basic steps are as follows:

Creating a Topic

Prewriting or Writing a Rough Draft

Conferencing with the Teacher about the Rough Draft

Writing the Final Draft

Editing the Final Draft

Publishing the Final Draft

The student then shares the final, published draft of the story or composition with the class by sitting in the "Author's Chair" while reading it. The "Author's Chair" should be a chair in the classroom that is used only for this sharing. When the concept of "Author's Chair" is adapted to content writing, the student should write mainly expository compositions related to the topic under study in social studies or science, go through the steps of process writing that were summarized earlier, and share the composition with the rest of the class while sitting in the "Author's Chair." Many teachers have found the concept of using an "Author's Chair," although easy to implement, very helpful for motivating students to write on a variety of topics.

CONTENT JOURNAL WRITING AND LEARNING LOGS

An interesting strategy involves having students write regularly in a journal under headings such as *"The Two New Ideas that I Learned This Week in Social Studies (Science) and How I Can Apply Them to My Life"* or *"How I Felt About*

My Progress in Math (Social Studies, Science) Class This Week." Although these entries can be read by other students or by the literacy or content teacher, they should not be graded but instead appreciated for their introspective qualities.

Learning logs, which are sometimes called content journals, are a fairly simple yet effective way to motivate all students to write in content classes. They are used to stimulate thinking. Usually students write in their logs every day either as a during-class activity or as an out-of-class assignment. Students should write entries that persuade, that tell of personal experiences and responses to the content material, that give information, or that are creative and spontaneous. Here is a sample of a learning log assignment that can be used in the content fields:

Read _____, and in your learning log write (*the teacher selects one of the following*:)

- any items from the assignment that are especially interesting to you
- any items from the assignment you cannot understand
- any items from the assignment you agree with
- any items from the assignment you disagree with
- ways in which this assignment relates to your own life
- why you think the material in this assignment is important
- several new concepts you learned from this assignment
- what you think will happen next in the assignment (if applicable)
- several items you would like the class to discuss after reading the assignment
- why you think _____ is important
- what you think the author of the material was like
- your reaction to _____
- a summary of this chapter (section, book)

Reproducible Learning Log

The following is a reproducible learning log that can be used after a student has read a content selection. You can duplicate and use this learning log in its present form or modify it in any way you would like. It is relevant for upper primary-grade students and above.

LEARNING LOG FOR A CONTENT ASSIGNMENT

	Predictions	*Concepts*	*Questions*	*Personal Opinion*
	What may happen in this material?	**What have I learned from reading this material?**	**What don't I understand yet about this material?**	**What do I think about this material?**
Date				

A READING RESPONSE JOURNAL

A *reading response journal* may be very applicable in content reading. Very briefly, it simply provides a student with the opportunity to respond to his or her reading in a written form. Obviously, a student can write some type of response to almost any content reading assignment. It is most relevant to literature, social studies, and science. It may be somewhat less applicable in math. The student in the upper primary grades and above can keep a reading response journal in a variety of formats. Some commonly used formats are a looseleaf notebook or a folder of some type. The student simply records the title and author of the book, story, unit, or chapter on a sheet of paper and then writes his or her reactions to it. These reactions can be in the form of a critical response, an applied response, personal experiences related to the topic, or an emotional response.

A sample sheet from a reading response journal in a looseleaf format might be the following:

Title _____ **Author** _____ **Date** _____

Now that you have read the book (story, unit, chapter) write a response to it. The response can include anything you like about the content, what you thought about it, or what it taught you.

THE GLOBAL METHOD

The *Global Method* is one content-oriented version of the language-experience approach (LEA). The content areas of social studies and science may be made more relevant by using this approach. In this strategy students are encouraged to observe things around them, record their observations (in pictures or writing), and associate what they have observed with their past experiences and prior knowledge. Students keep an observational notebook in which they record things observed at school, at home, on trips, or anywhere else they happen to go.

Later the students organize their observations. The teacher then encourages them to draw conclusions about word parts in words selected from their observational notebook. This has the advantage of students working with words they already can identify and for which they have meanings. This then adds to their decoding skill while they are learning important, relevant content in social studies or science.

CONTENT-AREA LANGUAGE-EXPERIENCE APPROACH (LEA) AND TRANSLATION WRITING

In *content-area language-experience approach (LEA)* the emphasis is given to organizing information about a certain content topic, most likely from social studies or science, and then reporting that information in an expository manner. This activity is most appropriate for primary-grade students and older disabled readers or learning-handicapped students. The process is very similar to traditional LEA in that students react to a motivator (stimulus), dictate a passage about that motivator, and then learn to read the passage as well as learning word identification skills from the dictated passage.

However, content-area LEA always is based on a specific content-related topic, perhaps the topic of a thematic unit the class is studying at that time. For example, the students can dictate a passage about a trip to a local planetarium or about a class pet. It also can be based upon pictures and study about a topic such as dinosaurs (a very popular topic among primary-grade children).

However, the passage always should be dictated in an expository, not a narrative, mode. This mode emphasizes detached, objective listings, comparisons, or sequences of objects or events. Since primary-grade children are often very egocentric, this activity should help them to perceive objects and events in a more detached manner, which also can be an important goal of this activity.

To best meet the goals of content-area LEA, the teacher always should have a clear topic and set of questions prepared before each lesson. For example, the classroom rabbit may be the topic for the dictated passage. In order to motivate exposition, you might first stress only what the rabbit eats. You can ask such questions as the following: "What does our rabbit eat?" "What kinds of foods would not be good for her?" "What would happen to our rabbit if she were not given enough of the right kinds of food to eat?" Then the teacher should write the answers to these questions in a paragraph form. An example of a dictated paragraph about this topic might look like this:

THIS IS WHAT MUFFIN EATS

Muffin eats carrots, lettuce, and rabbit food. Muffin likes carrots the best. Muffin could never eat pizza, chocolate cake, or candy. If Muffin tried to eat them, she might get sick and die.

The dictated passage can be expanded on another day to include where Muffin lives, her size in comparison to other animals, what she drinks, the type of cage she lives in, and when she goes to sleep. Of course, the original passage and additions to it should be reviewed often to improve reading fluency and review word identification skills. Students always should be encouraged to focus on the animal itself and not their own relation to it. As facts are listed and discussed, students then become more accustomed to passages that do not follow a story format, thus preparing them for expository writing in the intermediate grades and beyond.

Translation writing is similar to LEA because students respond to a motivator (stimulus), produce a written passage, and then work with that passage. However, there is an important difference between these two activities. *Translation writing is based on a specific content passage,* while content-oriented LEA is based on whatever motivator you or the student selects. While the goal of translation is for students to write a passage that parallels the original content material as much as possible, in LEA students produce an original passage at the beginning.

Translation writing is *converting or rewriting information* from content material into a "translated" or rewritten version. Until students become accustomed to this activity, the teacher should only select short content passages. The teacher also must be careful to choose content passages that are at the appropriate reading level.

First present the important vocabulary of the passage to be translated and explain the concepts they represent. Next present short sections of the passage to your students in one of several different ways. Have the students read the text independently if they are able to do so. However, you can pair above-average and below-average readers so that disabled readers or learning-handicapped students have the opportunity to listen to the good readers. The teacher also instead can read the material to the group of students. In addition, upper-grade students can come to the classroom to read the material. In any case, it is important that all students read along as the passage is presented so that they become accustomed to the structure and format of their content textbooks.

Next, the students convert the content passage into their own words either individually, with a partner, or in groups. This is done by dictating the passage to someone as is done in a typical LEA lesson. *A good way to record the dictation is to place each sentence on a strip of paper or tagboard.* In this way each separate idea can later be reviewed separately. After translating a part of the book, have the students listen again to that part in order to evaluate what they have dictated. The translated version then can be changed if incorrect information was included or omitted.

After a group of students has completed a translated version of a part of the content textbook, that version should be saved. The translation can be copied into students' notebooks or put into a group folder. In any case, the translations are very helpful both for review and for future classes to use.

THE REAP TECHNIQUE

Another content writing strategy is the *REAP Technique,* which is designed to improve students' comprehension skills by helping them to synthesize an author's ideas into their own words and to develop their writing ability as an aid to the recall of the concepts they gained from reading. The REAP technique is based on the idea that a student comprehends most effectively when asked *to write the ideas gained* from a passage he or she has read. It may be thought of as an alternative to the Directed Reading Activity and the Guided Reading Procedure (the latter was discussed and illustrated in Chapter 4). The student must internalize a text-based understanding by using this strategy.

The REAP technique consists of these four main steps:

- **R**—Reading to discover the author's ideas
- **E**—Encoding the author's ideas into one's own language
- **A**—Annotating these ideas in writing for oneself or for sharing with others
- **P**—Pondering the importance of the annotation

The most important aspect of the REAP technique deals with helping students to develop the ability *to write annotations about what they have read.* Therefore, the discussion of the REAP strategy follows these steps:

- teaching students to write annotations
- writing annotations
- thinking about the annotations that were written

When a student writes annotations, he or she must interact with the ideas of the author to synthesize them into his or her own language.

There are several different types of annotations the literacy or content teacher can find out about by checking the journal article cited later:

- summary annotations
- thesis annotations
- question annotations
- critical annotations
- intention annotations
- motivation annotations

The students must be taught how to write annotations by using these four steps:

- recognizing and defining
- discriminating
- modeling
- practicing

Finally, the student must think about the annotations to process them. (Adapted from M. G. Eanet and A. V. Manzo, "REAP—A Strategy for Improving Reading/Writing Study Skills," *Journal of Reading* 19, May 1976, pp. 647-652.)

The REAP technique probably is the most useful for students in the middle school and above by relating reading and writing and by offering students a way to interact with their textbooks. Although the annotations may serve as a foundation for critique writing in English classes, the writing of annotations can be a difficult and time-consuming task for even good and average readers. However, it can be a valuable technique if it is used appropriately.

USING BIOPOEMS AND CINQUAINS IN CONTENT WRITING

The *biopoem* is an interesting writing strategy that can easily be adapted to the content fields. A biopoem is a type of poem in which the subject is the writer himself or herself. Here is one pattern for writing biopoems:

Line 1: First name

Line 2: Four traits that describe the author

Line 3: Relative ("brother," "sister," "daughter," "son," etc.) of author

Line 4: Lover of _____ (list three things or people)

Line 5: Who feels _____ (three items)

Line 6: Who needs _____ (three items)

Line 7: Who fears _____ (three items)

Line 8: Who gives _____ (three items)

Line 9: Who would like to see _____ (three items)

Line 10: Resident of _____

Line 11: Last name

In addition, a biopoem can be adapted to different content fields as the following example in elementary social studies clearly indicates. In this modified version, the subject is the state of *Illinois*. The first name is not the name of the author of the biopoem, but rather is the name of the state. The second line adds three descriptive words about Illinois, and the third line adds to this list. In this version, the poem is shortened to contain only seven lines. In a sense, the biopoem is a biography of the state of Illinois.

Illinois

Flat, fertile, hot, cold

Prosperous, industrial, optimistic

Farmer, laborer, worker

Corn, soybeans, insurance

Lincoln, Stevenson, Springfield

Midwestern

As was briefly described in Chapter 3, a *cinquain* (pronounced sĭng-kăn′) is a five-line poem with the following pattern: the first line is a noun or the subject of the poem, the second line consists of two words that describe the first line, the third line consists of three verbs (action words), the fourth line has four words that convey some feeling, and the fifth line is a single word that refers back to the first line in some way.

Cinquains provide middle-upper level students with a very interesting way of motivating them to write about what they have learned in literature, social studies, science, or mathematics. Here is an example of a cinquain that was constructed about *tornadoes* from the content area of science:

Tornadoes
ugly, destructive
moving, swirling, destroying
are to be feared
funnel

Reproducible Form for Writing a Cinquain

Although a student obviously can write a cinquain on any sheet of paper, here is a reproducible form that may motivate your students to write a cinquain on a subject of their choice. You can duplicate and use it in its present form or modify it if you like.

MY CINQUAIN

Write your own *cinquain* (five-line poem) on the lines below. You can select any topic that you have been studying about in literature, social studies, science, or math that you want.

_____
title

_____
two adjectives

_____
three verbs

_____
four words that convey a feeling

_____
a single word that refers back to the first line

WRITING HEADLINES FOR NEWS STORIES

An interesting content writing strategy that my teacher-trainees often have used involves writing headlines for current news stories from either the local newspaper or a well-known newspaper. The newspaper is a highly motivating resource that lends itself well in thematic unit teaching as well as in classrooms using more traditional approaches. Most students in the middle school and above find various sections of the newspaper very interesting and informative. In addition, a number of local newspapers are able to offer teachers either free copies or copies at a reduced subscription rate.

When a student is to write headlines for news stories, the teacher usually clips a number of relevant, current news stories. He or she then cuts the headline off each news story. Then the student is given several of these news stories to read. After reading each news story, the student writes a headline for it on a separate sheet of paper. After writing a number of headlines, the student compares his or her headlines with the actual newspaper headlines. The student then discusses with peers or the teacher which is the more appropriate headline for each story and the reasons.

THE CONTENT-FOCUSED MELODRAMA

The *content-focused melodrama* is a very interesting content writing strategy that a history or literacy teacher can use when teaching history to students in the middle school and above. Very briefly, the procedure is as follows:

1. First, the teacher identifies important issues that are found in the unit. For example, in a unit dealing with the *Revolutionary War* some important issues for discussion might include *the Boston Tea Party, the midnight ride of Paul Revere, the British Redcoats, the signing of the Declaration of Independence,* and *various political figures.*

2. During the first several days of the unit, the teacher introduces each potential topic to the class. This topic introduction can use videotapes, guest speakers dressed in clothing of the Revolutionary War Period, demonstrations, realia of the period, or reader's theater. Book talks also can be used in the introduction. A book talk involves dramatic readings from both fiction and nonfiction books that help develop understanding of important historical events from the Revolutionary War period. For example, with the Revolutionary War Period, books such as *My Brother Sam Is Dead* (Collier, 1974 {junior fiction}), *The Mystery Candlestick* (Bothwell, 1970 {junior fiction}), and *Revolutionary War Weapons* (Coley, 1963 {nonfiction}) could be used.

3. When the topics have been introduced, students should be allowed to choose their own topic. When the teacher allows students the opportunity to select their own topic, they feel empowered and therefore their motivation and attention are improved. However, in order to avoid conflict, you can have students write their first, second, and third choices of topics on a piece of paper and hand it in anonymously.

4. When the teacher has collected and sorted the student topic requests, he or she then forms groups based upon the student choices. In the unit suggested above there might be several groups of students interested in the Boston Tea

Party, a few interested in the signing of the Declaration of Independence, and so on. Probably none of the groups should be larger than about five or six so that the group discussions are the most profitable.

However, the students probably will need some training and direction when they begin implementing melodramas. Each group should have an elected leader and a recorder. Rules for group behavior also should be discussed. Perhaps preliminary role playing of both positive and negative behavior may be helpful. However, each group should develop its own rules if possible. The ultimate goal always is effective group collaboration and cooperation.

5. Then the group is ready to produce its melodrama. When content-oriented melodramas are first introduced in a history class, it usually is helpful for the teacher to provide some concrete examples that show what a melodrama is. One way of doing this is to show the class a movie in which features of melodrama are easy to identify. Some possible examples of movies might be *Little Women* with either Katharine Hepburn or Winona Ryder or *High Noon* with Gary Cooper.

Producing a content-oriented melodrama involves writing the plot, developing the characters, and constructing the scenery. The writing probably is most effective when it follows these *process writing steps:* prewriting which involves conducting all of the research, writing the first or rough draft, conferencing with peers and/or teacher to evaluate the first draft, writing the final draft, and editing the final draft for complete accuracy.

When the students have had the opportunity to develop their melodrama scripts, they perform the plays for the class. After the performance, the teacher can lead a class discussion to compare and contrast the melodramas with the actual historical facts as they are known. This helps students think critically and helps avoid the possibility of students learning inaccurate information about the topic. (Adapted from "Content-Focused Melodrama: Dramatic Renderings of Historical Text," by R. B. Cooper and G. Chilcoat, *Journal of Reading* 34, December 1990, pp. 275-276.)

WRITING EXPOSITORY PARAGRAPHS

Writing expository paragraphs is a way to teach expository text structure as well as to strengthen the reading-writing connection. Give students directed practice in writing a paragraph with a directly stated main idea and supporting details. Have each student select an appropriate topic, activate his or her prior knowledge about the topic, and look for additional information on the topic.

Then have the student categorize the information that has been gathered and give a main idea about one of the categories. Then the student lists supporting details for the main idea and combines the main ideas and details into a short paragraph. If you wish, classmates then can evaluate each other's paragraphs for clarity and accuracy. After feedback has been received from classmates, the student may want to rewrite and edit his or her paragraph.

WRITING THE "EYEWITNESS ACTION" NIGHTLY NEWS

A motivating activity is to have students take the information learned in a unit in a content field and *to write a news program* based on that information. Have students independently or preferably with a partner(s) write a script that presents the information in a creative, interesting way. Then videotape the "news anchorperson" to replay to the class. Other students can act out "on the scene" accounts of important news happenings related to the newscast.

The students involved can design their own costumes, use the school's camcorder or bring one from home, and possibly get a blank videotape or used videotape from a local video store. Therefore, this activity need not be either expensive or difficult.

WRITING A ONE-PARAGRAPH ESSAY

Although a number of students in the middle school and above are able to understand their content textbooks at least to some degree, they often have considerable difficulty writing an essay about what they have read. When they are required to write the important facts from their reading in an organized pattern such as listing, cause-effect, or comparison-contrast, they may have a great deal of trouble. Teaching students to write a *one-paragraph essay* may help students to overcome this difficulty.

The one-paragraph essay begins with a general question that is then followed by information that structures the response. The general question is followed by a *thesis statement* so the students have a clear idea of what they are writing. After the thesis statement, the number of items to be included in the essay are given. Finally, the number of sentences your students are to write in order to explain each item is given. As an example, if in science you are studying the *Milky Way,* then you might ask the following question: "What are two of the most common constellations in the Milky Way?" Tell the students they should list the two most well-known constellations in the Milky Way, and then tell them they should write two or three sentences to explain each of these constellations.

If you are studying the Civil War, the question "What were the main causes of the Civil War?" may be asked. Then give your students this thesis statement: "Historians give several major reasons for the Civil War" (the secession of the southern states, ending slavery in the South). Notice that the number of items to include in this essay is provided in the thesis statement of this example. Next, tell the students to describe each reason with two or three sentences each. The following essay then might be written.

The Main Causes of the Civil War

Historians often give two major reasons for the Civil War that occurred in the United States in the 1860s between the North and the South. Prior to the Civil War, the owning of slaves was quite common in the South, and many Northerners were very much opposed to this practice. When the United States government criticized Southerners for continuing to keep slaves, some of the Southern states decided to secede from the United States and to form their own country with Jefferson Davis as President. The Civil War was fought in an attempt to keep the United States together and ultimately to free the slaves in the South.

As you can notice, a one-paragraph essay gives students structure for writing. For those students who need help with organizational skills more than that provided by a thesis statement, number of needed items, and number of sentences for each item, you might list each item in the appropriate order. In the example above, you could tell the students to first discuss secession and next to discuss the freeing of the slaves in the South. However, students who cannot write their own paragraph independently should have the opportunity to dictate their paragraph as is done in LEA. You may wish to give above-average readers only the thesis statement and have them decide how many items to write about and how much detail they should include in the paragraph.

NOTETAKING AND SUMMARIZING

Both *notetaking and summarizing* involve a very similar process. Teaching students how to take notes and how to summarize helps them *to identify the important information* in a content passage. Perhaps helping students to learn to locate the important information in a content passage may be more helpful than the actual notes and summaries students produce as a result of the notetaking and summarizing. Although having a set of notes or a summary helps a student to remember important information on a particular topic and enables him or her to review it later, learning how to create notes and summaries helps a student to identify the important information while reading about any content topic.

Since notetaking and summarizing are very complex study strategies, they cannot be learned in one or two sessions, but rather must be learned and practiced over a long time period. Students need direct guidance and many experiences with these skills. *Modeling* notetaking and summarizing is probably the most important element in teaching these two strategies.

As students are to read various content passages, the teacher should occasionally "walk students through the process of taking notes or writing summaries" with the help of a *listening guide*. In a "walk through" the teacher provides a rough outline of the passage that omits certain important points. The students should have a copy of the outline at their desks, and you can place a copy on an overhead transparency. Then read brief portions of the passage aloud, while the students follow along in their content textbooks. The length of the content passages depends upon factors such as your students' attention span, prior knowledge, reading ability, and interest. After reaching a logical stopping point, stop and complete the outline on the transparency with the light turned off as the students fill in their identical outlines at their desks. Next turn on the overhead projector and compare what you have written with what the students have written. This helps your students to recognize good notes. If you want, your students can change their notes so that they are more like your notes. Then turn off the light and read the next part of the passage to your class as they read along. This *read-compose-compare-change procedure* should continue throughout the content passage.

The modeling described here should be alternated with opportunities to compose notes and summaries independently or with a partner(s) so that the students do not come to depend on your help too much. In addition, the amount of structure provided by the listening guide should be fazed out over time. This indicates that you provide most of the information in the outline at the beginning, but you gradually remove more and more of the points during the school year until your class begins with a blank page. In addition, the rough outline you provide as a listening guide during this activity need not follow the rigid format of a traditional outline. Major and minor points should be listed, but labeling each point with Roman numerals, upper-case letters, numerals, or lower-case letters does not have to be used if a student does not want to do so.

Using Computer Software in Content Writing

There are a number of computer software programs that can be used effectively in content writing instruction or practice. Since publishers are constantly developing new software, it is difficult to provide a list of contemporary, relevant software.

Chapter 3 listed some sources for purchasing computer software, and you are encouraged to refer to that chapter if you wish.

One valuable reference tool for teachers interested in purchasing computer software is *Swift's Educational Software Directory* (Austin, Texas: Sterling Swift). The Minnesota Educational Computing Consortium (MECC) is a large distributor of educational software with an extensive catalog of offerings that is a useful resource. In addition, reviews in periodicals such as *Electronic Learning* and *The Computing Teacher* may be helpful to literacy and content teachers in locating appropriate computer software for use in content writing.

The Guided Writing Procedure

The *Guided Writing Procedure* is a strategy that uses the *process of writing* as a way of helping students in the middle school and above learn content textbook material. Writing fluency (the processes of writing) is taught along with content material. This is an extension of the concept that the processes of reading and listening can be taught in conjunction with content material.

The Guided Writing Procedure involves several specific procedures that take several days of content instruction. Two general steps usually are involved:

- Informal diagnosis of prior content knowledge and written expression
- Teaching content and written expression

Here very briefly are the steps a content teacher can apply while using the Guided Writing Procedure:

1. *Informal Diagnosis of Prior Content Knowledge and Written Expression—* Have the students brainstorm any thoughts they have related to the content topic to be studied. As an example, the following ideas related to the content topic of the *study of the United States Congress* could be suggested:

House of Representatives   Senate

term of office   Speaker of the House

House Whip	veto
appropriation	committee
seniority	chairmanship
legislative branch	majority leader
minority leader	sanction

Record everything the students say on the chalkboard or a transparency.

Then have the students vote on which ideas are the important ones and which ideas are details. Organize the ideas into an outline or a graphic organizer (see Chapter 3) on the chalkboard or a transparency. The outline should help students to organize and group their thoughts. Have the students write one or two short paragraphs using the outline or graphic organizer as a guide. Then collect these first drafts and have the students read the content material.

The teacher should examine the students' paragraphs quickly and analyze them for organization of ideas, style, and mechanics. A *Concept and Writing Checklist* (see the reproducible) can be used to record the information for each student.

2. *Teach Content and Written Expression*—One or several days should have elapsed since students wrote the first draft. The teacher then displays a composite of a number of first drafts on the chalkboard or a transparency. A first draft should be used that contains inaccurate information as well as inappropriate writing criteria. The class or group should use the checklist and textbook information to edit the illustrative paragraph.

Each student then should use the checklist to help analyze his or her own first drafts. They should edit both for content and written inaccuracies. Then the second draft is collected, and a follow-up quiz is given on the material read. The teacher should examine the second drafts and compare them to the checklist results. The Guided Writing Procedure is a unique way to introduce and teach content material. Students also may examine examples of text written by professional authors. An example is found in the activity sheet that follows. (Adapted from Carl Smith and Thomas Bean, "The Guided Writing Procedure: Integrating Content and Writing Improvement," *Reading World* 19, January 1980, pp. 290-298.)

Reproducible Example of the Guided Writing Procedure

The chapter now includes a reproducible activity sheet based on the Guided Writing Procedure. It is at about the fifth-grade level and is about lions from the content area of science. You may duplicate and use it in its present form or modify it in any way you wish in the light of the interests and needs of your own students.

ACTIVITY SHEET BASED ON THE
GUIDED WRITING PROCEDURE
(Approximately Fifth-Grade Level)

Read the following passage about *lions* silently. Although it is factually correct, it contains some inaccuracies in the organization of ideas, style, and writing mechanics. Here is a checklist you may want to use in analyzing this passage. You should complete the checklist after reading the passage. You may refer back to the passage if you wish, and you also may work with one or more partners in completing the checklist.

Concept and Writing Checklist
+ = Acceptable
0 = Needs Improvement
? = Cannot tell

Criteria

ORGANIZATION OF IDEAS

Clear topic _____

Supporting details/examples _____

Logical flow _____

Comments _____

STYLE

Show variety in:

Word choice _____

Sentence length _____

Comments _____

MECHANICS

Complete sentences _____

Capitalization _____

Punctuation _____

Spelling _____

Comments _____

ACTIVITY SHEET BASED ON THE
GUIDED WRITING PROCEDURE
(Approximately Fifth-Grade Level)

(cont.)

LIONS

Lions may well be the most admered animals on earth because of thier strength and beauty and fearless nature. In fact the lion is called "the King of the Beests."

Although lions are called the kings of the animals they certenly do not live the lives of kings but insted they must work very hard to survive. Since lions are meat eaters or *carnivores* they must hunt other animals for food and that is not always easy to do. in fact when food is scarce a lion may go for days without eating at all. However a lions body is made for catching pray since they have wonderful hearing and eyesite and have strong musls in thier legs to help them jump. Lions often work together when they hunt since by doing this they increese thier chances of getting food and although most of the hunting is done by a team of female lions when the prey is killed the male lions usually drive away the female lions and eat first or take the "lions share" and the females and cubs do usually get enuf to eat to.

Lions are members of the big cat family that also includes tigers, lepards, and jagers and the main difference between the big cats and all other cats is that big cats can roar but not pur. A family of lions is called a *pride* and lions are the only cats that live in large family grups and a pride of lions usually contains between four and thirty lions that includes several females and thier cubs and one or more males. Each pride has its own terrtory or area in which it lives and surprisingly the lions in a pride enjoy being together and are very affectonate and when they meet they often say "hello" by rubbing thier heads together.

Baby lions are called *cubs* and cubs are born in a *litter* of from three to five cubs and a lion cub is blind and totaly helpless at birth and weighs less than five pounds. In a pride all of the females take care of the cubs and a mother lion carries her baby in her mouth just like a mother house cat.

Most of the lions in the world today are African lions living on the grasy plains of Africa and they are *endangered* because people are taking away thier homes or *habitats* since they are turning more and more land into farms ranches so that it is harder and harder for the lions to live. However, goverments in Africa have set aside specal lands where lions can live safely and they are called *preserves*.

Answer Key for "Lions"

The passage on lions is factually correct. The responses included here are only for illustrative purposes.

Organization of Ideas

Clear topic	+
Supporting details/examples	+
Logical flow	+

Comments _____ This seems to be quite well organized. _____

Style

Shows variety in:

Word choice	0
Sentence length	0

Comments _____ This passage has two many and's in it. _____

Mechanics

Complete sentences	+
Capitalization	+
Punctuation	0
Spelling	0

Comments _____ This passage has both punctuation and spelling errors. _____

THE GIST PROCEDURE

The *GIST Procedure (Generating Interactions Between Schemata and Text)* is a strategy that can be used to improve students' abilities to comprehend the *gist or main ideas of paragraphs* by providing a prescription for reading from group sentence-to-sentence production to individual or partner(s) entire-paragraph gist production. It is a very useful strategy because *it relates reading and writing* (an important aspect of the whole language philosophy), guides student summary writing, and improves learning from content materials.

There are two versions of the GIST Procedure: *a paragraph version* and *a short passage version*. Very briefly, here are the steps of these two versions:

Paragraph Version

1. *Choose the appropriate paragraphs.* Choose several paragraphs containing three to five sentences each of which has a gist or main idea.

2. *Students read the first sentence.* Have the students read the first sentence of the paragraph so that they can retell it in their own words. The sentence

can be written on the chalkboard or overhead transparency with blank lines underneath it. The students then write their summaries on the blank lines.

3. *Students generate their summaries.* The students retell in a statement of 15 or fewer words what they read in the sentences.

4. *Reading the first two sentences.* The students read the first and second sentences and retell them in the same number of words used for the first sentence alone.

5. *Generate a summary of sentences one and two.* The students then should generate a single sentence of no more than 15 words that summarizes both sentences one and two.

6. *Continue with the procedure for the rest of the paragraph.* The procedure is continued until the students have produced a single statement of 15 words or fewer that best summarizes the paragraph.

7. *Move beyond a sentence-by-sentence approach to a paragraph approach.* Students are encouraged to produce their own gist statements on an individual basis across a variety of different kinds of paragraphs.

Shorter Passage Version

1. *Select appropriate passages.* The teacher selects a short passage at an appropriate reading level that contains paragraphs, each of which has a gist or main idea. The teacher then writes the passage on an overhead transparency.

2. *Read the paragraph.* All of the paragraphs are covered over except for the first one. Blank lines are written on the chalkboard, and the students are told to read the paragraph so that they can retell it in their own words in one statement of 20 words or fewer.

3. *Students generate summaries.* When students have finished reading the paragraph, the teacher removes the transparency, and the students are told to start writing their summaries. The students write and edit the summary until it is complete. They must write the summary from memory. The teacher should enforce the 20-word rule.

4. *Students read and summarize subsequent paragraphs.* The teacher erases the chalkboard, and the students read and summarize the first two paragraphs in not more than 20 words. The same procedures are used throughout the entire passage.

5. *Generate summaries for the entire passage and develop the independence in the use of this procedure.* This strategy should be used with many different kinds of short passages until students become competent at efficiently producing gist statements. The students then probably should respond to the entire passage rather than paragraph-by-paragraph. Students should be encouraged to produce gist statements on an individual basis or with a partner(s) if you wish. (Adapted from James W. Cunningham, "Generating Interactions Between Schemata and Text," in *New Inquiries in Reading Research and Instruction*, edited by J. A. Niles and L. A. Harris, "Thirty-First book of the National Reading Conference [Washington, D. C.: National Reading Conference], pp. 42-47.)

Reproducible Activity Sheet Using the GIST Procedure

The chapter now contains a ready-to-duplicate GIST Procedure that was constructed about *the civil rights March on Washington* from the content area of social studies at about the sixth-grade level. You can duplicate and use it in its present form if you would like or modify it in any way you wish. However, even more important, it can serve as a model for constructing GIST Procedures from the content materials your students must learn. My teacher-trainees have found it to be a very effective strategy in improving comprehension of content material as well as in relating reading and writing. It also is highly motivating to students.

ACTIVITY SHEET USING THE GIST PROCEDURE
(Approximately Sixth-Grade Reading Level)

Read the following paragraphs about the civil rights *March on Washington* to yourself. After you have read each paragraph, you will be asked to write a *summary* of what you have read.

THE MARCH ON WASHINGTON

There was a time in the American South when African-Americans faced unfair discrimination every day. Black children could not go to school with white children but rather had to go to different, very inferior schools. Black people could not use public libraries, pools, or parks. Black adults could not get good jobs or even vote for public officials. Many of the laws that governed life in the South were laws of *segregation*—separating the races.

Now *write a summary of the paragraph in no more than 20 words*. You may work with a partner if you want to.

_____

_____

_____

A. Philip Randolph was one of the first African-Americans who tried to win human rights for black people. He was deeply commited to this cause, and one of his first successes was managing to get the all-black union named the Brotherhood of Sleeping Car Porters (BSCP) admitted to the American Federation of Labor (AFL), an otherwise all-white group of unions. This enabled the black railroad Pullman car porters to earn more money and have better working conditions. Even as early as 1941 Randolph wanted to have a march on Washington to try to end discrimination against African-Americans.

Now *write a summary of the two paragraphs in no more than 20 words*. You may work with a partner if you want to.

_____

_____

_____

However, the fight for racial equality really began in the 1950s when the United States Supreme Court ruled that segregation in schools was unconstitutional, and Rosa Parks, a black seamstress, was arrested for refusing to give up her seat on a bus in Montgomery, Alabama, to a white man in 1955. The 1950s also brought many organizations to prominence that were formed to promote equality for blacks—the National Organization for the Advancement of Colored People (NAACP), Southern Christian Leadership Conference (SCLC), Student Nonviolent Coordinating Committee (SNCC), the Urban League, and the Congress of Racial Equality (CORE). Undoubtedly the most influential black leader of that time was Dr. Martin Luther King of the Southern Christian Leadership Conference (SCLC).

ACTIVITY SHEET USING THE GIST PROCEDURE
(Approximately Sixth-Grade Reading Level)

(cont.)

Now *write a summary of the three paragraphs in no more than 20 words.* You may work with a partner if you want to.

_____

_____

_____

_____

The plan for the actual March on Washington for Civil Rights began in July, 1963, when the leaders of the major civil rights organizations in the United States met in New York City. They agreed that the march would be held in Washington, D.C. on August 28, 1963, and would take place on the mall and begin at the Washington Monument and end one mile away at the Lincoln Memorial. The organizers of the march agreed that the tone of the march would be positive with no confrontation or violence. Instead, it would be a massive display of both black and white citizens demanding equal justice and equal rights right then.

Now *write a summary of the four paragraphs in no more than 20 words.* You may work with a partner if you want to.

_____

_____

_____

_____

The actual March on Washington took place on Wednesday, August 28, 1963, a late summer day with the temperature in the 80s. Unbelievably, an estimated 250,000 people participated in the march. They were black and white, young and old, wealthy and poor, male and female, Jew and Gentile, and powerful and powerless. They walked shoulder to shoulder and hand in hand for the cause of civil rights in which they believed. The march was peaceful, impressive, and moving. Undoubtedly, the highlight of the march was Dr. King's famous *"I Have a Dream"* speech which ended with this statement: *"Free at last, free at last, thank God Almighty, we are free at last."* However, unfortunately Dr. King's dream still has not been realized more than thirty years after the March on Washington. Hopefully, his dream finally will be realized during your lifetime.

Now *write a summary of the entire passage in no more than 20 words.* You may work with a partner if you want to.

_____

_____

_____

_____

Answer Key for "The March on Washington"

The following answers are included only for illustrative purposes. Many other possible summaries also are acceptable:

> Black people were unfairly segregated in the American South a number of years ago in a number of ways.
>
> A. Philip Randolph was one of the first African-Americans who tried to end segregation and win equal rights.
>
> Significant progress was made during the 1950s to end segregation because of the work of civil rights organizations and demonstrations.
>
> A March on Washington was planned to focus attention on segregation and to demand equal rights and justice right then.
>
> The March on Washington took place on August 28, 1963, and consisted of 250,000 people marching for civil rights.

USING K-W-L PLUS TO MOTIVATE WRITING AN EXPOSITORY SUMMARY OR REPORT

As you may remember, both K-W-L and K-W-H-L were described in detail in Chapter 4. They are both study strategies that are very useful when students are reading and studying content material, especially social studies and science. K-W-L is an acronym for *What I Know—What I Want to Learn—What I Have Learned,* while K-W-H-L adds the component *How I Can Find Out.*

Ellen Carr and Donna Ogle have added a *writing component* to K-W-L that my teacher-trainees have found very effective and motivating with students. (See their article "A Strategy for Comprehension and Summarization" in *Journal of Reading,* 30, April 1987, pages 626-631.) *K-W-L Plus* helps students to organize information they have learned from using either the K-W-L or the K-W-H-L worksheet to *write a summary or report* of some kind.

When students have finished recording what they learned and the "L" section of the worksheet is finished, the students organize their learning by using a mapping or webbing technique (see Chapters 3 and 4). The material contained in the "L" section of the worksheet can help students to identify appropriate categories, and the specific information learned can be attached to the appropriate categories. The webbing technique used in K-W-L Plus can replace the traditional outline students commonly use when writing a report or summary. Students usually can construct a semantic map (web) more easily than they can a traditional outline, and most students like constructing it much better. They also find it very effective in helping them write a summary or report.

Reproducible Passage and Semantic Web to Motivate Writing an Expository Summary or Report

The chapter now contains a reproducible K-W-L worksheet, a passage from science about Australian marsupials at about the fifth-grade reading level, and a partially completed semantic web based on the information contained in that passage. The students are to write an expository summary or report that is based upon the information contained in the semantic map.

You can duplicate and use any of the material in this section in its present form or modify it in any way you wish. More important, it should serve as a model for you as to how to use K-W-L Plus to help your students remember and write about the content material they are required to learn.

K-W-L PLUS ACTIVITY
(Approximately Fifth-Grade Level)

In a few minutes you are going to read a passage about *Australian marsupials*. Before you read this passage, you should try to complete the *K— What I Know* and *W—What I Want to Learn* portions of this K-W-L worksheet. You can complete these parts of the worksheets independently or with a partner(s). Then *read the passage* to yourself and *complete the L— What I Have Learned* portion of the K-W-L worksheet. Then complete *the partially completed semantic web* that is found after the passage either independently or with a partner(s). After completing the semantic web, you should *write a summary* of the material that is found in the map. When you have finished writing the summary, *read it silently* to be sure it is all right.

K	W	L
What I Know	**What I Want to Learn**	**What I Have Learned**

K-W-L PLUS ACTIVITY
(Approximately Fifth-Grade Level)

(cont.)

Now read this passage about *Australian marsupials to yourself.*

THE MARSUPIALS OF AUSTRALIA

You may be wondering what a *marsupial* is. *Marsupials* are a group of mammals that are furred and warm-blooded, and the female marsupials nourish their young with milk. However, they are very different from most other animals in the way in which they have their young and in their skeletons and teeth. The babies of marsupials are born at a very early stage of development and then complete the rest of the development within a fold or pouch of skin called the *marsupium,* the organ from which the group takes its name.

Although many of the commonly known marsupials are found in Australia and Tasmania, some of them are found in parts of North and South America. However, not all Australian mammals are marsupials.

As mentioned earlier, the young marsupial is born when it is very tiny and undeveloped. It has no usable ears or eyes, and its back limbs and tail are just stumps. However, its front legs are strong and equipped with sharp claws. When it is born, a young *joey* crawls through the fur on its mother's stomach to her pouch. When it is safely in the pouch, it finds a nipple and sucks. Not all marsupials have a deep pouch like the kangaroo, but in some it is just a fold of skin. In such species the joeys are hauled along between the mother's hind legs and later cling to her fur.

Of course, the most common and widespread of Australia's marsupials are *kangaroos.* As kangaroos rely on grasses and limbs for their food and water, many die during a drought. *Wallabies* are examples of medium-sized marsupials while *kangaroo rats* are examples of small marsupials. Both are grazing or browsing *herbivores* or plant-eating mammals. *Tree wallabies* or *tree kangaroos* (as they can be called) have fur on the neck and shoulders with a ruff on it that lets the rain run off as the animal huddles in a tree with its head down.

The *koalas* of Australia are protected by the law and certainly are very appealing animals. However, they are rather slow-moving, stupid creatures that spend most of the daytime sleeping in a eucalyptus (gum) tree and feeding on eucalyptus leaves and shoots at night. A koala gets its entire water supply from eucalyptus trees and from dew.

Another marsupial is the *wombat,* a herbivorous, burrowing mammal. It has a dark, thick coarse coat and powerful front legs and shoulders with strong curved claws. The teeth of wombats grow throughout their life as do those of rodents.

The only marsupial that lives in the United States and southern Canada is the common *American opossum.* It is mainly nocturnal and eats both animal and plant matter. The young spend about two months in the mother's pouch, and then she carries them on her back for awhile. They are quite common on suburban and small-town streets and roads and often are killed by cars and trucks as they run across the streets and roads at night.

The marsupial species of today will only be able to survive if they have a habitat in which to live. That may not be the case if city suburbs and agriculture take away the places where they now live. That would be a shame, don't you think?

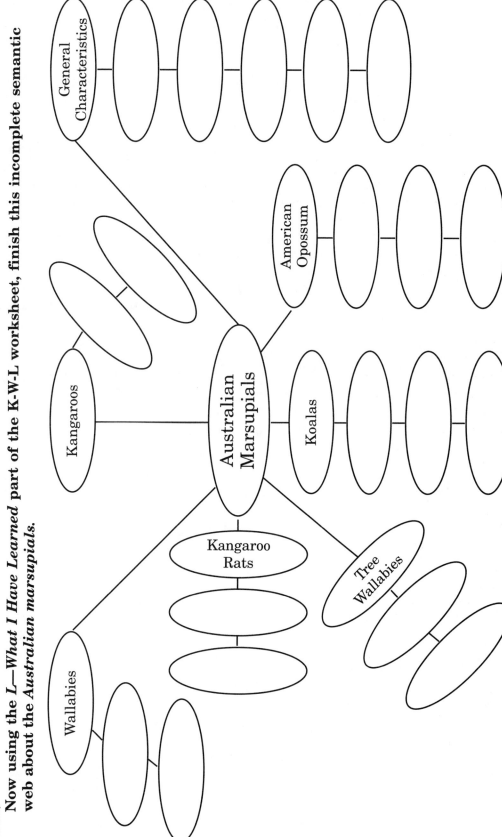

Name _____ Grade _____ Teacher _____ Date _____

K-W-L PLUS ACTIVITY
(Approximately Fifth-Grade Level)
SEMANTIC WEB

(cont.)

Now using the *L—What I Have Learned* part of the K-W-L worksheet, finish this incomplete semantic web about the *Australian marsupials.*

General Characteristics

American Opossum

Kangaroos

Australian Marsupials

Koalas

Kangaroo Rats

Tree Wallabies

Wallabies

323

Answer Key for "The Marsupials of Australia"

The summary included here about Australian marsupials is only a model of what a student(s) could include. Any summary that is based on the material included in the L—What I Have Learned portion of the K-W-L worksheet should be considered correct.

Marsupials are warm-blooded, furry animals that give milk to their babies. However, they are very different from other animals in that their babies are born very small and undeveloped.

A baby marsupial is called a joey and when it is born, it crawls into its mother's pouch and sucks, or else it is hauled between her hind legs if she doesn't have a real pouch.

Kangaroos are the most common of Australia's marsupials. They eat grasses and limbs. Some other Australian marsupials are wallabies, tree kangaroos, and tree wallabies sometimes called tree kangaroos.

Koalas are cute, but rather dumb animals that can only eat eucalyptus leaves and shoots. The only North American marsupial is the American opossum, an animal that eats both other animals and plants. It often gets killed while it runs across streets and roads at night.

We need to protect the homes of all of the marsupials if they are going to survive.

Ready-to-Use Strategies and Activity Sheets for Adapting the Literacy-Study Skills to the Unique Demands of Literature, Social Studies, Science, and Mathematics

Do you believe that a competent reader of literature and social studies materials also will be a competent reader of scientific and mathematical material? Obviously, the answer to that question is a very definite "No!" I, along with countless others, can attest to the fact that each of the four major content fields has both unique specialized vocabulary terms and reading and writing requirements that must be presented and practiced while using that particular content material. As I have written earlier in this resource, I am a good example of an excellent reader in literature and social studies, a competent reader in science, but a disabled reader of mathematical verbal problems. Perhaps you have a number of students with similar problems. This chapter is designed to help teachers adapt various reading and writing skills to the unique demands of the four major content fields so that students may be able to attain at least a fairly good degree of competence in all of them.

After reading the chapter, any literacy or content teacher will have a wealth of ready-to-use strategies and materials that he or she can use in presenting and reinforcing all of the important reading and writing skills that are needed for success in the content areas of literature, social studies, science, and mathematics. This should save the teacher countless time and effort as well as help each student to achieve as much success as possible in comprehending and remembering the important material in the various content fields. We can afford to do no less for our students. Any number of students in the intermediate grades, middle school, secondary school, and college as well as some adults are simply unable to read certain content fields effectively. We must improve our literacy-study instruction in these areas, perhaps especially in science and mathematics.

DESCRIPTION OF THE MORE GENERAL LITERACY-STUDY SKILLS

There are a number of somewhat general literacy-study skills in which students gradually should gain competence. These skills are relevant to success in all of the content fields of literature, social studies, science, and mathematics to a greater or lesser degree although their use may have to be modified somewhat depending upon the content area. This part of the chapter first very briefly describes these more general literacy-study skills, provides suggestions for improving ability in them, and if applicable, explains how to modify them slightly for use in literature, social studies, science, and mathematics.

Study Strategies

The use of a study strategy can help students understand and remember content material more effectively than would be the case without the use of this kind of strategy. Although the study strategies have different names as is explained shortly, each of them usually involves the use of some type of *preview* prior to reading, *formulating questions or purposes* for the reading, and later *reviewing* the material trying to relate it to prior knowledge or prior experience in that topic.

Undoubtedly the most well-known of the study strategies is *Survey Q3R—survey, question, read, recite, and review.* Survey Q3R was developed by Francis P. Robinson during World War II to help military personnel understand and remember the material they had to read. Survey Q3R is based on an *information-processing theory of reading.* Each part of Survey Q3R is designed to facilitate the processing of incoming print so that the student can deal with it effectively.

Although *Survey Q3R* must necessarily be varied depending on the content in which it is used as is explained in later sections of this chapter, it contains the following general steps:

1. *Survey or Preview:* The students survey an entire textbook chapter to gain an overall impression of its content. In this survey or preview, they may read the introduction and summary of the chapter and the first sentence in each of the paragraphs. They also may examine the pictures, maps, graphs, diagrams, tables, and other aids included in the chapter. **Note:** This survey or preview is the most useful aspect of Survey Q3R. It always should be used in reading content material even when no other part of this study technique is used. The use of the survey or preview alone will greatly add to comprehension and retention of any content material.

2. *Question:* The students pose questions they want to read to answer during this step. They turn each subheading into a question and also formulate additional questions to read to answer.

3. *Read:* The students read the entire chapter *on a selective basis* to try to answer the questions they have posed. In this selective reading, they try to fill in the gaps in their reading by capitalizing on their prior knowledge. This step of the procedure helps them to become *actively involved in the reading.*

4. *Recite:* This step applies only to one section at a time. After the students have read a section at a time in a purposeful manner, they can recite the important information from that section in either an oral or a written form, depending upon which is more efficient for them.

5. *Review:* This step applies after the students have completed the chapter. They try to review the important concepts, generalizations, and facts they gained from the chapter. They often can use the written notes they may have made in the fourth step of this procedure. (Adapted from Francis P. Robinson, *Effective Study.* New York: Harper & Row, 1961.)

As stated earlier, there are a number of variations of the Survey Q3R technique. Most of them use a survey or preview of the reading, some type of self-questioning technique, setting purposes for the reading, and a review step to fix the important information in mind. Some of the other acronyms for this technique are *Survey Q4R, PQRST, POINT, OK4R,* and *C2R.* In any case, the survey or preview of any of these variations is always its most important aspect.

Flexibility of Reading Rate

The improvement of reading rate and *flexibility* is an aspect of the reading-study skills that can aid in a student's comprehension and retention of content materials especially beginning in the middle school and above. It always should be emphasized only for those students who have good basic word-identification and comprehension skills. The concept of reading flexibility should certainly be pointed out to average and above-average readers as one important way to improve their understanding and retention of content materials.

A student's rate of reading always should depend upon the *difficulty of the reading material, his or her purpose for reading it, and his or her prior knowledge about the topic of the reading material.* This concept is called *reading flexibility* and is of much greater importance than is *reading rate or speed.*

Most reading specialists have described the following reading rates:

- *Skimming:* Skimming is reading for a general impression of the reading material. It is a reading rate of more than 1,000 words per minute. It generally is most applicable in the survey or preview portion of a study technique, reading very easy reading material such as a "light" novel or some parts of a newspaper, or skimming any type of reading material to gain an overall impression.

- *Scanning:* Scanning is moving one's eyes very rapidly to find a specific detail such as a name, a place, or a date. Since all of the words are not perceived in scanning, it is impossible to estimate the rate of scanning.

- *Rapid Reading:* Rapid reading is reading material, such as a novel, for main ideas. It often is at a rate of over 400 words a minute.

- *Study-Type Reading:* Study-type reading is reading mainly for facts and details in content areas such as social studies and science. It usually is at a rate of 250 to 350 words per minute.

- *Careful, Analytical Reading:* Careful, analytical reading is reading and rereading very carefully for details. It is perhaps best exemplified in reading mathematical verbal problems and in reading very difficult scientific material. It is probably at a rate of about 75 to 150 words per minute.

As stated earlier, reading flexibility can be stressed with students at the middle-school level and above. Such students always should be given opportunities to learn to vary their reading rate depending on the difficulty of the material and their purposes for reading it. If students are not exposed to the importance of reading content materials *flexibly,* they may well read every type of content material in the same word-by-word manner even though some types of content material such as an easy novel should be read much more rapidly. Students should be encouraged to read easy, interesting material in which comprehension is no problem in thought *units* or groups of words, skipping unimportant portions of the material instead of reading in a word-by-word manner as is often the case.

Teaching Parts of Content Textbooks

Content textbooks are often composed of similar sections, usually including a title, copyright page, preface, table of contents, reference list, index, and glossary. In addition, each chapter within a content textbook often contains a title, introduction, headings, subheadings, conclusions, questions, and references. Although not all books and chapters have these parts, most social studies and science books contain them as well as some literature and mathematics textbooks.

Understanding the information presented in each part of a content textbook can help students to understand the material that is presented. As an example, the copyright page can tell whether the information contained in the book is probably out of date or whether it undoubtedly is up to date. The preface can point out the purposes for which the book was written, while the table of contents presents an outline of what material the book contains and helps to set expectations regarding what will be found when reading it. Each book part contains important information that can help the reader.

Lessons that teach students about the parts of books and how they can help the reader should be a part of both reading and content instruction. Students need to be made aware of the various parts of books, the information that each contains, and their uses. Here are several strategies that can be used for this purpose:

- Have students predict what specific information may be found in various chapters by using the table of contents. Write the predictions on the chalkboard. Then have students locate the appropriate pages in the content textbook to check their predictions.

- Give students a list of specific items found in various chapters, sections, and subsections. Have students match the items on the list with the titles in the table of contents. Discuss reasons for the matches that were made and check the appropriate sections to see if the matches were correct.

- Have students look at several copyright pages and tables of contents from books in the same subject area (either social studies or science textbooks). Using the table of contents, have students compare differences in topics. Then, using the copyright pages, have students attempt to match copyright pages to table of contents. The teacher may have to give students some guidance by pointing out to students which topics may be relatively new to that field and would not have been included in earlier textbooks.

- Discuss the difference between a glossary and a dictionary. As you know, a glossary contains definitions for words that appear in that book, while a dictionary includes many other definitions as well as more general terms. Locate sentences in the textbook that contain content-specific vocabulary terms and have students look up their meanings in the glossary. Then have them read the paragraph that contains the term to see if the definition is appropriate.

- Compare pages in an index and glossary of a content textbook. Have students brainstorm the differences that are written on the chalkboard (glossary contains definitions, index contains page numbers, etc.). Discuss the purposes of each one and how the differences help to meet these purposes.

USING THE SCHOOL LIBRARY/MEDIA CENTER TO
IMPROVE COMPETENCY IN CONTENT LITERACY-STUDY SKILLS

School libraries/media centers are essential to the effective teaching of content literacy-study skills whether the teacher uses thematic units of instruction or traditional content teaching. Literacy or content teachers and librarians/media specialists should work together as teams to help students develop the skills they need to use libraries/media centers effectively.

The librarian/media specialist should show students the locations of books and journals, card catalogs, and reference materials such as dictionaries, encyclopedias, atlases, and the *Reader's Guide to Periodical Literature.* In addition, he or she should explain the procedure for checking books in and out and describe the rules and regulations of behavior in the library. The librarian/media specialist also should demonstrate how to use the library card catalog, how to use the *Reader's Guide,* and how books are arranged in the library under the Dewey Decimal System. He or she also can display posters around the library/media center to remind students of the check-out procedures and library rules.

By having literacy or content teachers discuss the reasons for using the library/media center and explaining the reasons why students may need to use the library card catalog, Dewey Decimal System, and the *Reader's Guide* before students actually visit the library/media center, the teacher can prepare them effectively for a first visit. While they are still in the classroom, the students should learn that cards in the library card catalog are arranged alphabetically and that the card catalog contains *subject, author,* and *title cards.* Sample cards of each type can be drawn and placed on a bulletin board. Students in the middle school also can benefit from a lesson that explains the use of cross-reference cards. All of these are illustrated in Figure 6-1.

The teacher also can construct a model of a library card-catalog drawer and have the students practice using it. Students may enjoy constructing the three main types of cards for several content-oriented tradebooks they have read and then alphabetizing these cards to make a miniature card catalog.

The resource *Looking it Up* can be used for teaching library skills to students in grades 2 through 5. This reproducible workbook contains eight units on a variety of topics related to library skills. It is available at the following address and toll-free telephone number:

Fearon Teacher Aids
P.O. Box 2649
Columbus, OH 43216
1-800-2442-7272

Here are two additional suggestions for practicing library skills:

- The teacher sends the students on a *scavenger hunt* that requires using the library by dividing the class into teams and giving the teams statements to complete or questions to answer. (**Example:** The author of *Animal Facts / Animal Fables* is _____.)
- The teacher gives students questions and asks them to indicate on a map of the library where they would go to find the answers.

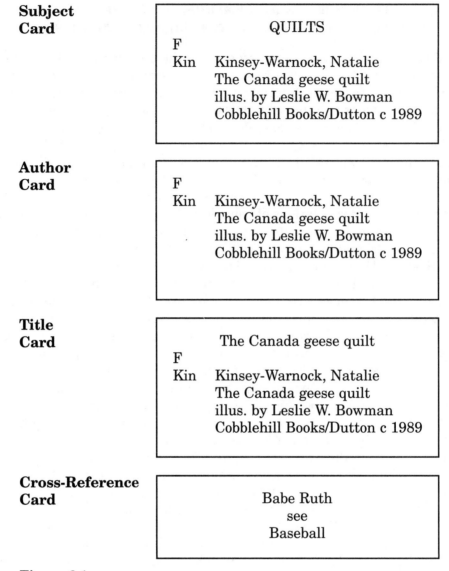

**Subject
Card**

QUILTS

F
Kin Kinsey-Warnock, Natalie
The Canada geese quilt
illus. by Leslie W. Bowman
Cobblehill Books/Dutton c 1989

**Author
Card**

F
Kin Kinsey-Warnock, Natalie
The Canada geese quilt
illus. by Leslie W. Bowman
Cobblehill Books/Dutton c 1989

**Title
Card**

The Canada geese quilt
F
Kin Kinsey-Warnock, Natalie
The Canada geese quilt
illus. by Leslie W. Bowman
Cobblehill Books/Dutton c 1989

**Cross-Reference
Card**

Babe Ruth
see
Baseball

Figure 6-1

The librarian/media specialist is a crucial ally for either literacy or content teachers as thematic units are planned. No thematic unit can be successful if the needed reading and reference materials are not available in an easy-to-locate and plentiful supply. The librarian/media specialist also can be very helpful as students search the library for needed material as the unit progresses. In addition, librarian/media specialists are equally helpful if content materials are presented in a more traditional manner.

SEVERAL RESEARCH STRATEGIES THAT CAN BE USED TO IMPROVE COMPETENCY IN THE LITERACY-STUDY SKILLS

Here are several creative strategies for teaching needed reference skills for content reading and writing:

- *Reference Match.* After discussing and demonstrating various types of reference materials, provide a list of reference materials and a separate list of information found in those materials. Have students match the information to the source. Here is an example:

thesaurus	_____	1. used to find out which states are bordered by the Mississippi River
atlas	_____	2. contains synonyms of a number of words
encyclopedia	_____	3. computerized source of many different kinds of information
encyclopedia on CD-ROM	_____	4. contains information about famous people
		5. maps
		6. graphs

- *Library Hunts.* Each week post a problem that requires students to use reference skills in the school library/media center. You can ask students questions such as these:

  What is the Dewey Decimal Number for information books about dinosaurs?

  Where would you find a book about *Shaquille O'Neal*?

  Where would you find a book by *Bonnie Busenberg*?

  What are the titles of one fiction and one nonfiction book?

  What are the titles of all of the books contained in this library that were written by *Judy Blume*?

- *Atlas Information.* Have students use an atlas to find information such as which states share borders, the capital of each of the states, the name of a very large city in each state, the population of various cities or states, and so forth.

- *Topic Sort.* Place a number of topics in a box. On the chalkboard have a drawing of the spines of an encyclopedia. Have students choose a topic and state which volume they would use to find information on that topic.

1	2	3	4	5	6	7	8	9	10	11	12	13	14	15	16	17	18	19	20	21
A	B	C-Ch	Ci-Cz	D	E	F	G	H	I	J-K	L	M	N-O	P	Q-R	S-Sn	So-Sz	T	U-V	W X Y Z

- *Newspaper Fact Hunt.* After discussing the general purpose of an index, provide newspapers for a discussion of the various newspaper parts and the newspaper index. Have students use the index to find answers to such questions as these:

  Where would you find out if anyone had found a lost dog or cat?

  What page(s) are the comic strips found on?

What page of the newspaper generally contains the most important national and local news stories?

Where would you find out information about airline fares?

On what page would you find the local forecast and weather information about your state and the entire country (world)?

- *Dictionary Keys.* Present and discuss the concept of *key words* in dictionaries. Provide key words for a dictionary page on the chalkboard as well as words that would and would not be found on that page. Have students place the words in the proper order stating whether or not they would be found on the page simulated by the key words.

- *Card Catalog Search.* Visit the library/media center after having discussed the library card catalog. Then present a two-column list with information desired in one column and the type of card in the other column. Have students match the columns. Have students use the library card catalog to find out the needed information. Here is a brief example:

Author Card	_____	1. You want to find the book *Incredible Edible Science.*
Subject Card	_____	2. You want to locate another book by Patricia Maclachan.
Title Card	_____	3. You want to find a book that tells about life during the Civil War.

GENERAL GOALS FOR TEACHING LITERATURE UNITS

The literature program should encourage students to learn about their literary heritage; expand their imagination; evaluate various kinds of literature; increase awareness of different types of language; develop a love for literature; develop preferences for different types of literature; and grow intellectually, emotionally, and socially.

These goals can be best met by reading aloud to students on a daily basis and providing them with opportunities to read and respond to different types of literature. Teachers can teach literary skills through units on a particular genre of literature such as poetry or short stories or can integrate literature with social studies, science, and mathematics in a thematic unit appropriate for that grade level.

When developing literature programs, teachers should plan diversity in students' exposure to literature rather than allowing them to have only random encounters with different kinds of books. Teachers can organize instruction by genres (forms or categories), literary elements, or topics in order to vary students' experiences. In addition, teachers should introduce students to the specialized vocabulary and skills they need to develop an appreciation of the different types of literature.

Literature consists of a number of different genres or literary forms including realistic fiction, historical fiction, biographies, autobiographies, poetry, plays, informational books, fantasy and folklore, novels, short stories, and essays. Historical fiction, biographies, autobiographies, and informational books all may help students to solve problems in their own lives as well as to understand the problems of others better.

Biographies and autobiographies enable students to learn about the lives of others in the hope that what they learn from reading can serve as a positive role model for them or help them to solve similar types of problems in their own lives. In addition, biographies and autobiographies integrate very well into units in social studies, science, and possibly mathematics. Poetry encourages students to explore their emotions, and plays offer the experience of dramatizing favorite stories. Obviously, informational books contain valuable knowledge that is very applicable in thematic units in social studies, science, and mathematics. Often the material contained in informational books seems more relevant and interesting to students than does the material in the typical content textbook. It can make the material seem more "alive" than does the typical textbook.

Both modern fantasy and folklore allow students to escape into worlds of imaginary characters and events. Folklore presents many possibilities for introducing different literary forms. Many students, especially in the intermediate grades, enjoy tall tales, and the students can try to locate the exaggerations in the stories. Another form of folklore is the fable, which is usually characterized by brevity, a moral, and the use of animal characters that are designed to represent human characters. Students can practice identifying the morals of the fables before they read the ones stated in the books. Myths, *pourquoi* (why) tales, some Native American folklore, and Rudyard Kipling's *Just So Stories* provide explanations for universal origins. These stories are excellent ways for students to understand different cultures and become familiar with children's classics. Short stories give students an abbreviated version of a fictionalized topic, while an essay deals with a subject or theme from a limited or personal point of view.

To understand literary passages, students should be able to recognize and analyze plots, themes, characterization, settings, and authors' styles. The *plot* is the overall plan for the story; the *theme* is the main idea the writer wishes to convey; and *characterization* is the way in which the writer makes the reader aware of the characteristics and motives of each person in the story. The *setting* consists of time and place, and the *style* is the writer's mode of expressing thoughts. Teacher-directed questioning can make students aware of these literary elements and help them to understand the interrelationships among them. Here are some concepts related to major story elements:

1. *Setting*—Teachers should point out how time and place affect the plot, characterization, and mood of stories. Stories should be true to their settings. For example, characters behave differently today than the way they behaved a long time ago, and settings in different parts of the country and in different countries may result in significantly different behavior on the part of the characters.

2. *Characterization*—Students who examine literature with strong characterization find that writers develop their characters through dialogue, actions, interactions with others, and insights into their thoughts and feelings as well as by description.

3. *Plot*—Students should analyze short, simple stories to see how writers introduce their stories, develop them through a series of incidents, create interest and suspense, and reach satisfying conclusions.

4. *Style*—Students should examine written material to analyze the author's choice of words, sentence patterns, and manners of expression.

5. *Theme*—The concept of theme is rather abstract. Perhaps the teacher can select two trade books or stories that have the same theme but have different
   settings, plots, and other elements to allow students to see how the same
   theme can be developed in different ways.

Figurative language is one aspect of literature that is very difficult for a
number of students to understand. Most students need considerable help if they
are to comprehend figurative language well. Some types of figures of speech that
may cause students difficulty are as follows:

- *Simile*—a comparison using *like* or *as*
- *Metaphor*—a direct comparison *without* the words *like* or *as*
- *Personification*—giving the attributes of a person to an inanimate object or ab-
  stract idea
- *Hyperbole*—an extreme exaggeration
- *Euphemism*—substitution of a less offensive term for an unpleasant term or
  expression

Teaching students to recognize and understand *similes* usually is not particularly difficult because the cue words *like* and *as* help to show the presence of
a comparison. However, metaphors may cause more problems. A *metaphor* is a
comparison between unlike things that share some attribute or quality. Sometimes students do not realize that the language in metaphors is figurative; sometimes students do not have sufficient background knowledge about one or both
of the things being compared; while sometimes students have not learned a
strategy for interpreting metaphors.

Although the two things being compared in a metaphor may seem to be
incompatible, students must think of past experiences with each, searching for a
match in attributes or qualities that could be the basis of a comparison. Visual
aids may be helpful in this process. For example, a comparison chart such as the
one in Figure 6-2 can be used:

COMPARISON CHART

Woman	*Dog*
✓+	alive
–	four legs
✓	two eyes
–	barks
–	fur coat
✓	walks

–	indicates dissimilarity
✓	indicates similarity
✓+	indicates *important* similarity

Figure 6-2

As is the case with many other strategies, the teacher should "think-aloud" for students about the operation of metaphors and their purposes, asking them questions related to the process being demonstrated. Group discussion of the comparison chart may help to activate students' prior knowledge about the items that are being compared, while the chart helps to make similarities more apparent.

USING LITERATURE-BASED UNITS FOR CONTENT TEACHING

One or several trade books can serve effectively as the basis for a literature-based unit that integrates all of the content areas in a meaningful way. The only problem with using literature-based units for content teaching is that the students may grow tired of a trade book while doing all of the related activities. However, this problem probably can be eliminated by choosing extremely interesting trade books that lend themselves well to this type of integration and not necessarily having students do all of the suggested activities. In this way a literature-based unit is similar to basal reader teacher manuals. Both only should be used as suggestions of possible activities that can be chosen.

I have selected a very interesting fantasy trade book on about the fourth- or fifth-grade reading level entitled *The Indian in the Cupboard* by Lynne Reid Banks (Doubleday, 1980) and constructed activities that can be done based on this trade book from the content areas of science, social studies, math, writing, art, music, and health/PE. In addition, this graphic organizer includes some discussion questions and the titles and publisher of three other related books by Lynne Reid Banks. Very briefly, the story is about the fantasy of a nine-year-old boy named Omri who has plastic figures and animals "come to life" when he puts them in a magic cupboard and locks it with a special key. It is a charming book that many students will enjoy very much.

Besides serving as a source of many activities from different content areas based on this trade book, the graphic organizer should also serve as a model for you about how to construct a literature-based unit from any trade book you think is relevant and appropriate for your students.

STRATEGIES FOR IMPROVING COMPETENCY IN THE VARIOUS ASPECTS OF LITERATURE

The chapter now very briefly *discusses a number of strategies that can be used for improving competency in the various aspects of literature.* Each strategy may have to be adapted somewhat depending upon the type of literature genre.

Using Survey Q3R While Reading Literature

As was explained earlier in this chapter, the study technique of Survey Q3R can significantly help students to understand and remember the content material they have to read. The general steps of Survey Q3R are as follows—*survey, question, read, recite,* and *review.* When Survey Q3R is used while reading literature, it must be varied somewhat from its traditional format. For example, the *survey* step can be used very effectively while reading a novel, a short story, an essay, and poetry. Since few of these literary forms contain subheadings, students usu-

Science:
- Explain electricity as though the person had never heard of it.
- How could Little Bear start a fire without matches?
- Why might the birch tree die after Omri cut off strips of its bark?
- What could a rat eat?

Math:
- Make a timeline showing when Little Bear may have fought with the English against the French and the Algonquin Indian tribe.
- Count the number of plastic figures and animals that the magic cupboard brought to life.

Art:
- Make a longhouse or a tepee like the ones mentioned in this book.
- Illustrate your favorite scene from this book.
- Draw a picture of a Western town in 1889 like the picture that Boone drew.

Music:
- Play a record of Indian music.
- Learn to do a traditional Indian dance.
- Listen to a song that was popular in 1889.

Health/PE:
- Make a list of the foods that Little Bear and Boone ate. Was it a balanced diet or not?
- Write a short report about the possible dangers of becoming "blood brothers" today.

*Book: *The Indian in the Cupboard*, Doubleday, 1980.
Author: Lynne Reid Banks
Illustrator: Brock Cole
Grade: 4th or 5th Grade

Social Studies:
- What kind of home did the Iroquois Indians live in?
- What were the three main foods of the Iroquois Indians?
- Describe a Western town of 1889.
- How did a person become and Indian's blood brother in the 18th or 19th century?

Writing:
- Pretend you are Omri. Write a thank-you card to Patrick both before and after Little Bear came to life.
- Write a short story about what Little Bear would do if he were brought back to life again. Compare your story with the book *The Return of the Indian*.

Other Related Books (also by Lynne Reid Banks):
- *The Return of the Indian,* 1986
- *The Secret of the Indian,* 1989
- *The Mystery of the Cupboard,* 1993

Discussion:
- What would be the advantages and problems for you of having plastic figures come alive?
- What would have been the disadvantages of living in Little Bear's time?
- What elements of this book make it a fantasy? What parts of it might be true?

*Thank you to Vivian Carter, Children's Librarian at the Normal Public Library, Normal, Illinois, for suggesting the book *The Indian in the Cupboard* for use in a literature-based unit.

ally must formulate their own purposes for reading in the light of their prior knowledge and the type of genre. In addition, the final step of Survey Q3R may be valuable for summarizing what was learned from the reading.

Teaching Figurative Language in Literature

Here are several strategies for teaching such figurative expressions as similes, metaphors, personification, hyperbole, and euphemism.

- Show a metaphor such as "Joey is a clown" together with the more explicit simile "Joey acts like a clown" and explain that metaphors have missing words that link the things being compared (such as "acts like"). Other sentence pairs also can be shown and explained.

- Students can be asked to find the missing word in a metaphor such as "He's top banana at the place where he works." Students then can offer guesses and explain their reasons aloud.

- The teacher then explains that people have words related to different topics stored in their minds. Examples of words can be modeled by the teacher and then given by the students. At this point students can try to select the attribute related to the new metaphor. After two incorrect guesses the attribute "boss or supervisor" can be supplied and the reason for this choice given. This process then can be repeated with another new metaphor.

- As more metaphors are presented, the teacher should do less modeling and give more and more control of the process to the students. After the teacher explains each type of figurative language and models its interpretation, have students interpret it under supervision, and then provide independent practice activities. In most cases, teachers should take examples of figurative expressions from the literature that the students are actually reading and use these expressions for constructing practice activities.

- Show students pictures of possible meanings for figurative expressions found in their reading materials and ask them to accept or reject the accuracy of each picture. Have them look carefully at the context in which the expression was found before answering. (As an example, if you illustrate the sentence "Betsy is as stubborn as a mule" with a picture of Betsy standing beside a mule, students should reject the accuracy of the picture.)

- Have primary-grade children draw a picture indicating the literal meaning of several figurative expressions. For example, have them draw a picture showing the literal meaning of each of these figurative expressions:

Bobbi's head is a computer.

My mother's new car turned out to be a lemon.

When my father saw my report card with its low grades, he gave me a tongue lashing.

I'm a real chicken when I see blood.

My father always has been as strong as an ox.

- Have students write an actual meaning for a number of idiomatic expressions such as the following:

The car *came out of nowhere* and hit the large tree.

Andrea's *head is always in the clouds.*

I have been *down in the dumps* all week.

Keep what I just told you under your hat.

Sallie *got up on the wrong side of the bed today.*

Ever since I won the award, *I've been walking on air.*

Andy *stole the spotlight yesterday.*

All I ever get from him is a *song and dance.*

We're not *out of the woods yet.*

I have a *fat chance* of getting that math assignment done on time.

- Ask students to select the best explanation of a figurative expression found in their reading materials and ask them to accept or reject the accuracy of each picture. Have them examine the context before answering. For example: "The night was growing old, and there still were many places that we wanted to go" means:

  a. It was very late at night, and there were still many places to go.

  b. The night was growing old just like a person grows old.

  c. Night was over, and there were still many places to go.

- Give each student a copy of a poem that contains figurative language and have the class compete to determine who can locate all of the figures of speech first. You may require students to label all figures of speech properly as to what kind they are and then to explain them.

- Have the students participate in an "idiom search" in which they look in all types of reading materials and try to locate as many examples of idioms as they can. Students must then define each one in a way that corresponds with its usage.

- Select a cartoon with a figure of speech and have the students answer questions about the cartoon to determine if they can comprehend it. You also can have the students look for other examples in newspaper comics with figurative language and ask them to cut out the examples and bring them to school for discussion.

Note: An excellent resource for locating many similes, metaphors, idiomatic expressions, common word idioms, proverbs, "Murphy's law and others," and euphemisms is the following:

Edward B. Fry, Jacqueline E. Kress, and Dona Lee Fountoukidis, *The Reading Teacher's Book of Lists,* second edition. Englewood Cliffs, New Jersey: Prentice-Hall, 1993, pp. 87-97.

Teaching Some Specialized English Skills

English textbooks usually cover the areas of *listening, speaking,* and *writing* and generally are composed of a series of sections of instructional material followed by practice exercises. The specialized vocabulary includes such terms as *noun, pronoun, determiner, verb, adverb, adjective, manuscript, cursive,* and *parliamentary procedure.* The concepts presented in the informational sections are very comprehensive; each sentence usually is very important for comprehending; and examples frequently are given. Students need to be encouraged to study the examples because they help to clarify the information presented in the narrative portion of the textbook.

Teachers should plan oral activities in class to accompany the listening and speaking portions of the English textbook because such practice allows students to *apply the concepts immediately* and helps them to retain the material. It also is helpful to have students apply the concepts encountered in the writing section as soon as possible in relevant situations to help retention.

Composition instruction can form the basis for reading activities. Students read to obtain information to include in their compositions, and they read to learn different styles of writing. As an example, they should read poems to absorb the style of writing of poetry before attempting to write poetry. The writing workshop also can be used to encourage writing in English (create a topic, write a rough draft, have a conference about the writing with the teacher or a peer[s], rewrite the final draft, edit the final draft, and publish the writing).

English classes are often the place where formal vocabulary instruction takes place. Trade books can be the basis for many helpful vocabulary lessons. They can offer instruction and practice in such elements of English as figurative language, synonyms, antonyms, and homonyms.

The Extendi-Character Strategy

The objective of this activity is to promote identification of particular qualities of characters in short stories and to extend imaginative thinking. It probably is most applicable with middle-school students and above. Before the activity is attempted, students should have read a variety of short stories with various characters and have had classroom instruction in characterization.

Since it often is difficult for students to obtain a clear picture of a particular character in a novel or short story, students can be asked to extend the scope of their awareness of the character through imagination. The teacher should compose fictitious circumstances into which students can project characters they have met in the short stories they have read.

Here are some examples of this activity:

Your character's older sister is leaving to go to college. What will your character do to adjust to this situation?

Your character has been involved in a minor traffic accident for which he or she received a traffic ticket. What kinds of statements will he or she make to the police officer?

Your character has met a person who said that he or she will lend the character some much-needed money for a high rate of interest. What will your character do?

A blizzard has spoiled your character's plan for an important business trip out of town. How will your character cope with this change of plans?

Your character has received a letter saying that a cousin he or she does not like will be spending the summer. How will your character react to this news?

Your character's father has died suddenly. How will your character adjust to this change in his or her life?

Then have the students match the situation created by the teacher with one of the characters they have read about in the short stories. They then compose two or three paragraphs in answer to the question.

The Clued-In Strategy

This strategy is designed for students of literature at the middle-school level and above. It requires a student to extract pieces of information from his or her reading and then to apply them in a new way. This skill should help students to sort facts from his or her reading and to locate a common element among those facts to produce new learning.

From the reading background of the class choose some common elements such as characters, theme, author, or any other factors that are significant to the selections. Place each clue verse in an envelope and mark the envelopes beginning with number one. The clues provided later in this section should serve as examples for you.

Divide the class into groups and give each group several envelopes marked in sequence beginning with number one. Each envelope should contain a clue or problem. When that problem is solved and the correct answer has been written on it, each group is entitled to open envelope number one. The answer to number one must be known before number one can be begun, and so forth. If the problem cannot be solved, the teacher provides the answer to the group on request and gives them a two-minute penalty. Since this is a timed race, it is possible that the winning group may be the last group to finish if it did not need to ask for an answer and thus be penalized. You should allow five minutes for each clue in a 40-minute period.

Here are some examples of clues that could be used in this activity.

One:

This poet from New England has a last name that can be associated with one of his most famous poems.

Two:

This reporter, novelist, lecturer, and "ham" used a pseudonym for his real first name which really was "Sam."

Three:

The famous novelist for young readers who writes about real-life situations and has a last name that rhymes with "broom."

Four:

This play written by William Shakespeare contains the very famous line: "*Et tu, Brute.*"

Five:

This poet and author wrote a poem about the city of Chicago and a well-known biography about the sixteenth president of the United States.

Answers to clues:

1. Robert Frost

2. Mark Twain (Samuel L. Clemens)

3. Judy Blume

4. Julius Caesar

5. Carl Sandburg

Games for Use in English Units

There also are several games that can be used for reinforcement of various concepts in English. Here is a description of several of them:

Grammar Whiz Quiz

GRADE LEVEL: 5-6

NAME OF GAME: Grammar Whiz Quiz

OBJECTIVE OF GAME: To enable students to apply grammatical skills and to follow directions

STUDENT PREPARATION: The students should have had some work in a grammar unit.

TEACHER PREPARATION: Prepare a gameboard or adapt a gameboard you are already using. You also probably can use a generic gameboard of some kind. Construct the *question cards* (see the examples below).

PROCEDURE: Two or more students can play this game. The first player rolls the dice and moves his or her marker along the board the number of spaces indicated by the dice throw. The student follows the directions on that space. When the direction says to select a card, he or she chooses a card, reads it aloud, and makes a response. The student shows the back of the card to another student to verify its accuracy. If the player has answered correctly, he or she moves the marker one space forward and waits for his or her next turn. If he or she answers incorrectly, the student retains the card and tries to answer the same question when it is his or her turn again. If correct, the student moves forward one space. The player who completes the entire circuit on the gameboard first is named *Grammar Whiz.*

EXAMPLES OF CARDS FOR GRAMMAR WHIZ:*

1. The elderly <u>gentleman</u> fell on the sidewalk and apparently broke his hip. What is the underlined word in this sentence called? (**noun/subject of the sentence**)

2. My English teacher certainly <u>is</u> a very talented person. What is the underlined word in this sentence called?(**verb/linking verb**)

3. I became very frightened when the car stopped ahead of me so <u>suddenly</u>. What is the underlined word in this sentence called? (**adverb**)

4. The boys ran <u>furiously</u> to escape from the ferocious dog that was chasing after them. What word does the underlined word modify? (**ran**)

5. Sandra fell <u>over</u> a chair as she was hurrying to her seat in class. What is the underlined word in this sentence called? (**preposition**)

*The answer to each question appears on the back of the card.

6. My kitten scratched my little <u>sister</u> on the hand when she tried to pet it. What is the underlined word in this sentence called? (**noun/direct object**)

7. I hope <u>that I will be able to go to the concert on Saturday evening</u>. What are the underlined words in this sentence called? (**subordinate clause**)

8. <u>Running that fast</u> certainly is not a wise thing to do. What are the underlined words in this sentence called? (**gerund phrase/subject phrase**)

9. Jimmy knows that <u>he</u> is a very good student in arithmetic. What is the underlined word in this sentence called? (**pronoun**)

10. My dog usually sleeps <u>under the bed</u> in the evenings. What are the underlined words in this sentence called? (**prepositional phrase**)

11. What are the three main tenses of English? (**past, present, and future**)

12. How can you recognize an infinitive phrase? (**An infinitive phrase begins with to and ends with a verb.**)

13. Don't play with the monkeys. What is the subject of this sentence? (**It is "you" which is understood since it is not stated directly in the sentence.**)

14. It is a sunny day today, <u>and</u> I feel very happy about that. What part of speech is the underlined word? (**conjunction**)

15. Her father forced her <u>to go</u> to the library today. What part of speech is the underlined phrase? (**infinitive phrase**)

16. Name any four prepositions. (***in, into, over, under, around, through, to, above,* or any others**)

17. Emily <u>has been going</u> to church almost every Sunday her entire life. What are the underlined words called? (**verb phrase**)

18. My mother <u>will be</u> sixty years old next month. In what tense is the underlined phrase? (**future**)

19. The green <u>grass</u> in spring certainly is very lovely. What part of speech is the underlined word? (**noun/subject of the sentence**)

20. Nakisha would like to go to the ballet on Sunday, <u>but</u> she must be out of town that day. What part of speech is the underlined word? (**conjunction**)

What's in a Picture?

GRADE LEVEL: Middle School Level

NAME OF GAME: What's In a Picture?

OBJECTIVE OF GAME: To enable students to learn descriptive adjectives that are beyond their present speaking vocabulary and to promote the use of a dictionary and/or thesaurus and the ability to read and follow directions.

STUDENT PREPARATION: The student should have had some training in the use of an appropriate dictionary or thesaurus.

TEACHER PREPARATION: Prepare a gameboard or adapt a gameboard you are already using. You also probably can use a generic gameboard of some type. Cut out attractive pictures from magazines that show situations that lend themselves to out-of-the-ordinary descriptive words. Make a card(s) to accompany each picture and select three words from which students are to choose one. Select words in such a manner that only one can be an appropriate descriptor.

PROCEDURE: Two or more students can play this game. They roll dice and move markers accordingly. When a player's marker stops on a Pick-a-Card space, he or she selects a card, chooses the appropriate picture, and reads the card aloud, shows the picture to other players, and then makes a response. He or she shows the back of the card to other players to verify his or her accuracy. If the player has answered correctly, he or she moves the marker ahead one space. If he or she has answered incorrectly, he or she is not allowed to see the definition but instead looks up the various words in the dictionary so he or she can answer on the next round. Then he or she can move ahead one space. The first player to finish the game can be called the ***Vocabulary Champ.***

EXAMPLES OF CARDS FOR WHAT'S IN A PICTURE?"*

1. Look at this picture. How could the girl in the picture be described?

   callous

   exuberant

   secluded

2. Look at this picture. What word best describes it?

   triumphant

   maudlin

   hazardous

3. Look at this picture. How can the people in the picture be described?

   estranged

   flamboyant

   agitated

4. Look at this picture. How can the scene in it be described?

   abominable

   enigmatic

   preposterous

5. Look at this picture. What word best describes it?

   ludicrous

   meritorious

   frolicsome

6. Look at this picture. How could the girl in it be described?

   credulous

   benevolent

   captivating

7. Look at this picture. How can the scene in it be described?

   obnoxious

   perilous

   sentimental

*The correct response is on the back of the card.

8. Look at this picture. How can the man in it be described?

   burly

   apprehensive

   taciturn

9. Look at this picture. How can the girl in it be described?

   feminine

   animated

   aloof

10. Look at this picture. How can the picture be described?

    incomprehensible

    abhorrent

    grandiose

11. Look at this picture. How can the men in it be described?

    hilarious

    aristocratic

    ghastly

12. Look at this picture. How can the scene in it be described?

    bloodcurdling

    barbarous

    commonplace

13. Look at this picture. How can the flower in it be described?

    exquisite

    pompous

    languid

14. Look at this picture. How can the building in it be described?

    hostile

    forlorn

    ardent

15. Look at this picture. How can the women in it be described?

    cantankerous

    amorous

    vivacious

Describe the Animals

GRADE LEVEL: Middle School

NAME OF GAME: Describe the Animals

OBJECTIVE OF GAME: This game has the following four main objectives:

- to enhance vocabulary through writing
- to emphasize the relationships between nouns and adjectives
- to encourage the writing of imaginative anecdotes
- to encourage the use of the dictionary and other references

STUDENT PREPARATION: None

TEACHER PREPARATION: Choose adjectives that are outside students' speaking vocabulary but may well be encountered in reading. As examples:

irate	overwrought
villainous	squeamish
maladroit	gallant
phenomenal	dexterous
compassionate	titian
hazardous	ingenuous
fractious	pretentious
appalling	irresolute
tranquil	apathetic
arduous	contemptible

Put the words on slips of paper or cards and place them in an envelope. In a second envelope place cards containing the names of various animals, such as the following:

cheetah	dingo
koala bear	rhinoceros
hippopotamus	llama
giraffe	gazelle
kangaroo	grizzly bear
crocodile	leopard
fox	cape buffalo
porcupine	fox
raccoon	antelope
muskrat	elephant

Provide dictionaries that have many illustrations and encyclopedias in print and on computer disk for the students. Put the materials together with a set of directions in a file folder.

PROCEDURE: Have the student draw one card from the animal envelope and five cards from the adjective envelope. Using the animal as his or her central character, have the student create a 50-word anecdote incorporating the five descriptive words.

VARIATION: As an alternative, the adjectives and names of animals can be dittoed for use with an entire class. In this case, each student would select his or her own animal and five descriptive terms.

Ready-to-Duplicate Activity Sheets for Improving Competency in Literature (Language Arts)

The chapter now contains four ready-to-duplicate activity sheets that are related to improving competency in literature (language arts) at the fifth- and sixth-grade levels.

A TYPICAL TELEPHONE DIRECTORY
(Approximately Sixth-Grade Level)

This activity sheet will help you to practice how to get information from the *Yellow Pages* of a telephone directory. *Let your fingers do the walking* through the Yellow Pages by completing this sheet *with a partner*(s). The first column contains a *situation* in which you would need to use the *Yellow Pages of your local telephone directory*. Fill in the remaining three columns about each situation with your partner. The first two situations have been completed for you as examples.

Situation	Service/Product Needed	Found Under	Name/Phone
Your wristwatch appears to be broken.	watch repair shop	Clocks—Service & Repair	Watkins Jewelry & Repair 555-3011
You want to locate a kennel in which to board your dog for a weekend.	dog kennel	Dog & Cat Kennels	Critter Care of Bloomington— Normal 555-6709
You want to build a deck on the front of your house.			
You want to try to rent a saxophone to see if you would like to learn to play it.			
You need new heels put on a pair of shoes.			
You want to hire someone to type a term paper for you.			
You want to find a lawyer to start a lawsuit because of an injury you received as a result of an accident.			

A TYPICAL TELEPHONE DIRECTORY
(Approximately Sixth-Grade Level)

(cont.)

Situation	Service/Product Needed	Found Under	Name/Phone
You want to get your hair cut.			
You want to have some drapes made to order for your living room windows.			
You want to buy some material so that you can make yourself a new dress.			
You want to buy some geranium plants for Memorial Day.			
You want to have a package professionally packed.			
You have had blisters and calluses on your feet lately and you want to find a foot doctor to examine them.			
You need to have a new roof put on your house.			
You need to have your income tax figured.			

Answer Key for "From a Typical Telephone Directory"

Although no answer key is possible for the last portion of this activity sheet since the answers to the last column will vary depending upon the local telephone directory the students are using, sample answers are given for the second and third columns of the activity sheet. *They should be thought of only as sample answers.*

a lumber yard	Lumber—Retail
a store that rents musical instruments	Musical Instruments—Dealers
a shoe repair shop	Shoe Repair
typing service	Typing Service
lawyer	Attorneys
beauty shop	Beauty Salons
draperies	Draperies & Curtains—Retail & Custom Made
dress material shop	Fabric Shops
greenhouse	Greenhouses—Retail
packing store	Packaging Service
foot doctor	Podiatrist
roofer	Roofing Contractors
tax return preparer	Tax Return Preparation

FEELINGS ABOUT WORDS
(Approximately Fifth-Grade Level)

Words have no feelings in themselves, but they do take on *negative or positive meanings* when they are used by people. Words that are positive to some people may be negative to others, depending on the experiences in people's backgrounds. Therefore, there are no right or wrong answers for this activity sheet. *Look at each word, decide how you feel about it, and put a check mark ✓ in the column that best represents your feelings.*

	Positive Feeling	Negative Feeling	No Feeling Either Way
1. Reading at the age of three			
2. Stepchild of an alcoholic			
3. Excellent scholar			
4. Husband and father			
5. Politician			
6. Very poor child			
7. Jokester			
8. Television celebrity			
9. Very well educated			
10. Extremely wealthy			
11. College graduate			
12. Television and movie actor			
13. Sports star			
14. Fugitive from justice			
15. Defendant			
16. Son of an immigrant father			
17. Astronomer			
18. Professor			
19. Television performer			
20. "Superstar" in science			
21. Raised in an aristocratic family			
22. Child of divorced parents			
23. Unmotivated student			
24. Had an eating disorder			
25. Mother			

Answer Key for "Feelings About Words"

Note: There are no right answers. The words contained in this activity sheet are based on the lives of the five following contemporary people:

1-5	President William Clinton
6-10	Bill Cosby
11-15	O. J. Simpson
16-20	Carl Sagan
21-25	Princess Diana

THE USE OF HETERONYMS
(Approximately Sixth-Grade Level)

As you know, a *heteronym* is a word that has a different sound and different meanings but the same spelling. All of the heteronyms contained in this activity sheet contain more than one syllable. *In column I write each heteronym with the accent indicating the meaning that you have chosen. In Column II write a phrase containing the word as you have accented it.* You may use a dictionary and work with a partner(s) if you wish.

Heteronym	Column I	Column II
1. content		
2. invalid		
3. object		
4. minute		
5. conduct		
6. digest		
7. contract		
8. converse		
9. address		
10. compound		
11. desert		
12. complex		
13. discount		
14. relay		
15. attribute		
16. convict		
17. present		
18. defect		
19. advocate		
20. upset		
21. contest		
22. upgrade		
23. compress		
24. buffet		
25. compact		

Answer Key for "The Use of Heteronyms"

Note: Since students' responses will vary greatly, no answer key is included for this activity sheet.

USING FIGURATIVE LANGUAGE
(Approximately Fifth-Grade Level)

Each sentence on the left contains an *idiomatic expression* or figurative language. *Rewrite each sentence without the idiomatic expression so that it has the approximate same meaning.* You can work with a partner(s) on this activity sheet if you would like. The first two sentences have been done for you as examples.

1. We need to *clear the air.*

2. Don *gets cold feet* when he has to give a speech in class.

3. Lily was *down in the dumps* all day yesterday.

4. Money always *burns a hole in Kay's pocket.*

5. Tell Barry to *drop me a line* when you see him.

6. Do you *get the picture*?

7. Reading that book certainly *opened my eyes.*

8. Jeanne certainly doesn't *know the ropes.*

9. *Keep it under your hat.*

10. Evelyn is not *out of the woods* yet after her surgery.

11. I was *walking on air* last Wednesday afternoon.

12. He *lost his temper* for no good reason.

13. Sarah *took the rap* for her friends.

1. We need to talk openly about the subject.

2. Don gets very apprehensive when he has to give a speech in class.

3. _____

4. _____

5. _____

6. _____?

7. _____

8. _____

9. _____

10. _____

11. _____

12. _____

13. _____

USING FIGURATIVE LANGUAGE
(Approximately Fifth-Grade Level)

(cont.)

14. Katie certainly *got up on the wrong side of the bed* today.

14. _____
    _____.

15. Mr. Larsson's new car really *hugs the road.*

15. _____
    _____.

16. My father quit smoking *cold turkey.*

16. _____
    _____.

17. I'd give *my right arm* to own a Corvette.

17. _____
    _____.

18. The party was *for the birds.*

18. _____
    _____.

19. Brian's *not playing with a full deck.*

19. _____
    _____.

20. Anita takes *forever and a day* to get ready.

20. _____
    _____.

Answer Key for "Using Figurative Language"

Note: The answers included in this answer key are only illustrative. Many other correct sentences are possible for each example.

3. Lily was depressed all day yesterday.

4. It is hard for Kay to have money without spending it.

5. Tell Barry to write me a letter when you see him.

6. Do you understand what I mean?

7. Reading that book certainly has helped me to understand the situation.

8. Jeanne certainly doesn't understand what is going on.

9. Don't tell anyone about that subject.

10. Evelyn is not out of danger yet after her surgery.

11. I was very happy last Wednesday afternoon.

12. He became angry for no good reason.

13. Sarah accepted the blame for her friends.

14. Katie is having a bad day today.

15. Mr. Larsson's new car certainly handles well.

16. My father quit smoking immediately without any difficulty.

17. I'd really like to own a Corvette.

18. The party was not very good.

19. Brian doesn't seem to know just what he's doing.

20. Anita takes a very long time to get ready.

GENERAL GOALS FOR TEACHING SOCIAL STUDIES

It obviously is very important to the continued success of a democratic society that students achieve a mastery of the various elements of social studies. As you know, social studies consists of the study of history, geography, political science, sociology, and economics. It is crucial that students especially in middle and secondary schools master the most important elements of these content areas in order that they may attain a productive and satisfying life. Unfortunately, however, much of the material in social studies is extremely difficult for many students in middle and secondary schools to comprehend.

As an example, many of the social studies content textbooks are written well above the reading level of many of the students who are to read them. For example, a typical fifth-grade social studies textbook may possibly be written on the sixth-grade or even the seventh-grade reading level. Thus, it is exceedingly difficult for both average and below-average readers to understand the material effectively. Indeed, often only the above-average readers in a class can understand the material effectively.

Thus, one of the general goals of teaching social studies is that of enabling students to understand the important technical terms that are contained in this content field. For example, such technical terms as *democracy, communism, so-*

cialism, capitalism, latitude, longitude, and *hemisphere* are very difficult for students to decode. In addition, some of the terms in social studies differ from those used in general conversation. As an example, when a student hears that the president is in the process of selecting a *cabinet,* it may mean to him or her that the president is going to choose *kitchen cabinets.* That is why one major goal of social studies teachers always should be to ensure that students clearly understand the concepts are represented by these terms.

Another goal of social studies should be how to teach students to interpret the maps, charts, and graphs found in social studies materials. Although these aids are extremely important to the complete understanding of the material, they are not always easy for students to comprehend. Social studies materials also provide teachers with one of the best ways of teaching *critical thinking* and *reading.* All social studies materials should be read very critically, with students being encouraged to compare material from different sources, analyze possible propaganda techniques, check copyright dates to determine timeliness, and be cognizant of outdated geography materials that show incorrect boundaries or place names. Certainly the former Soviet Union is a prime example of this concept.

Another goal for teaching social studies is to help students to evaluate the accuracy and authenticity of material. Fictionalized biographies and diaries are excellent for teaching students this important concept since authors have invented dialogue and thoughts for the characters to make the material seem more realistic. Teachers should lead students to see that these stories attempt to add life to facts but are not completely factual by having them check in various reference books for accuracy of dates, places, and names. Sometimes an author's foreword or postscript will offer clues to the fictional aspects of a story. As an example, sometimes only the historical events mentioned are true. Students also should know that authors use first-person narrative accounts to make the action seem more personal, but that in reality the supposed speaker is not the one who did the writing. In addition, any first-person account offers a limited perspective because the person speaking cannot know everything that all the characters in the story do or everything that is happening at once.

Another very important goal of teaching social studies is to have students look for an author's biases and also to check to see how much the author depended on *actual resources* if a bibliography of sources is given. Editorials and letters-to-the-editor also are very good sources of material for teaching students to search for an author's biases.

Other goals of teaching social studies require students to recognize cause-effect relationships, to recognize comparison-contrast relationships, and to grasp chronological sequence. Social studies materials often are written in a very precise and compact expository style in which many ideas are expressed in a few lines of print. For example, authors may discuss a 100-year span in a single page or even a single paragraph or may cover complex issues in a few paragraphs even though entire books instead could be devoted to these issues.

THE IMPORTANCE OF TEACHING SOCIAL STUDIES IN THEMATIC UNITS AS MUCH AS POSSIBLE

Social studies should be taught in *thematic units of instruction* as much as possible. In the past social studies typically was mainly taught from a single social studies textbook at either the primary-grade, intermediate-grade, middle-school, or secondary-school level. As stated earlier, often this single textbook was one or more reading levels above the reading levels of many of the students who were supposed to read it. In addition, it often was not written in a particularly appealing or reader-friendly manner. Instead, it may have consisted of a series of rather uninteresting facts that simply were to be memorized without being very relevant to students' daily lives.

Fortunately, however, social studies teaching at the primary-grade, intermediate-grade, and middle-school levels often now includes a substantial amount of *thematic unit teaching*. This probably is less true at the secondary-school level. Thematic unit teaching in social studies is an attempt to integrate other content areas such as language arts, science, mathematics, and often art, music, and drama into learning social studies material. Undoubtedly, a true middle school with its integrated, team-teaching approach best illustrates thematic unit teaching.

When thematic unit teaching is used in social studies, the social studies teacher—in consultation with language arts, science, and mathematics teachers—selects one important *theme or unit* that is going to be studied for a particular time period such as perhaps four weeks. One possible topic for a fifth-grade middle school class might be that of *Tropical Rain Forests*. Then the entire important content about tropical rain forests would be learned by the students themselves with the teachers acting mainly as *facilitators* of learning instead of merely lecturers or presenters. Some, if not all, of the content and ways of learning it is selected by the students themselves with teacher guidance if necessary. The students would use the content areas of literature, social studies, science, mathematics, art, music, and drama in the implementation of learning about tropical rain forests. Much of the learning about tropical rain forests would involve active direction and participation by the students themselves working independently, in groups, or with the entire class by using material from all of the different content areas when appropriate.

Thus, the material the students learn in the thematic unit teaching of social studies usually is much more relevant and meaningful to them than that learned in traditional teaching. In addition, thematic unit teaching integrates material from all of the content areas in a very comprehensive way and involves active student involvement in learning the appropriate content, usually much more effectively than is the case in traditional content teaching. Students also are encouraged to read appropriate material on their own level instead of being required to read material that is far too difficult for them as is often the case in traditional teaching. Reading materials such as content textbooks at various reading levels, trade books at different reading levels, newspapers, magazines, reference books of various kinds such as print encyclopedias and encyclopedias on CD-ROM at the appropriate levels are used in learning the material for the unit. Students therefore also are encouraged to work with students with different reading levels, which is especially helpful to the below-average readers who are so often required to regularly read only with other below-average readers, thus causing them to have a low self-esteem and a dislike for reading.

In summary, thematic unit teaching should be used to present social studies content as much as possible in the primary grades, intermediate grades, middle school, and even secondary school if possible. It generally is much more effective than is the traditional teaching of social studies through the use of a single textbook or several textbooks even if such strategies for improving comprehension as DR-TA, K-W-L, K-W-L Plus, or the herringbone technique are used.

USING MULTICULTURAL LITERATURE IN THE TEACHING OF SOCIAL STUDIES

Although multicultural literature of various types obviously can be used in many different content areas such as literature and science, social studies certainly lends itself very well to using multicultural trade books of various types perhaps especially in the study of historical and geographical units. Multicultural trade books add great interest to the material covered in the content textbook and inform students about people and cultures that are different from their own.

In a useful article Donna E. Norton suggests presenting multicultural literature in a sequence including traditional literature, traditional tales from one area, autobiographies, biographies, historical fiction, contemporary fiction, biography, and poetry. (Donna E. Norton, "Teaching Multicultural Literature in the Reading Curriculum," *The Reading Teacher,* no. 44, Sept. 1990, pp. 28-40.)

Here is a partial list of multicultural literature that might lend itself to use in various kinds of social studies thematic units. Complete annotated bibliographies of all of these trade books can be found in various reference books that are contained in the children's and young people's section of any local public library or any university library.

African-American Literature

Bryan, A., *Beat the Story-Drum, Pum-Pum.* New York: Atheneum, 1980.

Bryan, A., *Turtle Knows Your Name.* New York: Atheneum, 1989.

Carew, J., *Children of the Sun.* Boston: Little, Brown and Company, 1980.

Clifton, L., *Everett Anderson's Goodby.* New York: Holt, Rinehart and Winston, 1983.

Courlander, H., *The Crest and the Hide: And Other African Stories of Heroes, Chiefs, Bards, Hunters, Sorcerers, and Common People.* New York: Coward, 1982.

Ferris, J., *Go Free or Die: A Story of Harriet Tubman.* Minneapolis: Carolrhoda, 1988.

Greenfield, E., *Sister.* New York: Crowell, 1974.

Grifalconi, A., *The Village of Round and Square Houses.* Boston: Little, Brown and Company, 1986.

Haley, A., *A Story, a Story.* New York: Atheneum, 1970.

Hamilton, V., *Junius Far Over.* New York: Harper & Row, 1985.

Hamilton, V., *The People Could Fly: American Black Folktales.* New York: Knopf, 1985.

Hamilton, V., *Anthony Burns: The Defeat and Triumph of a Fugitive Slave.* New York: Knopf, 1988.

Harris, J., *Jump Again! More Adventures of Brer Rabbit.* San Diego: Harcourt Brace Jovanovich, 1986.

Hurmence, B., *A Girl Called Boy*. New York: Clarion, 1982.

Knutson, B., *Why the Crab Has No Head*. Minneapolis: Carolrhoda, 1987.

Langstaff, J., *What a Morning: The Christmas Story in Black Spirituals*. New York: Macmillan, 1987.

Lester, J., *How Many Spots Does a Leopard Have? And Other Tales*. New York: Scholastic, 1989.

McKissack, P., & McKissack, F., *A Long Hard Journey: The Story of the Pullman Porter*. New York: Walker, 1989.

Meltzer, M., *The Black Americans: A History of Their Own Words*. New York: Crowell, 1984.

Miller, D., *Frederick Douglass and the Fight for Freedom*. New York: Facts on File, 1988.

Patterson, L., *Frederick Douglass: Freedom Fighter*. Champaign, IL: Garrard, 1965.

Patterson, L., *Martin Luther King, Jr. and the Freedom Movement*. New York: Facts on File, 1989.

Steptoe, J., *Mufaro's Beautiful Daughters: An African Tale*. New York: Lothrop, Lee & Shephard, 1987.

Taylor, M., *Let the Circle Be Unbroken*. New York: Dial, 1981.

Hispanic Literature

Aardema, V., *The Riddle of the Drum: A Tale from Tizapan, Mexico*. New York: Four Winds, 1979.

Beals, C., *Stories Told by the Aztecs: Before the Spaniards Came*. New York: Abelard-Schuman, 1970.

Belpre, P., *Once in Puerto Rico*. New York: Warne, 1973.

Bierhorst, J., *The Monkey's Haircut and Other Stories Told by the Maya*. New York: Morrow, 1986.

Bierhorst, J., *Doctor Coyote: A Native American Aesop's Fables*. New York: Macmillan, 1987.

Blackmore, V., *Why Corn Is Golden: Stories About Plants*. Boston: Little, Brown and Company, 1984.

Cisneros, S., *The Horse on Mango Street*. Houston: Arte Publico, 1983.

Clark, A. N., *Year Walk*. New York: Viking, 1975.

De Gerez, T., *My Song Is a Piece of Jade*. Boston: Little, Brown and Company, 1981.

dePaola, T., *The Lady of Guadalupe*. New York: Holiday, 1980.

Griego y Maestas, J., & Anaya, R. A., *Cuentos: Tales from the Hispanic Southwest*. Santa Fe: Museum of New Mexico, 1980.

Hinojosa, F., *The Old Lady Who Ate People*. Boston: Little, Brown and Company, 1984.

Krumgold, J., *... and Now Miguel*. New York: Crowell, 1953.

Lattimore, D., *The Flame of Peace: A Tale of the Aztecs.* New York: Harper & Row, 1987.

Marrin, A., *Aztecs and Spaniards: Cortes and the Conquest of Mexico.* New York: Atheneum, 1986.

Meltzer, M., *The Hispanic Americans.* New York: Crowell, 1982.

Mohr, N., *Felita.* New York: Dial, 1979.

Mohr, N., *Going Home.* New York: Dial, 1986.

O'Dell, S., *The King's Fifth.* Boston: Houghton Mifflin, 1966.

O'Dell, S., *The Captive.* Boston: Houghton Mifflin, 1979.

O'Dell, S., *The Amethyst Ring.* Boston: Houghton Mifflin, 1983.

Pena, S., *Kikirki: Stories and Poems in English and Spanish for Children.* Houston: Arte Publico, 1981.

Phillips, B. L., *The Picture Story of Nancy Lopez.* New York: Messner, 1986.

Prago, A., *Strangers in Their Own Land: A History of Mexican-Americans.* New York: Four Winds, 1973.

Roberts, M., *Henry Cisneros: Mexican American Mayor.* Chicago: Children's Press, 1986.

Rohmer, H., & Wilson, D., *Mother Scorpion Country.* San Francisco: Children's Book Press, 1987.

White, C., *Cesar Chavez, Man of Courage.* Champaign, IL: Garrard, 1973.

Native American Literature

Anderson, B., *Trickster Tales from Prairie Lodgefires.* Nashville: Abingdon, 1979.

Baker, O., *Where the Buffaloes Begin.* New York: Warne, 1981.

Baylor, B., *The Desert Is Theirs.* New York: Scribner's, 1975.

Cleaver, E., *The Enchanted Caribou.* New York: Atheneum, 1985.

dePaola, T., *The Legend of the Bluebonnet.* New York: Putnam, 1983.

Esbensen, B., *The Star Maiden.* Boston: Little, Brown and Company, 1988.

Freedman, R., *Buffalo Hunt.* New York: Holiday, 1988.

Gobel, P., *Star Boy.* Scarsdale, NY: Bradbury, 1983.

Gobel, P., *Buffalo Woman.* Scarsdale, NY: Bradbury, 1984.

Grinnell, G. B., *The Whistling Skeleton: American Indian Tales of the Supernatural.* New York: Four Winds, 1982.

Hamilton, V., *In the Beginning: Creation Stories from Around the World.* San Diego: Harcourt Brace Jovanovich, 1988.

Highwater, J., *Anpao: An American Indian Odyssey.* New York: Lippincott, 1977.

Highwater, J., *The Ceremony of Innocence.* New York: Harper & Row, 1985.

Highwater, J., *I Wear the Morning Star.* New York: Harper & Row, 1986.

Hudson, J., *Sweetgrass.* New York: Philomel, 1989.

Marrin, A., *War Clouds in the West: Indians & Cavalrymen, 1860-1890.* New York: Atheneum, 1984.

Monroe, J., & Williamson, R., *They Dance in the Sky: Native American Star Myths.* Boston: Houghton Mifflin, 1987.

Morrison, D. N., *Chief Sarah: Sarah Winnemucca's Fight for Indian Rights.* New York: Atheneum, 1980.

Mowat, F., *Lost in the Barrens.* Toronto: McClelland & Stewart, 1966, 1984.

O'Dell, S., *Sing Down the Moon.* Boston: Houghton Mifflin, 1970.

Robinson, G., *Raven the Trickster.* New York: Atheneum, 1982.

Sneve, V. D. H., *High Elk's Treasure.* New York: Holiday, 1972.

Sneve, V. D. H., *Jimmy Yellow Hawk.* New York: Holiday, 1972.

Sneve, V. D. H., *When Thunder Spoke.* New York: Holiday, 1974.

Speare, E. G., *The Sign of the Beaver.* Boston: Houghton Mifflin, 1983.

Spencer, P. U., *Who Speaks for Wolf.* Austin, TX: Tribe of Two Press, 1983.

White Deer of Autumn, *Ceremony: In the Circle of Life.* Milwaukee: Raintree, 1983.

STRATEGIES FOR IMPROVING LITERACY-STUDY SKILLS IN SOCIAL STUDIES

There are a number of strategies that can be used for improving literacy-study skills in social studies. These strategies will be very briefly described now in this section of the chapter.

Survey Q3R

As was stated in an earlier part of this chapter, Survey Q3R is a very useful study strategy that can be used to help students understand and remember content material more effectively than would be the case without the use of this kind of strategy. Survey Q3R is especially effective as a strategy for helping students to comprehend and retain the important information from social studies textbooks at various levels. When it is used in the content area of social studies, the following steps are normally followed which are the typical steps contained in Survey Q3R:

1. *Survey or Preview:* The students survey the entire textbook chapter to gain an overall impression of its content. In the survey or preview, they may read the introduction and summary of the chapter and the first sentence in each of the paragraphs. They also may examine the pictures, maps, graphs, diagrams, tables, and other aids contained in the chapter. **Note:** The survey or preview part of Survey Q3R always should be used in reading social studies material even when no other part of this study technique is used since the survey or preview alone will add greatly to the comprehension and retention of the material.

2. *Question:* The students pose questions they want to read to answer during this step. They turn each subheading in the social studies textbook chapter into a question and also formulate additional questions to read to answer.

3. *Read:* The students then read the social studies chapter *on a selective basis* trying to answer the questions they have posed. In this selective reading, they try to fill in the gaps in their reading by capitalizing on their prior knowledge. This step of the study technique helps them to become *more activity involved in their reading.*

4. *Recite:* This step applies only to one section at a time. After the students have read a section at a time in a purposeful manner, they can recite the important information from that section either in an oral or written form, depending upon which is more efficient for them.

5. *Review:* This step applies after the students have finished the entire chapter. They try to review the important concepts, generalizations, and facts they gained from the chapter. They may use the written notes they have made in the fourth step of this procedure if they wish. (Adapted from Francis P. Robinson, *Effective Study.* New York: Harper & Row, 1961.)

As also stated earlier in this chapter, any of the variations of Survey Q3R are equally useful in the comprehension and retention of social studies materials. However, the *survey or preview* part of any of these variations always is its most important aspect.

Map Reading and Map Thinking

Social studies teachers should give special attention to the development of graphical literacy—the ability to read maps, graphs, pictures, and diagrams. One of the more important of these graphic skills is that of *map reading.* Many maps appear in social studies textbooks although they may also be found in science, mathematics, and literature books. As early as first grade, children can begin developing skills in map reading usually by learning how to read simple maps of their school or their neighborhood. This simple map reading serves as readiness for the more sophisticated map-reading skills students must learn in the intermediate grades, middle school, secondary school, and college.

The first step in map reading is *to examine the title* to determine what area is being presented and what type of information is being given about the area. The teacher should emphasize the importance of determining the information conveyed by the title before moving on to a more detailed study of the map. The next step is to teach students how *to determine directions.* By helping them to locate directional indicators on maps and to use these indicators to identify the four cardinal directions, the teacher makes students aware that north is not always on the top of the map nor south at the bottom of the map, although most maps are constructed in this manner.

The students next should learn how *to interpret the map's legend.* The legend contains an explanation of each of the symbols used on a map, and unless the reader can interpret these symbols, he or she will be unable to understand the information the map contains. A more difficult task may be learning *to interpret the map's scale.* Since it obviously would be impractical to draw a map to the actual size of the area represented, maps obviously must be greatly reduced in size. The scale shows the relationship of a given distance on the map to the same distance on the earth.

Students in the middle school also should learn to understand about such concepts as *latitude and longitude, the Tropic of Cancer and the Tropic of Capri-*

corn, the north and south poles, and the *equator.* Students also should become acquainted with such map terms as *gulf, bay, continent, delta, isthmus, peninsula,* and *hemisphere.*

Thematic maps show the distribution of a particular phenomenon over a particular geographic area. They include maps that focus on political boundaries, land elevation, weather, and population distribution. Each of these types of maps needs special instructional attention if students are to benefit sufficiently from reading them. In addition, students need to practice reading critically about the information that maps can provide.

Here are a few suggestions for teaching map-reading skills. As with most literacy skills, these skills are best taught when the students must read maps for a real purpose in one or more of their classes. Map skills always should also be immediately applied to these authentic materials after instruction takes place.

- To teach children about directions on maps, give them pictures of directional indicators that are tilted in different ways with *north* indicated on each one. Model the location of other directions based on the knowledge of where north is for one of the indicators. Then let the students fill in *S* for *South, E* for *East,* and *W* for *West* on each of the other indicators.

- To teach students to apply a map's scale, help them to construct a map of their classroom or their immediate neighborhood to a specified very simple scale. During this lesson, you must provide step-by-step guidance.

- Demonstrate the use of a map's legend. Then have the students practice using the map's legend by asking them questions such as the following:

  In what city is the state capital of Wisconsin located?

  In what city in Nevada do you see a symbol for a college?

  What is one national monument in the state of South Dakota? Near what city is it located?

  What is the name of the air force base that is located near the city of Tucson, Arizona?

- Have students demonstrate that they understand such terms as *equator* and *continent* by locating these features on a map.

- Give the students a map of their city and have them try to locate the approximate location of their homes on the map.

- Have the students use the computer program *Street Atlas USA* (Freeport, Maine: Delorme Publishing Company) to locate the street on which their school or home is located. This is an extremely motivating technique to use for learning map reading. It is much more motivating than the use of the typical map.

- Have the students look at a map in their social studies textbook and ask them questions such as the following about the map. These questions are based on a *thematic map about precipitation.*

  1. What is this map about?

     a. temperature

     b. precipitation

     c. population

2. What is the scale of miles on this map?

    a. two inches represent fifteen miles

    b. one and one half inches represent fifteen miles

    c. one inch represents fifteen miles

3. How much precipitation does the "brown meadow" receive per year?

    a. 4″ to 7″ per year

    b. 15″ to 20″ per year

    c. 7″ to 15″ per year

4. How much precipitation does the "winter range" receive per year?

    a. 4″ or less per year

    b. 4″ to 7″ per year

    c. 7″ to 15″ per year

5. Which has more precipitation?

    a. the winter range

    b. the summer range

    c. the home ranch

Newspapers

The *newspaper* is one of the most versatile sources of reading material that either social studies or literacy teachers can use. The use of the newspaper has many unique advantages that cannot be found in any other type of reading material. For example, when students read a newspaper, they learn to read for different purposes than is the case with other reading materials and also are able to read material that has real relevance and appears adult-like, which is highly motivating for them.

In addition, in a sense the newspaper is a living textbook for social studies through which students can learn about tomorrow's history as it is happening. Different sections of the newspaper require different reading skills. Here are some of the sections of the newspaper and the unique reading skills that are required for effective comprehension of each section:

- *News Stories*—Locating main ideas and important supporting details (who, what, where, when, why, and how), recognizing sequence, recognizing cause-effect relationships, making inferences and interpretations, and drawing conclusions

- *Editorials and Letters-to-the-Editor*—Discriminating between fact and opinion, determining an author's point of view, determining an author's biases, recognizing various propaganda techniques, recognizing cause-effect relationships, making inferences and interpretations, and drawing conclusions

- *Comic Strips*—Placing a number of items in sequence, understanding a unique style of writing and illustrations, improving comprehension by completing speaking balloons that have been whited-out, interpreting figurative language, interpreting idiomatic expressions, recognizing cause-effect relationships, making predictions, and drawing conclusions

- *Advertisements*—Detecting propaganda techniques, distinguishing between fact and opinion, making inferences, drawing conclusions, and improving critical thinking and critical reading skills

- *Entertainment Section*—Interpreting the TV schedule, determining significant details, and critically evaluating the material presented

- *Weather*—Reading maps, charts, and tables

Most regular newspapers vary somewhat in difficulty from section to section. Teachers can use a readability formula such as the Fry Readability Formula or any readability formula that is available on computer to determine an *approximate reading level* of various sections of the newspaper.

Student newspapers such as the *Weekly Reader* (Columbus, Ohio: Field Publications) and *Know Your World* (Columbus, Ohio: Xerox Education Publications) are most often used in elementary classrooms. However, *Know Your World* is geared toward students who are ten to sixteen years old but are reading on a second- to third-grade reading level, while *Weekly Reader* has a separate publication for each grade level.

A social studies or literacy teacher can begin newspaper study by determining what students already know with a *Newspaper Inventory*. Such a ready-to-use Newspaper Inventory is included in the next section of the chapter.

After evaluating the results of the inventory, here are some activities that may be relevant in helping students to read newspapers more effectively:

- Have students select news stories from a local, regional, or national newspaper. Then have them locate the *who, what, where, when, why,* and *how* in these news stories.

- Place a number of news stories with the headlines cut off and the matching headlines into a brown envelope and have students match the correct headline with the correct news story. If you wish, this activity can be made self-checking.

- Using news stories with the headlines cut off, have students write their own headlines, and compare these headlines with the actual headlines.

- Give students copies of news stories about the same event from two different newspapers. Have them locate the likenesses and differences between the two news stories and discuss in what ways they are alike and different.

- Have students compare an editorial and a news story on the same topic. Discuss with them the similarities and differences.

- Select editorials or letters-to-the-editor that have divergent opinions on the same topic. Have students locate the emotional language and propaganda techniques in each editorial or letter-to-the-editor and mark it.

- Cut apart several comic strips. Then have the students attempt to place the cut-apart comic strips in correct sequence. Each student can then read the comic strip in the correct sequence to make sure it is correct.

- Select a comic strip and white-out the dialogue found in the speaking balloons. Have the student fill in each balloon with dialogue that makes sense. If you wish, you can obtain another copy of the original comic strip, and the student can compare his or her version of the dialogue with the actual dialogue that was found in the original comic strip.

- Have the students try to solve the crossword puzzles contained in the newspaper.

- Have students locate advertisements that illustrate various types of propaganda techniques.

- Have students learn how to use the index of the newspaper to find on what page to look for various items included in the newspaper such as the weather, the obituaries, the comic strips, the editorial page, etc.

- Have students look through the newspaper for possible typographical errors, and then discuss the effect of these errors on the material in which they have appeared.

- Have students look in the sports page for *synonyms* for the terms *won* and *lost.* Help them to determine the most appropriate synonyms for these terms and why they are used in place of the more common terms.

- Have students locate examples of the following types of columns if they appear in a newspaper to which a student has access:

how-to-do-it column

"Dear Abby" or "Ann Landers" (or a similar type of column)

household hints column

medical advice column

- Have students search grocery advertisements from several stores for the best buy on a specific item.

- Have students look in the classified advertisements and decide on what kind of job they would like to have or what kind of house or car they would like to purchase. It also is helpful to have them write their own classified ads following the abbreviated model language found in the classified ads in the newspaper.

Note: One of my teacher-trainees once tutored a seventh-grade boy who asked that the first reading material of each tutoring session be the obituary section of the local newspaper. He very much enjoyed reading each obituary carefully noting the birth and death dates, the occupation of the deceased, the cause of death (if it was included), and the number of survivors. I was never able to determine the reason for his interest in the obituaries. He seemed to be a well-adjusted boy although he was a reluctant reader.

Ready-to-Duplicate Newspaper Inventory

The chapter now contains a reproducible newspaper inventory that is most applicable at the intermediate-grade or middle-school level. You can duplicate and use it in its present form or modify it in any way you wish in the light of the needs and interests of your own students.

NEWSPAPER INVENTORY
(Intermediate-Grade or Middle-School Level)

Answer the following questions about your use of the newspapers that you read.

1. What are the names of the newspaper(s) that come to your home?

   _____

2. Do you read any newspaper on a regular basis? How often do you read that newspaper?

   _____

3. Put a check mark ✓ in front of the parts of the newspaper that you read on a regular basis:

_____ News Section	_____ Editorials	
_____ Letters-to-the-Editor	_____ Entertainment Section	
_____ Comic Strips	_____ Features	
_____ Advertisements	_____ Classified Ads	
_____ Obituaries	_____ Other Sections (Give their names)	

4. Where is the index in a newspaper?

   _____

5. Where is the weather in a newspaper that you read?

   _____

6. How do you locate the part of the newspaper that you want?

   _____ use the index

   _____ turn to each page

7. Write a brief definition for each of the following terms:

   a. byline _____

   b. AP _____

   c. UPI _____

   d. dateline _____

   e. editorial _____

   f. masthead _____

   g. letters-to-the-editor _____

   h. classified advertisements _____

   i. entertainment section _____

   j. obituaries _____

Graphic Aids

One important skill required for effective comprehension and retention in social studies is that of using *graphic aids*. Graphic aids usually are defined as interpreting a graph, a table, a chart, and a diagram. Instruction and reinforcement in the use of graphic aids can begin at the upper primary-grade level from appropriate social studies (or science or mathematics) materials and then can be extended and refined at the intermediate-grade and middle-school levels.

Edward B. Fry of Rutgers University has written an interesting article on *graphical literacy.* Fry stated that the use of graphs to communicate information has been in existence since before written language. He further wrote that literacy teachers (or social studies teachers [my belief]) should present graphical literacy because they are well equipped to do so. Fry presented an interesting taxonomy of graphs that any teacher interested in pursuing this topic should explore. He also gave these suggestions for improving graphical literacy: selecting textbooks that have a good selection of graphs, asking comprehension questions about graphs, talking with students about the importance of interpreting graphs so that they can understand what they are reading, grading the graphs in students' papers, and having a graphing contest (Edward B. Fry, "Graphical Literacy," *Journal of Reading* 34, February 1981, pp. 383-390).

A *graph* is a graphic aid that has been constructed to show some kind of quantitative relationship. To interpret a graph, students should determine what kind of information can be obtained from it and the unit of measurement that was used in reporting the information. Graphs can be introduced in the primary grades in a simple form and then refined and extended in the intermediate grades and middle school. Here are the four main types of graphs:

1. *Picture graph (or pictograph)*—This kind of graph is used to express quantities through pictures.

2. *Circle (or pie graph)*—-This kind of graph shows relationships of individual parts to the whole.

3. *Bar graph*—This kind of graph uses vertical or horizontal bars to compare quantities. Vertical bar graphs are easier to read than are horizontal ones.

4. *Line graph*—This kind of graph shows changes in amounts.

Here are examples of these four types of graphs:

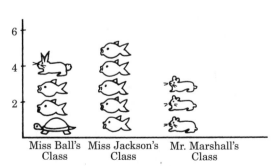

PICTURE GRAPH

Number of pets in the three first grades at Sheridan School.

PIE GRAPH

Weather in Milwaukee, WI during March, 1996.

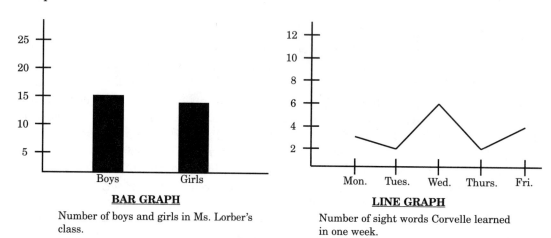

BAR GRAPH

Number of boys and girls in Ms. Lorber's class.

LINE GRAPH

Number of sight words Corvelle learned in one week.

One of the best ways to help students learn to read graphs is to have them construct their own meaningful graphs that they can easily understand such as the following:

1. A picture graph showing how many dogs stayed at Claudia's Kennel on July 4, 5, and 6, 1996.

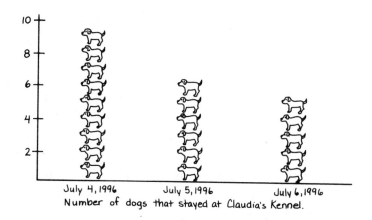

July 4,1996   July 5,1996   July 6,1996
Number of dogs that stayed at Claudia's Kennel.

2. A circle graph showing the percentage of each school day that a child named Jason spends sleeping, eating, at school, watching television, and playing.

3. A bar graph showing the daily maximum temperatures for the week of July 14, 1996 in Winchester, Wisconsin.

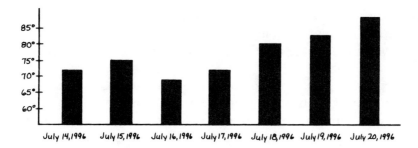

4. A line graph showing the precipitation in inches that fell during 1996 at Chicago, Illinois.

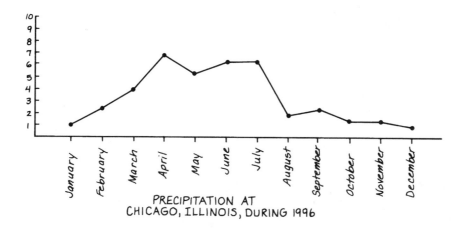

PRECIPITATION AT
CHICAGO, ILLINOIS, DURING 1996

(The next section of this chapter contains several reproducible graphs and questions about them that can be duplicated and used in their present form.)

Tables that appear in social studies reading materials may present problems to students because it may be difficult to extract facts from a large mass of available information. The great amount of information presented in a small amount of space on a table can confuse students unless the teacher provides specific instruction and practice in reading tables.

The titles of tables normally contain information about their content. In addition, since tables are arranged in columns and rows, the headings can provide information. To discover specific information, students must locate the intersection of an appropriate column with an appropriate row. Students also should learn that a special kind of information can be found in tables, and that this information can be used comparatively. The teacher should model how to read tables, verbalizing the mental processes involved in locating the information. Then the students can be asked to read a table and answer related questions about it.

Children in the primary grades can construct their own simple tables about events and tasks that are familiar to them. Intermediate-grade and middle-school students can learn to interpret the tables found in their social studies textbooks. Students at this reading level can learn to make comparisons from different kinds of data and draw valid conclusions from the data. Tables may be used in social studies textbooks to present information such as mileage between various cities, average temperature, and heights above sea level. Students also should have valid reasons for interpreting a table. As in the case of the other content reading skills, interpreting tables is more motivational and meaningful for students who have a valid reason for obtaining the information that is contained in the table.

Both *diagrams* and *charts* are commonly used in students' social studies textbooks in which they may be used to clarify new vocabulary terms or illustrate concepts. A diagram contains labels that are designed to help students interpret it. Either a *flowchart* or *timeline* is a graphic aid that shows the flow, organization, or sequence of a social studies concept in some way. Either may be easier to interpret than the traditional chart found in content textbooks. As you know, a timeline is quite commonly found in history textbooks.

In summary, teachers should discuss the various graphic aids, model their use, and provide students with meaningful, valid opportunities to learn how to use them in their social studies materials.

Name _____ *Grade* _____ *Teacher* _____ *Date* _____

BAR GRAPHS
(Approximately Fourth-Grade Level)

Examine the following two bar graphs carefully. They show the monthly average *temperature* and *precipitation* in the desert city of *Las Vegas, Nevada.* After you have studied the two graphs carefully, answer the questions on the next sheet. You may work with a partner on this activity sheet if you wish.

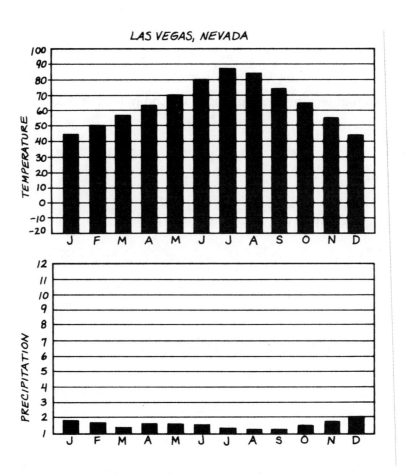

BAR GRAPHS
(Approximately Fourth-Grade Level)

(cont.)

QUESTIONS:

1. What is the hottest month of the year in Las Vegas?

   a. June

   b. July

   c. August

   d. September

2. What is the mean temperature in Las Vegas for the month of May?

   a. 78 degrees

   b. 70 degrees

   c. 80 degrees

   d. 74 degrees

3. What is the coolest month of the year in Las Vegas?

   a. December

   b. November

   c. January

   d. February

4. What is the wettest month of the year in Las Vegas?

   a. December

   b. January

   c. February

   d. March

5. Which of the following best expresses the total precipitation for the year in Las Vegas?

   a. under fifteen inches

   b. under twelve inches

   c. under twenty inches

   d. under two inches

6. Which are the three driest months of the year in Las Vegas?

   a. January, February, March

   b. April, May, June

   c. July, August, September

   d. October, November, December

Answer Key for "Bar Graphs"

1. b
2. b
3. c
4. a
5. b
6. c

CIRCLE GRAPHS
(Approximately Sixth-Grade Level)

Examine the following two circle graphs carefully. Then answer the questions below them. You may work with a partner on this activity sheet if you wish.

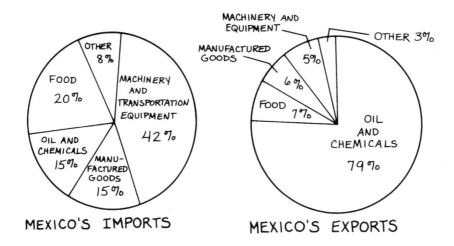

MEXICO'S IMPORTS   MEXICO'S EXPORTS

1. What is Mexico's *chief import*?

   a. manufactured goods

   b. machinery and transportation equipment

   c. food

   d. oil and chemicals

2. What is Mexico's chief export?

   a. manufactured goods

   b. machinery and transportation equipment

   c. food

   d. oil and chemicals

3. What percentage of Mexico's total imports is food?

   a. 18%

   b. 20%

   c. 25%

   d. 10%

4. What percentage of Mexico's total exports is food?

   a. 7%

   b. 8%

   c. 10%

   d. 12%

5. What percentage of Mexico's total imports is others?

   a. 9%

   b. 8%

   c. 10%

   d. 12%

6. What percentage of Mexico's total exports is others?

   a. 3%

   b. 5%

   c. 4%

   d. 7%

Answer Key for 'Circle Graphs"

1. b

2. d

3. b

4. a

5. b

6. a

The Guinness Book of Records

Many students in the intermediate grades and middle school are fascinated with the information contained in *The Guinness Book of Records* (Facts on File, 1996). Students at this level are very interested in the unique facts contained in this reference. It can provide them with much information that they will enjoy both for research about their schoolwork and for their personal pleasure. I cannot recommend this resource highly enough.

Reproducible Activity Sheets for Improving Competency in Reading-Study Skills in Social Studies

The remainder of this section of the chapter contains several ready-to-duplicate activity sheets that will enable students at various grade levels to improve their competency in the different reading-study skills that are required for effective comprehension and retention in social studies. You can duplicate and use any of these activity sheets in their present form or modify them in any way you wish in the light of the needs and interests of your own students.

THE GUIDE-O-RAMA
(Approximately Fifth-Grade Level)

(Carol Berkin, Joe B. Frantz, and Joan Schreiber, *America Yesterday and Today*. Glenview, Illinois: Scott, Foresman and Company, 1988. Grade 5. Chapter 14, "The Great Depression and the New Deal," pp. 302-317.)

Now that we have briefly discussed what you already know about the Great Depression and the New Deal and what you want to learn about this topic in social studies, read the chapter. It should help you better understand and remember the important ideas in the chapter if you use this Guide-o-Rama.

Page 303—First paragraph. You should understand and remember the term *depression* from this paragraph.

Page 303—Second paragraph. You should understand and remember the term *stock market* from this paragraph.

Page 304—Look at the picture on this page. On what street do you believe the stock market is located?

Pages 304-305—Write three probable causes for the Great Depression besides the stock market crash.

Page 305—Look at the picture on this page. What does the picture of the two men show you about the difficulty of obtaining a good job during the depression?

Page 306—Look at the *picture graph (pictograph).* What symbol stands for two million unemployed people in this picture graph (pictograph)? About how many people were unemployed in 1933 and in 1936?

Page 306—Second paragraph. Give a brief definition of the terms *bread lines* and *soup kitchens.*

Page 307—What group of workers were both the *last hired* and *first fired* during the depression? Why do you believe this happened?

Page 309—Third line. Who was the president of the United States when the depression began?

Page 309—Sixth paragraph. What was President Franklin D. Roosevelt's work and his years in office called?

Page 310—Look at the picture on this page. How did the Civilian Conservation Corps (CCC) help the United States recover from the depression?

Page 310—Second paragraph. What was the main purpose of the Works Progress Administration (WPA)?

Page 312—"Linking Past and Future." What does the acronym *TVA* stand for?

Page 313—First paragraph. What is probably the most important of the New Deal programs that remains today?

Page 314—Look at the political cartoon "It's In the Bag." What political parties do the *donkey* and the *elephant* represent?

© 1997 by John Wiley & Sons, Inc.

Answer Key for "The Guide-O-Rama"

Page 304—Wall Street

Pages 304-305—Warehouses were filled with unsold products. Credit buying. Banking practices in which savings accounts were not insured.

Page 305—It was very difficult to find any kind of decent job during the depression.

Page 306—a drawing of a man and a woman. 1933—about twelve and a half million people. 1936—a little over eight million people.

Page 306—*bread lines*—Lines in which unemployed people stood waiting for free food. *soup kitchens*—Places in which free food was given away and in winter where people could get warm.

Page 307—black employees; they probably had only been hired when the employers could not find any suitable white employees.

Page 309—Herbert Hoover

Page 309—the New Deal

Page 310—It gave many unemployed workers a chance to get a good job and also to do useful work such as planting trees, fighting forest fires, and building parks.

Page 310—It provided good jobs to people who were out of work.

Page 312—Tennessee Valley Authority

Page 313—insurance for savings accounts in banks

Page 314—The donkey stands for the Democrats. The elephant stands for the Republicans.

REPRODUCIBLE MAP AND QUESTIONS
(Approximately Second-Grade Level)

Look at the map below.

What does this mean?

N

W—┼—E

S

It means that **north (N)** is toward the top, **south (S)** is toward the bottom, **east (E)** is toward the right, and **west (W)** is toward the left.

> **Now look at the map of Birch Lake. Then read the questions under it looking back at the map when you need to. You can write the answer to each question on the line. You can work with a friend if you want to.**

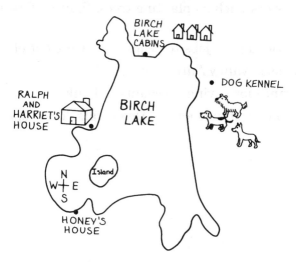

1. On what side of the lake are the Birch Lake Cabins found?

   _____

2. On what side of the lake is Ralph and Harriet's house?

   _____

3. On what side of the lake is Honey's house?

   _____

4. On what side of the lake is the dog kennel found?

   _____

5. Near what side of the lake is the island found?

   _____

FACT OR OPINION ACTIVITY SHEET
FROM SOCIAL STUDIES
(Approximately Fifth-Grade Level)

Read the following statements silently. Some of them are *statements of fact*, while some of them are *statements of opinion* about *"Life in the English Colonies."* If you believe that a sentence is a *statement of fact*, write an *F* on the line before the sentence. If you believe that a sentence is a *statement of opinion*, write an *O* on the line before the sentence.

LIFE IN THE ENGLISH COLONIES

_____ 1. In 1619 Jamestown was the only English colony in America, and about 1,000 settlers lived there or on nearby farms struggling very hard to build a new life for themselves on the land.

_____ 2. The thirty-five men and women who were traveling to the New World on board the ship the *Mayflower* were probably all extremely brave and had no fear at all of making the perilous journey to a dangerous, unknown land.

_____ 3. The *Mayflower Compact,* which the colonists signed before going ashore at Plymouth Rock, was an important step toward *democracy* in America since it gave the signers the right to make "just and equal" laws for the colony.

_____ 4. The English-speaking Native American named Squanto helped the Pilgrims learn how to plant corn and where to catch fish, and remained their good and loyal friend until he died.

_____ 5. The Puritans were justified in making a law that everyone in their colony must attend church on a regular basis whether or not they held the same religious beliefs.

_____ 6. The colonists all shared a common past since their ancestors had come from England, they all had the same language and customs, and they had the same respect for English laws and liberties.

_____ 7. The Quakers were wrong in that they believed priests and ministers were not needed to act between people and God, but believed that they could relate to God directly.

_____ 8. William Penn, a Quaker, promised *religious tolerance* for all, which meant that all people in the colony of Pennsylvania would be free to worship in the way in which they pleased.

_____ 9. It was acceptable for the colonists to take land from the Native Americans without having a treaty with them that would require them to purchase it instead.

_____ 10. Life in the Middle Colonies probably was much superior to life in Europe from which their ancestors had come.

FACT OR OPINION ACTIVITY SHEET
FROM SOCIAL STUDIES
(Approximately Fifth-Grade Level)

(cont.)

_____ 11. The people of the Middle Colonies worshipped in many different ways—they were Catholics, Protestants, and Jews.

_____ 12. The founders of Maryland, one of the Southern Colonies, were English Roman Catholics—Sir George Calvert and his son Cecil Calvert.

_____ 13. English colonists built a village that is now called Charleston in southern Carolina in 1670.

_____ 14. Since the colony of Georgia was in an undesirable location, it only attracted poor English people to live there since they undoubtedly would not have been welcome in any other colony.

_____ 15. The wide coastal plain of the Southern Colonies had both land and climate that were ideal for farming.

_____ 16. A plantation in the Southern Colonies in the 1700s and 1800s was a farm although since that time it has come to mean a large farm especially one on which tobacco, rice, or cotton is grown.

_____ 17. The indigo plant, which was grown in South Carolina, made a fine blue dye for cloth that was important since blue is the loveliest color for the dresses that the women wore who lived there.

_____ 18. Tobacco and rice were the chief exports of the Southern Colonies.

_____ 19. Many plantation workers were black people who had been kidnapped from their homes in Africa, a truly horrible, inhumane practice.

_____ 20. The indentured servants in the Southern Colonies probably had an even harder life in some ways than did the slaves in those colonies.

Answer Key for "Life in the English Colonies"

1. F	6. F	11. F	16. F
2. O	7. O	12. F	17. O
3. F	8. F	13. F	18. F
4. F	9. O	14. O	19. F
5. O	10. O	15. F	20. O

GENERAL GOALS FOR TEACHING SCIENCE

There are a number of goals and unique requirements in the learning of science that make it a very difficult content area for many students to comprehend and remember. One of the most important goals of teaching science is that of enabling students to identify and comprehend the very difficult technical vocabulary found in the vast majority of science materials. As an example, in the typical science textbook students may encounter such technical terms as *igneous, parietal bone, anvil, stirrup, carbon dioxide, hydrogen, atom, molecule, element, pollen, stamen, bacteria, virus,* and *inoculation.* Since science contains many words with meanings unique to it, science or literacy teachers must teach specific scientific concepts *before* students encounter them in their reading. Although context clues often help students to identify unknown vocabulary terms, context is not often so helpful in identifying and understanding technical scientific terms.

In addition, some of the vocabulary terms that have technical meanings also have more common meanings; for example, *solid, hammer, matter, solution,* and *salts.* In addition, science has several symbol sets. The symbols used in the following formulas along with the subscripted numbers in the formulas all must be mastered to read the scientific material correctly.

Compound	Formula	Phase of Matter
Water	H_2O	Liquid
Carbon Dioxide	CO_2	Gas
Salt	$NaCl$	Solid

Science also draws on several different disciplines for its knowledge base. It contains many words with either Latin or Greek *morphemes.* Thus, the study of the meaning of *prefixes, suffixes,* or *word roots* can be very useful in helping students to learn the meaning of unknown technical scientific terms.

A goal of teaching science also should be to help students understand and remember the science materials they read. One of the most important reading skills required is *reading to follow directions.* This is particularly important in laboratory exercises where even the smallest digression from the directions can result in an improperly conducted experiment. Experiments that must be read (and written) also have a text structure that is different from that found in other materials. Much scientific writing is presented in strict categories with understood requirements for what is acceptable in each. Here is a typical scientific problem-solving paradigm:

I. Statement of the Problem

II. Hypotheses

III. Procedure

IV. Observation

V. Collection of Data (Results)

VI. Conclusion(s)

This is a structure that students may not be familiar with before encountering it while reading scientific materials, and therefore it should be taught to them. Examining the organizational structure of scientific writing, it is easy to notice that reading in science requires organizing ideas so that relationships are clear and so that inferences can be drawn on the basis of the relationships. In addition, readers always must be able to understand the purpose of an experiment, read the list of materials to determine what must be obtained in order to perform the experiment, and determine the order of steps to be followed in conducting the experiment. Before they perform an experiment, students always should try to predict its outcome based on their prior knowledge. Later they should compare their predicted results with the actual results.

Reading scientific material also requires such comprehension strategies as *recognizing main ideas and important details, drawing conclusions, recognizing cause-effect relationships,* and *understanding sequential order.* It also is important for students to learn to read all scientific materials *very critically* and to check the copyright dates of scientific materials to ensure that the material is current. The *scientist's inquiring attitude* should be the same as that of the critical reader. It often also is necessary for students to be able to interpret such *reading aids as tables, charts,* and *graphs.*

In addition, science materials must be read slowly and deliberately, and rereading is often necessary to fully understand the information presented. I call this *careful, analytical reading* with a reading rate of perhaps 100-150 words per minute. Scientific materials generally are written in a very compact, expository style that often involves explanations, classification, and cause-effect relationships. Explanations in science often describe processes that may be illustrated by pictures, charts, or diagrams that are designed to clarify the written material.

As is the case with social studies textbooks, science textbooks are very often written at a higher level than the grade level for which they are designed. For example, a sixth-grade science textbook may well be written at the seventh-grade reading level or perhaps even higher. Thus, it is difficult for all but the able readers in a class and certainly is much too difficult for the below-average readers who may be reading at the upper primary-grade level if not even lower. One solution that may be feasible for average or below-average readers in a class is providing them with alternate materials to use for science instruction. Here is a partial list of some easy reading science materials:

Follett Beginning Science Books. Chicago: Follett Publishing Company

Natural Science Books. Minneapolis: Lerner Publications

Nature Club Series. Mahwah, New Jersey: Troll Associates

Nature Watch Series. Minneapolis: Carolrhoda Books

Our Planet Series. Mahwah, New Jersey: Troll Associates

Science Picture Books, by Herbert S. Zim. New York: William Morrow

Young Scott Science Books. New York: William Scott

THE IMPORTANCE OF TEACHING SCIENCE IN THEMATIC UNITS

As is the case in both literature and science, it is very helpful to teach the content area of science in thematic units as much as possible. Thematic or unit teaching enables students to easily understand the relationships between science and the other content areas. In the past and sometimes even today science usually was taught from a single textbook at either the primary-grade, intermediate-grade, middle-school, or secondary-school level. As mentioned earlier, often this single textbook was one or more reading levels above the reading level of many of the students who were required to read it. In addition, it often was not written in a reader-friendly way. Instead, it usually contained very difficult technical vocabulary and complex concepts that just were to be memorized without having particular relevance to the lives of students.

However, at the present time science teaching at the primary-grade, intermediate-grade, and middle-school levels may include some *thematic unit teaching.* Although this may be especially true at the middle-school level which uses an integrated, team teaching approach, it probably is less true at the secondary-school level. Thematic unit teaching in science is an attempt to integrate other content areas such as language arts, science, mathematics, and much less often art, music, and drama into the learning of science material.

When thematic unit teaching is used in science, the science teacher—in consultation with language arts, science, and mathematics teachers—selects one important *theme or unit* that is going to be studied for a particular time period such as about four weeks. One possible topic for a fifth-grade middle school class might be that of *The Solar System.* Then the entire significant content about the solar system is learned by the students themselves with the teachers mainly acting as *facilitators of learning* instead of being lecturers or presenters. Much, if not all, of the content and strategies for learning the material is chosen by the students themselves with teacher direction if necessary. The students use the content areas of literature, social studies, science, mathematics, and less likely, art, music, and drama in the implementation of learning about the solar system. Most of the learning about the solar system involves active direction and participation by the students themselves working independently, in groups, or with the entire class by using material from all of the different content areas when appropriate.

Therefore, the material the students learn in the thematic unit teaching of science usually is much more relevant and meaningful to them than that learned in the traditional teaching of science. In addition, thematic unit teaching integrates material from all of the content areas in a very comprehensive manner and uses active student involvement in learning the appropriate content, usually in a much more effective way than is the case in traditional content teaching. Students also are encouraged to read appropriate material on their own level instead of being required to read material that is much too difficult for them as is often the case in the traditional teaching of science. Reading scientific materials such as content textbooks at various reading levels, informational books at different reading levels, and reference books of various kinds such as print encyclopedias and encyclopedias on CD-ROM at the appropriate levels are used in learning the material for the unit. Therefore, students are encouraged to work with peers who have different reading levels, which is especially helpful to the below-average readers who are so often required to read only with other below-average readers, thus causing them to have a low self-esteem. As stated earlier, the typical chosen science textbook for any grade level usually is much too difficult for a number of the students at any grade level due to the technical vocabulary and difficult concepts that it contains.

To summarize, thematic unit teaching should be used to present science content as much as possible in the primary grades, intermediate grades, middle school, and possibly the secondary school. It well may be more effective than is the traditional teaching of science through the use of a single textbook or even several textbooks even if strategies for presenting technical vocabulary and improving comprehension are used.

SOME STRATEGIES THAT CAN BE USED IN THE TEACHING OF SCIENCE

This section of the chapter presents some strategies that can be used successfully in the teaching of science at various grade levels. They are adaptable to the teaching of science at various grade levels.

Survey Q3R (PQRST)

Survey Q3R (PQRST) usually can be used in its original form when reading scientific material. As stated earlier, Survey Q3R consists of the following steps:

Survey

Question

Read

Recite

Review

When Survey Q3R is used in reading scientific material, the final or review step may be enhanced by having the student summarize what was read by constructing a semantic map or web or by writing a brief outline of what was read. Either of these follow-up strategies can help a student firmly fix in his or her mind the important technical vocabulary and concepts that were gained from the reading. Therefore, the final step should help students to be better prepared to take a test on the chapter or unit when it is given.

The Inquiry Method

The inquiry method is a useful questioning strategy that is applicable in science classes. This strategy suggests that students ask questions about the content assignment in the form of *hypotheses*. The teacher then answers only *Yes* or *No* to each of the questions. If the students formulate enough correct question hypotheses, they eventually will arrive at the correct conclusion. Also the reading or science teacher always should encourage students to ask questions about the textbook material they must read by encouraging them to be critical readers. As an example, the teacher can ask the students to read a section of their textbooks as if they were investigative reporters. They should determine what kind of questions they would ask and why they would ask that type of question. The teacher always should stress the importance of asking questions about the textbook material while reading content books.

The Directed Reading Inquiry

The Directed Inquiry Activity (DIA) is based on the Directed Reading-Thinking Activity (DR-TA). This strategy seems applicable for study reading in science. As you may be aware, the Directed Reading-Thinking Activity (DR-TA) has the following main steps:

Making predictions from title clues

Making predictions from picture clues

Reading the material

Assessing the accuracy of the predictions, adjusting predictions as necessary

Repeating the procedure until all parts of the lesson have been covered

The Directed Inquiry Activity (DIA) suggests that students preview a part of the science reading assignment and predict responses to the questions *who, what, where, how,* and *why* which the teacher then records on the chalkboard. After class discussion of the ideas takes place, students read to confirm or alter their predictions. The predictions provide purposes for reading and, along with class discussion, provide the mental set needed for approaching the reading of scientific material.

Science Job Cards

In some instances teachers can relate *basal reader stories* to the study of science by making *science job cards* to be used as follow-up activities to stories. Here are several sample science job cards that should illustrate this strategy.

What season of the year and what type of weather was occurring in this story? Tell why you think this is true. Share your ideas with the reading group.

Are the animals mentioned in this story *carnivores* or *herbivores*? Tell why you believe this is true. Share your ideas with the reading group.

In this story what group of stars was Angie trying to follow at night when she was lost? Tell why you think this is true. Share your ideas with the reading group.

If the town in this story was destroyed by lava many years ago, what natural phenomena probably had occurred? Tell why you think this is true. Share your ideas with the group.

Language-Experience Approach

The Language-Experience Approach (LEA) can be very effective in helping below-average readers and learning-disabled students learn scientific content without having to depend entirely upon teacher lecture. Although LEA is primarily an emergent literacy (beginning reading and writing) strategy, it also is relevant in learning content material especially in a difficult-to-understand subject such as science.

When LEA is used for this purpose, it may consist of these steps:

- Introduction to the content in the chapter or unit by the use of a peer, volunteer, or the teacher reading the most important parts of the material aloud or tape recording it for the student. Experiments and demonstrations at this point also can greatly help below-average readers and learning disabled students gain an overall understanding of the material.

- If the student is severely disabled in reading, have him or her dictate an account of the science material presented by the reading, experiment, or demonstration. Then the dictation is transcribed by a classmate, volunteer, or less likely, the teacher. If the student is not so severely disabled in reading, he or she may well be able to write his or her own version of the material. As much as possible, the correct scientific terms should be retained even though they may be difficult for the student to identify. However, at least the content may be somewhat simplified.

- Then the student studies his or her own version of the chapter or unit instead of relying solely on the selected science textbook which likely is too difficult for him or her to comprehend.

- All of the transcribed or written accounts of the chapters or units should be bound together in some way so that the student can keep them over a period of time for additional study and reference. They then can serve as a permanent record of the material the student was to learn.

Note: The Language-Experience Approach (LEA) either can be used as part of thematic unit teaching in science or as part of a more traditional teaching of science that places major reliance on a single or several science textbooks.

Using Your Senses

This activity is designed to help students observe with their senses and to relate this activity to reading. For the sense of *touch* place a trash can in the front of the room that has been filled with objects of different shapes and textures. Make a hole in the lid of the trash can so that each student can come forward and stick his or her hand in the trash can. Each student then returns to his or her seat and writes about what and how he or she felt. After all of the students have completed the task, have a discussion on why they had a particular feeling about certain objects.

For the senses of *taste and smell* several blindfolded students taste and smell two objects that have nothing in common. As an example, they could taste a candy bar and smell an orange at the same time. The rest of the class then observes and reports their reactions. For the sense of *hearing* have the teacher or student make different sounds behind a screen that are unusual to the ear when the sense of sight is not being used. Some examples are as follows:

- ice being poured from one pail into another
- the opening of a can of carbonated soda

- a knife hitting a glass nearly full of water
- the dropping of a pen to the floor
- the rubbing of two sticks together

Each sound should be made twice so that students have a chance to write what they thought they heard. Then have a class discussion about the activity.

For the sense of *sight* place an object in a large circle formed by the students. The students then observe and record exactly what they see. They then exchange papers and critique their partner's observational powers, marking each statement with an *F for a fact* or an *O for an opinion*. For variation the teacher can have some students role-play a situation in the center of the circle.

Do the Details Fit?

The purpose of this activity is to help students identify main ideas and supporting details in science, to integrate factual information into concepts, and to classify information as a technique for study and review. The literacy or content teacher types or prints selected concepts on blue cards and examples or supporting details on white cards. If applicable, the white cards also can include diagrams and pictures of the scientific concept.

Here is an example from fifth-grade science:

BLUE CARD

The Solar System

WHITE CARDS

a group of stars known as "The Big Dipper"

a galaxy known as "The Milky Way"

the orbit of the earth around the sun

Mars, which is known as "The Red Planet"

a spacecraft

the planet that is surrounded by moons

the planet that is the furthest away from the earth

a comet

a space station

an astronaut

The student then spreads the sets of blue cards out on a flat surface. Then he or she places the white cards (which have been mixed up) under the appropriate blue cards. The student can check his or her answers if you wish from a prepared answer key and make any needed changes. The activity also may be used by teams by adding a scoring system.

Is There a Correct Answer?

This activity is designed to develop the skills of problem solving and predicting. The teacher prepares copies of incomplete fictitious incidents that relate to some area of science and to students' out-of-school experiences as well as three or four different endings to the episode. The students then decide which of the endings the character would be most likely to select and justifies his or her answer. When each student has made his or her selection, the student joins classmates who have chosen the same answer. The group then prepares a rationale for that response and presents it to the class. Here are several examples of incidents that could be used in this activity:

> A seventh-grade student sees one of his or her classmates buying a package of cigarettes from a vending machine and then starting to smoke one of them. Which of the following actions does the first student take?
> a. He or she says nothing about it to the other student.
> b. He or she says to the other student that smoking can lead to a number of significant health problems.
> c. He or she tries to take the package of cigarettes away from the other student so that he or she can throw them away.
> A third-grade student sees one of his or her classmates throwing a candy bar wrapper to the ground right outside of the school. Which of the following actions does the first student take?
> a. He or she picks up the candy bar wrapper and throws it into the nearest trash can.
> b. He or she tells the other student to pick up the candy bar wrapper since that is called "littering."
> c. He or she does nothing at all about the situation.

What Do You Think It Is?

The purpose of this activity is to enable students to test themselves on their familiarity with the names of *chemical compounds* that two or more elements form. Therefore, the activity is probably most applicable for the secondary-school level, although it is possible that it could also be used by some middle-school students.

The reading or science teacher can construct a list of pairs of elements and a list of scrambled word forms that are placed opposite the paired elements. Then from the list of scrambled compounds and the names of the elements, have the student(s) determine the name of the compound that the two elements form. If you wish, the student(s) then can check his or her (their) accuracy with an answer key.

1.	hydrogen and chlorine	doychrhorlci cida
2.	hydrogen and oxygen	hediydrxo
3.	silicon and oxygen	lciisno xdoiide
4.	copper, oxygen, and sulfur	ceppro lsuefat
5.	boron and hydrogen	nobro dhryditrei
6.	boron and fluorine	nbroo forureildit
7.	magnesium, carbon, and oxygen	sammuigen tenaaocbr
8.	hydrogen and oxygen	tawre
9.	carbon and oxygen	conrba xdodiie
10.	lithium and fluorine	lmuihlti fdorulie

Answer Key

1. hydrochloric acid
2. hydroxide
3. silicon dioxide
4. copper sulfate
5. boron trihydride
6. boron trifluoride
7. magnesium carbonate
8. water
9. carbon dioxide
10. lithium fluoride

Reproducible Materials in Science

The next section of this chapter contains several ready-to-use materials for reinforcing some of the technical vocabulary and content in science at different grade levels. You can duplicate and use any of these materials in their present form or modify them in any way you wish in the light of the needs and interests of your own students.

CLASSIFICATION ACTIVITY SHEET
(Approximately Fourth-Grade Level)

Here is a list of terms from some of the science materials we have studied in class this year. Read each term and then write it in the proper column under the heading *Animal, Vegetable,* or *Mineral.* You can use a science textbook, a dictionary, an encyclopedia, an encyclopedia on CD-ROM, or a thesaurus to help you. You also can work with a partner if you would like.

talc	photosynthesis	quartz
sulfur	muscles	sporophyll
epidermis	optic nerve	aluminum
basalt	pistil	stirrup
metamorphic	opthalmologist	chlorophyll
plankton	stamen	iodine
auditory nerve	retina	pollination
iris	calcium	hammer
sedimentary	stegosaurus	salt
granite	porpoise	reptile
ornithopod	sandstone	slate
coral	frontal bone	hornet
stingray	mummy	copper
ptarmigan		

Name _____ Grade _____ Teacher _____ Date _____

CLASSIFICATION ACTIVITY SHEET
(Approximately Fourth-Grade Level)

(cont.)

ANIMAL	VEGETABLE	MINERAL

Answer Key for "Classification Activity Sheet"

ANIMAL	*VEGETABLE*	*MINERAL*
mummy	photosynthesis	talc
muscles	sporophyll	sulfur
epidermis	pistil	quartz
optic nerve	plankton	sedimentary
stirrup	chlorophyll	basalt
opthalmologist	stamen	aluminum
iris	pollination	metamorphic
retina		iodine
hammer		calcium
stegosaurus		granite
ornithopod		salt
porpoise		sandstone
reptile		slate
coral		copper
stingray		
frontal bone		
hornet		
ptarmigan		

SPELLING CROSSWORD PUZZLE
(Approximately Fifth-Grade Level)

This activity sheet contains a *spelling crossword puzzle.* The longest word in the puzzle has been written in for you. You should try to write the rest of the words on this sheet from the science topic "Classifying Matter" on the puzzle. You should try until you can find a way to write all of them in. You may work with a partner(s) on this spelling crossword puzzle if you want.

Classifying Matter

ACROSS

phosphorus

mercury

tungsten

chromium

radon

manganese

arsenic

nucleus

sulfur

electron

fluorine

cadmium

neutron

bromine

DOWN

hydrogen

carbon

radium

substance

barium

compound

silicon

oxygen

platinum

SPELLING CROSSWORD PUZZLE
(Approximately Fifth-Grade Level)

(cont.)

Answer Key for "Classifying Matter"

REVERSIBLE CROSSWORD PUZZLE
(Approximately Sixth-Grade Level)

This activity sheet contains a *reversible crossword puzzle.* The crossword puzzle has the answers already filled in on it, but it does not contain the definitions or clues to the answers. Write the correct definition or clue beside the correct numbers both *across* and *down.* You can work with a partner(s) on completing the definitions or clues to this reversible crossword puzzle if you wish.

Beyond the Solar System

Answer Key for "Beyond the Solar System"

Note: The students' wording will be different. Be sure the definitions are correct.

ACROSS	*DOWN*
1. a group of stars that seem to form a picture	1. a device that separates light into a pattern of bands and colors
2. a huge cloud of dust, hydrogen, and helium	2. the brightness of a star
3. the violent explosion of a star that has a high mass	3. a huge rotating group of stars
4. everything that exists including space and all objects in it	4. a space craft that contains a powerful engine
5. the distance that light travels in one year	5. the part of the space shuttle that carries passengers
6. a body that orbits another body in space	6. the planet on which scientists are planning to build a space station someday

IMAGINARY SCIENTIFIC TERMS
(Approximately Sixth-Grade Level)

Here is a list of imaginary scientific terms. Using your knowledge of the meaning of common prefixes, suffixes, and word roots, try to determine an approximate hypothetical meaning for each of the terms and then write the meaning on the line beside the scientific terms. You can work with a partner(s) on the activity sheet if you would like to do so.

1. lunaphobia _____

2. atomcule _____

3. kineology _____

4. antipollen _____

5. coalite _____

6. botonarium _____

7. contrafungi _____

8. monofossil _____

9. micromonitor _____

10. circuitology _____

11. hydrovolcano _____

12. megasatellite _____

13. pseudostell _____

14. monembryo _____

15. myriabacteria _____

16. benecoral _____

17. macropistil _____

18. sonorology _____

19. planktonphobia _____

20. negluminous _____

21. hydrozoology _____

22. nonvore _____

23. polyglaciers _____

24. neofault _____

25. malion _____

© 1997 by John Wiley & Sons, Inc.

Answer Key for "Imaginary Science Terms"

Note: Any answer that approximates the answers given here should be considered correct.

1. fear of the moon
2. small atom
3. study of movement
4. against pollen
5. the mineral contained in coal
6. a place for plants
7. an agent against fungi (one- or many-celled living things)
8. one fossil
9. small (computer) monitor
10. study of (electric) currents
11. a water volcano
12. large satellite
13. false star
14. one embryo (undeveloped fetus)
15. ten thousand bacteria
16. good coral
17. a large flower pistil
18. the study of sonar
19. fear of tiny plants and animals that float in the ocean
20. not full of light
21. water animals
22. an animal that doesn't eat anything
23. many glaciers
24. a new break in the earth's crust
25. a bad atom that has gained or lost electrons

SCRAMBLED SCIENCE WORD PUZZLE
(Approximately Fifth-Grade Level)

Here is a list of *scrambled words* from the science topic "The Human Body." *Unscramble* each word and write it on the short line beside the scrambled word. Then write the *definition of the unscrambled word* on the longer lines beside it. You may want to use a science textbook, dictionary, or encyclopedia to help you locate the definitions. You may work with a partner(s) if you wish.

1. wrarom _____ _____

2. evtrbreae _____ _____

3. breceumlle _____ _____

4. shythopalaum _____ _____

5. mitslutnas _____ _____

6. stpedssrena _____ _____

7. apcrnesa _____ _____

8. turfaerc _____ _____

9. xelfer _____ _____

10. gmiltnea _____ _____

11. rohnomse _____ _____

12. etnodn _____ _____

© 1997 by John Wiley & Sons, Inc.

SCRAMBLED SCIENCE WORD PUZZLE
(Approximately Fifth-Grade Level)

(cont.)

13. snllhacuniego _____ _____

_____

14. rbnai _____ _____

_____

15. juaamrina _____ _____

_____

16. ormhpeni _____ _____

_____

17. iadeetsb _____ _____

_____

18. sdlgna _____ _____

_____

19. rbaistmen _____ _____

_____

20. ssslocoii _____ _____

_____

21. evern _____ _____

_____

22. vislep _____ _____

_____

23. abkcoben _____ _____

_____

24. gealitrac _____ _____

_____

25. recbmure _____ _____

_____

Answer Key for "Scrambled Science Word Puzzle"

1. **marrow**—a soft tissue inside bones

2. **vertebrae**—the bones of the backbone

3. **cerebellum**—the part of the brain that helps the muscles work together

4. **hypothalamus**—the part of the brain that releases many hormones

5. **stimulants**—drugs that speed up the action of the nervous system

6. **depressants**—drugs that slow down the action of the nervous system

7. **pancreas**—a large gland found under the stomach

8. **fracture**—a crack or break in a bone

9. **reflex**—a quick automatic reaction

10. **ligament**—strong bands of tissue that hold the bones at a joint together

11. **hormones**—the chemicals made by the endocrine glands that help control activities of certain body parts

12. **tendon**—a strong band of tissue that connects a muscle to a bone

13. **hallucinogens**—drugs that cause a person to hear or feel things that do not exist

14. **brain**—main order and control center of the nervous system

15. **marijuana**—a mild hallucinogen

16. **morphine**—a narcotic that slows down the actions of the nervous system and may cause sleepiness and confusion

17. **diabetes**—a disease caused because the pancreas does not make enough insulin

18. **glands**—organs or tissues that make or release chemicals

19. **brainstem**—the part of the brain that controls many actions that keep a person alive

20. **scoliosis**—a side-to-side curve of the backbone

21. **nerve**—a cell that can receive or send messages

22. **pelvis**—a group of large wide bones at the end of the backbone

23. **backbone**—a long row of connected bones in the middle of the back

24. **cartilage**—strong elastic tissue in the skeletal system

25. **cerebrum**—the part of the brain that controls all of a person's thinking

GENERAL GOALS FOR TEACHING MATHEMATICS

The content area of mathematics has specific goals and many inherent difficulties. As is true in science, mathematics has specialized vocabulary and symbolism. For example, young children must learn the terms *plus, minus, multiplication,* and *division,* while older students must understand such concepts as *pi, circumference, radius,* and *diameter.* In addition, mathematics contains a number of words with multiple meanings such as *base, planes, raising a number to its fourth power,* and *figures.* However, some mathematical terms have prefixes, suffixes, or word roots that a student can use as a help in determining their meaning. For example, the word *hexagon* is a figure that has six sides.

To help develop math vocabulary, a teacher can assign a mathematical term for each day that students must identify and then use in a sentence. As one variation that is most applicable in the primary grades, one student may "own" the word for the day, wearing a card on which the word is written and then giving a presentation about the word to the rest of the group. Students also might have to identify or illustrate math terms written on cards before they can line up for recess or engage in some other activity. In addition, the teacher can ask questions about what terms being studied apply to a particular problem or ask the students to dramatize the problems or meanings of math terms. Obviously, the meanings of prefixes, suffixes, and word roots and their application to mathematical terms can be studied. As has been stated earlier, one of the best sources of prefixes, suffixes, word roots, and their meanings is the following teacher's resource:

Edward B. Fry, Jacqueline E. Kress, and Dona Lee Fountoukidis, *The Reading Teacher's Book of Lists,* Third Edition. Englewood Cliffs, New Jersey: Prentice-Hall, 1993, pp. 117-139.

In addition to difficulties with math terms, students also have difficulties with a different symbol system and with reading numerals, which involves understanding place value. Students must be able to interpret such symbols as *plus, minus, multiplication,* and *division* signs as well as symbols for *union* and *intersectional, equal signs* and *signs indicating inequalities* among many others as well as such abbreviations as *ft., in., lb., qt., mm, cm,* among others. Symbols often are very difficult for students because some symbols have different meanings in other contexts; for example, "–" means *minus in math* but is a *dash in regular print.* Matching exercises such as are illustrated later in this chapter can help students to learn the meanings of symbols.

In addition, to read numbers students must understand *place value.* For example, they must understand that the number 432.8 has three places to the left of the decimal point (which they must be able to discriminate from a period), which means that the leftmost numeral indicates a precise number of *hundreds,* the next numeral indicates how many *tens,* and the next numeral indicates how many *ones.* In this example, the number is four hundreds, three tens, and two ones, or *four hundred thirty-two.* To determine the value to the right of the decimal point students must realize that the first place is *tenths,* the second place is *hundredths,* and so on. In this example, there are *eight tenths*; therefore, the entire number is *four hundred thirty-two and eight tenths.* Since this procedure involves not just merely reading from left to right as is typically the case, but reading back and forth, one can see that it can be very difficult for many students.

In addition, the reading of mathematical sentences also presents reading difficulties. For example, students must recognize numerals and symbols and then translate them into verbal sentences that make sense; for example, as in reading *27 ÷ 9 = 3* as *"twenty-seven divided by nine equals three,"* another difficult concept for many children to learn.

Calhoun Collier and Lois Redmond wrote that mathematics material is very concise and abstract in nature and involves very complex relationships. A high density of ideas per page appears in this type of material and understanding each word is very important since just *one word* may be the key to understanding an entire section. To understand mathematical materials and to help solve math word problems, Collier and Redmond suggested that students should do the following:

1. Read the material rapidly or at a normal rate in order to get just an overview and to determine the main points.

2. Read the material a second time, this time "more slowly, critically, and analytically" and determine the details and relationships involved.

3. Read some parts of the material a number of times if it is required, varying the purpose each time.

4. Determine the relevant operation.

5. Decide which operations must be performed to solve the problem.

6. Determine whether all of the needed information is given to solve the problem.

7. Read the numerals and operation symbols needed to solve the problem.

8. Adjust the reading rates to the difficulty of the material. Mathematical material, including math word problems, usually must be read at a slow, careful rate (Calhoun C. Collier and Lois A. Redmond, "Are You Teaching Kids to Read Mathematics?" *The Reading Teacher* 27, May 1974, pp. 804-808).

As stated earlier, I have always been a disabled reader of word problems in mathematics. Since reading word problems often poses a serious problem for otherwise able readers, imagine how extremely difficult trying to read them must be for disabled readers. William P. Dunlap and Martha Brown McKnight have written an interesting article about how to help students conceptualize math word problems. They wrote that one major problem that affects students' ability to solve a math word problem is the three-level translation of the vocabulary contained in that problem. They stated that students must be able to translate from the *general* to the *technical* to the *symbolic vocabularies*. They further stated that the translation process among the vocabularies is essential to the conceptualization of the message contained in that word problem. The authors then provided some concrete examples of these vocabulary translations (William P. Dunlap and Martha Brown McKnight, "Vocabulary Translations for Conceptualizing Math Word Problems," *The Reading Teacher* 32, November 1979, pp. 183-189).

Since students will need help in reading and analyzing math word problems, teachers usually should arrange such problems according to difficulty and avoid assigning too many of them at one time. Word problems require the basic comprehension skills of determining main ideas and details, noting the relationships among details, making inferences, drawing conclusions, analyzing the elements of the problem critically, and following directions. Here is one procedure students can follow in solving word problems:

1. Learn all the word meanings.

2. Determine what the problem is asking for.

3. Decide which facts are needed to solve the problem.

4. Determine which mathematical operations must be performed.

5. Determine the order in which the operations should be performed.

Sometimes students may find it useful to draw a picture of the situation contained in the problem or to manipulate actual objects for solving math verbal problems, and teachers should encourage these approaches when they seem appropriate. Teachers can observe their students as they solve word problems and decide when they need the most help: (1) with the problem interpretation (understanding problems that they are not required to read for themselves), (2) with the actual reading of the problems, (3) with the computation, or (4) with the integration of the three different skills in order to reach a solution. If you want, you can form small, flexible, short-term groups of students who need help in the three different areas of problem-solving.

Since story problems are not written in a typical narrative style, students often lack the familiarity with the text structure that is needed to comprehend them. Instead, the pattern writing for word problems is *procedural,* with important details placed at the beginning and the topic sentence placed near the end. This pattern does not help students set an early purpose for their reading.

According to D. Ray Reutzel, students may benefit from constructing their own story problems that are related to their experiences. This activity can help their comprehension of math word problems (D. Ray Reutzel, "C^6: A Reading Model for Teaching Arithmetic Story Problem Solving," *The Reading Teacher* 37, October 1983, pp. 28-34). A recent research study, for example, indicated that students who constructed their own story problems to solve performed better on tests containing math verbal problems than did students who only practiced textbook verbal problems. They found that students are likely to interpret story problems more effectively if they have constructed similar problems (Anne Ferguson and Jo Fairburn, "Language Experience for Problem Solving in Mathematics," *The Reading Teacher* 39, April 1986, pp. 504-507).

In addition, graphs, maps, charts, and tables often occur in mathematical materials. As has been discussed earlier in this chapter, students need specific instruction and practice in the use of these graphic aids in order to perform well on many mathematical assignments.

In summary, mathematics presents many difficult challenges for most students, even otherwise good readers. In addition, math verbal problems present an especially severe problem for many students. The strategies and materials contained in this section should help any literacy or math teacher present the important reading skills in all types of mathematics materials—including verbal problems—much more effectively.

USING THEMATIC TEACHING IN MATHEMATICS

As is the case in literature, social studies, and science, it also is helpful to teach mathematics in *thematic units* as much as possible. It is obvious that thematic or unit teaching in math enables students to use what they have learned and are presently learning in mathematics as a tool for solving important, meaningful problems. Currently, mathematics is sometimes taught along with the other content areas in themes or units especially in middle schools that use an integrated, team teaching approach. However, this is probably less true in the primary grades, intermediate grades, and secondary schools.

When thematic unit teaching is used in math, the mathematics teacher—in consultation with language arts, social studies, and science teachers—selects one important, relevant *theme or unit* that (usually from social studies or science) is going to be studied for a particular period of time such as four weeks. The entire important content of that theme is mainly learned by the students themselves with the teachers acting as *facilitators of learning* instead of being lecturers or presenters. Much, if not all, of the content about the theme is selected by the students themselves with teacher direction if necessary. Most of the learning about the theme or topic involves active direction and participation by the students themselves working independently, in groups, or the entire class by using material from all of the different content areas when appropriate. Therefore, the mathematical concepts and skills that students learn in thematic unit teaching usually are more relevant and meaningful than would otherwise be the case.

Mathematical verbal (word) problems can be a very important aspect of thematic unit teaching in math. As you are aware, the *whole language philosophy* states that school math should resemble real-world math as much as possible. Mathematics always should be a meaningful problem-solving, social activity, and a tool for success in everyday life. The math verbal problems that are used often should evolve from the thematic teaching of math and should be collaborative efforts between teachers and students. These math verbal problems should be integrated with literature, social studies, science, music, art, and drama whenever possible in thematic unit teaching.

In a variation of thematic unit teaching in math, the teacher identifies a curricular topic in math, and students then identify real-life problems. Students can formulate their own word problems that are related to the unit and then either solve them on their own or "publish" them for other students to solve. They also can generate new problems from old problems which deepens their understanding of math and integrates both prior knowledge and new knowledge. A student can generate a topic for a math verbal problem from one of his or her own interests related to the unit.

Writing story problems related to a unit also requires students to think about the unit outside of class. In addition to relating the story problems with social studies or science units, they also can easily integrate *reading and writing* with math. Students in the upper primary grades and beyond can initiate and sustain their own math problem-writing and solving with great enthusiasm. The writing genre required by writing math story problems is fairly easy to produce. This also helps students learn to conceptualize writing as a tool for learning. The solving of math verbal problems often focuses only on surface features while writing word problems requires students to go below the surface.

However, students need much teacher demonstration and guided practice about how to write the math story problems that are related to thematic units of instruction. Students also should practice writing math story problems that are related to thematic units on a regular basis to become adept at it.

TRADE BOOKS FOR RELATING MATHEMATICS WITH LITERATURE

The chapter now presents a comprehensive list of trade books that can be used to effectively integrate the learning of various math concepts with literature. I wish to express my thanks to Emily Long, Associate Professor of Education at Carroll College in Waukesha, Wisconsin, and one of my former graduate students in reading, for providing some of the trade books on this list. Using such trade books is a very effective way of presenting math concepts along with reading skills and is highly motivational.

Counting

Anno, M., *Anno's Counting Book*. Harper and Row, 1977.

Archambault, J., *Counting Sheep*. DLM Teaching Resources or Trumpet, 1989.

Bishop, C. H., *The Five Chinese Brothers*. Sandcastle Books, 1989.

Carle, E., *1, 2, 3 to the Zoo*. Philomel, 1990.

Ehlert, L., *Fish Eyes: A Book You Can Count On*. Harcourt Brace Jovanovich, 1990.

Falwell, C., *Feast for 10*. Clarion Books, 1993.

Giganti, P., *Each Orange Had 8 Slices*. Greenwillow, 1992.

Gordon, J., *Six Sleepy Sheep*. Penguin or Trumpet, 1991.

Grossman, V. and Long, S., *Ten Little Rabbits*. Chronicle Books, 1991.

Hulme, J., *Sea Squares*. Hyperion Books for Children, 1991.

Hutchins, P., *Don't Forget the Bacon*. Greenwillow, 1989.

Langstaff, J., *Over in the Meadow*. Harcourt, Brace, Jovanovich, 1967

Loomis, C., *One Cow Coughs*. Ticknor and Fields Books for Young Readers, 1994.

Mahy, M., *17 Kings and 42 Elephants*. Dial Books, 1987.

O'Keefe, S. H., *One Hungry Monster*. Little, Brown & Company, 1989.

Rees, M., *Ten in a Bed*. Joy Street Books/Little Brown & Company, 1989.

Schmidt, K. L., *Twelve Days of Summer*. Morrow Junior Books, 1991.

Tudor, T., *1 Is One*. Macmillan or Troll, 1956.

Wildsmith, B., *One, Two, Three*. Franklin Watts, 1965.

Zaslavsky, C., *ZERO: Is It Something? Is It Nothing?* Franklin Watts, 1989.

Operations

Addition and Subtraction

Adams, P., *There Were Ten in the Bed*. Playspaces International, 1979.

Anno, M., *Anno's Counting House*. Philomel Books, 1982.

Buringham, J., *Pigs Plus*. Viking Press, 1983.

Calmenson, S., *Ten Furry Monsters*. Parents Magazine Press, 1984.

Carle, E., *Let's Paint a Rainbow*. Philomel Books, 1982.

Christelow, E., *Five Little Monkeys Sitting in a Tree*. Clarion, 1985.

de Regniers, B., *So Many Cats!* Clarion, 1985.

Gisler, D., *Addition Annie*. Children's Press, 1991.

Le Sieg, T., *Ten Apples Up on Top*. Random House, 1961.

Merriam E., *12 Ways to Get to 11*. Simon & Schuster, 1993.

Rees, M., *Ten in a Bed*. Joy Street Books/Little, Brown and Company, 1988.

West, C., *Ten Little Crocodiles*. Children's Press of Chicago, 1987.

Multiplication and Division

Anno, M., *Anno's Mysterious Multiplying Jar.* Philomel Books, 1983.

Barry, D., *The Rajah's Rice.* W. H. Freeman & Company, 1994.

Chwast, S., *The 12 Circus Rings.* Gulliver/HBJ, 1986.

Geringer, L., *A Three Hat Day.* HarperCollins, 1987.

Hutchins, P., *The Doorbell Rang.* Mulberry Books, 1986.

Low, J., *Mice Twice.* Antheneum, 1981; Macmillan, 1986

Matthews, L., *Bunches and Bunches of Bunneys.* Scholastic Books, 1978.

Pinczes, E. J., *A Remainder of One.* Houghton Mifflin Company, 1995.

Pittman, H. C., *A Grain of Rice.* Bantam Skylark Books, 1986.

Trivett, J., *Building Tables on Tables: A Book About Multiplication.* Thomas Crowell, 1975.

Wright, H., *Four Threes Are 12.* Holt, Rinehart & Winston, 1964.

Geometry

Anno, M., *Anno's Math Games III.* Philomel Books, 1989.

Brown, M., *Listen to a Shape.* Franklin Watts, 1979.

Burns, M., *The Greedy Triangle.* Scholastic Books, 1994.

Carle, E., *My Very First Book of Shapes.* HarperCollins, 1974.

Clouse, N., *Puzzle Maps U.S.A.* Henry Holt & Company, 1990.

Crews, D., *Ten Black Dots.* Greenwillow Books, 1986.

Hoban, T., *Shapes and Things.* Macmillan, 1970.

Hoban, T., *Circles, Triangles, and Squares.* Macmillan, 1974.

Hoban, T., *Dots, Spots, Speckles, and Stripes.* Greenwillow, 1983.

Jonas, A., *Round Trip.* Scholastic Books, 1983.

Nakano, D., *Easy Origami.* Viking Penguin, 1985.

Orii, E., and Orii, M., *Simple Science Experiments with Circles.* Gareth Stevens, 1989.

Rand, T., *Arithmetic (Carl Sandburg).* Harcourt Brace Jovanovich, 1993.

Ross, C., *Circles: Fun Ideas for Getting A-Round in Math.* Addison-Wesley Publishing, 1992.

Saunders, K., *Hexagrams.* Tarquin (England), 1983.

Schwartz, D., *How Much Is a Million?* Scholastic Books, 1985.

Thompson, D., *Visual Magic.* Dial Books, 1991.

Thomson, R., *All About Shapes.* Gareth Stevens, 1986.

VanCleave, J., *Geometry for Every Kid.* John Wiley & Sons, 1994.

Westray, K., *Picture Puzzler.* Ticknor and Fields Books for Young Readers, 1994.

Yenawine, P., *Lines.* Delacourte Press, 1991.

Yenawine, P., *Shapes.* Delacourte Press, 1991.

Youldon, G., *Shapes.* Franklin Watts, 1986.

Problem Solving
Sorting (Classification)

Anno, M., *Anno's Hat Tricks.* Philomel Books, 1981.

Bodsworth, M., *A Nice Walk in the Jungle.* Viking Kestrel, 1989.

Carlson, N., *Harriet's Halloween Candy.* Picture Puffins, 1984.

Hoban, T., *Is It Rough? Is It Smooth? Is It Shiny?* Greenwillow, 1984.

Jonas, A., *Aardvarks, Disembark!* Greenwillow, 1990.

Moncure, J., *The Magic Moon Machine.* Children's Press, 1987.

Moncure, J., *My First Look at Sorting.* (series) Random House, 1991.

Spier, P., *GOBBLE! GROWL! GRUNT!* Doubleday & Company, 1971.

Spier, P., *Fast-Slow, High-Low: A Book of Opposites.* Doubleday & Company, 1988.

Patterning

Bayer, J., *My Name Is Alice.* Dial Books, 1984.

Carle, E., *The Very Busy Spider.* Putnam, 1989.

Emberley, B., *Drummer Hoff.* Treehouse Productions, 1967.

Geringer, L., *A Three Hat Day.* HarperCollins, 1985.

Martin, B., Jr., *Brown Bear, Brown Bear, What Do You See?* Henry Holt & Company, 1983.

Shaw, C., *It Looked Like Spilt Milk.* Harper & Row Publishers, 1947.

Graphing

Aker, S., *What Comes in 2's, 3's, & 4's?* Simon & Schuster, 1990.

Arnold, C., *Charts and Graphs: Fun, Facts, and Activities.* Franklin Watts, 1984.

Gardner, B., *Can You Imagine...? A Counting Book.* Dodd, Mead & Company, 1987.

Slobodkina, E., *Caps for Sale.* Scholastic Books, 1976.

Wilson, S., *The Day That Henry Cleaned His Room.* Simon & Schuster, 1990.

Measurement
Comparison

Cantienti, B., *Little Elephant and Big Mouse.* Picture Book Studio, 1981.

Carle, E., *A House for Hermit Crab.* Picture Book Studio, 1987.

Greenfield, E., *Big Friend, Little Friend.* Black Butterfly Children's Books, 1991.

Hoban, T., *Is It Larger? Is It Smaller?* Greenwillow, 1985.

Hutchins, P., *You'll Soon Grow into Them, Tich.* Greenwillow, 1983.

Kellogg, S., *Much Bigger Than Martin.* Dial (or Scholastic), 1976.

Manley, D., *The Other Side.* Raintree Publications, 1979.

Moncure, J., *The Biggest Snowball of All.* Children's Press of Chicago, 1988.

Myller, R., *How Big Is a Foot?* Dell Publishing, 1962.

Peterson, J., *The Littles* (and sequels). Scholastic, 1990.

Piendowski, J., *Sizes.* Little Simon, 1990.

Spier, P., *Fast-Slow, High-Low: A Book of Opposites.* Doubleday, 1972.

Youldon, G., *Sizes.* Frankin Watts, 1982.

Linear

Allen, P., *Mr. Archimedes' Bath.* Angus & Robertson (HarperCollins), 1980.

Avi, *The Barn.* Orchard, 1994.

Briggs, R., *Jim and the Beanstalk.* Putnam Publishing Company, 1980.

Butterworth, O., *The Enormous Egg.* (chapter) Dell Publishing, 1956.

Caple, K., *The Biggest Nose.* Houghton Mifflin, 1985.

Clement, R., *Counting on Frank.* Gareth Stevens, 1991.

de Paola, T., *The Popcorn Book.* Holiday House, 1978.

Johnson, T., *Farmer Mack Measures His Pig.* Harper & Row, 1986.

Kellogg, S., *Much Bigger Than Martin.* Dial (or Scholastic), 1976.

Lionni, L., *Inch by Inch.* Astor-Honor, 1960.

Myller, R., *How Big Is a Foot?* Dell Publishing, 1962.

Weight

Allen, P., *Who Sank the Boat?* Putnam Publishing Group, 1982.

Bendick, J., *How Much and How Many.* (revised edition) Franklin Watts, 1989.

Galdone, P., *The Three Billy Goats Gruff.* Clarion, 1973.

Time

Allington, R., and Krull, K., *Time.* Raintree Publishers, 1982.

Anno, M., *Anno's Sundial.* Philomel Books, 1987.

Anno, M. et. al., *All in a Day.* Putnam Publishing Group, 1990.

Apfel, N., *Calendars.* Franklin Watts, 1985.

Barrett, J., *Benjamin's 365 Birthdays.* Atheneum, 1978.

Carle, E., *All in a Day.* Philomel Books, 1986.

Cassidy, J., *The Time Book.* Klutz Press, 1991.

Cave, C., and McKenna, T., *Just in Time.* Clarkson N. Potter, 1989.

Florian, D., *A Summer's Day.* Greenwillow Books, 1988.

Gerstein, M., *The Sun's Day.* HarperCollins, 1989.

Hooper, M., *Seven Eggs.* Harper & Row, 1985.

Hutchins, P., *Clocks and More Clocks.* Macmillan, 1970.

Krensky, S., *Big Time Bears.* Little, Brown & Company, 1989.

Lessac, F., *Nine O'clock Lullaby.* Harper Trophy, 1991.

Maestro, B. and G., *Around the Clock with Harriet: A Book About Telling Time.* Crown, 1984.

Maestro, B. and G., *Through the Year with Harriet.* Crown, 1985.

Miles, A., *Annie and the Old One.* Little, Brown and Company, 1971.

Murphy, J., *Five Minutes Peace.* G. P. Putnam's Sons, 1986.

Neasi, B., *A Minute Is a Minute.* Children's Press of Chicago, 1988.

Russo, M., *Only Six More Days Left.* Greenwillow, 1988.

Trivett, D. and J., *Time for Clocks.* Thomas Crowell Publishers, 1979.

Wiesner, D., *Tuesday.* Houghton Mifflin, 1991.

Williams. V., *Three Days on a River in a Red Canoe.* Greenwillow, 1981.

Money

Adams, B., *The Go-Around Dollar.* Four Winds Press, 1992.

Adler, D., *Money.* Franklin Watts, 1984.

Briers, A., *Money.* Franklin Watts, 1987.

Cantwell, L., *Money and Banking.* Franklin Watts, 1984.

Danzinger, P., *Not for a Billion Gazillion Dollars.* Yearling Books, 1992.

Godfrey, N., *The Kids' Money Book.* Checkboard Press, 1991.

Herman, C., *Max Malone Makes a Million.* Henry Holt & Company, 1991.

Hoban, T., *26 Letters and 99 Cents.* Greenwillow, 1987.

Maestro, B. and G., *Dollars and Cents for Harriet: A Money Concept Book.* Crown, 1984.

Mathis. S., *The Hundred Penny Box.* (chapter) Viking Press, 1975.

Medearis, A., *Picking Peas for a Penny.* State House Press (or Scholastic), 1990.

Schwartz, D., *If You Made a Million.* Scholastic Books, 1989.

Zimelman, N., *How the Second Grade Got $8,205.50 to Visit the Statue of Liberty.* Albert Whitman & Company, 1992.

Place Value

Demi, *Demi's Count the Animals 1-2-3.* Grossett & Dunlap, 1986.

Du Bois, W., *The Twenty-one Balloons.* Puffin Books, 1989.

Dunn, P., and Lee, V., *How Many.* Random House, 1988.

Estes, E., *The Hundred Dresses.* (chapter) Scholastic Books, 1944, 1973.

Gag, W., *Millions of Cats.* Scholastic Books, 1928, 1956.

Hoban, T., *Count and See.* Macmillan, 1972.

Lee, J., *Animal 1*2*3!* Gareth Stevens, 1985.

Mathis, S., *The Hundred Penny Box.* (chapter) Viking, 1975.

Pinczes, E., *A Remainder of One.* Houghton Mifflin, 1995.

Richards, D., *Wise Owl's Counting Book.* Children's Press of Chicago, 1981.

Sloat, T., *From One to One Hundred.* Greenwillow, 1992.

Toban, T., *Count and See.* Macmillan, 1972.

Weiss, M., *Six Hundred Sixty-six Jellybeans! All That?* Crowell Junior Books, 1976.

Fractions

Bassett, J., *Gator Pie.* Dodd, Mead & Company, 1979.

Dennis R., *Fractions Are Parts of Things.* Crowell Junior Books, 1973.

Hughes, S., *Lucy and Tom's 1. 2. 3.*Penguin, 1987.

Khalsa, D., *How Pizza Came to Queens.* Clarkson N. Potter, 1989.

Leedy, L., *Fraction Action.* Holiday House and Trumpet Books, 1994.

McGrath. B., *The M and M's Counting Book.* Charlesbridge, 1994.

McMillan, B., *Eating Fractions.* Scholastic Inc., 1991.

Moncure, J., *How Many Ways Can You Cut a Pie?* Children's Press, 1988.

Pomerantz, C., *The Half-Birthday Party.* Houghton Mifflin, 1984.

Silverstein, S., *A Giraffe and a Half.* Harper and Row, 1964.

Wildsmith, B., *Brian Wildsmith's Puzzles.* Franklin Watts, 1970.

Statistics

Arnold, C., *Charts and Graphs: Fun Facts and Activities.* Franklin Watts, 1984.

James, E., and Barkin, C., *What Do You Mean "Average"? Mean, Median & Mode.* (middle school level) Lothrop, Lee & Shepard, 1970.

Mole, K., *Charts and Graphs.* Usborne Publishing Ltd. (England), 1994.

Parker, T., *In One Day.* (middle school level) Houghton Mifflin, 1984.

Riedel, M., *Winning with Numbers: A Kid's Guide to Statistics.* (middle school level) Prentice-Hall, 1978.

Srivastasva, J., *Statistics.* Thomas Y. Crowell, 1973.

Srivastasva, J., *Averages.* Thomas Y. Crowell, 1975.

TEACHER RESOURCES FOR RELATING MATHEMATICS AND LITERATURE

Braddon, K., Hall, N., and Taylor, D., *Math Through Children's Literature: Making the NCTM Standards Come Alive.* Teacher Ideas Press, 1993.

Burns, K., *The I Hate Mathematics! Book.* Little, Brown and Company (or Scholastic), 1975.

Burns, K., *Math and Literature (K-3).* Math Solutions Pub/Cuisenaire Company of America, 1992.

Griffiths, R., and Clyne, M., *Books You Can Count On: Linking Mathematics and Literature.* Heinemann Educational Books, 1988.

Tieseen, D., and Mathias, M., (Editors) *The Wonderful World of Mathematics: A Critically Annotated List of Children's Books in Mathematics.* National Council of Teachers of Mathematics, 1992.

Welchman-Tischler, R., *How to Use Children's Literature to Teach Mathematics*. National Council of Teachers of Mathematics, 1992.

Whitin, D., and Wilde, S., *Read Any Good Math Lately? Children's Books for Mathematical Learning, K-6*. Heinemann Books, 1992.

Whitin, D., and Wilde, S., *It's the Story That Counts: More Children's Books for Mathematical Learning, K-6*. Heinemann Books, 1995.

SOME STRATEGIES THAT CAN BE USED IN THE TEACHING OF MATHEMATICS

The chapter now presents some strategies that can be used to teach mathematics at various grade levels. They will have to be adapted to meet the requirements of students in different grades.

SQRQCQ

Although the Survey Q3R method can be effective with most expository (content) material, especially social studies and science, it is difficult to apply in its original form to mathematics. A similar plan developed especially for mathematical story (verbal) problems is known as SQRQCQ (survey, question, read, question, compute, question). As with Survey Q3R, the literacy or mathematics teacher should model SQRQCQ with the class and conduct whole-class practice before expecting students to try this procedure on their own. In addition, the teacher will need to remind students to use this strategy on a regular basis before they can be expected to use it consistently. The steps of this study strategy are as follows:

Survey—Read through the story (verbal) problem quickly to get an overall impression of what the problem is about.

Question—Then the student should ask him-/herself general questions related to problem solving, such as: "What is the problem to be solved?" "What do I need to find out?" and "What important information is provided in the story problem?"

Read—Read the problem again carefully, paying close attention to details and relationships that will help in the problem-solving process.

Question—Answer the question: "What mathematical operation(s) is needed to solve this problem?"

Compute—Do the computation associated with the operation decided on in the previous step.

Question—Answer the question: "Does this answer make sense?" If not, then the student may need to repeat some or all of the process.

(Adapted from Leo Fay, "Reading Study Skills: Math and Science." In J. A. Figurel [Editor], *Reading and Inquiry*. Newark, Delaware: International Reading Association, 1965.)

Using Newspapers and Magazines to Teach Mathematics

Clip some articles from current newspapers and magazines in which some type of mathematics is discussed; for example, metric equivalents, statistics, or comparison of numbers. Then paste the clippings on colored art paper and draw a line under each mathematical term and print the word near its position in the article. Then prepare a bulletin board for the new display. Using newspapers you can cut out letters for the title *People Talk Math Everyday*. Then mount the examples on the bulletin board.

By following the teacher's modeling, have students add their own clippings from newspapers and magazines that contain mathematical terms to the bulletin board. This activity shows students how relevant mathematics is in their daily lives.

Better-Buy Strategy

From sales advertisements in newspapers, clip two advertisements for each of fifteen nonfood household items, such as brand-name large or small appliances, sheets and pillowcases, or accessories. Mount each advertisement on a 3″ × 5″ index card. For each pair mark a + or − on the backs of the card. Prepare a posterboard similar to the one in Figure 6-3.

Then have the students shop through the sales items as they would through the newspaper. Have them select twelve items they would buy because of either their superior quality, quantity, or price and place the cards in the "Shopping List" envelope on the posterboard, placing the rest of them in the "Rejected Items" envelope. When each student has completed the activity, have him or her check his or her judgment against the teacher's judgment by checking the plusses and minuses on the backs of the cards and discuss the reasons for any differences.

Correct the Teacher About Charts and Graphs Activity

As stated earlier in this book, often the charts and graphs in all content textbooks, including mathematics, do not motivate students. Then the negativism associated with the charts and graphs in the textbook is transferred to all the material in the textbook. This activity is designed to use everyday resource materials as mediums for reinforcing the skill of chart and graph reading and to impress upon students the importance of interpreting graphic material.

Clip charts and graphs from newspapers and magazines that appeal to students in the middle school. Write a series of incorrect statements about each chart or graph and paste them under the appropriate chart or graph. Then have students either independently or with a partner(s) determine whether or not the teacher's statements are correct or incorrect and why. Later the student(s) can meet with the teacher to discuss the results.

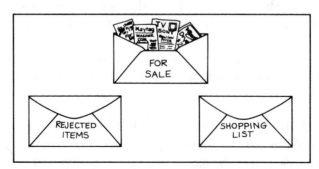

Figure 6-3

"Guesstimating"

A number of math students lack the ability to estimate an answer before computing a problem. Therefore, they give papers to their teacher with impossible answers and are unaware that their solutions are mathematically impossible. This activity gives students practice in "guesstimating" measurements, working with tangible objects to obtain the concept of estimating. It also enhances the skill of observing.

Display fifteen or more objects of different weights, lengths, and sizes. For each object prepare one question and make a copy for each student. Here are some examples:

- *a picture that is hung on a wall*—How many inches wide and how many inches long is it?
- *a clear plastic bag of hard candy*—How many pieces of candy are in the bag?
- *an onion*—How many ounces does it weigh?
- *an empty Mason jar*—How many cups of water does it hold?
- *a mathematics textbook*—How much does it weigh?
- *a large bag of potato chips*—How much does it weigh?
- *a closed dictionary*—How many pages does it contain?
- *a pail*—How many quarts of water does it hold?
- *a sack of oranges*—How much does it weigh?
- *an apple*—How much does it weigh?
- *a loaf of bread*—How many inches long is it?
- *a Sunday newspaper*—How many pages does it contain?
- *a piece of firewood*—How many inches long is it?
- *a bundle of spaghetti*—How many ounces are in it?
- *a paper bag*—How many inches long is it?

Add It in Your Head

This activity is designed to provide practice in the skill of estimating in an everyday situation. Have the student go shopping with a parent or relative when a number of small items are being purchased in a grocery store, a drugstore, or a discount department store. Without using paper and pencil, have the student keep a running estimate of items as they are placed into the shopping cart. Have the student include an estimate of the sales tax and then round-off for errors.

After the shopping has been completed, have the student tell his or her companion the estimate, which is then written on the back of the cash register receipt. On a selected date the class and teacher discuss what type of estimation errors were made most often and why. Then the teacher collects the cash register slips to study the errors and to identify students who need additional help in this skill.

Reproducible Activity Sheets for Improving Competency in Mathematics

The chapter now includes several reproducible activity sheets for improving competency in various elements of mathematics including specialized vocabulary.

The literacy or mathematics teacher can duplicate and use any of these activity sheets in their present form or modify them in any way they wish.

The literacy or mathematics teacher can use a variation of the cloze procedure to improve understanding of mathematical concepts and operations. When this instructional strategy is used, it must first be explained in detail by the teacher, then practiced by students under direct teacher supervision, and later practiced independently, or more preferably, by several students working together.

WORD SEARCH PUZZLE FOR MATHEMATICS
(Approximately Middle-School Level)

Below are the definitions of *eight words* that we have studied recently that are connected to *circles*. You should write the correct word beside each definition and then find that word in the word search puzzle. If you know a word that is defined, write it beside the definition and then find it in the puzzle. Or if you first find words in the puzzle, circle them and then write each word beside its definition. The words in the word search puzzle may be written forwards, backwards, up, down, or diagonally.

MATHEMATICAL TERMS RELATED TO CIRCLES

1. the continuous portion of a curved line

   _____

2. the line segment extending from the center of a circle to its circumference

   _____

3. the length of a straight line through the center of an object

   _____

4. the symbol π denoting the ratio of the circumference of a circle to its diameter

   _____

5. the perimeter of a circle

   _____

6. having a common center

   _____

7. curved or round like the exterior of a sphere or circle

   _____

8. a closed plane, every point of which is equidistant from a fixed point within the curve

   _____

WORD SEARCH PUZZLE FOR MATHEMATICS
(Approximately Middle-School Level)

(cont.)

X	B	I	O	R	T	B	M	J	U	I	W	E	M	L	Y	T	I	X	Z
Y	W	V	X	C	I	R	C	U	M	F	E	R	E	N	C	E	O	P	Z
O	I	E	B	B	V	M	J	G	Y	W	E	R	T	I	B	H	G	E	O
W	O	U	T	H	K	I	H	C	F	O	O	P	N	V	H	T	Y	E	M
X	I	U	W	E	N	M	B	I	P	Z	N	Y	E	R	N	B	H	Y	M
B	Y	T	R	E	W	T	U	R	C	R	A	O	Y	T	B	N	M	B	V
R	A	D	I	U	S	P	W	C	M	P	U	T	R	M	N	B	V	O	P
A	A	C	M	R	O	P	X	L	E	P	C	C	O	N	V	E	X	R	Z
Z	A	M	O	P	R	X	U	E	P	O	R	S	T	U	V	R	Z	Y	Z
I	P	X	I	O	R	U	P	X	I	Y	T	R	B	N	M	J	K	G	D
C	B	A	C	O	N	C	E	N	T	R	I	C	O	P	T	R	Y	E	W
T	Y	E	W	Q	V	B	M	J	H	Y	I	U	M	K	J	L	O	I	P
R	U	O	R	E	T	E	M	A	I	D	O	U	Y	T	R	B	N	M	O

Answer Key for "Mathematical Terms Related to Circles"

1. arc
2. radius
3. diameter
4. pi

5. circumference
6. concentric
7. convex
8. circle

```
X B I O R T B M J U I W E M L Y T I X Z
Y W V X C I R C U M F E R E N C E O P Z
O I E B B V M J G Y W E R T I B H G E O
W O U T H K I H C F O O P N V H T Y E M
X I U W E N M B I P Z N Y E R N B H Y M
B Y T R E W T U R C R A O Y T B N M B V
R A D I U S P W C M P U T R M N B V O P
A A C M R O P X L E P C C O N V E X R Z
Z A M O P R X U E P O R S T U V R Z Y Z
I P X I O R U P X I Y T R B N M J K G D
C B A C O N C E N T R I C O P T R Y E W
T Y E W Q V B M J H Y I U M K J L O I P
R U O R E T E M A I D O U Y T R B N M O
```

MODIFIED CLOZE PROCEDURE FOR MATHEMATICS*
(Approximately Lower Middle-School Level)

Here are a number of short passages that might be found in the lower middle-school mathematics textbook. Complete each modified cloze procedure independently or with a partner(s). An example has been completed for you as a model.

Example

Divide 25 by _____. Now _____ 25 _____ 1/5. Is _____ by _____ the same as multiplying _____ 1/5? Are these sentences _____?

   48 – 24 = _____ × 1/24

   81 – 9 = _____ × 1/9

Answers

Divide 25 by __5__. Now __multiply__ 25 __by__ 1/5. Is __dividing__ by __5__ the same as multiplying __by__ 1/5? Are these sentences __accurate__?

   48 – 24 = __48__ × 1/24

   81 – 9 = __81__ × 1/9

MODIFIED CLOZE PROCEDURE

1. Add 34 and 52. Now _____ 52 from 86. The _____ is 34. Then subtract _____ from 86. The answer _____ 52. Are addition and _____ reciprocal mathematical operations?

   34 + 52 = _____

   86 – 52 = _____

   86 – 34 = _____

2. Subtract 750 from 1121. The _____ is 371. Now add _____ and 750. The answer _____ 1121. Are addition and _____ reciprocal math operations?

   1121 – 750 = _____

   371 + 750 = _____

*In most cases every *fifth word or symbol* was omitted. However, there are some exceptions to this because of various considerations, such as it being too easy or difficult to complete that deletion.

MODIFIED CLOZE PROCEDURE FOR MATHEMATICS*
(Approximately Lower Middle-School Level)

(cont.)

3. Add 64, 64, and _____. The answer is 192. Now _____ 64 by 3. The _____ is
   192. Do you _____ it is easier _____ add the numeral 64 _____ times or to
   multiply _____ by 3?

   64 + 64 + _____ = 192

   64 × 3 = _____

4. Divide 80 by 4. Now _____ 80 by 1/4. Is _____ by 4 the same _____
   multiplying by 1/4? Divide _____ by 12. Now multiply _____ by 1/12. Is dividing
   96 _____ 12 the same as _____ by 1/12? Are these _____ accurate?

   80 ÷ 4 = _____ × 1/4

   96 ÷ 12 = _____ × 1/12

5. Is one-fourth of _____ pie the same as _____ of a pie? Would _____ rather
   have one-fifth _____ a pie or 1/4 _____ a pie? Why?

   one-fourth = _____

   one-fifth = 1/4 _____ doesn't it?

6. Add 921 and 265. Now _____ 921 from 1186. The _____ is 265. Then subtract
   _____ from 1186. The answer _____ 921. Are addition and _____ the same
   or different _____ operations?

   921 + 265 = _____

   1186 − 921 = _____

   1186 − 265 = _____

7. Subtract 72 from 288. The _____ is 216. Now subtract _____ from 216. The
   answer _____ 144. Now subtract 72 _____ 144. The answer is _____. Now
   subtract 72 from _____. The answer is 0. Now _____ 288 by 72. The _____ is
   4. Do you _____ the mathematical operation _____ division saves time in
   comparison _____ the mathematical operation of _____ subtractions?

   288 − 72 = _____

   216 − 72 = _____

   144 − 72 = _____

   72 − 72 = _____

   288 ÷ 72 = _____

MODIFIED CLOZE PROCEDURE FOR MATHEMATICS*
(Approximately Lower Middle-School Level)

(cont.)

8. Subtract 879 from 1021. The _____ is 142. Now add _____ and 879. The answer _____ 1021. Are addition and _____ reciprocal mathematical operations?

   $1021 - 879 =$ _____

   $142 + 879 =$ _____

9. Add 81, 81, 81, _____, and 81. The answer _____ 405. Now multiply 81 _____ 5. The answer is _____. Do you think _____ is easier to add _____ numeral 81 five times _____ to multiply the numeral _____ by 5?

   $81 + 81 +$ _____ $+ 81 + 81 =$ _____

   $81 \times 5 =$ _____

10. Is 1/9 the same _____ 9/1 or are they _____? Which is the larger _____? Is 1/25 the same _____ 25/1 or are they _____? Which is the larger _____?

© 1997 by John Wiley & Sons, Inc.

Answer Key for "Modified Cloze Procedure"

1. subtract; answer; 34; is; subtraction

    86

    34

    52

2. answer; 371; is; subtraction

    371

    1121

3. 64; multiply; answer; think; to; three; 64

    64

    192

4. multiply; dividing; as; 96; 96; by; multiplying; sentences (numerals, figures)

    80

    96

5. a (one); 1/4; you; of; of

    1/4

    or

6. subtract; answer; 265; is; subtraction; mathematical (math)

    1186

    265

    921

7. answer; 72; is; from; 72; 72; divide; answer; think; of; to; repeated (many)

    216

    144

    72

    0

    4

8. answer; 142; is; subtraction

    142

    1021

9. 81; is; by (times); 405; it; the; or; 81

    81; 405

    405

10. as; different; fraction; as; different; fraction

MATHEMATICS MATCHING ACTIVITY SHEET FOR
SYMBOLS AND ABBREVIATIONS
(Approximately Sixth-Grade Level)

This activity sheet contains mathematical symbols, abbreviations, and their definitions. Place the correct letter that is found in front of each definition in front of the symbol for which it is the definition. You should use each definition only once. You can work with a partner(s) if you want to.

_____ 1. ^{4}

_____ 2. mm

_____ 3. ×

_____ 4. ÷

_____ 5. $\overline{\times}$

_____ 6. <

_____ 7. >

_____ 8. °

_____ 9. m

_____ 10. C

_____ 11. %

_____ 12. cm

_____ 13. .

_____ 14. rt.

_____ 15. F

_____ 16. ☐

_____ 17. ∠

_____ 18. √

_____ 19. (

_____ 20. :

a. meter

b. Fahrenheit

c. kilometer

d. to the fourth power

e. angle

f. equality sign

g. is less than

h. gram

i. is greater than

j. square root

k. division sign

l. rectangle

m. the mean

n. degree

o. parentheses

p. centimeter

q. Celsius

r. percent

s. decimal point

t. right

u. fraction

v. trapezoid

w. multiplier

y. millimeter

z. ratio sign

Answer Key for "Symbols and Abbreviations"

1. d	**6.** g	**11.** r	**16.** l
2. y	**7.** i	**12.** p	**17.** e
3. w	**8.** n	**13.** s	**18.** j
4. k	**9.** a	**14.** t	**19.** o
5. m	**10.** q	**15.** b	**20.** z

MATHEMATICS VOCABULARY EXERCISE
(Approximately Fifth-Grade Level)

Fill in the blanks for the correct word for each clue given. The letter you are given is placed correctly in the word "MATHEMATICS." Each word must have the correct number of letters as designated by the blanks.

M _ _ _ — the sum of all the scores (or grades or measures) divided by their number

_ _ _ _ _ _ A — a shorthand of expressing a rule by the use of symbol or letter designations

_ _ _ T _ _ _ _ _ _ _ — the process of finding the difference between two numbers

_ _ _ _ H — the number of the digit that is in the first decimal place

_ _ _ _ E _ _ _ _ _ — the result obtained by taking a given hundredth part of a base

_ _ _ M _ — a number that cannot be divided by any number except 1

_ _ A _ _ _ _ _ — the quotient of two whole numbers that is not a whole number

_ _ _ T _ _ _ _ _ _ _ _ _ — a short method of adding a number to itself a given number of times

_ I _ _ _ _ — the symbol that indicates subtraction

_ _ C _ _ _ _ — relating to number 10

_ _ _ _ S _ _ _ — the process of finding out how many times one number goes into another number

© 1997 by John Wiley & Sons, Inc.

Answer Key for "Mathematics Vocabulary Exercise"

MEAN

FORMULA

SUBTRACTION

TENTH

PERCENTAGE

PRIME

FRACTION

MULTIPLICATION

MINUS

DECIMAL

DIVISION

ROMAN NUMERAL "BRAIN TEASERS"
(Middle-School Level)

This activity sheet contains some "brain teasers" that use Roman numerals. Read each brain teaser and then substitute the correct Roman numeral for its Arabic equivalent. You can use the chart of Roman numerals on this activity sheet if you want. Then think of a word for the definition given in the equation. Combine the Roman numeral with the word to formulate a *new word* for each example. You can work with a partner(s) if you want. An example has been given.

ROMAN NUMERALS

I = 1	C = 100
V = 5	D = 500
X = 10	M = 1,000
L = 50	

Example: 6 + become destroyed = related to a snake

VI + PERISH = <u>VIPERISH</u>

1. 100 + jump = cut into pieces

   _____ + _____ = _____

2. 50 + a conjunction = ground or soil

   _____ + _____ = _____

3. 5 + an article (in grammar) = a means of transportation

   _____ + _____ = _____

4. 10 + a beam of radiant energy = a special type of photograph used in medicine

   _____ + _____ = _____

5. 100 + to grow older = a box or enclosure having some openwork

   _____ + _____ = _____

6. 1,000 + an item that appears in a newspaper = carried away by intense anger

   _____ + _____ = _____

7. 100 + containing little or no fat = free from dirt

   _____ + _____ = _____

8. 1,000 + to give assistance = a female servant

   _____ + _____ = _____

ROMAN NUMERAL "BRAIN TEASERS"
(Middle-School Level)

(cont.)

9. 50 + the past tense of eat = being tardy

   _____ + _____ = _____

10. 100 + a tree belonging to the olive family = money paid promptly after purchasing

   _____ + _____ = _____

11. 1,000 + an alcoholic beverage = a person of the masculine sex

   _____ + _____ = _____

12. 100 + spoken by the mouth or in words = a deep pink color

   _____ + _____ = _____

13. 50 + a type of snake = a structure that is used for climbing

   _____ + _____ = _____

14. 100 + the whole amount or quantity of = to speak loudly

   _____ + _____ = _____

15. 1,000 + a fall-blooming leafy herb = one having authority over another

   _____ + _____ = _____

Answer Key for "Roman Numeral 'Brain Teasers'"

1. C + HOP = CHOP
2. L + AND = LAND
3. V + AN = VAN
4. X + RAY = XRAY
5. C + AGE = CAGE
6. M + AD = MAD
7. C + LEAN = CLEAN
8. M + AID = MAID
9. L + ATE = LATE
10. C + ASH = CASH
11. M + ALE = MALE
12. C + ORAL = CORAL
13. L + ADDER = LADDER
14. C + ALL = CALL
15. M + ASTER = MASTER

Strategies for Improving Test Construction and Test-Taking Skills in the Content Areas

Did you enjoy taking tests of various kinds when you were in elementary school, high school, or college? Most of you probably would have to answer "No!" to that question. I was one of those rare people who enjoyed taking tests and usually could raise my grade in any class on a final exam since I became "psyched" and did very well. Fortunately, I had good test-taking skills and did not experience the damaging test anxiety that plagues some students. Yet test-taking skills, "testwiseness," and relieving test anxiety in the content fields can be taught to students, and this certainly should occur. The information contained in this chapter is designed to help literacy and content teachers do just that. It also is designed to help content teachers construct tests in their field that will more effectively assess what students really have learned in that class, certainly one of the major reasons for giving tests.

After reading this chapter both literacy and content teachers should be much better prepared to help students develop both test-taking skills and "testwiseness." The improvement of these two aspects of taking tests in literature, social studies, science, and mathematics should enable students to perform much more effectively on tests and to greatly alleviate their test anxiety.

WHY STUDENTS NEED TO TAKE TESTS AND THE IMPORTANCE OF GIVING VALID TESTS IN THE CONTENT AREAS

Fortunately or unfortunately, tests are a part of life in school. Tests are given for a number of reasons. Some of them are as follows:

- Teachers want to know how much students have learned after studying a chapter or unit in a content field such as literature, social studies, science, or mathematics.

- Teachers want to evaluate just how effective their lessons in a content study or unit have been.

- Teachers want to diagnose the strengths and weaknesses of a student in his or her content field.

- Teachers, school districts, school boards, and parents want to compare a student's performance in a content area with those of other similar students.

- Students want to learn how well they are doing in comparison with their own past performance and the performance of other students in a content field.

- If a student performs poorly on a test, it should be a warning signal to him or her that he or she should obtain assistance from the teacher about the content covered on that test.

- If a student performs well on a test, it should reassure him or her that he or she has mastered the material covered in that content unit or chapter.

It is obvious that the tests given in the content classes of literature, social studies, science, and mathematics evaluate a student's mastery of the instructional objectives and material evaluated by that test. Unfortunately, this may not always be the case. Test scores are dependent upon many factors such as a student's prior knowledge, motivation, interest, attitudes toward the test and the teacher, physical or emotional health, and classroom climate, among countless other extraneous factors. However, all of these factors being equal, which they obviously never are, both test-taking skills and "testwiseness" can help students reflect what they really know on a test. That is why it is so important to give all students instruction in both test-taking skills and "testwiseness" so that they will be able to achieve at their optimum level. The strategies and reproducible materials contained later in this chapter will help any teacher to do this effectively.

TEST-CONSTRUCTION TIPS FOR BOTH LITERACY AND CONTENT TEACHERS

Obviously, it is very important for both literacy and content teachers to construct the fairest, most comprehensive, and valid tests possible to ensure that these tests evaluate those concepts and understanding that should be evaluated. This often can prove to be a fairly difficult task for a teacher. However, the following suggestions will help you.

Designing Content Tests for All Types of Students

- Test, teach, and then retest if possible to enable students to do as well as possible in a content class.

- Construct the test in a logical sequence, placing the easier items at the beginning and progressing through the most difficult items at the end of the test.

- Use test items that best reflect the techniques used to teach the content material.

- Type and copy the test so that it is very easy to read. If possible, for best results, use a laser printer.

- Prepare a study guide or practice test that matches the design and format of the actual test.

Constructing the Best Possible *Test Directions*

- Keep the directions simple by not including unnecessary words that may just confuse students.

- State the directions in a sequential order or place them all at the beginning of each separate test section.
- State only one direction in each sentence.
- Underline the word <u>Directions</u> *or the entire portion of the test devoted to directions* to call students' attention to it.
- Do not use words such as *always, never,* or *not*. If you have to use them, be sure to underline them.
- If the directions contain more than one statement, list them vertically so that students can read them more easily.

Constructing Multiple-Choice Items

- Avoid using unnecessary words that do not help a student to select the correct answer.
- Be sure the last word in the question stem is grammatically compatible with all of the items.
- Do not include options that are obviously incorrect.
- Do not include two or more answers that are both so nearly correct as to be confusing for the student.
- State the question and the responses in simple terms.
- Avoid using many answers that state "all of the above" or "none of the above."
- Avoid using many items that require students to pick more than one option as the correct answer.
- Avoid using such words as *either* or *or*.
- Avoid using two options with essentially the same meaning since test-wise students know that neither one can be correct.
- Avoid creating two options with opposite meanings since test-wise students know that one of the options must be wrong.
- Avoid hiding the correct option in the *B* or *C* position since test-wise students guess options *B* or *C* much more often than *A* or *D*.

Constructing True–False Items

- Avoid stating questions in the negative.
- Avoid using such terms as *all, always, none,* or *never.*
- Avoid items that are obviously designed to "trick" students.
- Avoid long, complicated sentences that are subject to many different types of interpretation.
- Avoid trivial statements or statements that are not really assessing students' knowledge.

Constructing Matching Test Items

- Place all matching items on choice selections on the same page of the test.
- Place a blank next to each item for the letter of the correct answer.
- Arrange all of the blanks on the same side of the questions.

- Have only one correct answer for each item.
- As it is confusing, do not have students draw a line to the correct answer.
- Keep all matching items as brief as possible to avoid confusion.

Constructing Completion or Fill-in-the-Blank Items

- Write simple and clear test items.
- Do not use statements taken directly from the textbook, as taken out of context they are usually too general and ambiguous to be used as test items.
- Construct all blank lines of the same length.

Constructing Essay Items

- Define any unclear terms in the item.
- Select questions that emphasize the domain level of the students; for example, *list* is on the knowledge level, while *predict* is on the interpretive level.
- Be sure students know the meaning of such clue words as *list, enumerate, describe, define, discuss, explain, compare, contrast, criticize, diagram, illustrate, evaluate, justify,* and *summarize.*

Reproducible Teacher Checklist for Designing an Effective Test

The chapter now includes a reproducible teacher checklist devoted to designing an effective test in any content field. If it seems applicable for your use, you can duplicate it and use it in its present form or modify it in any way you wish.

TEACHER CHECKLIST DEVOTED TO DESIGNING A CONTENT TEST

After you have read each question, place a check on the appropriate line. Using this checklist should help you determine if you have constructed a valid test for use in a content class.

Yes No

1. If you have emphasized certain study strategies to your students, have you asked questions on this test that will emphasize these strategies? For example, if you have encouraged students to recognize comparison–contrast relationships, have you constructed some test items that call for an understanding of these relationships? __ __

2. Do the items included on this test reflect your objectives in teaching the content effectively? __ __

3. Have you included SCORER or PORPE as a strategy for reminding students how they should use effective test-taking skills? __ __

4. Have you included a significant number of items that require higher-level thinking and responses such as interpretive, critical, and applied questions? __ __

5. What type of responses are you requiring from students? A balance of different kinds of responses usually is the most effective with production responses being preferred, if possible. __ __

6. Have you placed most of the easier items near the beginning of the test and the more difficult items near the end of the test? __ __

7. Have you written your test items so that comprehension is dependent on the learned material rather than on students' prior knowledge? __ __

8. Is the weight of the test to the final course grade completely clear to students? Is the weight of each item on the test clear? Is the weight of parts of an item clear within that item? __ __

9. Have you used some alternatives to traditional test items such as statements instead of questions? Have you tried to incorporate writing into the test if possible? __ __

10. For objective tests, have you constructed different types of items such as multiple-choice items, true–false items, matching items, completion, or fill-in-the-blank items? Why or why not? __ __

11. For essay tests, have you included the proper descriptive words such as *list, enumerate, compare, describe, define, discuss, explain, compare, contrast, criticize, diagram, illustrate, evaluate, justify,* and *summarize* to motivate students to respond in the appropriate way? __ __

12. Does the test have a good format? For example, is it easy to read and understand, uncluttered, and well spaced? Does it look like a professional test as much as possible? This is especially important for such "at-risk" students as learning-disabled and slow-learning students. __ __

HOW TO PREVENT TEST ANXIETY

As you know, test anxiety can greatly hinder a student's performance on a test. I once had an experienced kindergarten teacher in a graduate class about emergent literacy who obviously was a very competent teacher. However, on the midterm exam in the class she did very poorly. Certainly her test score did not accurately reflect her real knowledge of either concepts or attitudes. She told me later that she suffered from extreme test anxiety which had proven to be a great handicap to her in elementary school, secondary school, college, and now graduate school.

However, there are some strategies that literacy and content teachers can use to minimize, if not entirely eliminate, test anxiety. Anxiety can be reduced and learning enhanced if teachers prepare students for specific tests and if students learn how to study for and to take tests wisely.

A number of middle-school and secondary-school students distrust the validity of the tests they must take because they believe teachers may try to trick them with unfair questions on tests or mainly are interested in constructing tests that are designed to result in students receiving low grades. Two strategies teachers can use in minimizing students' test anxiety are (1) providing students with exact information about what a test will include and (2) giving students practice tests that are very similar to the actual tests they must later take to earn grades. These can be called a "practice pop quiz."

The "practice pop quiz" is a test that is designed to *review rather than test* recently learned information. The purpose of the quiz is to stimulate interest and to practice the actual test format. Tests may not be so unpleasant once the anxiety over being evaluated is removed. These "practice pop quizzes" also may be more motivating than simple reviews for a test which are so much more commonly used. In addition, students appreciate test simulations because they know the teacher is really attempting to prepare them for the actual tests that are to follow.

"Practice pop quizzes" can be part of daily lessons and written on the chalkboard, or they can be more comprehensive tests of which each student has his or her own copy. In either case, the quiz can follow this format:

> "Today we are having a Practice Pop Quiz on the unit about 'Astronomy' that we have been studying in science. This quiz will not in any way affect your grade in this class, but it will give you some practice in taking a test like the one you will have in the class, and it will give you an idea of how well prepared you are for the test on this topic when you must take it. When everybody has finished the test, you may score your own test and you will receive one (two, three, etc.) point(s) for each correct answer."

The "practice pop quiz" can be either open-book or closed-book depending upon your objectives and the type of material. Later the questions on the quiz can serve as a guide to classroom study and to further review for the actual test.

In addition, students can further reduce their test anxiety by learning the test-taking strategies and "testwiseness" skills that are now described.

TEST-TAKING SKILLS AND "TESTWISENESS"

Although test-taking skills and testwiseness are somewhat similar, there also are some important differences between them. *Test-taking skills* are long-term study strategies while *testwiseness* is a set of strategies students can use while taking exams. Some test-taking skills are frequent reviews of content textbook material, class notes, and other assigned materials. It also includes the concept that short study sessions are more effective than a few long cramming sessions.

Perhaps testwiseness has been best defined by Millman, Bishop, and Ebel when they wrote that testwiseness is the "capacity to utilize the characteristics and formats of the test and/or the test-taking situation to receive a high score. Test wiseness is logically independent of an examinee's knowledge of the subject matter." (J. C. Millman, C. H. Bishop, and R. Ebel, "An Analysis of Test Wiseness," *Educational and Psychological Measurement* 25, May, 1965, pp. 707-727). Therefore, *testwiseness* refers to some principles that can be applied to content exams independently of subject area knowledge. To be testwise is to be able to exploit the flaws that are commonly found even in good teacher-made tests and apply logic, common sense, and good organization skills in test-taking situations of all kinds. It is obvious that testwiseness alone will not result in good grades in elementary school or high school. There is no substitute for studying hard. However, testwiseness skills can help students to do better on classroom content tests. Although some educators do not approve of teaching testwiseness to students, it seems to make sense that if students are equally testwise, no student has an unfair advantage, and differences in performance should be attributable only to different degrees of content understanding.

Therefore, it seems apparent that both test-taking skills and testwiseness should be taught to all students beyond the upper primary grades, if not before. To not do so unfairly penalizes those students who have not figured out both test-taking skills and testwiseness independently through logic and trial and error.

STRATEGIES FOR IMPROVING ABILITY IN TEST-TAKING SKILLS AND "TESTWISENESS"

Test-Taking Skills

Here are some test-taking strategies that either literacy or content teachers may want to present to students:

When You Are First Told About a Test

- Ask your teacher as much about the test as you can.
- Find out the exact day on which the test will be given.
- Ask your teacher to tell you how many items will be on the test and what the items will consist of (multiple choice, true–false, matching, completion [fill-in-the blanks], essay).
- Ask your teacher to provide you with some sample items like those on the test, if possible. Although not all teachers will do this, some of them will usually only if they are ask to do so.

The Evening Before the Test

- Study only for a short time. Do not attempt to cram for the test, as it probably only will confuse you.
- Make certain you have all of the supplies you will need to take the test (sharpened pencils, paper, a watch, and a calculator if it is needed and allowed).
- Try to get a good night's sleep.

The Day of the Test

- Eat a good breakfast.

- Reassure yourself that you can and will do well on the test. Try not to approach it with apprehension even if it will be a fairly difficult test. Try to think positively!

- Make sure you have all the materials you need for the test.

- Do not cram during the last few minutes before a test since this can cause you to forget important information that you already have learned. Cramming also causes you additional test anxiety.

Improving "Testwiseness"

Multiple-Choice Tests

- Read and follow all of the directions for the test very carefully.

- Read the question and try to decide what type of question it is: fact, main idea, or vocabulary.

- Decide what you think the answer might be before you read any of the options.

- Read all of the options before answering the question.

- Read the question again, this time with the answer you selected to see if it sounds correct.

- When one of the options is "All of the Above," it usually is the correct option.

- Options with a qualifier such as "Most" usually are correct.

- Options with absolute statements such as "All" or "None" are usually incorrect.

- Try to use your time well so that you have time to finish the entire test and then go back over it to check your answers.

- Omit any items you are not at all sure of and come back to them when you have finished the test to avoid not finishing the entire test.

- Always make a calculated guess if you are not sure of the right answer, unless there is a penalty for an incorrect answer. Never leave a multiple-choice question blank.

- Try to eliminate any options that obviously cannot be correct.

- Watch for options that do not match the question stem grammatically since they are usually incorrect.

- You may be able to find the answer to one multiple-choice question in the stem of another multiple-choice question.

- When two options are similar, neither one is likely to be correct.

- The most general option is likely to be the correct one.

- The longest or most complete option is likely to be the correct one.

- The option containing familiar language is likely to be the correct one.

- The option containing technical language is likely to be the correct one.

- When two of the options are opposite, one of them is always incorrect, and the other is usually, but not always, correct.

- As a last resort, select an option that is not the first or the last choice since options *B* or *C* are somewhat more likely to be correct than options *A* or *D*.

True–False Tests

- Read all of the directions carefully.
- Budget your time so that you are able to finish all of the items.
- Always make a calculated guess if you do not know the answer. Never leave a true–false item blank, unless there is a penalty for an incorrect answer.
- Longer statements are somewhat more likely than shorter statements to be true.
- Assume the teacher is asking straightforward questions.
- Be aware of such words as *all, none, always,* and *never.* These words usually indicate the statement is false.
- Be aware of such words as *usually, generally, sometimes,* and *seldom.* These words usually indicate the statement is true.
- Assume absolute statements are *false* while qualified statements are *true.*
- Assume an answer is true unless the statement can be proved false.
- Be certain *all* parts of the statement are correct before marking it true.
- Watch for *negatives* such as *not* or the prefix *in,* as a negative can completely change the meaning of a statement.
- Simplify a statement that contains a double negative by eliminating both negatives.

Matching Tests

- Read all of the items in both columns before answering.
- Determine if you can use a choice more than once.
- Begin by making the easiest matches.
- Make all the correct matches possible before guessing at any of the other matches.
- Cross out items in both columns as they are used.
- Make the best guess you can for the remaining items unless there is a penalty for an incorrect answer.

Completion or Fill-in-the-Blank Tests

- Read the entire sentence or paragraph.
- Decide which word could best fit in the blank.
- Write an answer that grammatically fits the blank.
- Use the length of the blank line as a clue unless all of the blank lines are the same length.
- Read the entire sentence again including your choice to be sure it fits and sounds correct.
- If the blank comes at the beginning of the sentence, be sure to capitalize the word.

Essay Tests

- Read and restate the question or statement in your own words before trying to answer it. If you cannot do this, ask the teacher if he or she can explain it.

- Budget your time so that you are certain to complete the test. Determine how many points each essay question is worth. Spend more time on the questions that are worth the most points.

- Make a brief outline before you write your answer to help you organize it more effectively.

- Consider the meanings of the following essay test directions both before and during the writing:

  List, Outline. *List* tells you to present information in an item-by-item series, usually with each item being numbered. *Outline* tells you to provide the main points in a specific format, usually using both letters and numbers.

  Critique. *Critique* tells you to summarize and to evaluate.

  Discuss, Describe, Explain. All of these direction words tell you to write as much as you can about a question or statement.

  Diagram, Illustrate. These two direction statements tell you to make a drawing with each part labeled.

  Compare, Contrast. *Compare* tells you to tell how two or more items are connected. *Contrast* tells you to indicate how they are different.

  Criticize, Evaluate, Justify. These three direction words require you to reach a conclusion about the value of an item(s). *Criticize* and *evaluate* each require you to think about the positive and negative aspects of an item(s) before reaching a conclusion about it. *Justify* requires you to give reasons for an action or decision.

  Relate, Trace. *Relate* tells you to indicate how two or more items are connected, while *trace* tells you to state a series of items in some logical order.

  Summarize. *Summarize* tells you to write a brief statement that indicates something about all of the important ideas.

- Unless the directions state otherwise, never write a minimal answer. Teachers expect you to elaborate and provide full explanations and details on essay answers.

- Be sure to answer all parts of the question.

- Try to write directly to the point of the question.

- Use diagrams and illustrations when appropriate to explain an answer.

- Write as neatly as possible since a teacher cannot give credit for an answer that he or she cannot easily read.

- Proofread each answer for spelling, grammar, and organization. Remember that the grading of essay questions is mainly subjective, and a carelessly written answer may lower your grade.

- If you run out of time before the test is finished, list all of the information you know about that statement or question to receive partial credit for it.

READY-TO-IMPLEMENT STRATEGIES FOR IMPROVING BOTH TEST-TAKING SKILLS AND "TESTWISENESS"

The chapter now presents a number of strategies that can be used for improving test-taking skills and testwiseness. Both literacy and content teachers should find these strategies effective and simple to use.

The Five-Day Test Preparation Plan

The *Five-Day Test Preparation Plan* will help all students better prepare to take a test. The plan is divided into two parts.

Part One—Getting Ready.   Here are some of the things all students can do to best prepare to take any test:

- Ask the teacher what type of information will be included in the test.
- Ask the teacher what types of questions will be included on the test (multiple-choice, true–false, matching, completion or fill-in-the blanks, or essay).
- Use a study strategy such as Survey Q3R and take appropriate notes from the reading materials.
- Use an appropriate note-taking strategy.
- Schedule their time to begin studying about five days before the test.

Part Two—Preparing for the Test.   Here is the five-day test preparation plan:

- *Day Five*—Students should review their textbook notes for all of the assigned chapters in the textbook that will be included on the test. Students also should review their written class notes from the lecture and class discussions. The teacher should be asked to explain any information that is still unclear or unknown by a student.
- *Day Four*—Students should study the information in their textbook notes and class notes. They should begin to memorize this information by reviewing it at least three times during this day.
- *Day Three*—Students should rewrite both their textbook notes and their class notes in a briefer form. Encourage students to use abbreviated language while rewriting their notes. The rewriting gives students a multimodal review of the information they have to learn.
- *Day Two*—Students should write questions they think might be on the test. They should then write answers to these questions using their rewritten textbook and class notes as necessary.
- *Day One*—This is the day the students take the test. On this day students should review their rewritten textbook and class notes before the school day begins. A good time to do this might be at breakfast or while riding to school on the bus.

(Adapted from Stephan A. Strichart and Charles T. Mangrum, *Teaching Study Strategies to Students with Learning Disabilities.* Boston: Allyn and Bacon, 1993, pp. 301-302.)

Suggestions for Performing More Effectively on Any Objective Test in the Content Fields

Here are seven suggestions you can present to students that may help them to perform more effectively on any objective test in the content fields:

- *Relax*—Take two or three deep breaths and relax.
- *Budget Your Time*—Survey the entire test so you get an idea of what you will be expected to do on it.

- *Directions*—Read the directions carefully and underline all key words.
- *Easy Questions*—Answer all easy questions first.
- *Difficult Questions*—Place a light mark by all difficult questions and then go back to them after answering all the easy questions.
- *Continue to Relax*—Take deep breaths during the test whenever you feel the need to do so.
- *Reread*—Look over your test when you finish to double check your answers and to be sure you did not skip any questions.

The SCORER Strategy

The *SCORER Strategy* is a test-taking strategy that theoretically enables students to obtain higher scores on content tests than would otherwise be the case. The acronym stands for *schedule, clue, omit, read, estimate, review*. High SCORERS follow these steps:

- They *Schedule* their time while they are taking a test.
- They identify the *Clue* words to help them answer the questions. Usually the directions should contain the clue words.
- They *Omit* the hardest items at first.
- They *Read* carefully to be sure they understand and fully answer each question.
- They *Estimate* what should be included in the answer, perhaps by writing down some notes or an outline for the answer.
- They *Review* their responses before turning in the test.

Teachers should teach the steps of SCORER to students and then write the acronym into the test directions or include it as a reminder on tests. Students could even be asked to write how they used the SCORER Strategy while taking the test. This strategy gives students the responsibility to take a test carefully in an organized and thoughtful manner. It can be useful as part of the construction of any test. (Adapted from R. Carmen and W. Adams, *Study Skills: A Student's Guide to Survival.* New York: Wiley, 1972.)

The PORPE Strategy

The *PORPE Strategy* is a very useful study strategy that helps students to prepare for essay tests. The acronym PORPE stands for *predict, organize, rehearse, practice, evaluate*. It provides a step-by-step process to guide students' independent studying for an essay test. Here is a detailed description of each PORPE step.

- *Step One: Predict.* When students have finished a reading assignment in a lesson or unit in which an essay test will be given, have them create probable essay questions, emphasizing those that require interpretive thinking such as analysis, comparison, or contrast. You probably should first be sure that students thoroughly understand the *key words* used in essay questions. (See an earlier section of this chapter.) You should also model the question prediction step. Following this teacher-directed help, ask students to create their own predicted essay questions and share these either in small groups or with the entire class.

- *Step Two: Organize.* In preparation for responding to predicted essay questions, students should outline, map, or use an advance organizer to organize the information they will use in their written response. The teacher should first model this step, and students can share outlines, maps, or advance organizers.

- *Step Three: Rehearse.* The concept in this step is to develop a long-term memory for the information in the outline, map, or advance organizer that needs to be remembered at the time of the essay question answers. Students can self-test by giving the overall organizational structure of the outline, map, or advance organizer and writing it from memory.

- *Step Four: Practice.* Students are asked to write the answers to their predicted essay questions from memory. However, before actually writing, they should construct the outline, map, or graphic organizer of their rehearsed response to guide the structure and content of their essay questions.

- *Step Five: Evaluate.* An important final step is for students to evaluate their practice essay answers. You may want to provide students with a checklist that contains the criteria for a good essay response.

(Adapted from M. L. Simpson, "PORPE: A Study Strategy for Learning in the Content Areas," in E. K. Dishner, T. W. Bean, J. E. Readence, and D. W. Moore (Editors), *Reading in the Content Areas: Improving Classroom Instruction.* Dubuque, Iowa: Kendall/Hunt Publishing Company, 1992, pp. 340-348.)

Reproducible PORPE Checklist to Help Students Evaluate Essay Test Responses

The chapter now contains a ready-to-duplicate checklist that can help students evaluate their essay test responses. You can duplicate and use it in its present form or modify it in any way you like in light of the needs of your own students.

PORPE CHECKLIST FOR EVALUATING ESSAY TEST ANSWERS
(Middle-School and Secondary School Level)

Here is a checklist you can use to evaluate your essay test answers after you have written practice essay questions and responses using the PORPE Strategy that we have studied and practiced in class.

	Above Average	Average	Below Average
1. I answered the essay question in a direct way.	❏	❏	❏
2. I included an introductory sentence that restated the essay question or took a position on the question.	❏	❏	❏
3. I organized the essay question answer with major points or ideas that were very obvious for the reader to easily understand.	❏	❏	❏
4. I included relevant details or examples to prove and clarify each point in the answer to the essay question.	❏	❏	❏
5. I used transitions to help the reader.	❏	❏	❏
6. I had good knowledge of the content required by the essay question, and my answer made sense.	❏	❏	❏

A Test PAR

A *PAR,* which stands for *preparation, assistance,* and *reflection,* is a framework for content reading instruction. However, this framework also can be successfully applied to the taking of a test in a content class. When a test PAR is used, the first questions on the test might be as follows:

- How did you go about studying for this test?
- How much did you study for this test?
- How well do you think that you might do on this test?

The student's answers to the test questions should indicate how well he or she prepared for the test. Before the content teacher returns the graded test, a second set of questions should be asked. These questions can include the following:

- Now that you have taken the test and before it is returned, was this test what you expected and prepared for?
- What grade do you think that you probably will receive on it?

These questions can help the student to take responsibility for studying and providing a good test response. The third set of questions should encourage reflection. They are answered after the teacher has returned and gone over the test with the students.

- Now that you have gone over your test, do you think you studied enough?
- Was your grade a good representation of your learning? Why or why not?
- What have you learned from this test about taking tests?

Such a three-step process becomes part of the test-taking procedure and should encourage students to take responsibility for showing what they have learned. If teachers use a test PAR on a somewhat regular basis with students, a student should begin to take a more active role in his or her learning. Teachers also may learn quite a bit about how students feel about studying for and taking tests. This information can help teachers in both teaching and reviewing for tests and in constructing tests. When a student writes the answers to the questions, this also provides him or her with additional opportunities to write for real purposes.

However, for a test PAR to be effective, teachers must grade and return tests promptly. The answers should be reviewed so that students can use the test as a learning opportunity for later tests. Only if these conditions are met can an environment for true reflection be encouraged. One of the requirements for designing good tests is to use previous tests as the basis for constructing new tests. Students learn how to take an individual teacher's tests by learning that teacher's testing style. Teachers also should learn how to design effective tests by learning their students' test-taking styles. Did the students need better directions? Did they use appropriate and effective study strategies? Do they need reminders about certain test procedures?

Mnemonics

Mnemonics are memory aids such as Survey Q3R or PQRST. Using the initials of a series of important details to remember can help students to remember them. A common mnemonic is used to learn the names and order of the notes on the lines of a treble clef: *Every Good Boy Does Fine (EGBDF)*. Mnemonics probably is the most helpful with learned disabled students.

Reproducible Activity Sheets Related to Test-Taking Skills and "Testwiseness"

The chapter now contains several ready-to-duplicate activity sheets that may help students to improve their test-taking skills and "testwiseness." You can duplicate and use any of these activity sheets in their present form or modify them in any way you wish in the light of the needs of your own students.

ACTIVITY SHEET USING MNEMONICS FROM SOCIAL STUDIES
(Approximately Middle-School Level)

As you have learned in class, *mnemonics* are memory aids. Create your own mnemonics to help you remember the following facts from *social studies*.

1. The names of the three branches of the United States government:

   legislative, executive, judicial

   _____

   _____

2. The names of the first five presidents of the United States:

   Washington, Adams, Jefferson, Madison, Monroe

   _____

   _____

3. The names of the last five presidents of the United States:*

   Ford, Carter, Reagan, Bush, Clinton

   _____

   _____

4. The first names of the last five first ladies of the United States:*

   Betty, Rosalyn, Nancy, Barbara, Hillary

   _____

   _____

5. The names of three famous Americans who were assassinated during the 1960s:

   John Kennedy, Martin Luther King, Robert Kennedy

   _____

   _____

6. The names of the two major political parties in the United States:

   Democrat, Republican

   _____

   _____

*These lists may change, of course, depending on the outcome of the 1996 Presidential election. The teacher may have to revise these questions if necessary.

ACTIVITY SHEET USING MNEMONICS FROM
SOCIAL STUDIES
(Approximately Middle-School Level)

(cont.)

7. The titles of the two most important members of the United States Senate:

   Majority Leader, Minority Leader

   _____

   _____

8. The name of the most important member of the House of Representatives:

   Speaker of the House

   _____

   _____

9. The name of the body that actually votes for the President and Vice President of the United States:

   The Electoral College

   _____

   _____

10. The names of two of the most famous scandals in American politics:

    Teapot Dome, Watergate

    _____

    _____

Answer Key for "Using Mnemonics"

Note: The following answers are included for illustrative purposes and are only representative of the possible mnemonics that can be used.

1. Let's eat jello.
2. What are Jack's main missions?
3. Frank can't run but climb.
4. Betty rode no big hills.
5. Katie (Kennedy) made (Martin) katsup (Kennedy).
6. Don't run.
7. Mary likes my looks.
8. Sam offered the hat.
9. Try eating cabbage.
10. Tony drives wisely.

MULTIPLE-CHOICE TEST ABOUT
MULTIPLE-CHOICE TESTS
(Approximately Middle-School Level)

This multiple-choice test evaluates your knowledge about *multiple-choice tests*. Put the letter of the correct answer on the line in front of each question.

_____ 1. Before you read any of the options (answers) for a multiple-choice question, you should

　　　a. try to think what the right answer might be

　　　b. try to think what a wrong answer might be

　　　c. check your watch to see if you have the time to finish the test

　　　d. all of the above

_____ 2. Before you actually answer the multiple-choice question, you should

　　　a. write the proper letter of the first item that seems correct to you

　　　b. read all of the options (answers)

　　　c. make a guess as to the correct answer

　　　d. think about what a wrong answer to the question might be

_____ 3. After you have answered the item, it is helpful to

　　　a. think again what all the correct answers might be

　　　b. check your watch to see if you have time to finish the test

　　　c. read the three options (answers) again that you believe are incorrect

　　　d. read the question again with the answer that you selected to see if it makes sense

_____ 4. When one of the options (answers) in a multiple-choice question is "All of the Above," it usually is

　　　a. incorrect

　　　b. correct

　　　c. the wrong answer

　　　d. a trick question

_____ 5. When you read a question with an answer that you do not know, it usually is best to

　　　a. not answer it all

　　　b. skip it and come back to it later so that you are able to finish the test

　　　c. make a guess right then as to the correct answer

　　　d. none of the above

© 1997 by John Wiley & Sons, Inc.

MULTIPLE-CHOICE TEST ABOUT
MULTIPLE-CHOICE TESTS
(Approximately Middle-School Level)

(cont.)

_____ 6. If you don't know the answer at all to a multiple-choice question, it usually is best to

    a. leave the item blank

    b. make a wild guess as to the answer

    c. make a calculated guess as to the answer

    d. ask your teacher what the answer might be

_____ 7. When you take a multiple-choice test, it usually is most helpful to

    a. select the option (answer) in the "a" position

    b. select the option (answer) in the "b" position

    c. eliminate any obviously incorrect options (answers)

    d. select the option (answer) "None of the Above"

_____ 8. When you take a multiple-choice test, it is helpful to

    a. watch for options (answers) that do not match the question stem grammatically

    b. select the option (answer) that is the most difficult to understand

    c. select an option (answer) that is very similar to another option (answer)

    d. select an option (answer) that is the opposite of another option (answer)

_____ 9. The correct option (answer) on a multiple-choice test is likely to be the

    a. shortest or least complete

    b. longest or most complete

    c. one that sounds the most nearly correct

    d. one that is not correct grammatically

_____ 10. As a last resort on a multiple-choice test, you should

    a. select either options (answers) "a" or "d"

    b. select option (answer) "a"

    c. select option (answer) "d"

    d. select either options (answers) "b" or "c"

Answer Key for "Multiple-Choice Tests"

1. a		**6.** c	
2. b		**7.** c	
3. d		**8.** a	
4. b		**9.** b	
5. b		**10.** d	

Name _____ Grade _____ Teacher _____ Date _____

TRUE–FALSE TEST ABOUT TAKING TRUE–FALSE TESTS
(Approximately Middle-School Level)

Read each of the items on this true–false test about taking *true–false tests*. Write a *T* in front of each item that is *True* and an *F* in front of each item that is *False*.

_____ 1. Always make a calculated guess if you don't know the answer to a true–false question unless there is a penalty for an incorrect answer.

_____ 2. Shorter statements are somewhat more likely to be true than are longer statements.

_____ 3. Words such as *all, none, always,* and *never* usually indicate the statement is false.

_____ 4. Words such as *usually, generally, sometimes,* and *seldom* usually indicate the statement is true.

_____ 5. Assume that absolute statements are *true* while qualified statements are *false*.

_____ 6. Assume that an answer is true unless the statement can be proven *false*.

_____ 7. Be sure *all* parts of the statement are correct before marking it true.

_____ 8. *Negatives* such as *not* or the prefix *in* are not considered important when answering true–false questions.

_____ 9. Simplify a statement that contains a *double negative* by eliminating both negatives.

_____ 10. Reread all of the items and answers when you are finished to make certain they are correct and none were omitted.

Answer Key for "True–False Tests"

1. T	6. T
2. F	7. T
3. T	8. F
4. T	9. T
5. F	10. T

MATCHING TEST ABOUT TAKING MATCHING TESTS
(Approximately Middle-School Level)

This matching test evaluates your knowledge about _matching tests_. Put the letter of the correct answer on the line in front of each statement.

_____ 1. what you should do *before* beginning to take a matching test

_____ 2. what you should do when you begin to take a matching test

_____ 3. what you should do before guessing at any of the matches

_____ 4. a very helpful strategy you can use when you are taking a matching test

_____ 5. a helpful strategy for you to use if you simply do not know an answer on a matching test

a. make all the correct matches possible

b. read all of the items in both columns

c. make the easiest or most obvious matches

d. make the best guess you can unless there is a penalty for an incorrect answer

e. cross out items in both columns as they are used

Answer Key for "Matching Tests"

1. b   4. e
2. c   5. d
3. a

COMPLETION OR FILL-IN-THE-BLANK TEST ABOUT COMPLETION OR FILL-IN-THE-BLANK TESTS
(Approximately Middle-School Level)

This completion or fill-in-the-blank test evaluates your knowledge about *completion or fill-in-the-blank tests*. Write the omitted word on the line in each sentence.

1. When you are attempting to take a completion or fill-in-the-blank test, you always should read the entire _____ or paragraph first.

2. Next decide what _____ could best fit in the blank.

3. Write a _____ correct word that fits in the blank.

4. Use the length of the _____ line as a clue unless all of the blank lines are the same length.

5. Read the entire sentence again including your choice to be sure that it fits and sounds _____.

6. If the blank comes at the beginning of the sentence, be sure to _____ the word.

Answer Key for "Completion of Fill-in-the-Blank Tests"

1. sentence
2. word
3. grammatically

4. blank
5. correct
6. capitalize

ESSAY TEST ABOUT TAKING ESSAY TESTS
(Approximately Middle-School Level)

This essay test evaluates your knowledge about *essay tests*. Write a comprehensive answer to each of the essay questions.

1. Briefly describe the meaning of each of these key essay test words:

    a. list

    b. explain

    c. compare

    d. evaluate

    e. summarize

2. Summarize the things you should do before writing the answer to an essay question to help you organize it more effectively.

3. Explain how diagrams and illustrations can help you enhance your answer to an essay question.

4. Summarize what you should do to proofread the answers to your essay questions.

5. Discuss what you can do if you run out of time before you have finished writing the essay test.

Answer Key for "Taking Essay Tests"

Note: It obviously is not possible to write a comprehensive answer to each essay question that will match the responses of different students. However, the answer to each essay question should include some of these main points.

1. **a.** Present information in an item-by-item series.

    b. Write as much as you can about a question or statement.

    c. Tell how two or more items are connected.

    d. Think about the positive and negative aspects of an item(s) before reaching a conclusion about it.

    e. Write a brief statement that indicates something about all of the important items.

2. Make a brief outline or semantic map (web) to guide your response to the essay question.

3. They can enhance the answer to the essay question and make the answer more comprehensive and thorough.

4. Check each answer carefully for spelling, grammar, and organization. Be sure you have written as neatly as possible so that the answer can be easily read.

5. List all the information you know about the statement or question to receive partial credit for it.

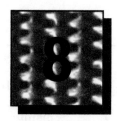

Ready-to-Use Strategies and Materials for Teaching Content Reading and Writing to "At-Risk" Students

If it is difficult for a number of average readers to understand and remember the material found in some content textbooks, think how much more difficult it must be for those students who are today characterized as "at-risk." Although I do not like to use any kind of label for students, perhaps the term "at-risk" is as inoffensive as any other. "At-risk" students often are thought to be those students who are learning-disabled, attention deficit hyperactivity disordered (ADHD), ESL, limited English proficient (LEP), bilingual, culturally or linguistically diverse, mildly mentally handicapped, visually impaired, hearing-impaired, or speech or language disordered.

This chapter is designed to help literacy and content teachers more effectively present content reading and writing skills to those students who can be called "at-risk." As you can imagine, this often is not an easy task since these skills sometimes are difficult for even average and above-average readers. However, all "at-risk" students can be helped to perform more effectively in content reading and writing if they are given the proper kind of assistance.

After reading this chapter literacy and content teachers should be able to present content reading and writing skills very effectively to various types of "at-risk" students.

A DESCRIPTION OF DIFFERENT KINDS OF "AT-RISK" STUDENTS

Pellicano defined "at-risk" students as "uncommitted to deferred gratification and to school training that correlates with competition, and its reward, achieved status" (R. Pellicano, "At Risk: A View of 'Social Advantage,'" *Educational Leadership,* 44, September 1987, p. 47). In general, the following is a brief comparison of expected and exhibited school behaviors of a number of "at-risk" students, especially those who are learning-disabled, attention deficit hyperactivity disordered, or possibly culturally or linguistically diverse.

Expected Behavior	*Exhibited Behavior*
good listeners	inattentive listeners
good readers	reading below grade level
good writers	disinterested in writing and often exhibiting poor writing mechanics
self-controlled	impulsive
initiators	low motivation
independent	dependent or disinterested
organized	disorganized
high self-esteem	low self-esteem
able to delay immediate gratification for long-term rewards	desire immediate gratification
good social skills	poor social skills

learning-disabled

The term *learning disability (LD)* was first used in 1963 by Samuel Kirk to refer to students who—despite apparently average or above-average intelligence—had great difficulty with school learning. Since then the most common definitions of learning disability include the following features:

- a significant gap between expected achievement levels (based on intelligence test scores) and actual performance in at least one area (reading, mathematics, spelling, writing, etc.)

- an uneven profile in achievement with achievement in some areas being very high and in others, very low

- poor achievement apparently not due to environmental factors

- poor achievement not due to low intelligence or emotional maladjustment

The federal government's definition of learning disability states the following:

> "specific learning disability" means a disorder in one or more of the basic psychological processes involved in understanding or in using language, spoken or written, which may manifest itself in an imperfect ability to listen, think, speak, read, write, spell, or do mathematical calculations. (*Federal Register* 42, Number 250, December 29, 1977, p. 65083.)

In addition, a learning-disabled child *may,* but not necessarily, exhibit some or all of the following behavioral characteristics that sometimes are used to help in making the identification: hyperactivity, distractibility, perceptual problems, attention problems, and ineffective learning or problem-solving strategies.

Attention Deficit Hyperactivity Disordered

The term *attention deficit hyperactivity disordered (ADHD)* is a fairly recent term in special education. A child normally is given this label if he or she exhibits a number of the behavioral characteristics of a learning-disabled student to a fairly or very high degree in addition to possible other behaviors. ADHD students are those children who often act out, draw undue attention to themselves, have a very low attention span, may be aggressive, or generally get into difficulty at school.

They are the students who often are placed on a mood-altering drug such as Ritalin® to control their undesirable behavioral characteristics so that they can learn in school. Their behavior can be so disruptive that they not only are unable to learn themselves in school but may hinder the learning of other students. Although the use of Ritalin® may make them more manageable and able to learn in the school situation, the original disruptive behavior may often reoccur as soon as they stop taking it. The hope is that a child who is diagnosed as ADHD may demonstrate fewer symptoms as he or she grows older. This, however, may not happen in every case.

ESL, LEP, or Bilingual Students

ESL students are those students who speak English as a second language. They make up the most rapidly expanding population in North American schools. Students who have been labeled as *bilingual* are very different in their language and literacy competencies. Some of them may be fluent in their home language only, but not able to read and write it. Others may have strong backgrounds of knowledge and skills obtained through education and experience in their home country. Other students may have had few educational opportunities in their home country. Others may have a fair mastery of oral English but will continue to have serious difficulties in written English. Therefore, there are great differences among students who have the designation *bilingual,* a term that to be useful must be defined more precisely. Students who are acquiring English as a second language may possess strong potential for fluency and literacy in two languages. However, the extent to which this potential may be realized depends upon their educational opportunities at home, in their community, and perhaps—most important—in school.

Within the category of bilingual students, the following four main categories sometimes are recognized:

- *English-dominant students with a home language other than English:* These students may need to improve their academic achievement in English-speaking schools while continuing to develop the home language skills and cultural ties their parents want them to maintain.

- *Bilingual, bicultural students are generally fluent in both languages.* Bilingual education enhances their academic experiences while reinforcing the cultural and linguistic identity of their families.

- *Limited English-proficient (LEP)* students probably are the most typical of those receiving bilingual and ESL instruction. They do not have sufficient English language skills to achieve in a regular classroom and need specific instruction for developing linguistic and academic skills.

- *English-speaking monolingual students with no language minority background:* Since the law requires classes to be integrated, English-speaking students who have no knowledge of other languages may also be in bilingual classes. They may help to socialize minority students and also benefit from exposure to a second language such as Spanish.

The literacy or content teacher often can easily identify ESL students simply by listening to them speak, since their speech in English may be more limited than other students and their oral language heavily accented with the sounds and intonation patterns of their native language. However, the teacher must make this evaluation over a period of time since the student may simply be reserved or shy and not wish to talk much at first.

Culturally or Linguistically Diverse Students

Almost every major language has a number of different *dialects*. Dialects are alternative language forms often used by regional, social, or cultural groups. Although dialects are understandable by speakers of the same language group, they are different in several ways: sounds (*aks* for *ask*), vocabulary (*soda* for *pop*), and syntax (*He running.* for *He is running.*). All dialects are equally logical, precise, and governed by rules. However, usually one dialect becomes the standard language form in a society because it is used by the educationally, socially, and economically advantaged members of that society. In the United States the standard language is called *Standard American English (SAE)*. It usually is thought to be the form of English spoken by newscasters in most parts of the country. It normally is the ultimate goal of schools to teach standard American English to all students because they must compete in a society that recognizes this as the standard form of speech. However, each student's diverse dialect always should be respected while attempting to add standard American English on a gradual, tactful basis.

A common nonstandard dialect in the United States is *Black English*. However, Appalachia and the Northeast also each have a clearly definable dialect. Although the speakers of each of these dialects share certain language conventions, there may be some degree of variation within the dialect. Here are the more common characteristics of Black English.

Language Element	*Standard American English*	*Black English*
	Phonological Differences	
Initial		
th—t	thin	tin
th—d	this	dis
str—skr	stream	scream
thr—tr	three	tree
Final		
r—no sound	door	doe
l—no sound	pool	poo
sk—ks	ask	aks
th—f	teeth	teef
sks—ses	husks	husses
General		
Simplify final consonant blends	talked	talk
	looks	look
	best	bess
i—e before nasals	pin	pen

Language Element	Standard American English	Black English
	Syntactic Differences	
Dropping *to be* verbs	Latasha is working.	Latasha working.
Using *be* for extended time.	I am always late.	I be always late.
Subject—predicate agreement *to be* verbs	I am playing.	I is playing.
	There were three dogs.	There was three dogs.
Third-person singular verbs	Yetti studies hard.	Yetti study hard.
Irregular verbs	Yavanda flew in an airplane.	Yavanda flied in an airplane.
Double negatives	My sister doesn't want any.	My sister don't want none.
Omission of indefinite article	Play me a song.	Play me song.
Use of *more* for comparatives	My brother is smaller than I	My brother is more smaller than me.

Here are the major differences between Standard American English and Spanish:

Language Trait	Standard American English	Spanish
	Phonological Differences	
a—e	bat	bet
a—e	gate	get
i—e	hid	heed
b—p	bar	par
z—s	fuzz	fus
j—ch or y	June	chun or yun
th—d	this	dis
th—s	think	sink
	Syntactic Differences	
Negatives	My mother is not at home.	My mother is no at home.
	The men do not go to work.	The men no go work.
	Please don't go.	Please no go.
Tense	The principal will see you now.	The principal see you now.
	I learned many things yesterday.	I learn many things yesterday.
Use of *be*	My sister is twenty.	My sister have twenty years.
	I am thirsty.	I have thirst.
Omission of determiner	My father is a farmer.	My father is farmer.
Omission of pronoun		
in questions	Is it nine o'clock already?	Is nine o'clock already?
in statements	It is dark now.	Is dark now.

Culturally diverse students are students who belong to an ethnic or minority group that differs from that of white Anglo-Saxon Americans. In addition to African-American (black) and Latino (Hispanic) students, Native Americans and Asian-Americans usually are considered to be culturally diverse or members of a minority group. Such students—in addition to having a dialect that is different from that of standard American English—may differ in their values, and their orientations toward and interest in school.

Multicultural education means developing an understanding and appreciation of various racial and ethnic minority groups. This awareness should permeate the entire curriculum, and students should be taught with consideration for their cultural heritage, their language preferences, and their individual lifestyles.

Mildly Mentally Handicapped

The American Association on Mental Deficiency (AAMD) has defined *mental retardation* in the following way:

> Mental retardation refers to significantly subaverage general intellectual functioning existing concurrently with deficits in adaptive behavior and manifested during the developmental period. (H. J. Grossman, Ed., *Manual on Terminology and Classification in Mental Retardation, 1973 Revision.* Washington, D.C.: American Association on Mental Deficiency, 1973.)

According to this definition, two elements must be present for a child to be categorized as mentally retarded or mentally handicapped (I prefer to use the later term in writing and teaching): intellectual functioning that is significantly below average and inadequate adaptive behavior. According to the AAMD, "subaverage general intellectual functioning" indicates that a student must have an IQ score on the most commonly used individual intelligence test (WISC-R) of *69 or below.* Children who have IQs between 70 and 85 are sometimes called *slow learners,* and literacy instruction also should be adapted for them. However, they normally are not called mentally retarded or handicapped.

In evaluating adaptive behavior, the AAMD indicates that the educator consider the age of the child in making this judgment. In early childhood, sensorimotor, communication, self-help, and socialization skills are evaluated. In middle childhood and early adolescence, learning processes and interpersonal skills are evaluated.

Usually both mentally retarded or handicapped students and slow learners possess some of the same learning characteristics to a greater or lesser degree. Although they usually progress through the same developmental stages as do all other students, they normally do so at a slower rate. This is especially true in the academic tasks of literacy such as reading, writing, and spelling. They usually also have the following other characteristics that must be considered when planning a literacy program for them:

- delayed language development with a higher frequency of speech and language problems

- short attention spans with possible distractibility

- poor short-term memory especially in words, ideas, and numbers (their long-term memory tends to be somewhat better).

- difficulty in grasping *abstract* concepts but less difficulty in grasping concrete ideas

- deficiency in oral and silent reading, locating main ideas and significant details, using context clues, and higher-level comprehension

- ability to learn sight words and graphophonic (phonic) analysis with appropriate instruction that has sufficient meaningful repetition

Visually Impaired Students

Visually impaired students include the legally blind and partially sighted. A person who is considered *legally blind* has visual acuity that is less than 20/200. With the better eye, a legally blind person can see at least 20 feet (or less) what a normally sighted person can see at 200 feet, even with the best possible correction. A partially sighted person has visual acuity that is between 20/70 and 20/200 with his or her better eye.

Legally blind persons are not necessarily completely blind. Eighty-two percent of the legally blind have sufficient vision to be able to read print with the assistance of large print books or magnifying glasses. Only twenty-one percent of the legally blind use only Braille for reading. Over one-half (fifty-two percent) use large- or regular-print books for most or all of their reading. About one-tenth of one percent of school-age children in the United States are believed to be visually impaired (United States Department of Education, 1984).

Visual impairment usually does not greatly change a child's language development as hearing impairment may do. The intelligence (IQ) scores of the visually impaired are not significantly different from those of their normally sighted peers. It appears that visual impairment has little direct effect or either linguistic or cognitive functioning (D. P. Hallahan and J. M. Kauffman, *Exceptional Children [Second Edition]*. New York: Prentice-Hall, 1982).

Visually impaired persons may compensate for their limitations by listening skills, greater attention, and tactile sensations. Teachers should be able to recognize behaviors that may indicate a student's possible visual problems. Although visual screening takes place today in almost all, if not all, elementary schools, once in a while undetected vision problems occur. I have seen this happen a number of times with students who are tutored for reading problems. The following symptoms may indicate a student needs additional vision testing:

- squinting
- rubbing eyes often
- holding reading materials very close or very far away from the eyes
- having red or watery eyes
- covering one eye when reading
- having crusty material around eyes and lashes

With proper instruction, the majority of visually impaired students can make very good progress in literacy in terms of their intelligence and home environment in addition to the many other factors that may influence literacy achievement.

Hearing-Impaired Students

Hearing-impaired students have reduced sensitivity to sounds in their environment because of genetic factors, illness, or some type of trauma. Usually hearing-impaired students are not sensitive to sounds softer than about 26 decibels (dB, a unit of measure for the relative loudness of sounds). A classification system used by the Conference of Executives for American Schools for the Deaf defines degrees of hearing impairment as follows:

Category of Hearing Impairment	*Amount of Hearing Loss*
mild	26-54 dB
moderate	55-69 dB
severe	70-89 dB
profound	more than 90 dB

Persons with hearing losses greater than 90dB usually are considered *deaf,* while those with less hearing losses usually are thought to be *hard of hearing.*

In addition to knowing the degree of hearing loss, it also is helpful to know *when* the hearing loss took place. It is obvious that the earlier the hearing loss occurred, the less likely that a child will have adequately developed language skills. Since effective reading comprehension depends greatly on adequate language ability, the student with a hearing loss that occurred at an early age may experience considerable difficulty with reading comprehension, perhaps especially with the higher levels of comprehension. This may be especially true if the hearing loss has gone undetected for a long period of time. About two-tenths of one percent of school-age children are thought to be deaf and hard of hearing (United States Department of Education, 1984).

Some hearing-impaired students compensate by using amplifying devices, speechreading (lipreading), and sign language or finger spelling. Some hearing-impaired students receive an oral communication program dependent upon amplification and speechreading, while others receive a manual communication program dependent upon sign language and finger spelling.

Recently most students receive a total communication program that incorporates *both oral and manual* aspects. In any case, the hearing-impaired students are dependent upon the *visual information* in a classroom for obtaining information. This may include the literacy or content teacher's facial expression, lip movements, and written information around the classroom.

Although the vast majority of, if not all, schools today screen students for hearing impairments, some students with mild or moderate hearing losses may go undetected. You may request additional auditory testing for any student who has the following symptoms:

• has frequent earaches, head colds, or sinus infections
• has difficulty following oral directions
• often asks to have directions and explanations repeated
• is easily distracted by external noises
• has poor oral language development

- mispronounces words
- may have great difficulty with graphophonic (phonic) analysis
- gets tired easily during listening tasks
- is thought to be learning-disabled, mentally handicapped, or emotionally disturbed

Speech and Language Disorders

Students who have *speech disorders* produce oral language abnormally in *how* it is said, not in what is said. There are several classifications of speech disorders:

- phonological disorders (substituting *w* for *r*)
- voice disorders (unusual pitch, loudness, or voice quality)
- disorders associated with abnormalities of the mouth and nose (for example, an orofacial cleft)
- disorders of speech flow (stuttering)
- disorders associated with the muscles associated with speech production

On the other hand, students who have *language disorders* have difficulty expressing their ideas in oral language or have difficulty understanding the ideas expressed by other people. Children who have language disorders may not have developed verbal language, may use words in abnormal ways such as echoing words spoken to them, may have delayed oral language development, or may have interrupted language development.

According to the federal government, about three percent of school-aged children have speech disorders and about one-half of one percent have language disorders (United States Office of Education, 1975; United States Department of Education, 1984).

Some students with speech disorders may do quite well with literacy activities, while students with language disorders may have a difficult time developing proficiency in reading comprehension since literacy is very dependent upon adequate language proficiency.

A literacy or content teacher may want to consider the follow elements before referring a student to a speech pathologist:

- substantially less mature oral language than that of his or her peers
- inability to tell a story with all of its elements
- making substitution or omissions of sounds such as /*w*/ for /*r*/ or /*l*/, /*b*/ for /*v*/, /*f*/ for *voiceless* /*th*/, /*t*/ for /*k*/, voiceless /*th*/ for /*s*/, /*d*/ for *voiced* /*th*/, and *voiced* /*th*/ for /*z*/
- difficulty being understood by other students
- speaking much more rapidly than other students, thus causing difficulty in being understood
- pitch, loudness, and quality very different from those of other students
- particular difficulty in understanding and following directions

STRENGTHS AND WEAKNESSES OF "LABELING" A STUDENT IN ANY WAY

There are both inherent strengths and weaknesses in giving a student any of the "labels" that have just been described. As a former elementary classroom teacher and not a special educator, I feel ambivalent about this.

Here are some of the *major strengths* of labeling a student:

- It should enable him or her to receive the most appropriate instruction possible.
- It should enable the student's school to receive extra financial reimbursement which theoretically should help the student receive this additional appropriate instruction.
- It may help a classroom teacher to be aware that a student has special needs that he or she must attempt to meet as much as possible.
- It may enable the student to be placed—at least part of the time—with students who have similar educational needs.

Here are the some of the *major weaknesses* of labeling a student:

- *It may limit the achievement his or her teacher(s) think is possible—an example of the self-fulfilling prophecy.*
- It may stigmatize the student before either his or her teacher and/or peers.
- It may lower the student's self-esteem.
- It possibly may cause the student to be emotionally maladjusted.
- It may cause the student's teacher(s) to be less than enthusiastic about having him or her in class.

Thus, in summary, there are both advantages and limitations to the use of any of the "labels" described earlier in this chapter. A teacher(s) or school should be *very certain of a student's status* and the fact that "labeling" him or her will not cause any harm before doing it.

A BRIEF SUMMARY OF THE *INCLUSION PHILOSOPHY*

Inclusion is the most contemporary philosophy in special education. It has replaced mainstreaming in many schools as *the* way of organizing instruction for students with special needs. Inclusion is the ultimate result of The Education for All Handicapped Children Act, or Public Law (PL) 94-142. The most important part of PL 94-142 states the following:

> … in order to receive funds under the Act every school system in the nation must make provisions for a free, appropriate public education for every child … regardless of how, or how seriously, he may be handicapped.

In addition to requiring schools to provide a free public education for all handicapped students, two other provisions of this legislation affect classroom teachers of literacy: *individual educational plans (IEPs)* and the concept of a *least restrictive environment*.

Individual Educational Plans

Public Law 94-142 mandates that a multidisciplinary team consisting of trained educational specialists evaluate each exceptional student and potential exceptional student. This team then submits a report at a case conference meeting at which a representative of the school, the student's teacher, the parent(s), and other appropriate people are responsible for developing an IEP for the student. An IEP, according to federal guidelines (Education for Handicapped Individuals Act of 1975, p. 3), must include the following elements:

- a statement of the present levels of performance
- a statement of annual goals including short-term instructional objectives
- a statement of the specific educational services to be provided
- the extent to which each student will be able to participate in regular educational programs
- the projected date for the beginning and anticipated duration of the services
- appropriate objective evaluation procedures
- a schedule for determining at least annually whether or not the instructional objectives are being achieved

The Least Restrictive Environment

One of the most important decisions made at the group conference, in addition to whether or not to place the child in any type of special education program, concerns the recommended instructional environment. The IEP must state the extent to which the student will be placed in a regular classroom.

The *inclusion philosophy* indicates that as much as possible of the student's learning be done in a regular classroom setting with his or her own teacher doing much of the instructing. Any special education teacher often then becomes a consultant to the regular classroom teacher, providing him or her with instructional strategies and materials. In addition, the special education teacher may come into the student's classroom and work with the student on an individual basis or even teach a group of students or the entire class. The concept behind inclusion is to avoid singling out a learning-disabled, mildly mentally handicapped, hearing-impaired, visually impaired student, or any student with special needs. Inclusion also assumes that the student's own teacher can best present much of the required material to him or her with the *support of the special educator* without a pull-out program. Unfortunately, according to research, pull-out programs often have not resulted in long-term gains for students.

The following are some of the *main advantages* of inclusion:

- It enables students to participate in the regular classroom and school activities as much as possible.
- It may avoid stigmatizing students, since in a pull-out program they are otherwise separated from their peers and may feel isolated.
- It should teach all students to be tolerant of students who are different from them.
- Since the regular classroom teacher and the special education teacher work cooperatively in planning each student's program, he or she then should have the optimum learning experiences possible.

The following are some of the *main limitations* of inclusion:

- Regular classroom teachers must receive *true support from special educators* if inclusion is to be successful. Regular classroom teachers cannot be expected to know how to teach all types of "at-risk" students without appropriate, long-term support from special education teachers.

- "At-risk" students must be truly welcomed into a regular classroom by both the classroom teacher and the students so that they do not feel stigmatized or different.

- The educational opportunities provided for the other students in the classroom cannot be neglected by the need to help the "at-risk" students. All students need to be provided with the best possible appropriate educational experiences.

- The parents of "at-risk" students need to have the inclusion philosophy explained to them in detail before a school attempts to implement it to be sure they understand and support it.

STRATEGIES TO PRESENT READING AND WRITING SKILLS IN LITERATURE, SOCIAL STUDIES, SCIENCE, AND MATHEMATICS TO STUDENTS WITH SPECIAL NEEDS

The next part of the chapter presents a number of classroom-tested strategies that should help both literacy and content teachers better present reading and writing skills to "at-risk" students.

The Whole Language (Unit Teaching) Philosophy

As has been emphasized throughout this book, *whole language or unit teaching* probably is one of the best ways to teach content reading and writing skills to all students in the primary grades, middle school, and secondary school. Chapter 6 presented many specific strategies for using whole language in teaching literature, social studies, science, and mathematics. Many of the strategies discussed in that chapter are applicable for use with various types of "at-risk" students either with or without some modification. You should refer to that chapter for specific ideas about how to use whole language or unit teaching in teaching the required skills in all of the content areas.

The Language-Experience Approach

The *language-experience approach (LEA)* also was described in detail in Chapter 6. This approach is one of the most useful ways to teach emergent literacy skills to many kinds of "at-risk" students, probably especially to learning-disabled, attention deficit hyperactivity disordered, ESL, LEP, and culturally diverse students. However, it also is very effective with mildly mentally handicapped, visually impaired, and hearing-impaired students. Indeed, LEA probably is one of the most useful approaches that both literacy and content teachers can use with all students who have special needs. It is highly motivating, uses the student's own language patterns, and enhances creativity. My teacher-trainees have used it very successfully with learning-disabled students, attention deficit hyperactivity disordered students, ESL students, culturally diverse students, mentally handicapped students (including some trainable students), and various kinds of physically challenged students. It has proven to be successful, even amazingly so, with a number of students.

You should consult Chapter 6 for a detailed description about how to use the language-experience approach. The instruction contained in that chapter is applicable for most students, and you can modify it if needed in light of the needs of your own "at-risk" students.

Scaffolding Strategies

Scaffolding strategies are a change in delivery systems, which is especially helpful to students from all kinds of diverse backgrounds. Scaffolded instruction allows teachers to *mediate* learning experiences for students. A teacher who mediates serves as an *intermediary* in helping diverse or "at-risk" learners to negotiate meaning and overcome difficulties in textbook learning situations. Instructional scaffolding is a way to guide students in their development as independent learners.

Scaffolding serves to support students as they engage in various tasks that require reading and writing. The term "scaffolding" comes from the fields of construction and house painting in which scaffolds serve as supports to lift up workers so that they can achieve something that otherwise would be impossible. Instructional scaffolding provides the necessary support students need as they attempt new tasks in reading and writing. *Teachers model or lead* students through the effective strategies needed to complete the tasks. Scaffolding considers such things as the different needs of the diverse students in a classroom, cooperative learning groups, authentic materials beyond the textbook, and planning an active learning environment. Therefore, it gives students a better chance to be successful in handling the linguistic and conceptual demands found in content textbooks. Perhaps the most important element in scaffolding is *modeling.* You must not just tell students *what to do but rather tell them the strategies* to use to be successful in content reading and writing.

Inference-Awareness

Inference-awareness can be helpful in showing students how to locate information found only interpretively in content reading material. Inference-awareness can be used during reading to answer teacher-posed questions and to complete independent assignments. The steps contained in inference-awareness are as follows:

1. The literacy or content teacher *defines inference making* as using clues from a paragraph or selection along with what the author has meant but has not actually stated.

2. The teacher *models inference-making* by reading a selection from the content materials, asks an inference question, and then giving an answer and the reasoning involved in getting that answer.

3. In the next step, called *providing the evidence,* students join in the modeling process. The teacher asks a new inference question and gives the answers. Then students are asked to find supporting evidence that supports or refutes the teacher-provided answers in their content textbook. Students are encouraged to participate in discussion to explain the thinking processes used to find their responses. This form of teacher- and peer-supported guided practice can be a very beneficial intermediate step for "at-risk" students.

4. The next step is called *reversing the process* and requires students to write answers to inference questions with the teacher providing the evidence. A teacher–student discussion follows to justify responses and supporting evidence.

5. *Total student responsibility* is the final process in inference awareness. After the students are completely familiar with the steps of this strategy, the teacher only asks inference questions and the students do the rest. They answer the question, find supporting evidence, and explain their reasoning.

(Adapted from C. J. Gordon, "Modeling Inference Awareness Across the Curriculum," *Journal of Reading,* 28, April 1983, pp. 444-447.)

"Paper-Chase" Groups

"At-risk" students, as well as many other students, can receive a great deal of academic and affective support in establishing *"paper chase" groups.* These are groups that meet together on a regular basis to work on content assignments and share the work. In elementary school "paper-chase" groups typically contain from two to five members. Although membership in such a group is usually determined by the students themselves, it could be arranged by the teacher to achieve a balance of academic abilities and learning styles.

Cooperative Learning Groups

Cooperative learning groups are a variation of the "paper-chase" groups. In a cooperative learning group the content teacher usually gives from about four to ten students who have been grouped heterogeneously a topic to research and report on later. For example, a cooperative learning group in fifth-grade science could be composed of about six students—two above-average readers and writers, two average readers and writers, and two below-average readers and writers. This group of students could be requested to research the topic "The Planets" from astronomy.

The two above-average students can read about the planets from encyclopedias in print or on CD-ROM, above grade level science textbooks, and informational books; the two average students can attempt to read the material about planets found in their science textbook using some of the comprehension and retention strategies they have learned; while the two below-average students can read about planets from informational books on their independent reading level and then, with the help of the four other students, construct a mobile of the planets in their various positions rotating around the sun.

After completing this assignment, for which they should be given sufficient class time, all six students can share with the teacher and the rest of the class the information they have learned about planets and the mobiles that they have made. The use of cooperative learning groups helps each student experience a feeling of success and contribution toward the learning of the rest of the class. It is a very good way to motivate students to learn content material and to provide them with reading and writing tasks at which they are successful.

The Listen-Read-Discuss Strategy

The *listen-read-discuss strategy (L-R-D)* may provide the type of varied repetition that "at-risk" learners need to have success in content classrooms. It contains the following steps:

- *Listen.* The teacher begins by choosing a portion of the content textbook to be emphasized. The section is usually presented by lecture for about half the class period.

- *Read.* The students read the section just covered by the teacher in class.
- *Discuss.* Have a class discussion about the material the students have just read. This discussion should be to first answer questions about what was read and, second, to raise new questions of an applied (creative) kind. The questions may resemble questions such as these:

What did you learn from what you heard and read?

Which parts were difficult for you to understand?

What additional questions did the lesson raise for you?

(Adapted from Anthony Manzo and Ula Casale, "Listen-Read-Discuss: A Content Reading Heuristic," *Journal of Reading,* 28, May 1985, pp. 732-734.)

Text Lookbacks

Text lookbacks is an innovative term for what teachers have been telling students to do for a very long time in order to locate answers to questions or when they cannot understand content material they have read. A text lookback is simply when a student looks back through a content reading assignment to locate the answers to questions or to review what has been read. It is searching through content material with a specific purpose(s) in mind. It should be focused reading instead of reading without any real purpose.

Text lookbacks can involve skimming for a general impression, scanning for a specific fact such as a date or place, rereading one or more topic sentences, or reading specific paragraphs or sections.

ReQuest Procedure or Reciprocal Questioning

The *ReQuest Procedure* is a questioning strategy that has been used for many years. It was first explained by Anthony Manzo in 1969. To use this strategy, the teacher first tells the students to ask the types of questions about each sentence in a content selection that they think the teacher might ask. The teacher then answers each question as completely and fairly as possible and tells the students that they later must do the same. Then the teacher and student both silently read the first sentences. The teacher then closes the content textbook, and the student asks questions about that sentence that the teacher is to answer. Next the student closes the book, and the teacher asks questions about the material. The teacher should provide an excellent model for the student's questions. The questions should mainly be of the higher type such as interpretive (inferential or implicit), critical (evaluative), or applied (creative). After a number of additional sentences, the procedure can be varied to use an entire paragraph instead of individual sentences.

In this procedure questioning should continue until the student can answer the question: "What do you think will happen in the rest of this selection?" The ReQuest Procedure shows a student how to formulate and answer higher-level questions instead of just literal or explicit (lower-level) questions. The ReQuest Procedure also can be called *reciprocal questioning.* This strategy also helps students to *monitor their reading* more effectively than they might otherwise. (Adapted from Anthony Manzo, "The ReQuest Procedure," *Journal of Reading,* 13, November 1969, pp. 123-126.)

As stated in Chapter 4, one of my teacher-trainees used the ReQuest Procedure with a fourth-grade student named Matt who probably was learning-disabled. During a first semester of tutoring, another teacher-trainee usually had Matt complete worksheets to try to improve his interpretive comprehension skills. Since these worksheets usually were not motivating, Matt just rushed through each one of them, marking anything that he chose without reading each item. However, the next semester when his tutor used reciprocal questioning with Matt, for the first time in his school career he began to read content material carefully. He had experienced the most difficulty understanding and re-membering science materials. However, when he was allowed to ask his tutor questions about the material, he began reading it very carefully so that he could "trick" her if possible. Indeed, once in a while he asked her questions that she re-ally was unable to answer! According to the post test his tutor gave him at the end of the tutoring, he had made significant progress in comprehending content material and was reading on grade level.

SIP Strategy

The *SIP Strategy* capitalizes on the concept that students benefit from learning activities that require attention to content and active engagement in processing. This strategy should be especially useful for *learning-disabled* and *attention deficit hyperactivity disordered students.* The steps for SIP are as follows:

- **S** indicates to students that they should ***summarize*** the content of each page or naturally divided section of the content textbook. This summarization of the content textbook tells students to reflect on and interact with the content in producing a summarized version.

- **I** represents the concept of ***imaging.*** This indicates to students that they should form an internal visual display of the content while reading that pro-vides a second imprint of the textbook's content.

- **P** tells students to ***predict*** while reading. As each page or naturally divided section of a content textbook is read, students should pause to predict what they may learn next. While reading the section predicted, students verify, re-vise, or modify predictions according to what they have learned. This process of predicting and verifying can help students read entire selections and moti-vates them to maintain their interest.

(Adapted from C. Dana, "Strategy Families for Disabled Readers," *Journal of Reading,* 33, October 1989, pp. 30-35.)

EEEZ

The *EEEZ Strategy* encourages students to elaborate mentally on new content information to help long-term remembering. In the same article as cited above, Dana recommends:

> After reading, it is recommended that students review what they have read in the light of the purpose that was set for the [content] reading assignment. Students are told that after reading they should *'take it easy' (EEEZ)* and make an attempt to *explain (E)* the content in a manner commensurate with the purpose set for reading. They might have to answer questions, generate ques-tions, define a concept, or provide a summary. (p. 33)

The other concepts represented by the EEEZ acronym are as follows:

E: Explore the same content material as it has been described by other authors of different content textbooks or informational materials. These comparisons often help students to clarify important concepts.

E: Expand the subject matter by reading other content textbooks or informational materials that go beyond the content covered by the original textbook.

After expanding, students should respond to the original purpose for reading the assignment by the teacher and should embellish their responses with additional content discovered during the EEEZ process. (*Ibid.*)

Differentiated Content Assignments

There are a number of different ways to adjust single content textbook assignments to better meet the needs of "at-risk" students of various kinds. For example, *students with different reading abilities can be told to read for different purposes.* This can be done by assigning different directions, questions, vocabulary activities, or writing activities to different groups of students. For example, if a literacy or content teacher is studying a passage on tropical rain forests, one group of students can study about all of the elements that comprise tropical rain forests, another group of students can study about some of the practical ways the tropical rain forests of the world can be saved from destruction, and a third group of students can make a map showing the location of all the tropical rain forests in the world. All of these activities can be completed after reading or listening to the same content reading assignment. Although the activities vary from complex to simple, varying students' purposes for reading should not mean that the good readers always have higher-level activities, while below-average readers always have lower-level activities. You should try to involve all students in all levels of thinking as much as possible.

The amount of information different students must read and study can vary. Content assignments do not always have to cover one chapter at a time. As an example, one group of students that is able to be read by itself may be assigned a short section within a chapter, while another group of students can be assigned two or three sections. Sometimes the graphic aids provided in a chapter can comprise a reading assignment. However, whole-class discussion always should follow the directed reading so that all students are exposed to the important information contained in the chapter.

Different degrees of response structure is another way to vary content textbook assignments. For example, literacy and content teachers can vary the response structure by alternating students' tasks between *answering questions* and *verifying statements.* During a unit in science on blood, for example, this open-ended question may be asked: "How are white blood cells and platelets different?" This is an open-ended question that may require some interpretive thinking and writing ability. On the other hand, a more structured and easier task may be the following series of statements:

Mark the ways that white blood cells and platelets are different:

_____ An increase in white blood cells often means that the body is trying to fight off some type of infection.

_____ An increase in platelets often means that the blood is somewhat too thick and may clot quite easily.

_____ Platelets are much larger than white blood cells.

_____ A marked decrease in platelets usually means the blood is somewhat too thin and may not clot well.

_____ A marked increase in white blood cells may indicate a person has leukemia, while a marked increase in platelets may indicate a person has a risk of developing a blood clot somewhere in his or her circulatory system.

The preceding activities are several ways for literacy and content teachers to differentiate content reading assignments *while using a single content textbook* with a large group of students such as an entire class in literature, social studies, science, or mathematics.

"About Point" Strategy

The *"About Point" Strategy* is a way of having students in middle and secondary schools remember information from content textbooks while working in groups. To use the "About Point" Strategy, literacy or content teachers can have students reread a content selection and then decide in groups what the passage is *About* and what details—*Point*—support their answer. Teachers can provide study guides that follow this format:

This reading is ABOUT _____

_____

_____

and the POINTS are _____

_____

_____

An example of a completed study guide from a fifth-grade science textbook might look like this:

This section is ABOUT: <u>The different organs and processes that are involved in human digestion.</u>

And the POINTS are <u>The esophagus is a tube through which food passes in making its way into the stomach.</u>

<u>The stomach produces a number of different acids that help break food down so that it can be used or stored by the body.</u>

<u>The large and small intestines also are important in the digestive process.</u>

<u>Since the body is not able to use all the food that is eaten, the remainder is waste.</u>

Remembering Strategy

The *remembering strategy* is especially useful with learning-disabled and attention deficit hyperactivity disordered students while studying content textbooks.

These students can be taught a three-step remembering strategy. They should first carefully **select** the information that is the most important to remember. Next they should choose from a variety of techniques those that they will use to **remember** the information, and last they should systematically **review** the information. Very briefly, here is a summary of these three steps:

1. *Select.* Students select the information they need to remember, hopefully with the help of their literacy or content teachers. Sometimes, it may be necessary for students to rewrite information they need to remember, especially when the information is found in many different sources. In such cases, students collect and integrate the information before applying specific techniques for remembering it.

2. *Remember.* Students select the technique(s) they will use to remember the information. They choose techniques that are compatible with the nature of the information to be remembered. For example, students might use a graph to remember percentages, but might use a mnemonic device to remember important names. Here are some techniques that learning-disabled and attention deficit hyperactivity disordered students may use in helping them to remember information:

   association

   visualization

   application

   repetition

   mnemonic devices

3. *Review.* This step of the remembering strategy helps students to remember information over a period of time. Techniques for remembering information are not enough in themselves to insure retention. These three additional steps are important in the review process and should enable students to remember information more effectively both in the short- and long-term:

   - periodically *reread* information that is to be remembered

   - *recite* information or say aloud the information to be remembered (this is *verbal rehearsal* which is especially helpful for learning-disabled and attention deficit hyperactivity disordered students)

   - *rewrite* information in a concise form using key words and phrases rather then complete sentences; in this rewriting abbreviations also are often useful

(Adapted from Stephan S. Strichart and Charles T. Mangrum II, *Teaching Study Strategies to Students with Learning Disabilities.* Boston: Allyn and Bacon, 1993, pp. 8-12.)

Mnemonic Devices

A *mnemonic device* is any formal scheme designed to improve a person's memory. When used judiciously, a mnemonic device can be very helpful in enabling learning-disabled and attention deficit hyperactivity disordered students to remember content material. Here are several uncomplicated mnemonic devices that may be useful with LD and ADHD students:

- *Acronyms*—An acronym is a word made from the first letter or first syllable of other words that a person wants to remember. For example, *WASP* stands for "white Anglo-Saxon Protestant," *HUD* stands for "Housing and Urban Development," and *SAC* stands for "Strategic Air Command." Although an acronym can be a real word, it does not have to be one. However, an acronym always should be easy for a student to pronounce.

- *Acronymic Sentence*—When using this mnemonic device, students can make up sentences using words that begin with the initial sound of the items to be remembered. (Chapter 7 contained a reproducible activity sheet with acronymic sentences from the content area of social studies.)

- *Rhymes*—This simple technique is often taught to students in songs and verses. Undoubtedly the most popular rhyme that has been used for this purpose over the years is the following:

> Thirty days hath September,
>
> April, June, and November,
>
> All the rest have thirty-one
>
> Except February, which has twenty-eight.

  When students transform information into rhymes to help them remember, they can emphasize the cadence in the rhyme and form a mental picture of the rhyme. (Adapted from B. Adler, *The Student's Memory Book.* New York: Doubleday, 1988.)

- *Abbreviations*—As in the case of acronyms, abbreviations use the first letters of words to be remembered, but the letters do not form a word that can be pronounced. Some examples of abbreviations are *NBC* (National Broadcasting Company), *UPS* (United Parcel Service), and *FBI* (Federal Bureau of Investigation).

Adler (*Ibid.*) also has written about some concepts that students must be aware of if mnemonic devices are to be used successfully. These are especially important if mnemonic devices are used with learning-disabled or attention deficit hyperactivity disordered students:

> pay attention
>
> divide the material to be remembered into parts
>
> structure the material
>
> use your imagination when attempting to use a mnemonic device
>
> review the material often
>
> perhaps most important, try to enjoy using the mnemonic devices

Listener-Friendly Lectures

It is extremely important that content teachers present *listener-friendly lectures* if all types of "at-risk" students are going to be able to gain as much information as possible from the lectures. A listener-friendly lecture should help students take good notes by being well organized, distinguishing important from unimportant information, and relating new information to old information.

In addition, here are some other suggestions that should help content teachers present listener-friendly lectures:

- Provide advance organizers or semantic maps (webs) before the lecture to keynote the important concepts that will be in it.
- Use key words and phrases such as *first, then, finally,* etc.
- Repeat important statements and concepts.
- Pause once in a while so that students can catch up with their writing.
- Write important information on the chalkboard or a transparency.
- Provide a duplicated copy of the most important points in the lecture if you think it might be helpful.
- Adjust the pace of the lecture by observing the students as they take notes.
- Vary voice quality and tone.
- Use visual aids of various types whenever appropriate and possible.
- Write technical and difficult-to-spell words either on the chalkboard or a transparency.
- Ask questions during the lecture when appropriate.
- Encourage students to ask questions during the lecture when appropriate.
- Summarize the lecture after you have finished presenting it.
- Provide time at the end of the lecture for students to review their notes and to ask questions if necessary.

NoteTaking Strategies

Notetaking strategies often are very difficult for "at-risk" students to master. Yet effective note-taking strategies are very important if such students are to experience the optimum amount of success possible with content reading assignments and in listening to teachers' lectures. Students first must be prepared to take notes by having all the materials necessary to take good notes.

Once students are prepared to take notes, it is important for them to follow these important steps:

- Take notes on one side of the paper only so that notes can be laid side by side for study.
- Skip lines to show changes in concepts.
- Try to write only key words and phrases instead of complete sentences to save time.
- Always write down all of the information that the teacher emphasizes as important or writes on the chalkboard or a transparency.
- Do not worry about spelling, at least until the notes are rewritten later.
- Make certain that notes are as clear and legible as possible.
- Write notes in your own words with the exception of technical vocabulary (terms that cannot be changed).
- Try to include examples in the notes.

- Use the structure the teacher provides.
- Do not write down what is already known or understood.
- Rewrite rough notes if they will be easier to understand and more useful.

Use of Technology

Technology is one of the more effective ways of meeting the needs of students with various kinds of disabilities. For example, in the future overhead transparency projectors may be replaced by a video camera version called an ELMO. This device displays text material, graphics, and almost any image that is placed on its glass top on a video monitor. It is more adaptable than the overhead projector when presenting visual images.

Many devices that are based on closed-captioning will help increase hearing-impaired students' learning in the content areas. For example, an Optacon translates images to tactile Braille-like print or synthesized speech. Another device called the Talking Terminal is a database that reads material aloud. Visually impaired students will have many print-to-speech translators available. The Kurzweil Reading Machine reads aloud printed material placed on a glass desk. A student can pause it, rewind to hear a word, and control volume, pitch, and speech rate.

Strategies for Using Time Effectively

Time management may be defined as organizing and monitoring time so that tasks can be scheduled and finished in an effective and timely way. There are a number of strategies and materials that can be used to help various types of "at-risk" students use their time most effectively.

- *My School Calendar for a Semester*—This is a place for students to record the important due dates for tests, projects, reports, and papers of various kinds.
- *My Weekly Planner*—This is a detailed view of what students must do for a specific time period of the semester.
- *This Is My Daily Organizer*—Each late afternoon or evening before a school day, students should review their weekly planner and the notes from their classes for that day. In addition, they should determine what they did not finish that day. Next, they should record everything they have to do the next day and exactly when they will do it.
- *My Checklist of Study Habits*—This is a checklist of what "at-risk" students should do to develop appropriate study habits in the content fields.
- *My Study Location Checklist*—This is a checklist of appropriate elements to be included in the place at which "at-risk" students do their studying at home.

Reproducible examples of these time-management materials are found later in this chapter. You may duplicate and use them in their present form or modify them in any way you wish in light of the needs of your own students.

STRATEGIES TO PROMOTE MULTICULTURAL AWARENESS AND LINGUISTIC DIVERSITY

A number of strategies are specifically designed to help both literacy and content teachers promote *multicultural awareness* and *linguistic diversity*. Although many of the strategies and materials just described in this chapter are equally valuable with all kinds of "at-risk" students, the remainder of the strategies in this section are specifically designed to develop multicultural awareness and linguistic diversity.

Instructional Approaches for Limited English-Speaking Students. Here are the main instructional approaches for limited English-speaking students that are being used at this time:

- *Immersion Approaches*—These approaches make no special provisions for limited English-speaking students. As teachers instruct all students in oral and written skills in English, limited English-speaking students are expected to pick up as much as they can as rapidly as they can from immersion in English. This has been the traditional form of instruction to limited English-speaking students in our country, although it is not necessarily the most effective.

- *ESL Approaches*—These approaches teach limited English-speaking students oral English skills first before any reading instruction begins. Usually ESL approaches require that students leave the classroom for this instruction. Special ESL teachers work with students in structured oral drills to develop fluency in oral English. After students have begun to establish fluency in oral English, reading instruction is started.

- *Bilingual Approaches*—These approaches promote the development of reading and writing skills in the students' native language concurrently with either formal or informal instruction in oral English. After students have learned to read and write in their own language and acquired proficiency in oral English, reading instruction in English begins. Bilingual approaches require special teachers who are fluent in the native language of the children with whom they work.

Two-Sided Stories.   When using *two-sided stories,* have students write stories in their own dialects, writing several sentences and then drawing an illustration on the left side of the page. Then help them to rewrite the story in Standard American English on the other side of each page. This first may be done as a language-experience activity in which you write down the sentences dictated by students.

General Guidelines for Teaching Culturally Diverse Students.   Here are some general guidelines for teaching students who come from culturally diverse backgrounds:

- *Learn about their cultures.* Find out about their language and learn the cultural variations in their word meanings. Try to learn about the students' living conditions and what things they value. Try to determine any cultural traits that may affect how they learn. Show them you accept and value their diversity.

- *Participate in the community.* Try to become involved in cultural and recreational and community service projects. The students and their families will very much appreciate your interest, and you will come to know them away from the school setting.

- *Value their unique contributions.* Show an interest in what students bring to talk about and listen carefully to what they say. Try to build activities around their holiday celebrations. Provide opportunities for their families to share their cultural heritage through learning experiences in the curriculum.

- *Share your ideas with other teachers.* Observe the techniques used by other teachers whom the students like and respect. During inservice and faculty meetings, share ideas that obtain results.

- *Discuss universal concerns.* Show the students that all kinds of people have many things in common, such as loving their families and needing a place to live and food to eat. Use these commonalties in developing lessons and units.

- *Provide a supportive classroom environment.* Have your classroom environment reflect the different cultures represented in the classroom by displaying multicultural materials and by including instruction related to multicultural education.

- *Develop background knowledge.* Provide adequate background experiences for helping students comprehend stories when they lack the required prior knowledge. Locate ways to link stories, trade books, or content textbooks to familiar things.

- *Use multicultural literature.* Use trade books, informational books, and stories related to students' cultural background whenever possible.

(Adapted from the ASCD Multicultural Education Commission, 1977.)

> **Note:** Remember, Chapter 6 provides a comprehensive list of multicultural trade books. African-American, Hispanic, and Native American literature comprised this comprehensive list. You should consult Chapter 6 for this very helpful list.

Some Other Effective Ideas for Limited English-Speaking Students. Here are several other useful ideas for limited English-speaking students that both literacy and content teachers may want to consider using:

- Seat the student near the front of the room so that he or she can see and hear better and have less distractions.

- Speak somewhat more slowly and distinctly than normal but not in an artificial way.

- Use shorter sentences and fewer long words, and simplify concepts as much as possible.

- Use manipulative materials and concrete demonstrations as much as possible, especially in science and mathematics.

- Use visual materials such as pictures, videotapes, diagrams, dioramas, etc., as much as possible.

- Allow students to respond with only one or two words.

- Do not correct errors of vocabulary, pronunciation, accent, or structure.

- Do not expect perfection in English in too short a time period.

- Assign a compatible "buddy" to work with the student whenever it is required.

- *Provide a supportive classroom environment.*

LIST OF PROFESSIONAL RESOURCE BOOKS FOR TEACHERS OF "AT-RISK" STUDENTS

Here is a partial, but certainly not comprehensive, list of some of the professional resource books that teachers of "at-risk" students may find helpful. They are all available from:

Prentice Hall/The Center for Applied Research in Education
Order Processing Department
P.O. Box 11071
Des Moines, IA 50336
Call Toll Free: 1-800-288-4745
FAX: 515-284-2607

Barnes, David, and Barnes, Cheryle, *Special Educator's Survival Guide,* 1989.

Bernstein, Rosella, *Ready-to-Use Phonic Activities for Special Children,* 1993.

Davis, Diane, *Reaching Out to Children with FAS/FAE,* 1994.

Elman, Natalie Madorsky, *The Special Educator's Almanac,* 1984.

Flick, Grad, *Power Parenting for Children with ADD/ADHD,* 1996.

Harwell, Joan M., *Complete Learning Disabilities Handbook,* 1987.

Harwell, Joan M., *Complete Learning Disabilities Resource Library, Volumes I and II,* 1996.

Harwell, Joan M., *Ready-to-Use Learning Disabilities Handbook,* 1993.

Krepelin, Elizabeth, *Sound & Articulation Activities for Children with Speech and Language Problems,* 1996.

Mannix, Darlene, *Life Skills Activities for Secondary Students with Special Needs,* 1995.

Mannix, Darlene, *Life Skills Activities for Special Children,* 1992.

Mannix, Darlene, *Oral Language Activities for Special Children,* 1987.

Mannix, Darlene, *Social Skills Activities for Special Children,* 1993.

Mauer, Richard E., *Special Educator's Discipline Handbook,* 1988.

Pierangelo, Roger, *A Survival Kit for the Special Education Teacher,* 1994.

Pierangelo, Roger, *Parents' Complete Special Education Guide,* 1996.

Pierangelo, Roger, *The Special Education Teacher's Book of Lists,* 1995.

Rief, Sandra F., *How to Reach & Teach ADD/ADHD Children,* 1993.

Waring, Cynthia, *Developing Independent Readers: Strategy-Oriented Reading Activities for Learners with Special Needs,* 1995.

REPRODUCIBLE MATERIALS FOR TEACHING CONTENT READING AND WRITING SKILLS TO "AT-RISK" STUDENTS

The remainder of this chapter contains reproducibles for teaching content reading and writing skills to "at-risk" students that you can duplicate and use in their present form if they seem applicable to the needs of your students. You also can modify them in any way you wish.

STORY STARTER
(Approximately Fifth-Grade Level)

Read this short story to yourself. Then write one or two paragraphs in answer to the question that is asked at the end of the story.

Amy is a fourth-grade student at Sheridan School who has been taught the importance of recycling. However, everyone else in her family throws soda pop cans into the garbage, while Amy crushes each can that she has drunk from, saves it, and later takes all of the cans she has saved to a recycling center.

What do you think Amy should tell all of the other members of her family about the importance of recycling soda pop cans or do you think she shouldn't tell them anything at all about it?

Write your answer here.

_____

_____

_____

_____

_____

_____

_____

_____

_____

_____

_____

_____

_____

_____

_____

_____

_____

_____

SCRAMBLED PARAGRAPHS IN SCIENCE
(Approximately Sixth-Grade Level)

Put all of the sentences in each group in the correct order to make a good paragraph. Put the *proper number* in front of each sentence. Then *write a good paragraph* using all of the sentences in the correct order. In writing each paragraph you can use such *transition words* as *however, unfortunately, then,* or *finally* among many others.

"Where Plants and Animals Live"

A.

_____ Bushes make up the middle layer, and deer hide and give birth to fawns in this layer.

_____ Deer also eat the twigs and leaves that come from the middle layer.

_____ The bottom layer in the forest floor is where deer find mushrooms, moss, and grass to eat.

_____ Trees make up the top layer, and they are home to many different types of birds.

_____ A deer's forest habitat is composed of many different layers.

_____

_____

_____

_____

_____

B.

_____ Most deserts have a very short rainy season, after which the desert plants bloom.

_____ A place that receives little or no rain at any time during the year is called a desert.

_____ While saguaro cactus usually are very tall, most desert plants are quite small.

_____ The desert is a fascinating place with many unusual creatures such as gila monsters, kit foxes, cactus mice, and rattlesnakes.

_____ Many of the desert plants are called cactuses, and they can survive with very little rain.

_____

_____

_____

_____

_____

SCRAMBLED PARAGRAPHS IN SCIENCE
(Approximately Sixth-Grade Level)

(cont.)

C.

_____ A marsh is a place in which the soil is wet or covered with water.

_____ In a salt marsh, tops of cordgrass sway above roots sunk in soggy soil.

_____ A marsh that is covered with salt water is called a salt marsh.

_____ At high tide in a salt marsh a green crab makes a meal of worms and small clams in the water.

_____ Although the green crab and the fiddler crab share the same habitat, they live in different parts of it.

_____

_____

_____

_____

_____

D.

_____ A pool of sea water that is trapped at low tide is called a tide pool.

_____ Patches of rockweed half under water grow on the lower parts of the rocks.

_____ Their tightly closed shells keep the mussels from drying out.

_____ There often are rocks at the edge of a tide pool.

_____ The dark blue shells of mussels stick up from the water in the pools.

_____

_____

_____

_____

_____

SCRAMBLED PARAGRAPHS IN SCIENCE
(Approximately Sixth-Grade Level)

(cont.)

E.

_____ A starling on the ground can be seen picking at an apple core that someone has carelessly thrown away.

_____ A deserted lot in the city also can be a habitat for living creatures.

_____ Before a cat can kill a starling, the bird flies in a tree and eats a grasshopper.

_____ A gray cat puts one foot out of a broken fence and slips toward the starling.

_____ Then the starling turns and drinks water from a piece of broken glass.

_____

_____

_____

_____

_____

Answer Key for "Scrambled Paragrahs in Science"

Note: Students' paragraphs will vary, although they should all include the appropriate information.

A. 3, 4, 5, 2, 1
B. 2, 1, 4, 5, 3
C. 1, 3, 2, 4, 5
D. 1, 3, 5, 2, 4
E. 2, 1, 5, 4, 3

Name _____ Grade _____ Teacher _____ Date _____

"ABOUT POINT" ACTIVITY SHEET
(Middle-School or Secondary-School Level)

Read the material from your content textbook that your teacher has assigned. Then decide what the passage is *About* and what details or *Points* support your answer. Then complete this "About Point" Activity Sheet. You can work with a partner(s) if you want.

This reading is **ABOUT** _____

_____

_____

and the **POINTS** are _____

_____

_____

_____

_____

_____

_____

_____

_____

_____

_____

_____

_____

_____

_____

_____

_____

_____

_____

_____

LEARNING LOG
(Middle-School or Secondary-School Level)

Complete this *learning log* as you read the content textbook assignment your teacher has given you. The "Prediction" column of the learning log should be completed *before* you begin reading the assignment, while the *rest of it* should be completed *after* you have finished reading it.

PREDICTION: What may happen in this assignment?	CONCEPTS: What have I learned from reading this assignment?	QUESTIONS: What don't I understand about this assignment?	PERSONAL OPINIONS: What do I think about this assignment?
Date			

Name _____ Grade _____ Teacher _____ Date _____

MY SCHOOL CALENDAR FOR A SEMESTER

Fall or Spring Semester _____
  (Underline One)   Year

August, September, October, November, December, January, February, March, April, May, June

  (Underline One)

Monday	Tuesday	Wednesday	Thursday	Friday

MY WEEKLY PLANNER

My name is _____

This weekly planner is for the week of _____

	Sunday	Monday	Tuesday	Wednesday	Thursday	Friday	Saturday
7:00 A.M.							
8:00							
9:00							
10:00							
11:00							
12:00 P.M.							
1:00							
2:00							
3:00							
4:00							
5:00							
6:00							
7:00							
8:00							
9:00							
10:00							
11:00							

Name _____ Grade _____ Teacher _____ Date _____

THIS IS MY DAILY ORGANIZER

THIS IS MY DAILY ORGANIZER FOR _____ _____
(Day)   (Date)

7:00 A.M. _____

8:00 _____

9:00 _____

10:00 _____

11:00 _____

12:00 P.M. _____

1:00 _____

2:00 _____

3:00 _____

4:00 _____

5:00 _____

6:00 _____

7:00 _____

8:00 _____

9:00 _____

10:00 _____

11:00 _____

MY CHECKLIST OF STUDY HABITS

Read each sentence in this checklist and put an *X* on the line under the appropriate column: *Always, Sometimes, Never*. You should learn from evaluating this checklist how effective your study habits are.

	Always	Sometimes	Never
1. I begin by studying my hardest assignment.	_____	_____	_____
2. I review my previous notes before starting to study an assignment.	_____	_____	_____
3. I finish studying one assignment before going on to another one.	_____	_____	_____
4. I begin studying when I am supposed to.	_____	_____	_____
5. I do not daydream while I am supposed to be studying.	_____	_____	_____
6. I ask my friends not to call me or bother me during the time when I am supposed to be studying.	_____	_____	_____
7. I take breaks when I get tired from studying.	_____	_____	_____
8. I study in an area away from disctractions.	_____	_____	_____
9. I have a "study buddy" who I can call if I need help.	_____	_____	_____
10. I begin studying at least five days before I know I have to take a test.	_____	_____	_____
11. I keep working regularly on any of my long-term assignments.	_____	_____	_____
12. I don't "cram" for a test right before I am supposed to take it.	_____	_____	_____

Name _____ Grade _____ Teacher _____ Date _____

MY STUDY LOCATION CHECKLIST

Evaluate your *home study place* by reading each sentence in the checklist and putting an *X* on the line under the appropriate column: *Always, Sometimes, Never.*

	Always	**Sometimes**	**Never**
1. I have a quiet, private place to study at home.	_____	_____	_____
2. My home study place has good light.	_____	_____	_____
3. My home study place has a comfortable temperature.	_____	_____	_____
4. There is a desk or table large enough to hold all of the materials in my home study place.	_____	_____	_____
5. There is a comfortable chair to sit in at my home study place.	_____	_____	_____
6. I keep all the required work and reference materials in my home study place that I will need to complete my content assignments.	_____	_____	_____
7. There are no distractions of any kind at my home study place.	_____	_____	_____
8. My home study place is kept private from my brothers or sisters who might disturb me.	_____	_____	_____
9. I can use my home study place whenever I need or want to.	_____	_____	_____
10. I enjoy studying at my home study place.	_____	_____	_____